IT'S ALL PART OF THE GAME

A story describing 30 years in the antique business

John Clegg

Grosvenor House
Publishing Limited

This book is published by
Grosvenor House Publishing Ltd
Link House
140 The Broadway, Tolworth, Surrey, KT6 7HT.
www.grosvenorhousepublishing.co.uk

This book is a work of fiction. Any resemblance to
people or events, past or present, is purely coincidental.

A CIP record for this book
is available from the British Library

ISBN 978-1-80381-268-7
eBook ISBN 978-1-80381-269-4

DEDICATION

Alfreda Jessica Sciville; Peter Hayes; John Joe; Hannah, Johanna-Maria Deiwiks.

PREFACE

Often when relating or hearing tales from when the antique trade was in its pomp; busy antique shops in most market towns; Volvos piled high with furniture; frenetic business done on the opening day of major antique fairs, I often thought, someone ought to write all this down, before it becomes lost. I made a start on numerous occasions, but all came out as just a string of anecdotes, until chancing upon the solution, as found in this book; something that tied all together.

ACKNOWLEDGEMENT

Jennifer Elkin, Graham and Wendy Hayes.

INTRODUCTION

The story covers the period, roughly between 1974 and 2004, including details of initial blunderings, door-knocking escapades, the antique ring, impact of the Irish travellers, a house clearance in Australia, the trade-chain along which goods passed on their way to the final customer and a multitude of other particulars, only someone from within the antique trade could realistically provide.

PROLOGUE

When recently driving the country lanes, on my way to an auction held in a South Herefordshire village hall, my head wrestling with an intractable portion of a planned fiction, I chanced upon on a man, a good 30 years my senior, whose snippets of dealings from a past age, filled me with such fascination, I decided to abandon my intended story and pursue the trail that led to the contents of this book.

PART ONE

CHAPTER ONE

It was a pleasant drive up through the Wye Valley and I'd timed the run to miss the early morning Monmouth congestion, plus had also remembered the mobile speed trap, a large white van occasionally parked on a bridge at the summit of a long rise up the dual carriageway. A few, cruising leisurely past showed sudden red-light alarm, but alas, probably too late. I continued east, then north, following the scrap of a map I'd drawn, leading to a village hall sale I'd been told about. A friend had spotted the tiny advert in a local paper and on ringing the auctioneer, had realised some lots could be of interest. With my business being based on hiring out furniture and props for parties and weddings, with the proviso, all items must be from natural materials and recyclable, what my friend had gleaned, gave me the impetus to take a gamble on the trip being profitable. I always loved exploring that natural, largely unchanged part of the border country, plus as I drove, it gave a chance to wrestle with the plot of a book I had the notion to write. I'd already had one published and thought the second would duly flow, but the logic of one important twist in the tale simply refused to stand the test of credibility. Each time I thought I'd discovered the answer, I found myself muttering, 'Not even I believe that!'

The sale was being held in small village hall on the Welsh Marches and I'm aware there must be a more direct route, but hadn't dared risk entanglement in the myriad of lanes and anyway, even with going slightly the long way round, I still managed to arrive in plenty of time. I know I should use Satnav, but have always reasoned, you'll never learn the routes if not engaging the brain to find destinations and anyway, shortest routes can often take longer, especially when stuck behind a tractor. It was old fashioned stock I was seeking, with an old-fashioned attitude to match, even to the point of reading about the history of towns and villages I visited, not only out of interest, but also out of respect for their past. One snippet of information about this particular western pocket of Herefordshire had tickled me. Apparently, for any man of the cloth applying to work here in the early 1900's, a prerequisite was being bilingual in Welsh and English, as many of the locals only spoke a dialect known as Herefordshire Welsh. A good few place names still attest to that, but what a shame it has now died out.

Being a fine day, many of the early lots sat in rows, out in the village hall car park. I'd had to leave the van quite a way up the lane, beyond the line of cars, pick-ups and Land Rovers jammed in against the hedge. The atmosphere was quite convivial, with I'm sure most turning up out of nothing more than curiosity and a good excuse to chat to their neighbours. Most of the men were dressed in work gear and the favoured method of examining goods seemed to be a stick-prod or a sharp toe-ender. Those chatting in neighbourly groups kindly parted to allow me room, falling silent as if mystified when I upended items for examination. Needing to look for damage or woodworm wouldn't have occurred to those, not there to buy the furniture. The lots were numbered with the large red numerals on oval white paper discs, glued down with flour and water paste, which apparently, had always been the case at farm sales years ago. They can be a hell of a job to remove and so no chance of swapping lot numbers, an old dealer's trick, I'd been told, from back in the days when contesting for goods at the better auctions, had at times been tantamount to stylised warfare. Such small, interesting nuggets occasionally coming my way, had whetted my appetite to delve for more information regarding that frenetic time from the late sixties onward. A time when one after another, various parts of the globe developed antique fever, buying up stock from the British trade to ship to America, Italy, Holland, Germany and even Australia.

The trick I referred to, had apparently been used to deter certain dealers from leaving bids on the book. The number of a coveted lot would be swapped with that of another, similar but far inferior. The trade would then bid the latter up to way past its value, meaning a severe financial shock awaited the dealer, eagerly returning to collect his prize. I had been told that some traders were renowned for being particularly vicious when it came to deterring their opposition, even to the point of damaging goods lost to a rival, which on the one hand I found slightly repelling, but on the other, fascinating, being nothing like the genteel world I'd imagined.

Little did I know, that on this particular day I was to chance upon someone who would set me off on a trail of discovery, stretching back into the previous century and that the investigation would be that fascinating, I'd abandon plans for my proposed book and instead write this one.

I bought myself a mug of tea and a sandwich from the ladies in the little tearoom. The hot liquid, poured from a large brown pot, tasted better than any tea I'd drunk in years and the fresh cut ham sandwiches with their thin crunchy crusts, had a succulent addition of salad.

The wickerwork suite was my first lot of interest, which was bought quite reasonably, as was the stack of stoneware jars and even better, the items I'd dug out for conversion to lamps, cost virtually nothing. A rag-work rug was on the dirty side, but would look totally different when cleaned, but what I coveted above all, was a small, two-part miniature press cupboard, made from reclaimed timber. It was nothing more than odds and ends put together years ago in someone's shed, but it had a certain charm and on first spotting it, I couldn't help it, the little oddity raised a smile. It was knocked down to me for a mere £9.

At end of sale, with vehicles reversing in, followed by the mayhem as they edged their way back out, it was difficult getting my van in for loading. Trails of people struggled with various goods up the lane and outside the saleroom itself was a complete melee. When paying, I left contact details, for the auctioneer to notify me of any further venues and he commandeered a porter to help. I don't know why I was thus favoured, but wasn't complaining. The man was the youngest of the three white-coated assistants and had a fair idea of how to pack, understanding economy of space and the risk of one item damaging another. It was when tucking in the curious little cupboard with blankets, I realised I was being watched.

He was quite a tall man and although clearly advanced in years, still had a full head of hair, grey around the temples, glints of silver elsewhere, but otherwise surprisingly still dark in colour. He'd obviously recently returned from sunnier climes and his genial look, became instantly warmer when lit by a smile.

"That little cupboard you bought," he said pointing. "It takes me back a few years."

"Why, have you seen it before?"

He shook his head. "A man I worked for many years ago, bought a few lots very similar. I had to drive to Rhayader to collect it all. What struck me was, they were totally at odds with what he normally dealt in. Having said that, he sold it all instantly. You and he must have a similar eye." The final sentence was said with a merry glint.

It jolted me slightly, for when previously enquiring about characters in the antique trade, the successful ones had often been described as having an eye for the job. It was apparently, one of the top accolades a dealer could receive, bestowing far more than status derived from merely throwing sheer wealth at the job, for it meant they had a natural flair; something that couldn't be learnt or taught. You either had it or you didn't.

I was of course interested to hear more and told him, once my van was packed and driven down the lane for ease of get-away, if he didn't mind, I'd join him back at the carpark. My new acquaintance said he'd get the teas in and on returning I saw him emerge carefully holding a mug in each hand with two homemade cakes balanced on a plate between. To be clear of exhaust fumes and bustle, we made our way to the edge of the carpark.

He introduced himself as Mike and said he occasionally attended these country sales, more for old times' sake, rather than for what was on offer. He enjoyed chatting to the locals and reminiscing at how different such venues had been years ago.

I asked if he'd bought anything and pulling out a polished piece of wood from his pocket, he handed it to me.

"It was in a box of junk. You very rarely see them these days. Well in fact, they weren't that common fifty years ago."

The shorter slim, rectangular end, had a hole drilled down its length and faded greens, reds and yellows, adorned the tiny triangles of the cross-hatched decoration. The 5 inch longer section had been cut and polished to resemble a curved wooden knife blade.

"What was it for?" I asked. It was too curved to be a paper-knife.

"It's a knitting sheath," Mike answered, explaining, that when a needle was wedged in the hole and the blade tucked into a lady's waist band, it acted like a third hand. "Most were whittled to be given as love tokens and as you can imagine, in much less overt times, such a shape being accepted and knowledge of where it would later be inserted, would have brought a certain frisson."

"A little piece of folk art," I said handing it back.

"Well, when you think about it, so is that cupboard you bought. I know it's only homemade, but it captures a spirit of times gone by and also in its way, is entirely unique. You won't find another exactly like it."

We talked a little more, with me divulging an interest in old yarns regarding the antique trade and on leaving, almost as an afterthought, he suggested we meet up at another sale, due the following week, further north, just over the Welsh border. He said, he couldn't promise it would be profitable, but at least I'd get to hear more about the boss he'd once worked for and some of the tales from back in the old days, adding, "We might even be lucky enough to chance upon an old contact. You should find him interesting. His experiences stretch back even further than mine." He wrote down the details and disappeared off down the lane.

It was a bit of a gamble to drive that far beyond, what I called home territory, just on the off-chance of it being worthwhile, but I couldn't help it, I could feel myself getting hooked.

CHAPTER TWO

The sale in question was being held on a Saturday in the pretty market town of Montgomery, made all the more charming by it being a county town that never really grew. I drove into the broad market square and saw Mike waving me into the last vacant parking spot. He removed the traffic cone as I reversed in and putting it far side of pavement said, "We won't be needing that anymore."

After exchanging pleasantries, he apologised, saying he thought he'd wasted my time. Having viewed the sale, even rooting through all the boxes, he'd not found a single item of merit. He accompanied me up the townhall steps, told me there was more upstairs, then said he would disappear for a while, having need of a few groceries.

The only thing you could call a genuine antique was a circular, pale mahogany stand, with a marble-top insert. The auctioneer proudly showing onlookers, hooked a fingernail into a thin vertical crack and pulling the curved door open, said with a beam of triumph, "A pot cupboard." Suitably impressed onlookers, turning one to the other, couldn't have looked more astounded, had he pulled out a live rabbit from within.

Mike had been right, what had been advertised as an antique sale was no more than second hand clear-outs, which I must confess, suited me fine, but all I actually found, were a couple of wicker baskets and a Lloyd Loom linen basket minus its lid. They were early lots fortunately, for had they been upstairs they'd not have warranted hanging around for.

When I later pointed out my finds to Mike, he just said with a patient look, "Mmm, I see." Then obviously sickened by the sight of auctioneer going through his wonderous act of pot cupboard revelation once again, said, with sad shake of head, "Come on, I can't stand any more of this, there's 20 minutes before the off, I'll show you a place I love."

We walked along a street leading off the square and entered an emporium, like stepping back in time, Bunners. The more one looked, however, it was the setting that was the time-warp, not the goods. The kitchenware was top quality. I bought a mug and milk jug, both with striking floral adornment and could have stayed mesmerized for far longer than circumstances allowed. The staff were a no-nonsense, efficient delight, carefully wrapping and packing my purchases into a box and the little experience made my trip, already seem well worth the effort.

Walking back, I quickened my stride slightly, people were hurrying up the Town Hall steps, indicating the sale was underway. Mike pointing to an old shop front on the left said, "You'd never believe it, but I once collected two pieces of early yew wood furniture, a fine Georgian bookcase and 26 rushlights from inside that place."

What were rushlights? I didn't ask. I was in danger of missing my lots, but did make a mental note to look it up later.

Back in the Town Hall, the sale was indeed underway and even though packed, I managed to squeeze into a spot where the auctioneer couldn't miss my bids. He was selling as he walked along the rows and a clerk following, took down the details of those purchasing. I bought the lidless linen basket for a maiden bid of a pound, but had to pay a little more than usual for the two baskets. I had no use for what lay within, but it soon became obvious others had seen merit in the contents.

As a clerk's table had been set up downstairs, I was able to pay immediately and handing the receipt to a porter, was handed the two baskets. They were a fine rich, conker colour and had a pleasant bulge to their oval shape and once in my possession, I wasn't sorry I'd paid that little extra.

"Would you sell me that old food mincer?" The request came from a small grey-haired lady standing beside me. "And how much do you want for that brass pastry cutter and the cutlery?"

"Did you want that old can opener?" asked another. He was referring to a bull-headed rust speckled implement with a looped tail forming the handle.

"What's it worth to you?"

"Would you accept three quid?"

By the time I'd sold all the bits of interest, the baskets owed me nothing. Mike looking on, was shaking his head in disbelief and laughing.

"What do you want this old laundry basket for?" he asked, carrying it down to the pavement. "Do you have a lid for it?"

"It doesn't need a lid. It will make a good stand for a shrub."

"Another world," he answered with a wry look. "When I think of all the wonderful things I used to collect from here years ago,--- dressers, Georgian oak linen presses, bureaus, bookcases, coffers, corner cupboards, you name it---. That pot cupboard he's so proud of, would never have even figured in the reckoning. A bolder one with fluted moulding, maybe, but not that insipid piece of Victoriana. One of the shippers would have bought it to put in a container bound for America."

For a former van driver, he seemed to have picked up a fair knowledge from the man he'd worked for, which cheered me no end, for he was just the sort of contact I needed. I could sense a book forming in my mind. We put my purchases in the van and headed off across the street to a small tearoom. A group was shuffling about, making ready to leave and so we grabbed their table beside the shallow bay window.

"He doesn't seem to be here," Mike said, surveying the small room. "What do you fancy? I'll order it and nip out the back. On a decent day he sometimes sits outside."

He returned, shaking his head. A young girl brought us coffee and slices of barra brith, the Welsh name for a moist currant cake usually served with butter.

I said, "All those goods you told me you collected from here years ago? Who exactly was it for?"

"John Dodds. Sorry, I thought I'd already told you. He had a large shop in a border town, east of here. He was quite a big player back then, but I bet if he walked into one of these country salerooms now, no-one would even recognise him."

Sensing a certain wistfulness, I didn't comment, but instead said that my interest regarding antiques went a little deeper than I'd first divulged and finally confessed, "I'm thinking of writing a book."

He laughed. "Difficult unless you've lived through those times yourself. Doddsy himself, had always intended to do the same, but after a number of attempts, gave up. I've still got all his notes. He gave them to me one day. He said, 'Here, you have them, Mike, they're bringing back too many bad memories.'"

"Bad memories?"

"It wasn't all buying cheap and raking in a fortune, you know. You had to know what you were doing and there were some

12

incredibly tough times. On a few occasions I remember him looking white with worry, up to his neck in debt and yet having to keep up pretences, appearing as keen and hungry for the next lot as if business was booming."

"Would there be any chance of me seeing those notes?"

He was silent for a while,--- "Yes, I don't see why not. Can't do any harm. Most of those mentioned would be dead by now anyway. Here he is!"

I instantly turned, expecting to see John Dodds himself, but the man entering was slightly stooped, had white curled remnants of what once would have been a luxuriant mop and the smile he gave, although suddenly taking ten years off his wrinkled face, didn't lend him the demeanour of someone who had once been a renowned antique dealer. He was introduced as George and with a squeaking of chair legs, as those at the next table budged up a bit, we managed to squeeze him in. Mike making the introductions, told him of my interest in days of yore and I'm not exaggerating, his face instantly lit up. He had apparently been the driver for one of the legendary doyens of the antique trade, his services necessitated by the man's penchant for liquid refreshment. He told me, he'd be quite happy to divulge, but suggested, with some of it being of rather a sensitive nature, it might be better we repair to a less crowded setting.

"Well just tell him the swing door story," urged Mike. "You remember the one."

"Oh, THAT sale!"

We drew closer to listen and before George began, Mike explained that back in those days, a week's wage for the average working man was about £12 and so a ten-pound note would have been the equivalent to over £250 today. "Back in those days," he said, "if a

13

lot made over £100 pounds there was a round of applause. I'm not kidding, everyone would start clapping."

I obviously didn't take notes, but so not to lose the detail, wrote the following as soon as I got home.

George was brought what must have been his usual order, coffee and carrot cake and with an anticipatory grin, began by explaining, "It happened at an auction down in West Wales. The church hall, the venue for the sale, had one of those typical Gothic shaped doorways. This led into the porch and barring the way to the hall beyond, was this massive pair of swing doors. The place did have a small gallery, but was basically open to the rafters and absolutely packed with folks, almost as if the auction was like the circus come to town. You actually had to squeeze and weave your way between them, to get into the place. Meanwhile, my boss, Ben Evans, was doing his usual thing, carousing in the nearby hotel while a designated minion bought all the main lots for sorting out later."

"You mean by the ring?" I asked.

Mike giving a warning look, nodded in the direction of the nearby table.

"Well," said George. "The day had been going along quite pleasantly and as the booze flowed, Ben would occasionally ask me to nip into the hall and report back as to how things were faring. I told him, a few lots were safely in the bag, but there was this main item of interest, a Georgian mahogany, serpentine commode chest and I noticed him getting decidedly fidgety as the time for its sale approached. I was actually inside the hall when the lot came up and a number of the trade had abandoned their little get-together to squeeze themselves into advantageous positions, some even sitting up on a piano and pieces of furniture arrayed around the room."

"The auctioneer had one of those voices that could knock an old tin can over at twenty paces. He bawled, 'So what will you give me for this fine mahogany chest? Do I hear 20? 10? Come on start me at 5! Whose got a fiver, you know it's worth it!'"

George started to laugh as he said, "Just then, the swing doors burst apart, knocking folks flying and there swaying in the opening was Ben Evans. The place fell silent. Everyone was watching, completely transfixed. I can still see him now. This vision, with a single digit raised on high, slurring, '**One unnred pounds**,' before falling backwards into the vestibule."

"Well over two grand in today's money," Mike chipped in.

"Watching the doors still flapping, the auctioneer, stunned to silence, tapped his gavel and mouthed, 'Sold.' You can imagine it can't you. The whole place literally erupted with laughter. Some dealers were holding their sides, crying from the pain of it."

"Oh, there was another sale-----. I've just remembered. It was a few years later." George paused to partake of his coffee, then continued. "It was a sale in Ludlow. A well-known local historian had died and when they cleared his premises, a number of the items were that rare, a few of the London trade turned up. Some of the medieval pottery and metalwork, in actual fact was worthy of a museum and well beyond the knowledge of most of the local trade, but Ben knew his stuff and wasn't afraid to give it a go. On knocking a lot down to him, the auctioneer pronounced, 'Sold! To Mr. Ben Evans. Thank you, sir. The last of a dying breed.' It brought a few chuckles, but it was sad really, for the old guard with their immense knowledge was dying out and a new breed, buying unheard of things like, pine and Victoriana, was coming through."

Mike got up to pay and on returning, said we ought to go to a quieter spot. "Have you ever seen the castle?"

I hadn't, to which he replied, "George, we can't let him leave without seeing the castle."

We drove up in Mike's car and I was glad we hadn't elected to walk, for the slope was quite severe. There were only two other cars parked and following the path and exchanging greetings with two old dears who had been exercising their small dogs, we headed towards the splendid oak bridge that gave access to the ruins. George, pointing down to the packed rows of houses, said a massive county gaol had once dominated that part of town, but other than the grand entryway, little remained of it today. Pointing vaguely in a westerly direction, he said a Welsh castle had been built across the far side of the Severn to supposedly counter this English one and then pointing in the opposite direction, explained, to the north of what he called Corndon Hill, a small stone circle still stood.

Apparently, there had been an earlier castle predating this one, a motte and bailey, which he dismissed as being, "Just a bit of a bulge, lying over yonder. And if you look down there," he said, pointing to where a road arrowed north, "You can just make out the line of Offa's Dyke, cut through by that road to Welshpool."

"So for hundreds of years, this really was border country."

"Lord aah!" he said, laughing as he slipped into a bit of local parlance. "Those Welsh, they burnt the town once. The castle held out, but the town below us was toast. Clun got the same treatment."

"That would have been in Owen Glendower's day." I had quickly scanned the history of the area the day before.

"Yes, something like that," George replied. "I bet even Shrewsbury would have got scorched, had that battle gone the other way."

"What battle? What year was that?"

George couldn't remember and I'd left my phone in the van and so couldn't look it up.

"Shrewsbury's over that way." He said pointing north. Then after pause for thought, said, "That reminds me."

"Sounds like another Ben Evans story could be imminent," said Mike.

"It wasn't one of Hall's auctions, it was in another small saleroom as you head uptown, from down by the Welsh Bridge. Ben had done his usual trick, passing on instructions to the lads, leaving the day clear to partake in one of his favourite watering holes. He was in a bit of a state when I went to collect him and was not best pleased when one of the boys at last dared break the news. The main lot of the day, the Georgian mahogany wall shelves had not been netted. They had chickened out and let a dealer from Dorrington run off with the prize."

George laughed, "He was absolutely raving, 'You let that woman get the better of you!' I won't tell you what he called them, but you can imagine."

"So what happened?" I asked.

"I had to drive him to Dorrington didn't I---and there proudly displayed in the shop window were the wall shelves. I must admit, they were quite splendid. You didn't have to be an antique dealer to see that, but the trouble was, the shop was shut. Ben rang the bell, hammered on the door, but she was obviously either not there, or not willing to open the door to him. He was a gent when sober, but could be a nasty piece of work when he'd had a skinful. Well anyway, it was now opening time and so of course Ben needed a top-up. He kept sending me back to see if there was any sign of life in the shop and on the third visit, I noticed a light on, upstairs."

17

"Ben would get himself in a state," Mike chipped in. "They used to joke, if ever he dried himself out, he'd instantly shrivel and die."

"So, we went back to the shop and Ben rapped on the door. When the woman appeared, looking a bit nervous, I have to add, Ben asked her what sort of profit she wanted on the shelves."

"She told him and even now, I can see the way his eyes bulged in disbelief. Because of sheer intake of booze, it often lingered awaiting a vacancy below, giving his words a gargling accompaniment, with a tendency to dribble and as if harbouring a small oyster that defied swallowing, he burbled, 'George, the woman's stark staring mad! Take me from here this instant.' Near the door, he turned and asked, 'Now come on, do try and be reasonable, what do you really want?'

She repeated the price.

Accompanied by an angry stamp of foot, 'How can the likes of you, stuck in a little place like this, dream up a price such as that?'

'I just like them,' she said.

'Well fair enough,' says Ben. 'So do I, but do try and be reasonable, woman!' He was back in the middle of the hallway by now and swaying a bit, obviously suffering from the day's intake. 'The price you're asking,' he said clutching his chest, 'almost brought on a heart attack! Can you not find it within yourself to reconsider?'

'I'm sorry, but that's the price I want.'

I think the air must have got to him on that walk from the pub, sending all the alcohol coursing through his system, for he now started to stagger. He had quite a sway on as he wrote out the cheque. 'She's barking mad,' he growled and the flourish to his signature, sent him reeling in my direction. The woman watched aghast, as with legs crossing in rapid dressage mode, he ended up flat on his back in the hallway, the dull impact resonating from nearby clocks. With cheque held aloft, he instructed grandly, 'Pay the woman.'"

On our way back down into the town, George told us a couple more snippets, regarding Ben Evans, and in the main square, pointing to a grand Georgian town house, told us, "That was Ben's place."

We were saying our farewells when, he said, "Nearly forgot, it got besieged one night. It was after one of the Welsh sales. Ben had made off with the best lot and when the lads found out, they were furious. They came tearing into town like a posse, hammering on his door and demanding he put the thing up to them. A cab-leg lowboy, I think it was."

"What? The ring were demanding this?"

"Yes, they were furious and wouldn't leave the square until he let them in. They made such a racket, it left him with no choice."

When George had gone on his way, I said to Mike, "It sounds unbelievable."

"It's true," he said. "There are many more tales like that. Some more uproarious in fact, but most of what you just heard, happened way before Doddsy's time."

"So how long have you known George?"

For some reason the question took him a little off guard, but then he said, "Not long really. Just happened to bump into him a couple of years back."

We agreed to meet again. He said he'd ring and would remember to bring John Dodds's scribblings along with him. The goods I'd bought would barely pay for the day's diesel, but in another way, it had been well worth the trip.

Later, when back home, I looked up the battle of Shrewsbury. It had been fought in 1403 and although as I'd guessed, it had been in Owen Glendower's time, on that particular day, the man in question had been down on a bit of enforcing duty in Carmarthen. So nowhere near Shrewsbury, let alone close enough to torch it, as his followers had done to Clun and Montgomery. The Welsh castle, George had alluded to, turned out to be Dolforwyn, hurriedly put up by order of the self-declared Prince of Wales, Llywelyn ap Gruffyd, to counter English aggression. For some reason they hadn't dug a well and after being besieged by Roger Mortimer's forces, in the Spring of 1277, it capitulated through lack of water. Even though, the castle had supposedly been a bit of a rush job, I was amazed there had been such an oversight. The English moved in, dug a well and the villagers, formerly living beyond the castle walls, were resettled in what is now Newtown.

Then in the Summer of that same year, Edward 1 launched his decisive attack into North Wales and I was surprised to read, more than half his army had been recruited from South Wales. Seemingly, divide and conquer has ever been thus and in 1282, Llywelyn, the last native Prince of Wales, was somehow lured away from his army and killed by English lancers near Builth Wells. But not to worry, in 1301 King Edward had the bright notion of offering his adversaries compensation, another Prince of Wales, his very own son. I thought, no wonder they delight in beating us at rugby.

I also looked up rushlights. They were a form of free lighting. Rushes were cut and dried and their pith dipped in tallow. When lit and fed through pincers of a rushlight, it gave a dim and probably rather smelly lighting to a room. There were illustrations. Some had iron tripod supports, others, polished wooden stands, some hung from beams and yet others were for hammering into a beam. Top of the range could be adjusted for height and also had a tiny spike to hold a small candle.

I started making notes for my story and when writing a brief sketch of my new friend Mike, it suddenly dawned on me, considering he'd been nothing more than a general factotum, he seemed to have a fair deal of knowledge regarding the antique trade. Over time, I'd found need to employ people to deliver and collect for me and other than know how to handle and pack the goods, they didn't seem to show much interest in what the items were, or what they might be used for. I did try and explain on a couple of occasions, thinking it might make their job more interesting, but after seeing the glazed look of disinterest, I gave up.

This brought me to thinking about John Dodds himself and the question, if still alive, where was he now? His shop had apparently been, east of Montgomery. A vague description to say the least. I Googled his name and found a brief account of what he had specialised in and above it, a picture of a large premises in Ludlow. The business was obviously long gone and so what I was looking at was an ancient reference, still lingering on the internet.

The next meeting with Mike was in the charming market town of Tenbury Wells. I'd parked and a message came through on my phone to meet him at the Pump Rooms. I knew the rough location for I had read a little about the town the previous day.

"What are you grinning at?" he asked.

"It looks like it was designed by a committee. An exceedingly imaginative one at that."

"I know, isn't it marvellous? They built it in 1862," he said, prodding a piece of literature he was holding. "I didn't forget the notes you asked for," he added. "I left them in the car. It's parked in the main street."

It stood outside an interesting looking ironmonger's shop, the sort of premises that tempts with the notion, 'There must be something in there I need.' I was handed a massive crumpled brown envelope, stuffed with papers, but then Mike floored me somewhat, by saying, as much as he'd like to, he couldn't stay; he'd have to love and leave; "Pressing duties elsewhere."

I was obviously a little taken aback and as if by way of compensation, he suggested I take a look at another little architectural gem, his curved sweep of hand indicating it lay beyond the sharp turn, end of high street, behind me. Pointing in the opposite direction, to where a few pieces of second-hand furniture stood forlornly on the pavement, he said, that was the shop I needed to head for. "The man could well have the type of goods you're looking for and you might just find, he can tell you a thing or two about John Dodds." Apologising again, he gave a wave and drove off.

It wasn't what I'd expected at all and watching his car disappear from sight over the river bridge, I thought, what an enigma this man was turning out to be.

I took the trouble to look at the architectural gem he'd suggested, the old market hall and wasn't disappointed. It was a small, compact circular building with a light gothic touch, crowned by a roof with such an exaggerated overhang, it put me in mind of those massive sunshade hats, the Chinese wear in the paddy fields. Above all, with tiles matching the main roof, was a raised fenestrated lantern, to offer more light within.

The shop I headed for, now with very much a sinking feeling, was beyond the Regal, a remnant from when the movie world held such sway and with the shop not being too far from the river, I did glance in the window, but then walked the few extra yards to the stone bridge with its busy white painted railings. I think it's the only bridge I've ever seen with a definite bend in it and cars far side had to pause to allow a small truck through. Looking down at the unperturbed manner of the ducks busying themselves and then dreamily watching the river's flow, swirling around a shrub strewn island, I thought what a beautifully tranquil part of the country.

I retraced my steps and on entering the small shop, was given an affable greeting by the proprietor, who, although of quite generous build, had the slightly self-deprecating stoop of a man who'd probably spent too many years trying to persuade people to part with their cash. I described the type of things I was looking for and he said, chances could be, we'd both be in luck, but he'd have to close the shop and take me round to his store. I won't go into great detail about what I bought, but suffice to say, it made the trip worthwhile. The main thing of interest, which of course, I will dwell on; just as my friend Mike had informed me, this man could fill me in with a few more details regarding John Dodds. I had come to the firm decision; the man would be the central character in my antique saga.

Apparently, they had both started in the trade, about the same time, but whereas my new contact Clive, had been happy to keep pootling along, as he put it, John Dodds had expanded his business to such an extraordinary degree, he often dealt in items costing many thousands. Even when paying prices that would have given the average antique dealer a nose bleed, he would somehow, as if by magic, send the goods on their way into the trade.

In the early days, both had attended the auctions, held across the road in the old cattle market; now a supermarket, but he said, "As Doddsy progressed, even though he no longer attended the sales, the best items still seemed to end up with him."

He took me outside and pointing to small wrought iron first floor balcony said, "Can you imagine getting a massive pine cupboard from out of there? It was that wide, we had to take the sash window out to squeeze it through the frame. Short of building it in situ, makes you wonder how they first got it in there. Trouble was, moving it was part of the agreement and being a firm of solicitors, I could hardly mess them about. There was stuff in there like you wouldn't believe, partners desks, roll-top desks, bookcases, smoker's bow armchairs, a huge hallstand; sold Doddsy the lot. I made him promise mind you, he'd have to come back and help me out with that beast of a thing. It must have been at least 8 foot by 4, filled from top to bottom with pigeon holes; double doored and most of it pitch pine. It weighed a ton and pitch pine was not flavour of the month."

"Sounds like a nightmare." I looked up at the window, "Could have killed someone."

"It was Doddsy's idea. He parked his van, directly below on the pavement and having struggled, walking it inch by inch to the window, we tipped the thing on its back, slid it over the balcony and down onto his roof rack. Didn't do the balcony much good," he added laughing.

He carried on chatting, telling me of other deals, the seemingly endless van loads of pine, the sofa table deal, where there had been that much Regency furniture, he'd had to store it under a tarpaulin until John Dodds, buying the lot, had cleared it. He'd usually give him first chance if anything good was in the offing, for he would turn up immediately and as long as the price was right, tended not to haggle. He'd also once done him a great favour, speaking up in his defence when a pair of urns he'd bought had turned out to be a bit on the warm side.

I didn't quite understand how an uninvolved third party could defend someone's purchase of stolen garden urns. He coloured slightly at my query and so I left it at that, asking instead about others he'd known in the trade. He told me of a few who'd risen high, shooting stars, were apparently what they were known as. Seemingly unstoppable, until overcommitting and disappearing back to near anonymity. A couple of others went spectacularly bust. He told me of one unlikely success, a shipper, who unless by pure accident, had never bought a good lot in his life, the man being perfectly happy to make his living, filling containers with dross to be auctioned in America. "Well, you'd never believe it, one day in he waltzes, huge white shorts, fat as a barrel, fresh back from the States, as if he'd just stepped off his yacht moored in the river back there,--- a fully-fledged millionaire." Clive gave a wry laugh, "Most dealing in the better goods, never really got rich from it. Seems like you had to deal in junk to do that." Then returning to the self-deprecating wistful look, "Me? I'm just happy pottering along."

"And John Dodds?"

"Nobody really knows. Trading large as life one day---gone the next. There was a rumour, he'd ended up in California. Others say he's living in the Balkans, Serbia, Bulgaria? No-one really knows."

As I left, he gave me a name and phone number. "Leon Jones. That's who you ought to talk to. He'll tell you a thing or two about Doddsy."

"You seem to have the perfect setting here. Pretty countryside, charming market town, picturesque river," I said as I left.

"Don't let it fool you," he called. "A few years back it came roaring through here, a raging torrent. People were boating down the street. Took months to dry the shops out." With a cheery wave, he disappeared inside, to sit once more amid his second-hand furniture and nick-nacks.

Back at the van, I rang the number I'd been given and received a cheery reply in a comforting Shropshire burr. Leon told me, he'd be happy to have a chat, but unfortunately was currently at a fair in the south of England. I knew the one he was referring to; hundreds of vans in a field. I'd sometimes found a few decent items there, but had also been asked ridiculous prices. I thanked him and said I'd give him a call again. Meanwhile I had the scribblings to delve into, penned by the man himself, John Dodds.

CHAPTER THREE

With the goods I'd picked up the previous day, being of much better quality and condition than average, I decided to do as normal and advertise them for hire, whilst moving on lesser items in stock. Without such discipline, I would end up becoming snowed under. It was a fine day, ideal for taking flattering photographs, but really, I was itching to get back inside and withdraw the thick wad of papers from their crumpled envelope.

First though, just briefly, I'd found out a little more detail regarding the two buildings that had captivated the day before. My eye had deceived me, for apparently the market hall was slightly oval in shape, but my instincts had been right, it had been designed by the same architect who'd dreamt up the Pump Room, James Cranston and was built in 1858. The man, even though having adhered to the gothic taste of the time, had applied such imaginative touches, he would almost certainly have been an interesting person to meet in any age.

As I sifted through John Dodds' notes and fuller reminiscences, I realised, apart from immediate jottings, it would be some time before I could actually start writing the book itself. They seemed to be roughly in the right chronological order, but varied so much in style and content, I needed to sift through very carefully, to take notes, underline details and make cross references. I was embroiled in it for over a week and finally hit on the idea of colour coding, tying in reminiscences that had later occurred to him, with the appropriate earlier sections. I even found a couple of pieces of poetry.

When happy I at last knew my way around, what I'll loosely describe as a manuscript, I had to decide whether to use the actual words of John Dodds or my own. With some of the work being sketchy and many serious attempts at prose, full of alterations, I decided to do as I'd done with George's anecdotes and the tales Clive had told me; I would employ a little artistic licence. With all the information given, I'd try and imagine the scene, then put it all into in my own words, so please forgive me, as with not having taken notes, the various snippets you read above, were bound to have had a similar ring to them, but although bearing slight embellishments, they remain true to the essence of what I'd been told.

The earliest sections of the notes, in actual fact, appeared to be a later addition, as if John Dodds had suddenly realised, certain background details were needed as a foundation for the tale. They had been neatly written on blue notepaper, obviously all taken from the same pad. Even the piece they provide to keep the lines straight had been written on and included. Much of it went back to school and university days and reading through it made me realise, it was amazing John Dodds had even had such a thing as an antique shop in Ludlow. I won't go into all the details, but basically, he couldn't wait to get away from the place. The 1960's was rocking, but not back in that particular border town, where he'd felt trapped, with not even a car to make an escape.

There is one small tale I'll include: the day the rent man came to call, for it's not only relevant, but provides a snapshot, capturing the difficult economic conditions of the time.

John's mother, recently divorced from his stepfather, was bringing up two boys as best she could on the National Assistance allowance. She had taken a part-time job helping in an antique shop in town, but could only earn 30 shillings a week, for anything above that would jeopardize the weekly state benefit. Officials made regular calls and if having been given notice of an impending visit, one happened to be out at the time, serious questions were asked. You couldn't even nip to the local shop, for they could descend at any minute of the working day. John wrote,--- *The money provided was absolutely essential, but I was saddened to see mother in such demeaning circumstances.*

Gradually debt began to creep up, clothes and school uniforms had to be paid for and two growing boys fed, so with the worry of it all, the doctor had put her on Valium. The rent collector mentioned, was a genial soul and a good friend, but after letting payment drift for 6 weeks, he thought he'd better call and do what he was paid for.

That's the background detail, now I'll hand you back to John Dodds.---*I can see it now, that puzzled look, when my mother burst out laughing. She was almost crying with it, but finally managed to blurt, 'I don't have it.'*

'Oh dear. Why not?'

'I've spent it all.'

When he replied, 'You're joking,' she was laughing that much, she could hardly get the words out. 'I'm not joking. It's all gone, every last penny.'

Must have been the tablets. It seems she'd taken a dose, marched downtown and attended an antique auction in the town hall. The man was taken through to the hallway to view the damage and stood staring dumbstruck. Instead of six weeks' rent money, there were Staffordshire figures, a large pair of china swans, ruby glass, Nailsea glass, green Mary Gregory vases, decanters, a pair of lustres, large chemist's bottles with their pointed stoppers and all manner of other things.

Well putting it briefly, she made a whacking profit and doing more of the same got her out of the debt cycle and reliance on state aid.

As she began to make a name for herself, old vans would occasionally pull up with scruffy looking pieces of furniture, either binder-twined to the roof or protruding out the back and a deal would be done out on the pavement. She took a Saturday stall in the market hall and that's where a certain Marie came into the story. Seems she was one of, what he describes as the exciting, free-spirited crowd, who turned up at the house after the stallholders had packed everything away. The notes didn't make it clear, but I assumed her husband was also part of the merry throng. It didn't stop schoolboy Dodds from fantasising mind you. I'll give you one of his reminiscences:--- *That wicked spark of merriment in those huge brown eyes of hers, as if knowing exactly what I was thinking, brought on blushing, palpitations and confusion and yet I couldn't wait for her next visit.*

The sketchy outline of his university days and job in London aren't really relevant to the story, other than the request by his mother for a loan. Reading between the lines, with both her boys now having left home, her heart had gone out of the job. She had taken a small shop in town, but was hardly ever in it. The loan was for two oak four poster beds, a pair of brothers had stashed away in the roof of a barn. The beds were bought, sold and he had his money back.

I now moved on to the section written on pale blue airmail paper, the scrawled writing, sloping down the page. John Dodds had become thoroughly fed up with suburban London, had pulled out of an impending marriage that threatened to trap him there, had grown to hate his job, but had not one clue of where to go next. He'd tried window cleaning in his spare time, even freelance grave digging, but apart from giving him spare cash, it hardly seemed to offer a way into a new career. Strange thing is,--- in a roundabout way, it appears it did.

Trying to piece together the story, it seems his mother had sunk into debt once more, was thoroughly fed up with Ludlow, maybe even depressed and was now planning to join her two sisters up in Lancashire. The long and the short of it was, John gathered together all the columns of coinage he'd amassed from window cleaning, drove north and put down a deposit on a small terraced cottage for his mother. Needless to say, he'd probably had the good sense to convert the coinage into something more convenient. Problem over? It didn't seem like it. There were a few references to him now being saddled with a mortgage on a house, that for some strange reason, his mother hadn't moved into. He had done all he could to discover the reason and coax her into taking up the opportunity, but after what must have been at least six months back in the job he loathed, frustration spurred him into action.

I refer to a short piece, boldly written, describing how he'd handed in his notice, put all his possessions in the back of the Minivan and having driven north to Lancashire, had taken possession of the house. I smiled at his description of feeling unfettered and singing as he drove up the M1. I worked out, he must have been 26 at the time and although having completely burnt his boats, didn't seem the slightest bit worried. I scanned his notes again, but found no hint at this point, of him even dreaming of venturing into the world of antiques.

In fact, he got a job on a major construction project, a link road leading off the M6 to Kendal. I found some of his anecdotes entertaining, but with them not being relevant to John Dodds, the antique dealer, I've not included them. He did have a couple of liaisons with local young ladies, but these again are not relevant, although I will include one little tale.

He'd drawn plans, had them passed by the council, work was being done on the house and an extension containing new kitchen and bathroom was in its final phase. A young lady had been invited for a late coffee and on her requesting to use the new facilities upstairs, he'd given directions along with the warning to be mindful of a floorboard still not back in place, left open for the electrician to finish the job.

I'll give you his words:--- *I was sitting there relishing a drop of red, heard the toilet flush, then a screech as ladies leg appeared through the ceiling. 'That's buggered it,' I thought and went upstairs to ease my stricken date from the lath and plaster.*

Reading on through his notes I came to the bit where all were laid off the job for the winter. He'd had a grant for the extension on the house, but it hadn't covered all the costs and he'd used up most of his own funds. His attempt at signing on the dole had fallen on stony ground. The man weighing him up had said, '*You don't want us making your life a misery for just a few bob a week, do you?*'

John had said no and was sent on his way with a reassuring pat on the back, '*Someone like you won't find it hard to get a job. You'll thank me in the end.*'

Some comfort coming from a man at Lancaster Labour Exchange and when I checked; all this was happening in 1974, those dark days of the three-day week, when the country it seems, was on its knees. What a time to decide to leave a secure job in London!

This is where his mother comes back into the story, for on hearing of his plight, she drove up north with the sole purpose of introducing him to a certain Pete. No second name--- I checked. He was always referred to, as just Pete. The meeting took place on a Saturday morning in one of Pete's favourite haunts, a newish establishment on the outskirts of Morecambe. He earnt his living distributing illustrated leaflets displaying antique artefacts, which when returning later that same day, would supposedly be in the happy position of paying top price for. John explained, he didn't know the first thing about antiques, to which Pete had said, '*Don't worry you'll soon pick it up.*' Well, the drinks flowed, Pete regaled them with stories of his successes and John Dodds couldn't wait to get started, first thing Monday morning.

I won't go into detail, but taking you fast forward a couple of weeks and using John Dodds' notes as inspiration, will try and capture the scene.

On ringing his mother from the local call box and finding, she was rather keen to know how he'd got on, he'd answered, 'He's still got a cold.'

'What?'

'I've called there three times and each time he says he's got this stinker of a cold.'

'No he hasn't! He's just messing you about!'

'Honestly--- he doesn't look well at all. I actually feel a bit embarrassed pestering him."

'I'm coming up there.'

Which she did and the sight of her marching into the same pub they'd all met in the time before, registered as a look of shock and an attempt at damage limitation. Shuffling in his seat, Pete pulled his old beige mac a little tighter, flicked strands of hair from broad forehead and switching on a disarming smile, said with a blue-eyed blink of sincerity, 'Hello Jessica, what a nice surprise. What can I get you, love?'

'Never mind that!' she said, with a vehemence that made the glasses jangle. 'What about doing what you promised?'

'It's this cold Jessica,' he said, coughing and wincing as he rubbed his throat. 'Just can't seem to shake it off.

'Rubbish! You're just shilly-shallying!'

He'd just taken a sip of beer and nearly choked on it. 'Now Jessica,' he said trying to suppress a smile, 'What a thing to say!' He was actually laughing now, 'I've never shilly-shallied in my life.'

After a few drinks, the promise to make a start and sally forth door-knocking that following Monday, was finally made.

CHAPTER FOUR

So here we have it at last, John Dodds' first step into the mysterious labyrinth of the antique trade. Fortunately, his notes at this stage are fairly copious, helping me write the following in the first person.

I arrived at Pete's place bright and early, full of hope, expecting him to be ready for the off, but the man I'd met in the pub, so full of cheer and optimism, now looked completely dishevelled as if having been caught on the hop. As he was getting his children ready for school, I thought it best to sit down, quietly out of the way.

Finally he said, 'Been having a bit of trouble with the van.'

The fact it wasn't a problem, for I had a van of my own, was countered with, 'Well truth is, I'm a bit strapped for cash at the moment.'

'Well I've got a few quid on me.'

'How much?'

'Twenty-six pounds.'

Thinking for a while he gave a resigned smile and said, 'Fine, that should be plenty.'

Having dropped Paul, the youngest of his boys off at his grandmother's, we finally set off in my grey Minivan, with its small aluminium luggage rack, to invest my £26 in a new career, antiques. Our destination was Kendal.

As with most enterprises, John Dodds found things were not quite as simple as well lubricated reminiscences make them sound. They had a few minor triumphs, but it did seem a hard way to earn a crust. Most of their profits went on fuel, lunch and the obligatory four pints each to accompany it. As you can imagine, the smell of beer didn't go down too well when making enquiries on people's doorsteps.

When they did hit on finding jugs and basins, japanned coal boxes, silver plated tea sets, fish servers, plant stands, hall stands, chamber pots, display cabinets, mantle clocks and all the other things asked for by the shipping trade, Pete always insisted, they take them to the same man. One very difficult to deal with. Getting a profit out of him was like pulling a tooth and as his shop was near a natural beauty spot on the local river, it was the eponym for his name, 'The Crook of Lune'. Any attempt at negotiating a better price was immediately quashed by being led through to where lines of stock stood ready for his American purchaser, '*Here, help yourselves. The price you're asking would buy any one of these. Take your pick.*' With no funds in reserve, they were in no position to argue. If their haul wasn't cashed in each night, there was no money to go out with next day.

At one point of course, Pete had thought it a good idea, John should chance his arm at buying, so rather than calling for assistance every time something was offered for sale, he told him, to give it a go and buy the odd thing himself. As regards what happened, I'll hand you over to John Dodds.

---A very pleasant woman answered the door and asked my reason for knocking on it. I explained it was I who had delivered the leaflet earlier and enquired, did she have anything to sell?

My heart lifted as she said, in fact she did. Now was my chance! She returned holding an oak framed mirror and after assessing its value, I made an offer and became the proud owner of my first ever antique artefact. I returned with it to the van and Pete looking a little bemused asked, 'How much did she make you pay for it?'

'15 shillings,' I replied, immediately having that sinking feeling.

'Have you got the rest of it?'

'No, why?'

'It's the mirror off an Edwardian dressing table.'

He let me off lightly, saying we'd lose it in a deal somehow, but that was my first ever attempt at being an antique dealer.

On another occasion, our budding dealer, described how he'd not been too enamoured with Pete's intervention.

---An extremely attractive woman, in a rather short skirt, tight blouse and particularly high heels, considering the time of day, had invited me to step inside. Music was softly playing and on a coffee table lay a magazine with the centrefold fully on display. The woman, raising an eyebrow and smiling, asked how she might be of assistance. I could feel my heart pounding and was just about to reply, when a rapping on the door and Pete's sudden appearance, was not unlike a drenching from a bucket of cold water.

What might have happened, if Pete hadn't burst in on the scene, is left to our imagination.

Door knocking for antiques was not as easy as some tales of old make it sound. Sometimes they went for days without much success at all, but Pete's bright wit never seemed to dampen.

John Dodds had written:--- *It felt like nothing would change our luck. Nearing end of day, we walked up a house path together, not a thing we normally did as it seemed threatening, but it was the last in the row and to be truthful, I was quite happy to just go through the motions, get in the van and drive back home. However, as the door opened, my heart gave a jolt, for the tight white blouse, its buttons barely constraining what heaved within, belonged to a particularly attractive young lady. Pete went into his cheerful patter and then asked if there might be anything for sale?*

The woman shook her head and said, 'No, I'm afraid not.'

'We buy all sorts, y'know love. Pay good money. We buy washstands, jugs and bowls, barley twist tables, even big wormy chests.'

Her laughter had a marvellous rippling effect and Pete staring back, as if completely unaware of having said anything suggestive, wore a look of blue-eyed innocence, before slowly breaking into a smile.

On another occasion, with nothing to lose, we thought we might as well try our luck at a grand mansion commanding a rise at the end of a long gravel drive. Pete reached up and gave the door a drumming with the iron knocker. I winced and braced myself. A tweed skirted lady standing small in the opening answered Pete's enquiry with a haughty, 'Goodness, no! We don't sell to people at the door!'

With a look of complete sincerity he asked, 'What about those in the upstairs flats, love? D'you think they'd have something to sell?'

A shocked glint of mirth showed, before she had time to suppress it.

At this point in the notes, John Dodds' account becomes sketchy. There was reference to an attempt at selling their goods to dealers other than the Crook of Lune, but with the country still in a state of depression following the three-day week, times were hard. Not many buyers were coming over from America and as they walked along the lines of goods amassed in dealer's storerooms, row after row of things like hallstands and washstands, dusty shelving absolutely bulging with the very items they were trying to sell, they gave thanks for having been blessed with a certain amount of luck, thus far.

Antique jewellery, was still instantly cashable and when having gathered a decent quantity, they took it to a pleasant couple dealing in Kirby Lonsdale, avid buyers of sovereigns and anything Masonic.

They were often offered pine furniture, but having neither the funds, the place to store it, nor the vision to see what a craze it would become, they'd had to leave it behind; pine chests, bedding boxes, kitchen tables and even at one call, two pine tallboys, which I've been told, would later have been regarded as rarities.

They thought they'd had a touch of luck one day, for when striking out to the south of Morecambe Bay, they chanced upon a huge, ornate Victorian oak armchair, supposedly from Pilling village hall and in the same deal, an oversized cuckoo clock. The gamble on both helped lift their spirits, until time came to try and get rid of them.

John Dodds sounded quite down hearted. ---*Circumstances were beginning to become quite depressing. I still had more money than I'd started with, but we couldn't find enough deals of substance. Out of frustration one day we agreed to buy one of those dark, ugly, Edwardian spider tables. Trouble was it was up in an attic. The most we were likely to earn was 30 shillings, but at least it offered a ray of hope.*

'Pity you weren't here last week,' the woman said brightly. 'It was down here in the parlour, a bit of a nuisance actually and so my son popped it up into the attic.'

Popped it into the attic? Having hauled himself up there, using a chair and then my shoulders, Pete had it wedged in the rectangular opening and as he tried to push it through, flakes of white paint floated down. He then tried it top first with no greater success.

'How are you getting on up there?'

Pete, with a malignant spider table now blocking his route to freedom, bent down and through the remaining gap called, 'Fine, love, but are you sure he just popped it up here?'

'Oh yes, only took him a few seconds.'

Giving a growl, Pete wrenched the table free again and with great relief, made his escape to join me on the landing. Gazing up at the dark opening and dreaming of the 30 shillings profit, we decided to give it one last go. Pete, stood on the chair once more and pulling on a table leg, got the stubborn thing into the hatch where it became firmly wedged again. Wouldn't go up or down. More flakes of paint drifted down to join those already looking like a bad dose of dandruff. Gazing up at the four ugly legs and small adjoining shelf, now protruding just above head height, I asked a little concerned, 'Pete, what are we going to do now?'

'Oh, just paint it white and leave it there!'

Our stifled laughter brought another query from below, 'Are you two alright up there?'

Somehow, we did manage to extricate it and actually it seemed to change our luck, for we rattled along at quite a merry pace that evening with the van full. It was that packed, Pete had to almost wear the table, for with its legs protruding at an angle, encroaching on passenger seat and gear stick, it had him hunched up like Quasimodo.

Sounding like a ventriloquist he mumbled, 'Don't change gear just yet. I'm trying to light m'fag.'

I searched John Dodds' notes for more anecdotes and became aware, a huge amount of what they bought was a bit of a mystery to both of them. Much time was spent in Lancaster Library looking up factory marks, Chinese marks and impressed names on the underside of china objects they'd bought. Bottom corners of paintings were pored over, looking to see if a squiggle in the foliage was in actual fact a faint signature. Something that might make their fortunes. They chanced upon two traders, prepared to pay a little more than they'd been getting for their regular shipping goods. The one, if they happened to strike lucky, would drive all the way up from Bury and the other, a tougher prospect, had a lock-up unit on White Lund, an unattractive swathe of ground where travellers often camped.

Then I came across another two anecdotes. Only short, but they help capture the hit and miss nature of those days.

---*The day had brought meagre gains, a couple of jug and basin sets, a few coins and medals. The medals were just the usual, 'Pipsqueak and Wilfred,' as Pete called them and it always seemed a shame to scrap them, but as the one was worth more for its silver content than any collector would have given, we were left with no choice. On the last call of the day, our hopes were raised.*

We were in an old stone farmhouse and the woman said to her husband, 'Fetch sack from shed, Jack.'

Hauling in the sack he asked, 'Is owt in 'ere any good?'

It was packed full with copper kettles, jam pans, skillets, a spirit kettle and silver-plated trays and tea sets.

'Well,' says Pete scratching a temple and wincing, as if embarrassed at having to impart such bad news. 'I'm not saying we can't sell it, but you know how it is,--- these sort of things don't bring much these days.'

39

The day's success rested on the answer to the following. 'I'm sorry, I'd love to offer more, but how does five pounds sound?'

There followed a tense silence as each looked to the other, then finally, 'Well it's doing no good out in shed,' said the husband and the day was saved. I did have to spend many hours cleaning it all mind you and in places the copper had become that encrusted, it was a job to remove the verdigris without scratching the metal beneath.

The second little tale happened when they were on quite a good run.

---We had decided to return to Kendal and on an estate we'd not tried before, struck lucky even before finishing the leaflet distribution. Pete emerged holding a doll.

'That's it,' he said. 'We can go home now.'

Looking down at the small china face and grubby doll's clothes, I asked, 'Why?'

Making sure the previous owners couldn't witness, he thumbed up the hair on the back of the doll's neck to reveal the impressed maker's mark. The doll had quite a pretty face, but I found it hard to believe we'd hit the jackpot. It took a fair deal to persuade Pete, that now we'd started, we may as well finish the day's work, which was quite fortunate, for as so often happens when striking lucky, luck tends to continue for a while.

The doll, however, now posed a problem. Most dealers wouldn't have rated it and anyone who did, was not likely to tell us its worth. The whole of next day we spent either looking up doll maker's marks in the library or trying to get an idea from contacts, what price to ask. Pete had dreams of great reward and didn't want to give it away.

40

He used the trusted tactic, saying not that we owned a rare doll, but he did know where one could be found. Reactions to his description, were underwhelming to say the least and by the end of day two, our much-vaunted prize had become a bit of a burden, for whilst trying to ascertain its value, we hadn't earnt any bunce, as Pete put it. Then at last we met someone who gave us a pointer, divulging, a lady in Preston, renowned for buying antique dolls, would probably give us the best price.

When we entered her shop with huge dolls arrayed in seeming pristine condition, clothed and bonneted, limbs jointed, eyes that opened and closed, our little effort seemed pathetic. We came out of there glad of her £12 and the realisation, a better price is often gained from someone who hasn't a clue, rather than from someone who has.

This left the rest of the day free and so we thought we might as well go round the junk shops. The doll, bless her, had unwittingly led us to a day of bounty. For some strange reason, we'd chanced upon an untouched enclave; none of the shops had been stripped of stock by the shipping trade. Jugs and basins and washstands, yes, but not the things we'd found an outlet for. Still arrayed on shelves, were Napoleon-hat clocks, Westminster chimers, biscuit barrels and shoved into corners and back rooms were coal boxes, chamber pots, hearth tidies, plant stands and barley twist tables. We drove home with the larger items bound to the roof-rack with binder-twine and the booty in the back ringing success, at every bump in the road.

The sorting out was done in the usual manner, in a Morecambe pub. We always kept back a kitty for the next day and split the remainder equally. It was in these bay-side hostelries that a number of the dodgier coves hung out. Pete would occasionally divulge details of their colourful pasts, making me all the more wary, but a certain one, bereft of that whiff of petty criminality, had a rather pleasant countenance and magnetism that drew people in around him. Pete often joked with him and initially,

41

gave no hint as to how he fitted in with that particular crowd. The man had a ready wit and an easy manner, but I don't know what it was, there was something I couldn't quite put my finger on that put me on my guard.

Pete had been regaling all with some of his stories. He told the small throng of how one day, he'd chanced upon a full-sized, female, wax tailor's dummy. 'The motor was that full, I drove home with her lying, knockers up, strapped to the roof. You'll never guess what happened?'

'The law stopped you,' said one who'd more than likely had a few run-ins with the boys in blue. 'Thought you'd done her in and you was making off with the body.'

'No,' said Pete, laughing. 'It was a baking hot day and that's women for you! She began to melt, and I saw the cream of the day's profits dripping down the side of the car.'

The laughter was interrupted by the barman saying there was a phone call for that enigmatic man I mentioned. On returning, he said to Pete, 'Sorry mate, I've been called.'

It was later, with the two of us alone, Pete at last explained, that the fellow in question was a kept man, making himself indispensable to a wealthy male retiree, living alone up by the Wintergardens. That apparently, was how he made a living. He was a genius at it. He'd once come a cropper and been banged up for fraud mind you, but on release, had even conned his probation officer. 'She'd been that taken with him, can you believe it? She bought him a car.'

John Dodds, then gave brief details of another meeting with the man.---*All had had quite a bit to drink and with the two of us chatting out of earshot, he regaled me with a few of the stunts he'd pulled over the years. The alcohol had managed to loosen even his tongue and he boasted, that once having latched on to*

42

the right client, he was almost impossible to shake off, becoming the best friend they'd ever known, willing to do anything they required.

'Anything?'

'Anything. Just so long as that money tap remains turned on.' Then turning, his eyes fully locked on to mine, he said, 'Believe me lad, I can con anyone. Even you!'

John Dodds wrote, ---*That cold stare, gave him the look of a born predator.*

Meanwhile, down in Welsh border country, appreciation of her son's success, seems to have acted as a catalyst, for his mother decided to make the bold move and journey north, fully intent on joining the action. His enterprise had rekindled her antique dealing spirit and although over 50 years of age, for the first time ever, she would try her hand at door-knocking. Pete enjoyed her company and whether it was the enthusiasm she engendered, perhaps her ban on lunchtime quaffing, or maybe it was just pure luck; anyway, for whatever reason, they enjoyed quite a run of success, selling most of their finds to a man who could keep their assets liquid, Bruce, the dealer from Bury.

---*He was not a big man, barely five foot two and slight of build, but what he lacked in stature, he made up for with energy and heart, plus he had deep pockets. He worked on rapid turnover and the philosophy; 'small, quick profits trumped waiting for big hits.'*

One evening I was helping Bruce load a massive Edwardian inlaid mahogany cabinet onto his roof rack and remarked, it was a pity none of us had the capital to hang on to items of such quality. I'm not saying it was my taste, far too busy, but the marquetry absolutely oozed quality. If one small section, or the bowed glass door had needed restoration, it would have cost a good deal more than the £32 we'd sold the piece for.

'You can't really look at it like that,' Bruce said. 'It's supply and demand. We have to keep the money turning over and even though it seems like we're virtually giving some things away, we can only ever get the going rate.' As we re-entered the house, where Pete and my mother were now supping tea, Bruce continued, 'You have to keep it moving---you have to keep playing with it.' He added in all sincerity, 'The more you play with it the bigger it grows.'

I saw Pete's eyes widen as he tried his best not to choke on a biscuit.

So easy at that point to have come out with a quip, but we were too much in need of Bruce's regular money supply. So, when he blithely added in his northern chirpiness, 'It's true you know. The more you play with it the bigger it grows,' I refrained from replying, 'Really. Mum always told me, it makes you go blind,' knowing full well, if I had have done, that would have been the end of the dealings with our little friend, for it would have set her off and helpless laughter would have rung in his ears all the way back to Bury.

At this point, John Dodds' notes became a little sketchy, with just the odd comment such as, ---*Pete didn't turn up again today.* It's not clear if he and his mother continued door-knocking, but I assumed they must have done, for I found a note dated much later.---*We found Pete in his shop, which was a rarity. It was obvious there would be no shifting him and so we carried on alone. When he did eventually re-join us, his heart didn't seem to be in it and then to cap it all, he tripped when walking down a path. I was of course concerned, as it appeared he'd sprained his ankle, but my mother, with a withering look said, 'Come off it, Pete. Pull the other one,' which I thought was a bit harsh, but his sheepish smile indicated she'd been right, he'd been faking.*

I knew what the trouble was. Pete's wife was not well, in and out of hospital, with never ending rounds of chemotherapy treatment and he was obviously worried, plus whatever we now earned had to be split three ways. By the end of that week, sad to say, our little trio broke up, but my mother and I decided to persevere.

---She was particularly good with the older folk, John Dodds writes. She would sit and listen to their life stories, look at old family photos and whereas I was itching to be off, chasing the next opportunity she would say, 'Don't be so impatient.' She was right, for often, when passing former calls, we'd hear a rap on a window and be waved inside. Sometimes they'd rooted out something more to sell, or occasionally, would refer us to friends who also wanted us to call. Their attitude seemed to be, with the old stuff having been shoved away, forgotten and no further use to them, they might as well cash it in, as they could hardly take it with them. Not so sure the lady in the alms houses should have sold the oversized Georgian oak tripod table, mind you, but when she did, a few curtains must have been twitching, for over ensuing days, three of her neighbours decided to do likewise. They were the largest of their type I had ever seen, in fact would ever see, comfortably able to seat four people.

I noticed an asterisk and bottom of page, in tiny writing, probably added much later:---*With hindsight, being light oak in colour and from Victorian alms houses, they were almost certainly an example of the Georgian style being reproduced mid-19th C. Out of period.*

There were now quite a few references to someone called Thompson. Apparently, all the local trade complained of how he now dominated local sales. They couldn't get a look in, whether it be a humble towel rail or a Georgian bureau. Although living near Windermere, he actually bought for a dealer in Harrogate. No-one could work out how this Yorkshire dealer, Smith the Rink could consistently pay what seemed like too much money and yet never run out of the stuff. It didn't affect the mother and son outfit, for they carried on, not with leaflets, but cold calling and with venturing out into the country, they chanced on items of better quality. What his mother described as, *'proper antiques.'*

It prompted the pivotal notion of taking the stock south to her shop for sale. Trading conditions in Shropshire had vastly improved, meaning, in theory their goods ought to command a higher price. Also, as a bonus, the shipping trade there hadn't yet latched on to the sort of mundane items John Dodds could instantly sell in the north, meaning he could tour the shops around the Ludlow area and return to Lancashire with oak-cased mantle clocks, jugs and basins, biscuit barrels, small Edwardian barometers and anything with a barley twist to it. A classic two-way trade. On one particular journey, the wind got under a washstand door, sending it winging to bounce in the middle lane of the Thelwell viaduct. No chance of retrieving it, therefore. He wrote:---*It absolutely scared the life out of me, for it could have smashed through a car windscreen, wiping out an innocent family. Headline news! End of my career!* A lesson learnt for life? Not quite, I discovered as I perused his notes further.

There was one last door-knocking tale and then I assumed they altered their modus operandi, for after one unfortunate encounter, which I've included below, I found no further mention of such. Perhaps it had cured him. Remembering something I'd seen previously and shuffling through his papers once more, I found, not quite, but the next attempt at door knocking would be years hence.

---*It had been a long tiring, fruitless day and in a row of cottages over Bentham way, I was at last told there might be something for sale. An instinct made me wary, for the old lady looked a bit doddery, not quite with it and the place had a foul stench to it. She pointed to an armchair she was willing to sell. I bent, in order to turn it on its side, hoping to ascertain its age, but literally recoiled in horror.*

My mother appeared in the doorway, but being unable to speak, I waved frantically, warning her to approach not one step further. Joining her in the lane, I was still retching and hardly able to breathe.

46

'Whatever's the matter?' she asked.

Convulsed with spasms as if attempting to bring up my innards, I made it back to the car and finally, taking a deep breath, managed to gasp, 'That dirty old bag's been pissing in it!' before going into a fit of coughing and retching, my words having revived the memory of warm ammonia.

Sadly, there was only one more mention of Pete. He turned up one day, telling them he'd heard of an oak coffer for sale, at an hotel up at Shap. John suggested they go in his mother's estate car. It would appear more business-like compared to arriving in his Minivan. Pete joined them. The coffer was late 17th century and although on the hefty side, had an interesting pair of central cupboard doors where normally two panels would be. None of the three had much experience dealing in early oak and with the owners not willing to take a penny less than £40, Pete declined, but John and his mother, finding it a good colour and rather monumental, thought it worth a gamble. It was that big, it stretched the length of the estate car and they had to tie the back door down. With all three crammed in the front seats, they made their way back south, to drop Pete off.

John Dodds writes,---*It was the first time I'd heard the description, breaker. It was the term used by the oak dealer, we'd invited to peruse our find, back in Ludlow. I truly thought, that when he said, 'It's a good breaker,' I'd become acquainted with a new word describing a particularly rare type of coffer. I was crestfallen to hear, however, the interesting pair of doors we'd set such store by, had been fabricated at much later date and that also, there wasn't much call for what he described as, 'A wooden railway carriage,' these days.*

The bad news didn't stop there, for as a breaker, he was sad to inform us, the most we could expect was a tenner. Plan B had to be thought of and quickly, as it was a bit of a shop blocker.

John continues,---*I settled on the notion of entering it into a local sale and took it to Leominster, the saleroom being located at the time, in the cattle market. I met the head of the auction house, a genial man who introduced himself as Mr. Croft. All semblance of geniality left his face, however, the moment he espied what was being unsheathed from the back of my mother's estate car.*

'Hope you're not proposing to dump that here,' he said.

After a great deal of persuasion and willingness to offer the lot without reserve, he reluctantly entered it into the next antique sale.

It seems that something must have been looking after them, for two locals, having taken a shine to it, bid it up to over £40. After expenses had been deducted, they escaped from the deal having lost a mere £2, the equivalent of about £20 in today's money.

'You were lucky,' remarked Mr. Croft as the cashier handed me the cheque. He was obviously anxious to quash at birth any notion I might have, as regards repeating the exercise.

I smiled to myself as I read those words ringing back from the past. It was hard to imagine young John Dodds ending up as owner of the massive shop I'd seen on the internet.

Initially, they considered their base, to be still in the north, with just occasional journeys south to sell the better stock.--- *We were given a favourable deal by friends who ran the Bull Hotel and so we took rooms there, rather than stay at the shop in Old Street, where conditions were primitive, to say the least. I found it strange, that the town I once couldn't wait to escape from, now held such an allure. Whereas those in the north still wore collar and tie if invited to a party, some even doing so for a Saturday outing to the local, in Ludlow it all seemed far more Bohemian and exciting. To be honest, I could feel my blood coursing at the very thought of going back there.*

I again scanned the notes and realised, that although no longer door-knocking for antiques, they still occasionally revisited old northern calls, for as John Dodds writes:---*As goods that had once been considered unsaleable, suddenly came into demand, we could benefit, if able to remember where we'd seen the items. Also, with the Ludlow connection now giving us an upper hand, we could call round the local trade, taking a pick of their latest stock, far easier than those barren days we'd often had cold-calling.*

Here's an interesting snippet I found from the notes.---*We had experienced a middling day covering old ground. Often, the people who at first visit, appear willing to sell almost everything they own, can on return, with the rapport now lost, seem almost completely intractable. We struggled, but did manage to prise a few pieces free. On the final call, however, the couple looking glad to see us once again, had already put their wares, ready for sale in a shoe box and after a cup of tea and a chat, waved us off, quite happy with the couple of quid my mother had paid for their nick-nacks. Back at the car, I sighed and commented on it having been a tough day. Mother returned a smile.*

'What are you grinning at?' I asked.

With a wink she held up a slender item fashioned from wood. I enquired as to its use and she explained it was a knitting sheath, unusual in the fact it had a tiny aperture in the one end, a glass covered picture, no bigger than a child's fingernail.

I must admit, I gasped when I first read this, for it was a similar item that Mike, the one-time driver to John Dodds', had shown me at our first meeting. The notes went on to say, the box also held a Stevengraph and lace bobbins, some of which were of turned ivory with names inscribed. Again, an asterisk drew me to tiny writing, bottom of page.

Years later, when perusing the Pinto treen collection in the Birmingham Museum, I spotted an old friend, the knitting sheath from all those years ago.

As evident, when they'd courted disaster with the oak coffer, they had to be careful where they gambled their scarce resources and often went for the quirkier items, the trade had to offer, rather than the conventional. In the notes, I found reference to a Noah's ark, a small wooden tram, a piece of folk art in the form of a farmer aboard his carved and painted horse-drawn wagon, Victorian children's games, a japanned coal box, similar to those they'd sold for £3 each, apart from the fact, this one was emblazoned with a floral design that John's mother felt certain was Pontypool Tole ware.

At a shop near the river in Kendal, they often chanced on something a bit out of the ordinary:--- *Not least the owner*, John Dodds had written. Then continued with:---*On entering, one is instantly hit by the waft of potpourri, heaped in bowls dotted around the shop. Charles, the proprietor was surprisingly light on his feet for such a large man and with a manner, not unlike a dowager duchess, it would not have been hard to imagine him wearing dangly earrings and an all-enveloping frock. If anything happened to be needed, his partner Andrew would be dispatched to immediately attend to it. On one lucky visit we bought two large dough troughs, potpourri included and four slender, rectangular wooden boards, edges attractively fretted and the circular ends, pierced to simulate flowers. Each had two rows of vicious iron hooks arrayed along their length, on which to hang game. 'From a large estate in Cumbria,' Charles revealed as if letting slip a secret. We actually did quite well with them back in Shropshire and avidly bought more on our return. It was on the fifth visit, I commented, 'This Cumbrian estate must be quite massive.' We later found out they were Spanish.*

Judging by John Dodds' notes, Ludlow now became their base, with only the odd foray north being made. I'll hand you over to him again, but must confess, as before, I did tweak the descriptions a little.

---*We had toured the trade with fair success and one of the last calls was at a shop run by, The Potty Man as my mother called him. Outside his shop near Morecambe Town Hall, he had a row of chamber pots with joke inscriptions painted on the side. We bought a couple of minor items and he said, if we hurried, we might catch the sale being conducted next door. We wandered in and I couldn't see much of interest, but with a jab of a finger, my mother pointed to an oak armchair. 'It's an early one,' she hissed. I don't know how I'd walked straight past it, but I suppose, with it having such a simple panelled back and seat missing, in my ignorance, I'd taken it for a down at heel, Edwardian discard. It was only when I looked again, I noticed its generous girth, rich colour and proud stance. Obviously, my eye was not yet tuned in, enabling me to pick out gems lurking amongst the rubbish and alas it would take a good few years before the skill became second nature. Even then, one could still miss the odd lot.*

The local trade stood bunched in a threatening huddle, but when the item came up for sale, only one bid against us. As the price topped the vaunted ceiling of a hundred pounds, my heart was thumping, for the majority of our remaining capital was being bet on the one piece. The whole thing was way beyond my reckoning and I was on the one hand relieved, but on the other, quite stunned by the enormity of mother's final bid of £120, cowing our opposition into a grave shake of head.

We had paid and were leaving when the Crook of Lune bustling in, headed towards our adversaries. His anticipatory smile, on relishing the spoils, faded when witnessing his wave of enthusiasm, dashing resoundingly against their wall of glumness. There followed an intense exchange and as he eyed me departing with the chair, I noticed his face slowly transforming into a picture of puzzlement.

Back in Ludlow, my spirits were not dashed exactly, but definitely given a disconcerting dent. A trusted friend who had a haulage business, but was also a fair judge of antiques, spotted the chair tied to the roof rack and asked whether we would be willing to take £40 for it? Mother quickly put him in his place, causing his colour to heighten, but his attempt to regain a little dignity by explaining, the lack of a seat on such an item was a serious drawback, I did find rather unsettling.

There happened to be a sale on next day in the Regency Assembly Rooms and before the off, the trade tended to whip around the local shops in an attempt to beat the opposition to anything with a profit. Of course, the chair was homed in on, but all too aware most of our capital was tied up in it, I hesitated at being too ambitious with the asking price. At £180, I was told I was mad and when asking the next enquirer, £160, it brought, 'Huh! You'll be lucky!'

By mid-morning I'd begun to feel quite jittery, but then in came a dealer who said very quietly, having examined the chair, 'Now then young man, I would like you to think very carefully before you answer. How much exactly do you want for this chair?'

I took a deep breath and said, 'One hundred and forty-five pounds.'

'Now are you quite certain that is your best price?'

'Yes,' I said.

'Then you have just sold it.'

'Goodness, the town's busy this morning,' said my mother, looking windswept as she entered the shop. 'Where's the chair?'

'I've just sold it.'

'*You haven't! How much?*'

'*One hundred and forty-five.*'

'*Oh, well done!*'

I had not only recouped the bulk of our working capital, but that one item had gained us nearly as much as my weekly earnings would have done, when doing a proper job. Once all the other items from our latest foray north had sold, it brought on quite a glow; satisfaction mixed with relief and with the frisson of having successfully pitted one's wits, thrown in, it made the throng I joined in the Rose and Crown that evening, seem all the merrier.

CHAPTER FIVE

The notes now dwelt on how they coped in those early days, trying to revive the shop's fortunes. Again, I've filled out John Dodds' descriptions slightly, but my adaptation still contains the essence of what he actually wrote.

---*It was years prior Ludlow bypass having been constructed and on some days the traffic through town was incessant. On occasions, when a large truck laboured uphill, the whole shop window would vibrate. A newsagents situated at the top of the hill was constantly having part of its façade knocked off and to add to the mayhem, the wholesale drinks suppliers at the end of the narrow lane running up the side of the shop, needed regularly restocking and so on top of the constant back and forth of the large delivery vans, there came a juddering as an articulated lorry, that had stopped Old Street traffic in both directions, edged its way, reversing slowly up the lane. The two pubs in the bullring, were also restocked via this narrow artery, as was Boots the chemist. On some days of almost manic activity, Pepper Lane gave hint of street bedlam in mediaeval times.*

The shop consisted of the main selling area of about 12'x 12', a backroom of 10' x 8' with a door accessing the lane and there was a tiny space at the bottom of an enclosed stairway, barely enough to turn round in, but it did have a yellowed sink and Baby Belling cooker. A precarious stairway located between the two main rooms gave access to the cellar and although extremely damp, the slimy flagstone floor, had to be negotiated if one happened to be in need of the only lavatory. The first floor had two rooms, the one with barely enough room for a single bed, while the other, same size as the shop selling area below, afforded a good view of the main road and the Art Deco cinema opposite. The top floor had arguably the best room in the property, provided an outbreak of fire below, didn't trap the occupants. It again had a window overlooking the street and also a squint-hole that provided a constant supply of fresh air through the parted brickwork. Viewed from outside, the fracture ran down the gable end like a flash of forked lightening imprinted in the masonry. Another interesting feature could only be viewed if crawling through a hatchway leading into a triangular roof space halfway up the stairs. The beam supporting the roof valley was that rotten a finger could be poked into the wet pulp, but as unsavoury as this small space happened to be, it had to be regularly visited to drag out the oval zinc wash-pail for its contents to be emptied into the sink below. Failure to do so made the small cooking area extremely unpleasant and in fact dangerous to work in. The lead casing to the wiring needed a regular wipe-down and the linoleum floor covering became horribly slimy underfoot unless regularly mopped. The only form of heating came from a Calor gas stove, the sort that have a flimsy metal rear door, to allow access when exchange of gas bottle is required. On a winter's day with it going full blast, the air hung heavy, the window in the small back room ran with condensation and if polishing anywhere near it, especially when using the melted beeswax and turps mix favoured by the trade, the air became almost explosive. Friends calling in for coffee and a chat tended to tap on the side door leading from the alley. The heavy curtain would be drawn, the draught excluder removed and with a warning regarding of where best to tread, descending via the wooden step, they would be admitted into the den. Customers entering by way of the shop door, automatically sent the brass bell jangling and the curtain from the warm enclave would be parted to ascertain which of us should venture into the chill to offer assistance.

55

'Oh, it's that Mrs. Eddy. You go.'

Mrs. Eddy was a small, pleasant, bespectacled Yorkshire lady, with a shop in Leominster, mainly dealing in interesting metalware and treen.

'Why me?'

'You always do better with her than I do.'

I would moan saying, 'You just don't want to leave the warmth,' but would still venture forth to say something like, 'Mrs. Eddy, how nice to see you again.' Which of course, I meant, but also enjoyed the barely perceivable glint of eye, beyond the thick lenses.

It was when John's mother went down with a bad dose of some sort food poisoning, that he discovered the secret behind why she'd not moved north. When tidying, he'd chanced upon her latest bank statements and to his horror found she was over £3,000 in debt, a huge sum at the time. To give you an idea, the terraced house he'd bought in the north had cost only £2,200. He then went through the stock book and when totting up value of contents, discovered, apart from six main items, it didn't amount to much at all. Worse than that, all was old stock and therefore virtually worthless. The six items mentioned, were entered in at an overall cost price of £600. Of course, John Dodds was deeply worried and I'll give you his words.---*Once mother had recovered somewhat, I thought the time right to have a little chat regarding financial matters. Rather than discuss a possible rescue plan, however, she employed a diversionary tactic, her feathers having been severely ruffled by the audacity of my having looked into her finances. In defence, I said I'd simply found the bank statements pushed to the back of a drawer I was tidying and eventually she calmed down sufficiently for me to explain my plan. Having noted the date of entry in the stock book of the only six items of value and the fact they'd been in residence for two years, I reasoned, with them taking up valuable space, why not simply cut our losses and get rid of them? It would provide a little working capital and free up room.*

'I can't,' she told me, looking truly worried.

'Why ever not?'

'They don't belong to me.'

The revelation hit me like a hammer blow.

Mother continued, sounding completely desolate now, 'I said I would try and sell them for a friend, but the trouble is, none of the things are right. None of the trade have ever looked at them and you know what it's like trying to sell furniture privately.'

It was at this point, the enormity of the situation hit home. I had joined a business with a debt high enough to have bought the very building we were renting. First thing we had to do was vacate the rooms at the Bull Hotel. Obviously for financial reasons, but also, when making myself a sandwich in the hotel kitchen, I'd discovered the possible cause of mother's recent ailment. Pointing out the thick mould on the sandwich spread, however, had merely brought a shrug from the landlady and suggestion, I scrape it off. This in a way helped stiffen my resolve, for as awful as the facilities in the shop happened to be, we had to make the best of them if we were to have any chance of clearing the debt.

It wasn't difficult finding cheap bed and bedding and once the upstairs was thoroughly cleaned and walls painted it didn't feel quite so much like a slum dwelling. I rang the owner of the six spurious items of furniture and he had them collected, freeing up valuable floor space. All that was needed then, was to earn some money, not only to live off, but to staunch the flow going out in interest payments. I should have been worried sick, but having been blessed with a capacity to work and also belief in my own ability, I manfully set to, attempting to free the business from debt. The trouble was, I have to be truthful, other than having an eye for the odd thing that might appeal, I hadn't a clue what I was doing.

Going back and thoroughly checking John Dodds' notes. I was amazed to read how untroubled he'd been, seemingly, perfectly willing to take everything in his stride. He spoke of relief at having broken free of London's dull suburbia and initially seemed that content with being his own boss, in a job where you never quite knew what the next day would bring, it appears, that as long as each week brought in a little more than he would have earnt in his previous employment, he was quite happy to simply muddle along. He even fell in with the archaic, Thursday half day closing regime, sometimes inviting young ladies he'd met to join him whilst exploring surrounding locations of interest, of which there were plenty. As a student in the town, he'd done the same, but had been limited to the distance his ungeared, second-hand bike would take him.

I'll include one tiny excerpt from his notes.--- *An interesting walk beneath the Brown Clee, culminated in us sitting on the grass covered defences of Nordybank iron age hillfort, sharing a bottle of white wine, rose tinted by the sunset.*

There were a number of such outings briefly referred to, but no names mentioned until he caught sight a young local girl called Anne. There was no notion at this point of settling down with anyone, but this Anne he'd seen striding purposefully through town, had instantly drawn him as if by magnetic force.

He bemoaned the fact:---*If only mildly attracted, it seems fairly easy to engage alluring young ladies in conversation, so why, when you fancy someone like hell, is it so flaming difficult?*

Looking forward in the notes, I was surprised to see mention of a trip to Canada and New England. I searched further, attempting to discover how he'd managed to fund it. The trips north continued, but the shipping goods bought locally and sold there, now merely covered the travelling costs. It was what they bought off the Lancastrian and Cumbrian trade that brought the profits. There was mention of local calls that came their way. There was a lucky deal, when a grand looking brass coated bed, bought up near Abdon, once cleaning commenced back at the shop, turned out to be solid brass. People brought a few things in for sale, china, glass and jewellery mainly and a contact supplied modern rings and guard chains, bought from the Birmingham Jewellery Quarter, but even though enthusiastic and as one dealer put it, 'Having a bit of an eye for the job,' it was hard to see how John Dodds earnt enough in such a short space of time. I checked and worked out, he'd only been in the business 12 months and yet had not only lessened his mother's debt, but had also saved enough for the American jaunt.

His notes explained the motive behind such a seemingly rash move. A visit to the States, had apparently been an ambition since his early teens, a thing not many did back then. Hitch-hike to Greece, maybe; take a budget trip to the Costa Brava, yes, but not fly to the USA and hitch hike round Ontario and New England. His reasoning was, it needed to be done soon, for once past 30, with probably by then having mortgage commitments, it would not be possible. Thus, I did stumble upon the fact, he did have property ambitions in mind and surmised, maybe this could have been the spur that galvanised him into climbing his way up the trade echelon.

I smiled at one short anecdote, for it summed up his modest beginnings.---*I was down at Leon's shop and the dull looking chaise longue he unloaded, was avidly snapped up by a lady who said it would be ideal for her upholstery classes. I rushed back to the warren of houses above the cattle market to see if the thing, of equal ugliness, I'd been offered for £1 was still available. On spotting it still lurking, black and unappealing in the outhouse, I parted with a pound note and swinging the horsehair covered brute up onto my shoulders, walked with it, back through the town. Legs becoming wobbly, I was relieved to dump it in through the front door of the shop and even more relieved to sell it for £3 the following morning.*

It was pure accident, how I found how the American trip had probably been funded. I'd left my sheaf of notes, spread on the dining table and as I opened the door to let some air in, a gust of wind blew the whole lot onto the floor. Cursing, I was gathering and reassembling, trying to get them back into the right order, when I noticed a little section written on pale green notepaper. I realised it had previously been ascribed to the wrong portion. I checked again, but my instincts had been right, I'd given it the wrong colour code.

Abandoning further tidying, I sat down and started to read, totally engrossed. John Dodds had written the piece without alteration, meaning it was probably a fair copy of an earlier attempt and with it being full of Shropshire dialect, I'd not the slightest clue how to amend, I left well alone.

---It was one of those afternoons that fools you into thinking Winter is at last over. I was in the shop polishing and on hearing the door rattle, sending the bell dancing on its spring, I turned to see an absorbed looking Gary Lockyer standing in the opening. He was one of the youngest scions of a proud family of 18. His mother had been smock-bound since her teens.

As if asking someone ten foot tall, standing directly behind me and unbridled enough to blow hair out of place, he unleashed the enquiry, 'Is yer mum about?' He'd put his whole face into the effort of making the request, but with now standing mute and not looking the least bit likely to explain further, I summoned mother from the back room.

'Yes Gary, what is it?'

'Our mum says as 'er's got some stuff for yer and 'er wants yer there straight away.'

We locked the shop and walked through town to Mrs. Lockyer's, an unimposing house that fronted onto a communal yard. We were greeted at the door and on entering were told, as regards the person she normally sold to, a good friend of my mother's as it happens, there had been a big falling out. She didn't give details, but said, if it suited, she'd now be selling to us. My mother was rather hesitant and on explaining, she didn't want to appear to be going behind a friend's back was told, 'Dunner be so daft, Jessica. The falling out's nowt to do uv you.' Then with the arching of a brow, 'But if you inner keen to buy the stuff, it dunner matter, there's plenty us ul be.'

We were led a little further down the yard to where the pick-up had been unloaded. None of it was what you'd want to furnish your own home with, but all was instantly saleable and with a bare minimum of negotiating, the deal was concluded.

Back in the house, we were ushered beyond the kitchen, into what resembled an Aladdin's Cave. Jugs and bowls were arrayed along the side-cabinet and paintings leant against the wall. There were Staffordshire figures, ruby glass ornaments, a tantalus complete with cut glass bottles, a pair of lustres, oil lamps complete with shades, decanters, clocks, enamelled patch boxes and dealing with it all took the best part of a very enjoyable hour.

'No need to check those!' she chided. 'They'm all perfect.'

As one of the bowls I rapped, rattled, rather than making a ringing sound, she said, 'Trevor musta done that when-'ee was loading. They was all perfect when I bought 'em. I keep tellin 'im not to be so rough uv the stuff.' Trevor was another of the 18.

Finally we were offered the silver and the jewellery. 'Oh thaim all silver.'

My mother was peering at the hallmarks through her spyglass.

'They needs no checkin' Jessy. Thaim all silver. They've all got the little lion on.'

As she delved to produce goods from her huge handbag and went into the telling, that always accompanied the selling, her cigarette ash was flicked into its depths. Then finally came the jewellery. 'Don't go tellin' our Trevor I sold you any o this,' she said with a wink and gummy chuckle. 'This is my little deal.'

Small bundles tied in old handkerchiefs were rummaged from the depths and when unknotted, gold glinted and gems sparkled. I had learnt a little about jewellery styles and could see, amongst the Scottish agate brooches, sovereigns, gold charm bracelet, long guard chain, gold framed cameo and silver name brooches, there was a pretty Victorian pendant, Victorian rings, plus the possibility, of another three rings being Georgian.

We took the jewellery and silver back with us and I returned for the rest in the estate car.

'So 'elpin yer mum now am yer?'

I breezily explained to Mrs Lockyer, how I was quite enjoying it.

Looking as if she could hardly contain her mirth, 'So, yume learnin' the business?'

'Well doing my best.'

'That mum o yorn can be an 'andful, my lad,' she said with the wag of a finger, 'But 'appen you'll meet the right wench, strong enough.'

Seeing me now rather deflated, she placated with, 'Come round ere, about same time next Friday. Should av a few more bits by

then. That's if them Irish aven't 'ad it all. Thaim swarmin'
everywhere.' As I edged the car towards the narrow-necked yard
entry, I waved and she called, 'If I gets another load mid-wik, I'll
send our Gary round.'

With John Dodds' little composition on my lap, I sat there
thinking and came to the conclusion, this must have been the
change of fortune that had paid for the American trip. Each deal,
with his mother negotiating, would have been like a free tutorial
and also instrumental in putting the shop back on its feet. Strange
though, other than a few brief references, I could find no further
details describing such a dramatic change of fortune, nor any
notes regarding the American trip itself. With it having been such
a burning ambition, it seemed a strange omission.

Even though John Dodds was obviously learning fast, he admitted,
when visiting the local salerooms, he felt overawed and completely
out of his depth.---*As the early lots are being sold, the ring sit*
around the largest table available, playing cards. I find their
collective air of arrogance and disdain quite menacing. When
the furniture is offered, they don't stand together, but it's quite
obvious they're working as a group, for I've quite often heard
things such as, 'Leave it. Barry's on this one,' or from a dealer
frantically scanning the room, a concerned, 'Is this ours?'

Which could bring a reply such as, 'Yes, don't worry, Denny's on
it,' or 'Get your arm down, idiot! Docherty's got it covered.'

Obviously, they weren't without competition and with a fair
degree of tactical bidding, prices could rise to extraordinary
heights.

Following the sharp rap of gavel, I once heard, 'Well done, Barry.
He'll be owning that for a while.'

To which came the matter of fact reply, 'Well, you have to defend
your patch, don't you.'

But although some prices seemed staggering, even those of the very last lots, the ones John had hung on for, in the vain hope, by that time the ring would surely have run out of money, the group would still troop from the room, obviously with things to sort out.---*It all seemed quite daunting and I wondered if I'd ever learn enough to compete on their level. The whole experience felt like entering a minefield. How, for instance, can you tell a trade lot, from one fresh to the market, entered privately?*

It appears, some salerooms were peppered with trade mistakes, to be bid up to the reserve and then dropped on the unwary, so one couldn't assume that topping a reliable dealer's bid, guaranteed a profit, for the item being bid on could well be theirs. So, needless to say, apart from furniture from farm sales, very little of their stock in those early days came from major auctions.

Another reason for not crossing swords with certain members of the ring, was the fact it would have been counter-productive. It seems, one or two of them had befriended young Dodds, giving him the odd insight into why one thing was worth far more than another and along with a business card, the instruction would be given, if chancing on anything tasty, to give them a ring, for whilst on buying trips, literally racing each other around the trade, a few had become his best customers.

As I read these details, I realised I might have found his first point of ascent, the arrival at the first rung of the trade ladder and seemingly, not all were treading on his fingers, to prevent further progress.

Once free from winter, life in the shop became more bearable and there were descriptions of things being cleaned and polished out in the side alley. Night time could be a problem, however, as all the A49 traffic still filed through the middle of town and trucks crashing over the summit, a few yards up from the shop, sounded like they'd been dropped from space. Once awoken, the church clock, chiming every quarter hour, kept a record of how much sleep was being lost.

In an attempt to make up for lack of knowledge, John Dodds employed invention, with virtually unsaleable washing dollies being sold as toilet roll holders; leather horse collars, usually thrown in a deal for nothing, if polished and having glass inserted, sold well as wall mirrors and a number of stout oak boards he'd found stored in a barn loft, with the help of a carpenter friend, became coffee tables.

Also, he found a market in things, as yet, ignored by the trade. A row of Victorian cottages had been demolished and buying all the ornate brackets to the outhouse water cisterns, he found, if wire-brushed and painted and offered a pair at a time, sold well as shelf brackets. Needless to say, he never divulged their former use.

I winced as I read this next bit, for it described the pub down the road being under refurbishment and how all the old fittings had been torn out and left in the back yard. John Dodds had bought for next to nothing; all the advertising mirrors, prints proclaiming the efficacy of certain beverages, colourful leaded light windows, the doors with leaded lights that had led to 'Lounge Bar' and 'Smoke Room.' He'd even bought the old brass and polished mahogany beer pumps, the circular cast iron, mahogany topped pub tables, the Mitchell and Butler's trays and a toucan water jug. I could have wept, for these were the very things I was scouring the country for, to put back into pubs.

There was a description of a call up at Bitterley Station. The old line, leading from there into Ludlow, had been ripped up, but the platforms were still intact and a travelling family had claimed the station concourse to set up camp. All five lived in a caravan plus supplementary canvas tent and the goods they had for sale were stored in an old railway tool shed still left standing.

They called him, Mr. Dodds, which he found quaint and although the goods bought were of no great merit, brass and iron beds, cast iron cauldrons and kettles, they were cheap and sold immediately.

One of the three sons took him to a call nearby and they drove up the vertiginous ascent to Bedlam, a village outpost on the edge of Titterstone Clee's hilltop wilderness. At a house, where the road terminated far end, they were greeted and he was shown into an abandoned outside toilet where two triangular iron hay cratches and a small water pump lay in the cobwebbed interior. On successfully purchasing, he asked if anything else might be for sale. His escort waited while John was admitted to look at a dressing table, that if the price was right, they would consider selling. It was a 1950's varnished, three mirror affair, that he politely declined, but in the hallway was a Georgian oak, three drawer dresser base.--- *It stood, proudly displaying original brasses and patination glowed soft on the slight undulations, time had blessed it with, but needless to say, it was not for sale.* If one day, however, for whatever reason it should be, the man of the house, promised John Dodds, he would be given first chance. Small comfort, but they were good people and he thanked them. Truth be known, he'd not yet learnt enough to offer them a fair price.

---I re-joined my dark faced companion who had retreated beyond the gate, looking truly worried, as if his end could well be nigh and eying the ridiculously small terrier yapping at the bars, called out to the man I'd been dealing with, "Does it bite?" As we drove back down to Bitterley, he explained, biting dogs were a constant hazard in his line of work and that the most he'd been able to offer for the things, now in the back of the car, had been scrap value. The £2, I tipped him, came back over 100-fold from other things bought from that family.

I'll include a description of another call, because again it captures a little of the spirit of those times.

---It was a pleasant afternoon and my mother suggested we shut up shop and give old Pip a call. Pip was a grand old girl, living in a country smallholding, over Leintwardine way. We edged the car down the track and left it parked in the yard. Pip looked pleased

to see us, put the kettle on and said there might be a few old bits of rubbish lying around, we could sell. We were offered cake, but I found, with the kitchen so redolent of horse sweat, it required a determined swallow.

Pip brightly announced, she had spotted me in town, with a girl at my side; it had been Anne in fact.

'Looks a bit of a smasher,' she added beaming and then suddenly entreated, 'Come and look at my two fine beauties.'

We were shown around the barns, that acted as stables and then taken to the paddock where the two silky creatures grazed in the sunshine. Her dog had the closest thing to a smile a hound can manage, a cat entwined itself around my legs purring,--- the place seemed idyllic. Back in the house we were led into the parlour and she told me, 'Have a good old root in the cupboards. You're bound to find a few bits of old junk.'

I dug out the usual, biscuit barrel, fish servers in their original box, silver napkin rings, blue and white platters, an epergne in perfect condition, wrapped in tissue paper, but then came across strange coloured balls, that I later discovered, were water grenades for throwing onto small domestic conflagrations. From the depths of one cupboard, I brought to light, lumps of intertwined coloured glass and lifting the lid of the window seat, I found, wrapped in brown paper, four unusual hand-embroidered wall hangings of a rather bizarre nature.

'Oh those old things,' said Pip. 'They were done by a cousin of mine. Those lumpy glass thingamies were her doing as well. Strange girl. One of those arty types,' she confided. Then thinking for a moment asked, 'Why do fat woman always seem to sit with their legs apart?'

Mother and I both laughed.

67

'It's true though, isn't it? You don't want to look, but can't help it. Draws you like an open window. Anyway, I was with a friend, in the castle a few days ago--- there was a bit of a do on. People sat about tucking into picnics, and this friend of mine said, "Just look at her! She shouldn't be sitting there like that. She ought to be ashamed of herself!"'

'I'll soon sort her out,' I said and bending down, told her, "Hey! Just saw a mouse run up your knickers!" Well, that shifted her, I can tell you.'

Whilst carrying our purchases to the car, mother told me to look inside the small downstairs lavatory. Pinned to the wall, hand written, was Pip's last will and testament, beginning with, 'If you've discovered I've snuffed it---' Just outside the doorway was an interesting tall backed, pale green Arts and Crafts chair, unfortunately, not for sale.

By the end of the week, we'd sold all our purchases from dear old Pip, including the wall hangings and glass fantasies, that a dealer took a wild punt on, just as we had done.

As described earlier, John had once spent a rather pleasant afternoon with a young lady, reclining on the ramparts of an Iron Age hill fort, sharing a bottle of wine. Reading a later section, I saw brief mention of it again, but then, how a dampener had been put on the day by his mother's reminder, they'd a rendezvous with a group of ladies in Knighton. You might suggest, I'm easily pleased, but I did get a slight buzz of excitement on finding two separate entries in the notes did tie up, with the added detail in the second making it obvious, he was less than enamoured by the impending jaunt. He'd put:---*It's not as if the bulk of the jewellery was ours, the trays of rings were on sale or return.*

That solved another little mystery. I had wondered, with their limited resources, how had they'd managed to finance continually topping up a briefcase packed with trays of brand-new rings from the jewellery quarter?

His mother had been adamant, John should accompany her, saying, '*You know I always do better when you're there.*'

'*But I'm knackered.*'

'*You'll be alright after a bit of a livener.*

The little soiree had been arranged to commence at 7.30 in a Knighton hostelry. The hosts, arranging it were old family friends and it turned into quite a gathering. The drinks flowed, the jewellery sold and John Dodds kept notes as to who was having what and prices agreed.

'*There, that wasn't so bad was it,*' his mother had said as they drove from town.

---*Just then*, wrote John, *my blood ran cold, for we were being overtaken by a police car with light flashing. I pulled over and immediately got out to enquire the reason for being apprehended.*

'*Sounds like you're driving a flaming tractor! Open the bonnet.*'

Mother chose this very moment to lean across and offer a piece of her mind through the driver's-side window, but thankfully, although with obvious reluctance, my glare plus instruction to, 'Just shut up, mother,' was heeded.

The officer shone his torch on the gaping fracture in the manifold and then asked, 'Have you been drinking?'

I managed a rather rasping, 'Not really,' difficult to do whilst inhaling.

'*You smell like a flaming brewery. Consider yourself lucky I don't have a breathalyser in the car!*'

Come the day of my appearance in Knighton Magistrates Court, whilst waiting to be summoned, I exchanged reasons for us being there with a local, rangy looking habitue. On telling him the name of the arresting officer, he looked at me in astonishment. 'He didn't breathalyse you? F--- me! You were lucky. That f------g bastard's been the bane of my f------g life!'

It wasn't the first time I'd had the feeling someone was looking after me.

I never intended my rendering of the John Dodd's story to be just a string of anecdotes, but I must include this one.

---I was working on some horse hames. Even with brass acorn finials, they always took ages to sell, but having had them thrown in a deal for nothing, I thought I'd better make them presentable. I'd wire brushed the rust off out in the alley and was now black-leading. The shop bell rang and I went through to see our next-door neighbour, Mrs. Mills, standing in the doorway. She asked me to call round, for she'd rooted out a few things for sale.

When I later knocked on her door, she appeared holding a tray of various nick-nacks, including of all things, a Second World War hand grenade. Probably cost about three quid the lot and once priced, I placed the bits in the window. I'd handled polished brass shell cases before, selling them as stick stands, but never a hand grenade.

I went back to my polishing, but again was interrupted by the shop bell. It was a schoolboy in short trousers, enquiring the price of the piece of ordnance in the window. I'd put £1 on the ticket, but told him he could have it for 50 pence. With transaction complete, he left the shop and I was just writing the entry in the sales' book and laughing at the description, for as the grenade had been bought from Mrs. Mills, I'd given it it's proper title, Mills Bomb, sold for 50p, when my blood ran cold. I rushed to the shop door, but saw no sign of the boy. I attempted to carry on working, but simply couldn't, my mind being continually invaded by the image of an explosion and just a pair of smoking shoes where the boy had been standing. I must have knocked on Mrs. Mills's door at least ten times, desperate to know if the grenade had been disarmed. Along with the vision of smoking school shoes, I could see a banner headline, 'Antique dealer blows up innocent child.' Career over.

When, mid-afternoon, Mrs Mills finally answered the door and said, 'Of course it has been. You don't think I'd sell you a live bomb, do you?' I could have kissed her.

I read further and noticed, a regular visitor to the shop in those early days, had been an old boy called Harry. It was hard to see how he fitted in with running an antique business, but at least twice a week he'd call in, sometimes with farm eggs for sale, ensconce himself and drink the mug of tea provided. I finally found out who this Harry was. He'd been a drover, herding cattle and sheep over the ancient hilltop trails to be there ready for sale day in various local markets. John Dodds had found his tales fascinating and he must have been good at his job, for farmers would hardly have entrusted valuable livestock to someone who had the habit of losing the odd ewe or heifer. There was mention of nights camped out, the baking of tickled trout, having wrapped them tight in wet newspaper before consigning them to the embers. When the paper was peeled free, all the skin and scales came away with it. Old Harry obviously embellished the tales a little, but John Dodds found this survivor from another era, absolutely fascinating.

Around the pubs he listened to reminiscences from other old timers, those that had worked on the Wales to Birmingham water pipeline and others that had toiled up in the Clee Hill quarries. They all knew Harry of course, admiring him for being a tough old bird, for even in his seventies, he could still handle himself.

Apparently, at about that time, one young lad in the Tavern, as the Bull Ring Tavern was known for short, had chanced his luck, baiting old Harry and in a flash had found himself decked, sprawled flat on his back. He'd received a whiplash, straight right and not one jot of sympathy.

I've included this, for it helps set the scene of John Dodds's early years in the business, not a frenetic buying and selling, avaricious world, more a gentle rural entry into running an antique shop on the Welsh Marches. He had summed it up by saying,---*Those days were fun. But, I wondered, would it last?*

I'll just mention three more characters from those times and then I'd better continue with the main thread of the saga. From amongst the notes, I gained inspiration for the following.

For some reason, John Dodds seemed to get on well with the travellers and gypsies. One bronzed lady, face lined with character, used to pop in, asking him to call whenever she had gathered a few items for sale. She and other members of her clan were camped in Darky Lane, which I discovered, was the remnants of an ancient trail, probably dating back to the Bronze Age. He could never second guess what old Rose might have found, for he'd bought huge milk churns, sporting splendid brass plaques inscribed with the name of the farm; quality china; Staffordshire figures; hanging lamps; splendid brass oil lamps complete with shades, quite a mixed bag really.

Alerted by the calm curiosity of her Lurcher dog, she'd usually emerge from the old caravan, with its basic fittings and Queenie stove, but conclusion of the deal, would always be conducted in her show wagon, with its massive Royal Dux vases and gleaming cabinets full of Crown Derby china. She'd almost become like a friend and in the shop one day, asked to look at the jewellery. After trying on a few rings, replacing each back into its slot, with nothing apparently suiting, she went to leave, but on seeing John on the point of closing the jewellery case, gave a slow shake of head. Opening her hand, Rose revealed a ring she'd palmed and giving a wink, like a glint off a crystal ball, she admonished, 'You gotta be smarter than that m'lad!'

The second character, was known as Tater.--- *Tater Davies, used to earn a few bob delivering furniture on a hand cart, at the conclusion of the Ludlow antique auctions. In his odd mix of second-hand clothes, sometimes even sporting a lady's hat, he was a cheery soul and on the couple of occasions, when chancing upon him hitch-hiking back from Worcester races, I realised, as strange as it sounds, he must have been as well accepted there as back in Ludlow, for Tater avowed the Worcester race goers to be, 'My sort of folks,' which I'm sure they would have been thoroughly heartened to hear.*

One evening, I was driving past the end of Station Drive, bottom end of town and seeing him earnestly dipping his bike's front tyre in a puddle, stopped to ask, 'What are you doing, Tater?'

'Just raced the train back from Bromfeld.' (Bromfield) 'Coolin' 'em down a bit.'

The third character I discovered, was simply described as Percy and again I've written it, as a John Dodds original, even though a few touches of my own have been worked in.---*Percy, although not dressed like a gentleman of the road, I still think it fair to say, personal appearance was not high on his list of priorities. He often chanced upon odd items of interest and if the fancy took him, would even return to the pending work pile, amongst which languished our pieces we'd delivered for restoration. His workshops were a ramble of sheds round by the castle, in an area known as Dinham.*

I saw a later note had been squeezed in between the lines.--- *Property there would be in the hundreds of thousands now.*

Visiting Percy, that's if lucky enough to find him in his lair, was like time travel to converse with an ancient bard, which was all *very well, but when the urge to make haste restoring a piece of oak, instantly saleable once back in the shop, foundered against his wall of insouciance, laced with poetic quotations, I must admit, it could strike one as rather irritating. Burrowing amongst his piles of artefacts would usually unearth something of interest mind you; fragments of 17th century carving; huge Georgian keys; discarded gilt frames, perfect for lending advantage to daubs chanced upon.*

When later cross referencing the notes, I found, his brother was the very one whose eclectic collection had drawn interest from the London trade. The same sale, Ben Evans had been mentioned in dispatches.

I've included these snippets, because they seem truly from a lost age and I was just planning the next chapter in the John Dodds' story, when my phone went. It was Mike. He sounded quite excited. He'd chanced upon another wad of notes.

CHAPTER SIX

We met in the charming little town of Grosmont, Monmouthshire. It had a beautiful untouched feel and I'd been amazed to read, way back in time, this sleepy little place had once been the third most important town in South Wales. Its castle was the brainchild of Hubert de Burgh who also had nearby Skenfrith and White castles built, plus another fascinating footnote to history, he'd even been the power behind the abandonment of Montgomery's motte and bailey castle, for construction to commence on the stone fortress, whose slighted remnants still perch above the town today. From my brief spell of research, the day before, I realised what an impact Owen Glendower's uprising must have had throughout the central Welsh Marches, for although Grosmont castle had managed to hold out, the town itself had been razed to the ground in 1405.

Mike was as cheery as ever and we drove to the farm sale in his car, which was a wise move, for with the only lots of interest being at the end of sale, getting just one car clear of the place, against the inflow of Land Rovers and trailers, was hard enough. The meagre items we'd seen lotted up in the barn, simply weren't worth the time and effort spent waiting for them and giving profuse apologies, Mike said he'd pay for lunch.

First, however we visited the castle and I felt a little saddened, for the place that would have once engendered such power, was now just a genteel relic, practically ignored by those going about day-to-day business in the town. The church of St. Nicholas had a slight barn-like feel and pale in the dimness, as if having become encrusted by a slow accretion of limestone whilst slumbering, an ancient knight now lay grey, a huge enshrouded effigy.

While waiting for lunch in the hotel, Mike handed me the notes. Quickly scanning I said, "Don't worry about the sale being a waste of time, these notes are like gold." I couldn't wait to go through them properly for almost jumping from the pages were the names of Marie, Anne, Mrs. Lockyer and east coast American states. Resisting the impulse to start reading, I put them back in their envelope.

Mike said, "I had a quick look, but all of it is from before my time."

"You've no idea how important this is. It's the portion missing. I was puzzled as to why certain sections had been given such scant regard, now here they are."

"How far have you got with the story?"

"Early days in the small shop, top of Old Street."

"Oh that place. You can't imagine Mr. Dodds starting out there, can you? Sometimes, whilst on longer journeys, he'd talk about the old days, ruefully referring to the 'slum dwelling', as he called it. Basic, to say the least."

"Yes, ignoring the fact it did in fact have primitive wiring, it has the feel of something you'd expect from Dickens not the 1970's."

Lunch arrived and we had a glass of red apiece.

Back home I began studying the notes and with much of it predating what I'd already written, I wondered how to shoehorn the sections into the tale. I certainly didn't feel like starting again and spent a couple of days racking my brains, before coming up with the following, told in my own words, but hopefully not having lost John Dodds' slightly formal style.

---*With the warmth of the Spring morning giving me confidence, I decided to attend McCartney's antique auction, being held in a rather characterless building far side of the cattle market, bottom of town. Dealer's cars and vans filled the carpark, but the room was fairly empty. A few were examining the small items on the trestle tables and there were three I recognised, carefully peering at items handed them from the cabinets.*

Mr Wolfe, a regular caller at the shop, gave me a nod and smile of greeting. Although having countless years of experience and a knowledge, vastly superior to mine, he still treated me like an equal. I made a note of lots that were not only of interest, but more importantly, likely to be in my price range. Having finished viewing the furniture, some in front of the rostrum, but most arrayed around the room, I suddenly felt rather cowed, for those most likely to be the buyers of it, filed back into the hall.

I did buy a few early lots of interest, brass, copper and boxes with assorted contents beneath the tables and then ignoring the rugs and paintings, saved my efforts for the furniture, wanting to know how my valuations would fare, when compared with reality. On certain pieces, I was that wildly off the mark and so in fear of ridicule, I was careful none should see what I'd written in my catalogue, scribbling out my pathetic estimates and writing in the actual hammer price for future reference.

As if to rub salt in, a number of dealers still avid for action, jauntily left the room end of sale, to sort things out, probably in a huddle somewhere, hidden from view. I felt quite numb, devastated and remember giving myself a talking to, mentally that is, 'Come on! You've got a university degree. Learning the ropes shouldn't be that difficult.' I made the resolution there and then, that whatever I earnt from that already known, would be invested to learn the value of better-quality items I'd yet to handle. Taking one piece at a time, I would begin to learn. Difficult admittedly, for it wasn't in the trade's interest for me to walk away with any of the better lots. The words, 'Defending one's patch,' came to mind. They would do all they could to discourage the likes of me competing for furniture at the auctions.

Regarding my degree, as strange as it sounds, antiques had even played a part in my actual admission to university. Out of the blue I'd been offered an interview by the University of Surrey, which despite the name, was based in Battersea at the time, prior to the new campus being completed in Guildford. My invitation was courtesy of the clearing scheme. To save on costs, my mother had arranged a lift, travelling with a dealer I knew, Fred from Newent. He was quite a character and I always enjoyed his company. When a rival, in an attempt to keep him from attending a nearby sale, had sabotaged his motor, Fred commandeering a lift and managing to discover the culprit, had promptly laid him out in Ledbury saleroom carpark.

Anyway, I was dropped off at Fred's shop in Newent and with his wife managing to squeeze in alongside, we journeyed into the night, requiring a contortion on my part, to synchronise with every gear change. Amongst other things, the back of the van was taken up by a quivering display of stuffed birds in the huge amboyna cabinet, my mother was half shares in. We arrived at Bermondsey market early the following morning and dealers ghosting about, viewed items for sale by torchlight. Fred did well with all but the cabinet of birds. A few mocked, as they considered not only his price, but the item itself to be ridiculous.

One even returned to jeer, 'Those didn't exactly fly out, did they.'

Dawn was breaking by the time the deal was finally done, enabling us to lock the van and go for breakfast in a nearby pub. I was amazed to see the place absolutely heaving and alcohol being consumed, that early in the day.

We later visited Portobello and entering the establishment of the recent purchaser of the birds, were told by an assistant they'd been sold. They had also been sold from the next shop in the chain, but tracking them down to the third, there they stood, looking resplendent, just in from the shop doorway, sporting a price tag of more than double the amount Fred had sold them for. I must admit, I'm not a fan of taxidermy, but the cabinet was truly amazing and in the bottom section were slender drawers containing trays of bird's eggs.

It was during a mid-morning break in a Portobello café, that Fred asked, 'What time is your interview again?'

'Three thirty.'

He thought for a while and then told me it posed rather a problem. It meant we'd be leaving in the rush-hour and with all that stopping and starting, his old van would almost certainly overheat. 'Bit of a radiator problem,' he added. 'And by the time we reach High Wycombe, the traffic up that hill will be crawling. We could end up with a blown gasket. Look lad, ring them up.'

'What?'

'Ring them up and ask to have the interview brought forward.'

'I can't do that, Fred. I'm lucky to even get the interview.'

'Course you can. Bugger 'em! They can only say no.'

Full of trepidation, I went to the phone booth and rang the university.

'What did they say?'

'Two o-clock,' I answered.

'Good lad. You've got to learn; don't be frightened to open your mouth.'

So, having been up all night, I sat the short entrance test and endured the interview, facing a stern panel of three.

'How did you get on?' Asked Fred when I re-joined them in the small Battersea café.

'I've been accepted.'

'Well done lad. You've no idea what doors could now be open to you. Just be sure you make the most of it. Don't mess it up.'

I was quite surprised, for with his brusque manner, I'd expected him to favour a more hands-on approach to making one's way in life. Having said that, I suppose university was considered quite a step up, with less than ten percent of school leavers, gaining entry at the time.

After having successfully escaped London, before major traffic build-up, engine still happily whining away, we stopped for fuel. Fred would rather have got High Wycombe and its hill out of the way first, but with the van running almost on empty, it left him no choice.

The garage was busy, but we managed to pull in behind a car whose departure looked fairly imminent.

Fred thumping the steering wheel said, 'What's that flaming pillock doing?'

The man was almost on all fours peering under his car.

'What's the matter, mate?' Fred yelled.

'I've dropped sixpence.'

'Sixpence?' Fred, fishing in his pocket shouted, "Here's a couple of bob, now piss off!"

It was well after dark by the time we arrived home. There was a bit of bustle, dog rushing to greet, tea making and a fry-up for the wanderers' return and my mother was that keen to know how Fred had fared, regarding the amboyna cabinet, my university interview failed to even get a mention, which I have to admit, left me feeling like a bit of a spare part.

When I finally told her, she went 'Mmm?' as if in a bit of a dream, then, 'Oh well done, dear. I knew you'd sail through it,' before returning to the crucial matter of how Fred had done with the other items.

Leaving them to it, I ventured down town for a drink and having entered that heady zone beyond tiredness, ended up celebrating my next step in life at a party in one of the castle flats.

I won't trouble you here with details of university life, but in case you think it was all drugs and sex, I'll give you this quote. ---*Back in those days, the majority leaving the all-male, Ludlow Grammar School, were virgins. The most sexual of sexual encounters could be summed up by the archaic sounding, heavy petting.*

Further into the notes I had the impression young Dodds had at last accomplished the deed, for I chanced upon the self-mocking, ---*And to think I was once concerned, lest heavy petting should lead to pregnancy.*

Wonderfully innocent sounding times, even though it was actually the late sixties. I wondered, with him initially so glad to leave Ludlow, why he'd so often returned and then stumbled across the fact, each end of term, the hall of residence was rented out to foreign students. He'd had no choice and writes, ---*In my freshers' year, I was always excited by the prospect of returning to Ludlow, but after two days, couldn't wait to leave the place again.*

His mother, by this time, had taken the small shop in Old Street, but home was still a council house on the very outskirts of Ludlow.

I'll hand you back to the man himself.

---It was my second year at university and I was back in town for the Easter break. It always amazed me how much cheaper Ludlow was compared to London. I'd venture out with a pound note and bit of loose change and was always pleasantly surprised to find the pound note still intact in my pocket the following morning.

This next section is almost entirely in John Dodds' own words.---*It was after closing time and three of us thought we'd try our luck at the Tally Ho Club in Broad Street, which other than the happenchance of being included in a lock-in, was the only establishment in town that would still be serving drinks. I wasn't a member, but had gate-crashed the place that many times, the doorman, a pernickety old boy called Percy, rarely challenged me. Just to be on the safe side, however, we waited until seeing a few mounting the steps to gain entry and on joining them, sailed past the liveried doorman before he'd time to register who it was.*

It was close to floor mopping and chairs on tables time when it happened. I couldn't believe it, for in sailed Marie, looking beautifully wild, her dark locks a little windswept. I had heard she was now a single woman, but wondered why she had entered alone and so close to the club's closing time. Her face lit up on catching sight of me and of course, I bought her a drink and we started chatting. It was a short while later, I don't know what started it, but things began to get a little boisterous over in the seating area, a raised section, railed off from the small dance floor.

Marie, looking across in alarm said, 'I've got to get you out of here!'

'Why? Whatever for?'

'Drugs. I can smell them. Come with me!'

By that time, I certainly knew, what cannabis resin, smelt like when smouldering in a joint, but believe me, was not going to argue. She whisked me to her car and we rattled along to her little cottage out Peaton way. Now looking a little worried, she was at pains to entreat, not to be fearful, for she was only doing all this as a favour. If the place had been raided, I could have been arraigned with the rest, putting my reputation in tatters.

Her use of the word arraigned, rather than the modern parlance, 'busted', sounded a little quaint, but with it highlighting our age difference, I'd no notion of correcting her, besides, I was absolutely mind-numbed by this magnanimous so-called favour, offered by the lady of my youthful fantasies. Well, I won't trouble you with much detail, other than point out, after having consumed copious quantities of alcoholic beverage, a man is well aware he could be either a rampant hero, or alas, a drooping flop. Thankfully my constitution was such, that after that feeling of blessed relief, 'I'm in at last,' came the amazement at realising, even though shamefully inexperienced, what I was doing was the sole reason for her throaty noises and odd whimper, as if in slight discomfort. I felt like I'd literally died and gone to heaven.

It was about four when Marie woke me. She said she had to take me home. There were to be no ifs, or buts, for there would be hell to pay if she didn't get me back before dawn. What cold reality. I didn't give a damn for the consequences. I just wanted to remain there, totally, blissfully smitten, lying next to her. Anyway, I was driven home and despite the explosive greeting from the dog, managed to quieten him and slip between cool sheets, a prouder man than the one who'd exited them the previous morning.

Mother instinctively knew something had happened, but what, or with whom she as yet was not party to. In the ensuing days however, with Marie turning up out of the blue, setting my heart hammering, then watching the exchanges between us at the

Saturday market stall, she began to get the picture. So when Marie struggling with the zip on her jeans, said, 'It keeps coming undone.'

Mother snapped, 'Too much use, I shouldn't wonder!'

It was near the end of the Easter break and I was starting to feel depressed at having to part company with this beautiful, exhilarating woman in my life. We had packed both mother's and Marie's jewellery away at the close of the Saturday market. Mother had driven home, but Marie rented a lock-up unit down the back of The George, a large pub immediately behind the town hall. We thought we might as well drop in for a drink, but at that point, two laconic young men, hair styles obviously not achieved by simply combing, appeared as if looking for something.

On spotting their bold shirts, tight jeans, white slip-ons and slender leather satchels, Marie's eyes instantly sparkled and she said, 'You boys look as if you could be in search of jewels.'

They said, yes, they were in the jewellery trade and followed Marie down to the lock-up. Feeling rather in the way, I retired to a seat halfway up the narrow yard. I could hear the music of her laughter and after about half an hour, the two men, who from their accents, hailed from London, gave me a nod as they walked past. Marie, on spotting me, stood and stared for a while. 'Whatever's the matter, John?'

Feeling stupidly jealous, I didn't answer.

'Come on. Cheer up, I'll buy you a drink.'

We found a place to sit, for the market day fever had begun to abate.

Marie, carefully pouring half her tonic into the gin, to fizz and set the ice cubes in motion, asked again, 'So what's the matter?'

*'It sounded like you were selling yourself as well as the jewellery,'
I said glumly.*

*With eyes glinting across the bubbles, she smiled and said, 'It's all
part of the game.'*

I found other references to Marie, but with the huge age difference
and sheer chasm of mileage between them, they gradually drifted
apart.

I read through the notes describing the trip to North America and
although highly entertaining, I decided to not include details in my
book, for it would start to sprawl and I needed to concentrate on
John Dodds, antique dealer.

Alright, I'll include this one part, but only briefly.---*Out of
desperation, having been dropped off at a barely used exit,
I decided to risk hitch-hiking on the freeway, where if caught,
I would incur a heavy fine. Money I did not have. With rain
imminent, I headed for the shelter of a flyover and stood there
shivering, as an absolute deluge began to hammer down, giving
the feeling I'd taken refuge behind a waterfall. I literally prayed to
God, for a miracle to liberate me from the predicament. Minutes
later, a small car pulled up and I was invited to join the two male
occupants. They told me they were trainee priests returning to the
monastery where they had first received religious instruction.*

*I know God works in mysterious ways, but hadn't expected
anything that immediate.*

What happens next is the main reason for including this anecdote.-
--*I was offered a monastic cell for the night and was invited to
partake in the evening meal, but first there was to be a meeting
between my two new companions and their mentor.*

*We stood to greet his entry and of course he enquired, as to how
the two had fared since venturing forth the previous year. The*

conversation was quite jaunty, until a silence fell on the room. It went on for so long, I was almost on the point of blurting something regarding my own experiences, simply to fill the yawning gap. Thinking again, however, I realised it was their silence not mine and if they were happy with it why should I intrude? After another five minutes or so, as if all three had suddenly re-awoken, the conversation chimed up again.

Now comes the reason for this short tale's inclusion. John Dodds wrote:---*From that moment on, I was never again, daunted by silence.*

With further perusal of the notes, I began to puzzle; how were the deals in those early days financed? Apart from salerooms, few of the people John Dodds dealt with would have been interested in taking a cheque. They had limited funds and so how did they keep going? Also, did the trade operate on cash or cheques? Then I chanced upon two short extracts that gave me the answer. Again I've augmented details from the notes. Well, this is my book, when all's said and done.

One of the dealers to befriend John Dodds was a certain Mike from Hereford, who rang him one day, telling him he'd chanced on a house clearance and felt sure some of the items bought would be of interest. With Mike being further up the dealing pyramid than he was, John was slightly wary, but in fact ended up pleasantly surprised, for the deal had a lucky feel. Mike explained, 'I can sell the better lumps;' he dealt solely from a warehouse; 'but not the squitter.'

John hadn't felt insulted by the last word, for if the likes of Mike were willing to unburden themselves, by selling the lesser goods so cheaply, it was alright by him, as he'd found a profitable niche in the market.

Noticing John admiring his rather grand looking break-front mahogany bookcase, he said, 'The lads thought they'd dropped that on me. Had to ladle out a heap of cash, but I tell you what, it might take a while to sell, but you'll never be stuck with a good bookcase. Better than any cash stashed away.'

Rather daunted by being in the presence of such a noble piece, John tried to imagine the wad of notes necessary for its purchase. 'Cash, you say. What would have happened if you hadn't had enough on you?'

'Well, some would have let me pay later, but you can't do that too often. If you can't cough up, you're out on your ear.'

He then went on to explain how he'd made his money. Years back he'd latched onto the notion of attending ministry sales. After the war, the Ministry of Defence had a huge surplus of equipment to get rid of. Desks, chairs, tables, you name it, would be heaped into separate sections and you couldn't buy just the one item, say a desk, you had to bid for the whole stack of them, maybe as many as 50. Well of course, being just after the war, not many had the cash available and so most sales were attended by the same few. 'When the lads sorted everything at the end,' Mike explained, 'you could make a decent wedge by throwing in a few bids and coming away with virtually nothing. But if you copped a lot and couldn't pay,' he said with a laugh, 'that was it, barred. You'd never be allowed back in. And there were some rough customers, I can tell you.'

'But I can't see the point. If the buyer has to pay the ultimate price, why not just bid for it?'

'Whoever ends up with the lot automatically has 10% saving and if he's smart about it, when the shares are worked out, the weakest get their cut slashed to the minimum. If they kick up a fuss, they just get told to bid for themselves next time.'

'But surely, you can't just get paid for simply being there?'

'Well no, you did have to appear as if a serious contender and I always made sure I came away with at least one little deal. Just standing there and taking the money, you'd have soon been told to sling yer hook.' He went on to divulge, 'My big break came, when a porter I gave the odd tip to, told me to bid on a room stuffed full with mattresses. Well of course no-one wanted the scabby things and so they were knocked down to me for a pound. Having bought them, which brought a lot of piss taking, I can tell you, I was then duty bound to shift them. I couldn't believe it, hidden beneath were all the smokers-bow armchairs from an officer's mess. They weren't worth anything like they are today, but I still had the equivalent of six months wages, for the outlay of a pound. The porter was happy with his tip, the ministry couldn't have given a damn, they just wanted rid of the stuff and at last, I had my stash to compete for the better lots.'

Like I'd said, the little manuscript I now possessed was like gold, voices from the past and the next little gem involved another Mike. This one however was more old school and from the opposite direction, Shrewsbury.

There had been an auction in Ludlow Town Hall and the knockout afterwards had been that protracted, the last protagonists left standing, had drunk that much they were almost on their backs. This was in those very early days, when John and his mother still resided at the Bull Hotel. The Mike in question had become a good friend, having been a regular customer for all the decent glass and china, Jessica sold from her shop. He packed it into furniture his firm shipped to North America, for it seemed criminal not to utilise all that vacant space. Anyway, Mike was three parts gone by the time he lurched into the Bull Hotel. The carousing continued and it was well gone closing time, when an abusive side of his nature began to feature, growling at the landlady's sister, 'Sitting there with a face like that, you could empty the best pub in England.' It wasn't said, just the once, either. They could see he was becoming a bit of a handful, not likely to improve and was obviously too far gone to drive back to Shrewsbury, so after a little persuasion, they managed to coax him upstairs, undress and tuck him into a bed for the night.

It was about an hour later when the door to the lounge burst open and there stood Mike in droopy underpants and socks held up by garters, enquiring ferociously, 'Is this some sort of clip joint?' He took some convincing, but John, leading him back upstairs, pointed out where his clothes had been safely stowed. Mike, lurched towards his jacket, hanging from a bed post and peeping inside a pocket, breathed a sigh of relief. 'It's still there.'

It was the fattest wad of notes, John Dodds had ever seen. Mike was tucked in again, but next day, once more required John's assistance, driving him slowly round the town, as for the life of him, he couldn't remember where he'd left his car.

I had of course known, a good deal of cash must have been involved in the dealings done back in those times, but hadn't realised, just how much. This explained some of the, almost pass the parcel, trading, in the early days, John Dodds had had to engage in after each major deal with Mrs. Lockyer. He lamented on a number of occasions, of how they'd virtually had to give certain things away, but had no choice. If they didn't have the cash, each time Gary Lockyer appeared saying, 'Our mum's got some more stuff for yer,' she would have had no qualms about selling it to someone else.

John continued:---*She constantly complained about the Irish swarming everywhere, buying everything up and she had a perfect right to; convoys of them would occasionally drive through town; the whole tribe on the move; each truck absolutely laden with furniture. You might think, 'manna from heaven,' but dealing with them was a nightmare. Not really knowing the true value of anything, not helped by the fact I didn't either, they would ask a fortune and then harangue to the point of anger, swarming, until on one occasion, I retreated to the shop and fearing for my safety, locked the door. There were exceptions, but generally the whole process was far too stressful and I found it easier to deal with those who had built up a trading relationship with the saner ones.*

He returned to the subject of Mrs Lockyer.---*I don't know how she managed it, but every few days, we'd be called to haggle for her latest finds. Given sole buying rights did come with its downside mind you. There were certain things you didn't want at any price, but leaving them behind would have left the door open for a competitor and so as regards some items, it was more a matter of damage limitation than making a profit. How she knew the period of the furniture, puzzled me. She couldn't read or write and so how on earth had she learnt about Queen Ann cabriole legs and Georgian bracket feet? She did have some comical terms mind you, cross-bounded tops and gabriel legs, but seemed to instinctively know the age of what she chanced upon and what was more puzzling, when for some reason there was a price hike on a certain item, something innate told her to up her asking price accordingly. It was a complete mystery.*

Some stock bought from her could be mundane, or it could be sublime: huge floral urn on stand; elaborate cast iron garden furniture; impressive bull or horse paintings, with the animal named in bold lettering below; brass beds; huge Imari platters; cloisonne vases; Vienna wall clocks; carriage clocks; Webb's Stourbridge glass; signed Worcester porcelain; gold bracelets; sovereigns; pretty Georgian pendants, but there might also be the black couch with the stuffing hanging out. On the selling of such, the lady who'd been born in a gypsy caravan, would bring all her inherent skills to bear.

'Bit of a tidy-up and this will look a different thing. You'll have no trouble putting this right, my lad.' In a semi-recline on what she called a cheese-long she'd wax lyrical, 'I had a job buying this, I'll have you know. The old vicar said it's where he lay, composing his sermons.' With a wink. 'There's a load more stuff to come, from where this owd sofa came from. Buying it from out of 'is big glass conservatory was my way in. The gent says, we'm to give him a call when next passing. Set of chairs, big oak table,' parting fingers and thumb as if grasping the girth, 'Gert big oak top, that thick!'

On eying the scabby couch again, came the mental debate, *'I know I once carried similar through town on my back, but I don't want to be known for the things. How little can I give, so not to be stuck with it?'* Needless to say, the vicar supposedly reclining in his conservatory was pure invention and she was mistress of it.

Sometimes, when we hadn't enough money, Mrs. Lockyer would say, *'Oh that's alright. Pay our Trevor. You'll find him in the Tavern I 'spect.'*

We always made the pretence we'd simply not brought enough with us, but in fact had to resort to our only means of obtaining immediate cash, always made readily available so long as we ensured, it and the little extra was paid back, quickly as possible. With mother's debt and my lack of collateral, no bank would have funded us, but an ex-bank manager, who bought sovereigns off us, was always glad to help.

On finding Trevor, we'd sometimes be regaled with the latest saga. *'Remember Tuesday?'* he said. *'The day we 'ad that rain? Well where we was calling, it was abso-lute-ly pissin' it down and our mum ses, "Trevor, pull over to that orchard!" I'd noticed 'erd 'ad 'er eye on it, each time we 'appened to be passin'. Well anyway, with all that rain and the weight of them massive scrumps, the branches was absolutely groaning under the weight. It was like them scrumps was callin' to 'er. And so, there 'er was, busy 'elpin erself, stuffing all these apples down 'er front,--- when this big wet farmer's face come loomin'.'*

'Steaming red, he asks her, "Have you had quite sufficient, madam?"'

*'"What on earth do you think **you're** doing, out on a day like this?" Er says, lookin' most put out.'*

'The moosh still 'ad 'is gob 'anging open as we drove from there.'

On another occasion, Trevor had stopped the pick-up and grabbing a foraging chicken had rung its neck, to shove it, still flapping, down by his mother's feet. 'Well, our mum goes into this mad panic, wailing, "Trevor what have you done? You'll get us both locked up!"'

'Calm down,' I says, but 'er was still flappin' as bad as the bloody chicken, "Trevor, you'll get a year for every feather!"'

'After 'er and the chicken had calmed down a bit, 'er said, "That'll roast lovely with a bit of fat bacon."'

Her attitude to buying antiques was, 'If you canna beg it, then you dunner go stealing it.' The same gold standard didn't apply, as regards a few of her sons' activities it seems, for when one was given a custodial sentence for helping himself to scrap metal, she'd said to John in all seriousness, 'Well what does folks expect when they leaves stuff lying about?' Although of course, well known to the police, neither she nor Trevor ever featured in their enquiries regarding stolen property.

Having discovered that the trade back then, largely ran on cash, I was keen to discover how John Dodds transformed the business from in the main, running on squitter, as his Hereford friend had said, to becoming a well-known furniture trader. Searching through the notes, it seems there were many constraints to becoming upwardly mobile. The ring seemed to have a stranglehold on the better salerooms and those with anything notable to sell, tended to call the most prestigious dealers. Then, even if John had pushed the boat out, investing heavily on a good lot, he still stood the chance of being stuck with it, for being beyond the pocket of his regulars and the dealers much higher up the pecking order only calling on their main contacts, a huge percentage of his capital would then have been tied up until a complete maverick arrived, touring the shops.

It was in fact, although accidental, how he gradually latched on to the few better customers that helped him up out of the pit. Most of the old-school dealers, however, still ignored shops such as his, for fear of encouraging competition that would push up the price of items they were after. So even if tempted, by the sight of a particularly desirable lot having been placed out on the pavement, they still wouldn't stop to enquire, preferring to leave their main contact to deal with it. Then, if on examination, that piece happened to be merely above average, rather than top of the range, the pronouncement, "You should do very well with that," was likely to be heard, when in reality, the attitude was, 'Leave him with it. He won't want another bugger round his neck!'

There was also not much coming his way from the lesser traders, for if chancing on anything a bit tasty, they'd ring a mentor, wanting the kudos and their continued backing, rather than letting the lowly John Dodds have chance of it. Also, the sheer numbers trading at the time was quite staggering. Every village seemed to have its antique dealer, whether trading from home, barn or shop and to give you an idea of just how intense it all was, the little town of Clun, at one point, boasted four. What kept them all going, were other dealers from out of the area, calling to buy and supply the trans-Atlantic trade, with what the old school would describe as shipping junk. With so many constantly ferreting about, the pickings were thin, especially as many antiques readily available, still didn't sell. Stripped pine, as yet, hadn't come to the fore, Georgian mahogany wardrobes were shop blockers and even Victorian wind-out tables only sold as scrap.

At what a certain friend might call, the squitter level, John Dodds had found a ready source of cast iron kettles, trivets and cauldrons that a dealer over by Tenbury bought from the Irish. He also bought brass fenders, warming pans, copper kettles and jam pans to embellish the shop window, but the furniture there was usually on the hefty side, would have cleaned him out of cash and have taken a Herculean effort to manhandle into the shop. One steady earner, mind you were things still largely derided, brass and iron beds. He could buy the roof rack full for next to nothing, clean and paint them and make a massive profit when selling to the burgeoning Dutch trade.

There were of course, the occasional private calls, but they weren't frequent enough to provide a living, but he did discover the next best thing, a lady from Minsterly, who without the incumbrance of a shop, did occasional house clearances to supplement the family income. Although the youngest of her boys was John's age, she was still a girl at heart and they instantly got on, with the deals conducted, being more like banter than serious trading. He frequently rang for news of fresh stock and bought, glass, china, jewellery and the usual shipping fare, but try as he might, it didn't help his quest to learn about period furniture, for any she chanced upon was snapped up by a Shrewsbury trader who almost seemed camped on her doorstep.

To give an idea of how tough it was, trying to buy better furniture, John Dodds and his mother, having bought nothing more than a horse measuring stick, when standing all day at an Abergavenny auction, stayed on until late afternoon to purchase the only lot of note, a humble Georgian mahogany chest of drawers. The virtue of it being only three feet, two inches wide, tall on its bracket feet and a good colour, was undermined somewhat by it having patinated pine sides. It was borne home in triumph, however.

His mother was up north again, when he proudly returned from Mrs. Lockyer's with his first ever Georgian mahogany bureau. It was a bit on the bloated side, but there again, a bureau was a bureau, how could he miss with it?

The question, 'Where's the rest of it?' deflated him rather. He had wondered why the top board was a bit raw and was told, polished timber wasn't required, for that was where the bookcase top would have sat, bringing a balance to the thing. Worse than that, was his first ever coffer, bought as a solo effort. He writes:---*Once again, Mrs. Lockyer's eyes lit up when she saw me arrive alone.*

'Come uv-out yer mum again,' she chortled and in her proud, shoulders back, way of walking, led me down the yard to where the furniture was arrayed.

It was when she said those parting words, 'You'm a better buyer til yer mother,' I suspected something could be amiss. It wasn't until middle night that the truth suddenly struck. It woke me up in fact. What I'd taken to be an interesting structural design in the lower regions of the coffer, would once of course, have held two drawers. The enormity of the mistake was driven home, I felt, in an unnecessarily brutal manner. A dealer I'd invited into the back room, for a privileged perusal of my latest purchases, took one look and pronounced, 'If there's one thing sells worse than a mule chest, its one without its drawers!' I was sorely tempted to give the thing a good kick every time I walked past.

He went on to write:---There seemed so many dead ends that needed exploring, before knowing the profitable route to take. Butter churns seemed interesting relics until, whilst trying to circumnavigate, one got caught in the crutch yet again, by the handle; rectangular Georgian oak, gateleg tables only sold as scrap; iron-bound butter tubs, had an appealing look, but if allowed to dry out, fell to bits, defying all efforts to reassemble; cradles held an allure until realising the feeling wasn't generally shared and then on catching one's little toe on the protruding rocker yet again, came the vow, never to buy another.

Sets of dark varnished Edwardian chairs were readily available, but being usually of beech, could end up as wormy shop blockers. Most heavy Victorian furniture didn't sell, for the brief Australian boom had not yet started. Carnival glass, the more common Staffordshire figures, pale blue Wedgewood and late coronation mugs would gather dust; Grimwade and Shelley china didn't even feature and butter pats, you couldn't give the things away. Silver thimbles sold, but not if pierced by a pinhole and cloisonne was unsaleable unless absolutely perfect.

Half sovereigns were as highly valued as full sovereigns, however, as they were the perfect size for making into earrings and there were other little insights that could give one an edge. An innocuous looking tiny silver box in a collection, could be worth as much as the other ten it came with, being a vinaigrette; one stick, with small brass button just below the handle, revealing it to be a sword stick, could be worth more than all the rest in the stick-stand and a post card showing an ancient train crash, could be worth more than all the rest in the bundle.

Post cards? Yes the collecting phase was on the rise, gradually becoming, everything and anything. It had started way back with fairings and pot lids, graduating on to Goss china, pastil burners and then even disinterred codd-necked bottles, coloured medicine bottles and eye baths. Collectors of the latter, didn't seem the least put off by them varying only in colour, for they proudly displayed them in lines along shelves. A population that had been glad to turf out the old fashioned, after the war, was beginning to take an interest in buying some of it back again and at last it meant, a shop that had relied almost solely on the trade, could now sell the odd thing privately.

CHAPTER SEVEN

So, John Dodds had left two clues in his notes as to how it had been possible to inch his way up from the bottom rung on the antique dealing ladder. First was his strategy of investing profits, attempting to learn about the better items and second, how, by chancing his arm on those things of merit, it eventually brought him better customers. Without the latter, the next stage would have been near impossible, for as he explains, there was little chance back then of selling the better stock privately and most of the proverbial rich Americans that made it as far as the Welsh Marches, must have done so in the belief, their willingness to venture beyond the Cotswolds must surely lead to some sort of antiquated time warp, where the goods would be available for next to nothing. Some became quite affronted at being asked a price near the going rate, with one, in her pale tartan trousers, white slip-ons and see-through mac, actually slamming the door and marching off in a huff.

I chanced upon a section, which I've decided to include, for although the experience didn't exactly help John Dodds in his quest for knowledge of the better pieces, it has entertainment value and certainly gave his business a boost. Like many a brave enterprise, the eventual rewards are rarely those expected when first venturing forth and yet without such daring, the gains would have been nothing at all.

He did add in his notes, mind you,---*There's a very narrow dividing line between bravery and recklessness.*

Again, I've taken the liberty of smoothing out the account that had come into my possession, but hopefully without losing John Dodds' slightly formal, self-deprecating manner.

---*One day Trevor Lockyer came into the shop, dressed as usual in collar and tie, smart trousers, jacket buttoned and boots polished. 'Ood you be interested in an owd caravan?' he asked. 'I come across it over Worcester way. Dunner laugh, but the place is called Wyre Piddle.'*

It sounded quite exciting and so leaving mother to run the shop I let Trevor guide me to his latest find. He'd said, to just give him fifteen quid for his trouble, but how I dealt with it from there on was down to me. Half way there he divulged, he hadn't actually bought the vehicle, but assured me it wouldn't be a problem, 'The moosh uz said I can 'av it. Dunner worry, 'ee's as good as gold.'

I'd taken the trouble to look at the map before leaving and when we'd circumvented Worcester, I asked, 'Why are we heading this way? I'm sure Wyre Piddle is in that direction. This takes us to Upton Snodsbury.'

'Upton Snodsbury? Wyre Piddle? Fuck me! You couldna make 'em up! Anyway, we gotta go this way, cos it's the road I took when I found the place.'

'Are you sure it's Wyre Piddle we need to find?'

'Well aah! That's where the moosh said 'ee lived!'

It hadn't dawned on me until now, he couldn't read the road signs. Winding along the lanes, we eventually found the property and there in a wild tangle of hazel and plum trees, stood the old grey caravan, like a stranded pachyderm, quietly dreaming of liberation. It was of wooden construction and still had its original wooden wheels. Apart from the one rear wheel requiring attention, it seemed in fairly sound condition and I told Trevor, provided the owner would allow us to dismantle part of the decrepit panelled fence for its extrication, I'd take a gamble on it. With that part of the deal agreed, he went in search of the said owner.

Slowly approaching along the garden path, the man, a little bent and looking obviously unnerved by his visitor's assured manner, gave the odd wince at Trevor's way of conversing as if two fields lay between them.

'Now you does realise we'll 'av to 'eave it out from 'ere, into the lane.'

The man nodded.

'You knows we'm gonner 'ave to pull part of that fence down? You knows that dunt cha? Course 'ee does. Good as gold, just like I said.'

'As long as it's put back again,' came a frail voice of concern.

'Of course it ul be put back. When we'm finished, you'll never knowed we've even bin 'ere.'

So that was how I became the proud owner of a caravan. I won't call it a gypsy caravan, for Mrs. Lockyer was keen to put me straight on that one, pointing out one day. 'That aint no gypsy caat. My folks wouldn't uv bin sin DEAD in a thing like that. I should know, I was born in one. What you've got yourself there, is an owd roadman's wagon.'

It had been a struggle to slowly inch it, with a winch from the trees, but we did manage to edge it onto the car transporter. Fortunately, the latter came with a man proficient at handling it. Before we left, the previous owner approached, anxious that I should sign a piece of paper.

'Old wooden caravan, sold as seen, £4.'

It was, coming off the roundabout, heading in the Ombersley direction, that we thought we'd lost it. As luck had it, there was a layby and we pulled in to inspect the damage. The suspect rear wheel, probably with the shock of having been called into action after all those years, had given way and the waggon now lay at a drunken angle. Passing motorists slowed to look and I felt a sense of panic rising, not helped by the words, 'If this thing collapses in the road, we could be in big trouble.' We did manage to wedge the car-jack beneath the axle, shoring up any further inclination to lurch, but the thing was too massive to be returned to anything approaching vertical.

From hereon we crawled along, drawing attention at every village. In Ludlow, another jerked slippage brought gasps of horror from onlookers, but we finally managed to get the thing to creak and limp to the safety of a factory car park, where I'd been told I could leave it. Any sense of relief was short lived, however, as the shop phone went and I was summoned down to see the factory manager, a dour Scotsman. I told him, I'd been given permission to park it there, to which he replied, 'Not by me, you haven't! But dinner worry I'll soon have a fork-lift shift it.'

By apologising and appealing to his better nature, I gained a stay of execution, being granted three days to find it a new home. By the second day, with mother's help actually, a friend of hers offered a solution. We could tuck it in out of the way and work on it in the car park, to the rear of the Castle, the only pub in Richards Castle. With it being a possible draw to trade, the landlord looked quite taken by the idea.

The owner of the car transporter, however, was of a rather different frame of mind. 'You want that thing shifted again? Not really sure I like the sound of that,' but after a little persuasion and the fact it was such a short journey, although extremely reluctant, he offered his services again.

As regards renovating the old relic, it was of course now more than just a paint job and I'd not the slightest idea how to tackle it. This is where Trevor came to my aid. I happened to meet him in the Tavern and he said, his father-in-law had once travelled with the May Fair and one of his duties had been the upkeep of the vehicles, including renovation of their traditional decoration. So that is how an old boy named Mr. Reece came into the picture, with his tales of travelling with the fair from town to town.

I won't go into all the details regarding problems and renovation, other than say we put the raised roof section back on, a molly-croft, he called it; we cut out and patched the rot; created an interior, with cupboards and beds; applied chamfered wooden battens to simulate panels on the exterior and painted the whole thing as if being a showman's rather than the roadman's waggon it really was.

It still left the problem of the rear wheel, rotten beyond saving. Worse than that, I found it was not only more generously dished than you'd expect on such a utility vehicle, but also a nonstandard size. Incidentally, the interior fittings were fashioned from two pine wardrobes we'd scrapped. The stripped pine craze was just catching on in the Marches, but as yet, no-one wanted pine wardrobes.

Obviously, his next job was to find a wagon wheel to match the one still intact and with it having been far from easy, I thought it best to just summarise the details. Enquiries led him from farm to farm, but most of the wheels found leaning up against sheds, buried in nettles or still on rotting carts, were massive and when he did chance upon a carriage wheel it was always the wrong diameter.

He still came back with pine furniture, brass and iron beds and old brass-bedecked horse equipment, which of course was profitable, but the harder he searched, the more he realised from old timers he met, his chances of success were slender in the extreme. At a hamlet called Greete, not far from Ludlow, he was told he was 50 years too late, for back then the tiny community had boasted six wheel-rights. He did buy his first wheel-right's traveller from there mind you, a home-fashioned tool they used for measuring wheel circumferences.

One of his regulars, a dealer from Birmingham, told him he'd seen wagon wheels for sale outside a shop in Bewdley. When pressed for more information, the man had just shrugged as if to say, 'A wheel's a wheel ay it?'

There was nothing for it, but to go and look and at first glance he knew it had been a fool's errand. The things must have come off a cart requiring a team of oxen to heave into a slow trundle. Each one would have taken at least two men to lift and it wasn't as if he'd found a wagon wheel specialist, for the shop owner told him, these were the first he'd ever bought and would probably be the last. In an attempt to pay for the day, for it seemed like a fun item, he bought a factory clocking-in, clock. Apparently, another lesson learnt, for bottom of page, attention drawn by a large asterisk, he'd written, *'Some days are best, simply written off.'*

He writes:---*One day I'd followed dead-end leads almost down as far as Gloucester, but had drawn a blank at each farm I'd been sent to. Out of desperation I pulled onto a pub carpark, thinking the landlord might offer a spark of inspiration. His response was a blank look, before asking, what did I do for a living? I told him and he said, 'Follow me.'*

Back in Ludlow, the shop must have darkened as I pulled up onto the pavement, for mother suddenly appeared looking extremely concerned. 'John, whatever is that?'

'An oak corner cupboard.'

'I thought you'd bought a boat.'

'It's a Georgian one.'

'But it's massive! Who's going to buy a thing that big? Not sure it will even fit in the shop.'

'It only cost £2'

'A crumb of comfort I suppose.'

Once untied, we slid it to the pavement with a dull thud. 'Oh John what have you done? It's just the top half. The thing must have been a monster.'

'Perhaps this half opened up in the bedroom.'

'You may well joke, but somehow we've got to drag it inside.'

We moved a previous folly, the factory time-clock, to give a clearer run to the back wall and with not so much as the thickness of knife blade to spare, we somehow dragged it in, to be slid it on its back to the far lefthand corner. Between us, we managed to heave it upright. In idle moments over ensuing days, I dragged an old penny across portions of its frontage, flicking off old varnish, bringing some degree of satisfaction and finally, when polished, that entire corner of the room glowed as if the thing had settled nicely into its new abode. Although the front was a vast spread of plainness, the interior did have shaped shelves and immediately below the pair of panelled doors, there had once been a drawer. It would have been a comical little thing on such a brute, as the remaining aperture was no bigger than an average letter box. It turned out to be elm, by the way, not oak and of course went for scrap, such wide backboards being a godsend to a furniture restorer.

It appears, it was just as well it hadn't hung about, for close on its heels, when out hunting for wheels, a huge oval barrel was chanced upon. Fortunately, it was of no great depth, but its frontage, adorned with carved grapes and vines, was an imposing 5' in height. This did, it seems, dominate the shop corner for a while and yet if I'd have come across it, I'd have bought it in an instant, perfect for my hire business.

Not all the time was spent hunting wagon wheels, for there were calls to follow up and Mrs. Lockyer, although not as active as she had been, still found the odd few pieces. He writes: *I went round on a Sunday morning to collect the furniture bought the previous evening and had the feeling I'd interrupted a secret gathering. Even the Yorkshire Terrier looked concerned and long dark faces eyed me warily as Mrs. Lockyer hurriedly ushered me from the kitchen. I felt certain, whatever language they conversed in, would not have sounded much like English.*

A call chanced upon, was virtually on his doorstep. He had often noticed all the equipment scattered in a field near Brimfield and on impulse one day, called in to enquire about wagon wheels. The door was answered by a man in middle years, who said with a wry look, all the stuff strewn about had been his father's doing. He was happy to show John the wooden wheels he was aware of, but of course as ever, they were off lumbering farm carts. He suggested John should call back, on the off-chance of others lurking in the barns. Well, the long and the short of it was, there were no other wheels, but he and the old boy got on like a house on fire. He came away with his car laden with pig benches, pine furniture extricated from the old horse boxes, outbuildings and barn, plus no end of interesting tools he'd never seen the like of before; for instance, a horse balling iron. It was wrought iron, with a wooden handle. Forced flat between a horses' teeth, it would have been twisted to force the mouth open and a hole through the metalwork allowed the vet access, without having his hand bitten off. Thrown in the deal was the wooden tube, through which the medicinal tablet would have been blown down the animal's throat.

His new friend attended all the local farm sales, almost like a hobby. Antique dealers only tended to bother, when household furniture had a mention, end of advert in a local paper. Unbeknown to most, however, where things lurked in barns, even though in a previous life they would have been listed as household furniture, on most occasions they were just lumped together under the heading, 'dead stock'. John Dodds kept his eye on the man. Inadvertently, he'd found himself a good friend and a goldmine.

104

Sometimes, when the old boy was out, he'd be told to go and have a good root about and leave the stuff in a stack for a deal to be negotiated on the next visit. John dug out kettle sways, for the back of inglenook fireplaces, trivets, huge firedogs, adjustable iron hooks, old brass weights, stack of irons for marking sheep, a thatcher's needle, bushel measures, milk measures, turned lignum vitae horse tethers, bull nose-leads, table top butter churn, old flesh forks, spice tins and even a cast iron fireback. The latter was left until the son could help lift it.

A wheel was eventually found for the caravan, but as ever, it's never as simple as just slipping it on, with a bit of grease and finally seeing the back of the thing. The wheel's collar didn't fit the axle. He took the problem to an old timer in Bromfield nicknamed, 'Poon-iron,' on account of him having been a blacksmith and was told, "You'm gonna hafta re-bowk 'err." This involved hammering out the existing collar and wedging in the slightly slenderer version. One that perfectly fitted the caravan's axle. This was undertaken in the back yard belonging to a certain Mr. Birdy Price, a devotee of the turf and the noble creatures that raced thereon. He had even sold John, the oak floorboards from a spare bedroom when in need of a stake to lay on a red-hot tip. Anyway, for some reason, down Birdy's back yard lay an old turntable upon which the re-bowking could be carried out. Not easy of course, but it was finally achieved; after a fashion.

The wheel was rubbed down, primed, painted and secured on the caravan's axle. Luckily, a friend of his mother, a picture restorer by trade, occasionally held a collective sale at his studios in Erdington, Birmingham. The caravan standing in the drive, would be an interesting lot, perfect for drawing in the customers. The car transporter man was called into action again and as the vehicle was winched aboard, the replaced back wheel gave a bit of a saucy flick, but at least it stayed on. John had written,---*You've no idea how glad I was to see the back of the thing. It did make us a fair profit, but nothing like that gained from all the things found when searching for the wheel.*

Augmenting slightly, I give you the following.---*I happened to be passing the Greyhound Yard one day, just as Mrs. Lockyer was exiting, taking the short-cut through to a favourite haunt, The Smithfield Inn.*

It was strange to see her not enveloped in usual smock and apron. High heels gave her a precarious upright teeter and the dentures so rarely in place, added a broad white gleam as if suddenly becoming lodged from having inadvertently overwound a toy piano.

'I did alright on that caravan,' I said cheerfully.

The teeth, mainly reserved for weddings and funerals, proved a slight impediment, but words did escape, whistling slightly, "I oodna make an 'abbit of it, if I was you.'

CHAPTER EIGHT

---*The mahogany chest from Abergavenny had taken on a very settled look in the shop and from its vaunted position of being the very first thing mentioned to any trader calling, had slipped down the rankings to earn the odd muttering of, 'It's time that thing went.'*

John Dodds continues:---*One afternoon the shop bell rang and mother said, 'It's Deerstalker, you go.'*

From the notes, I gathered the man referred to, owned a massive pile over Leominster way and the fact he was always in tweed, topped by a deerstalker hat, was the reason for his appellation.

Here's John Dodds once more.---*He enunciated his words with distinct relish as if hoping their impact might elevate his stature, for he was not a big man and although generally thought of as pugnacious and contrary, for some reason mellowed somewhat when in my company.*

Other traders had expressed amazement I could even put up with him. They told me of a sale once held at his manor, where the auctioneer had been hampered by the man's insistence on vetting every potential purchaser before allowing the gavel to fall. If winning bids came from certain members of the trade, they were denied ownership. It had caused astonishment and hilarity.

107

Well for some reason, on this particular afternoon, Deerstalker, without the slightest prompting, homed in on the mahogany chest of drawers and provided it could be delivered post haste and fitted the alcove intended, he would be happy to make the purchase and hadn't even asked for a price reduction.

I almost beat him back home with it, but as we were carrying it up the stairs, his voice chimed from above, 'Oh! I say! You didn't tell me it had pine sides.'

There followed a long pause and fearing all was lost I peered round the chest and said, 'But they are beautifully patinated,' to which Deerstalker cheerfully declared, 'Not to worry. Where it's going, they won't be seen.'

It slipped into the alcove as if designed for it and Deerstalker's voice rang, 'I think it quite likes it there. It looks quite well don't you think?'

'Better than where it came from,' I thought and in fact, it did look the part, reflecting in the floorboards, but now all I wanted was his cheque and to be away from there. Having just been asked my opinion on a nearby tapestry, I could sense a grand tour pending, but thankfully was saved by the distant tinkling of a telephone.

What would I know about an ancient tapestry?

Back at the shop, mother said, 'well done' and with a knowing look, reminded me of the times, when running it single handed, she'd had to keep the male dealers interested enough to buy the goods, whilst still managing to keep their over amorous advances at bay. With them often being three parts cut at the time, it had been quite a battle.

Marie's words came back to me, 'It's all part of the game,' but by now, having taken that fully on board, I must admit, I had something a bit more voluptuous than Deerstalker in mind.

Reading further through the latest notes, given me by my acquaintance Mike, I saw three references to a large load of early oak that had been promised by Mrs. Lockyer. It was a clearance from an old farmhouse and at last it seems, John Dodds was about to get his hands on some of the decent stuff, the sort of items normally beyond his reach. This sounded interesting and I wondered if it heralded a breakthrough. Something that might help explain how he'd ended up in the big shop I'd seen. He wrote, that he'd been impatient, anxious to call mid-afternoon on the appointed Friday to see if the load had arrived, but his mother had told him not to pester, as they'd been given a solemn promise of first chance.--- *The assurance 'On our babbie's life,' had been said as a guarantee, even though the babby in question was now at least fifteen.*

We were met at the door by an admonishing, 'You shoulda been here earlier, Jessica. Where d'you get to? John Smith's 'ad it all!'

'But you promised!' Mother was almost in tears.

'No, t'inner my fault. You shoulda been 'ere earlier.'

'What? Has he had it all?'

'Aah. Took the lot.'

Mother and I felt absolutely eviscerated, but in all fairness, she then said, it was no good crying about it, we'd better see if we could rescue something from the disaster.

John Smith was Mrs. Lockyer's son in law and ran a scrap yard to the rear of my friend Leon's antique shop. His grin on seeing us, wasn't triumphant as such, more one of slight satisfaction at being prescient. We were shown into the shed, used for selling any antiques chanced upon, when purchasing scrap and selling iron gates around the farms. What lay within halted us in our tracks. It was an absolute body blow, the best cache of oak furniture I'd ever seen in my life, but making matters worse, even though probably bought for next to nothing, he was now asking sky high prices for it.

Mother trying a little charm, appealed to his better nature, but on realising it was getting her nowhere, finally told him he was nothing but an old rogue.

This he took as a compliment, his attitude softening slightly and perching on the long oak farmhouse table, he absolutely beamed, 'Now come off it, Jessica. You knows the stuff's worth it.'

'And I know you've begged it.'

'Now you know's as well as I do, Jessica, that inner the point and it's obvious you'm quite upset. Canner blame you there. I'd be exactly the same.' Giving the table a rap with his knuckles, 'Listen to that. Pure quality. What you has to ask yerself is,--- can you see a profit in it?'

'I know that, but at least be reasonable.'

'I am, but you inner lookin' at the stuff right, Jessy. What you'm seeing is dusty owd things in a shed. What you gotter imagine is,--- this table I'm sat on, not hemmed in by all this other stuff, but gleaming down the length of a panelled room. There'd be the 'ed of the family, way down that end, carving the turkey and all them twenty others, up this 'un, in their paper 'ats waitin' for a slice. This 'eer table, Jessica,' another rap of knuckles, 'is a gent. Worthy of pride of place in any mansion. You ooner get stuck uv a thing like this.'

'But------?'

'You canner miss with it, Jessy. You wants to get it bought!'

We had a short discussion and decided to ignore coffers, boxes, Georgian side-tables and chests, to home in on the table and an oak food hutch. The latter was boarded, had a panelled door, pierced in the upper, narrow horizontal panel with two rows of holes for ventilation and stood on tall stiles to an overall height of roughly five and a half feet. I hadn't a clue regarding its value, but it had the look of something you couldn't possibly leave behind. Homing in on these we managed to ease John down slightly on the price and he delivered them on his truck. I suspected, his was the vehicle used to remove all from the farm in the first place.

He helped clear a path for the table, which spanned virtually the whole depth of the shop.

'Whatever's you doin' uv a thing like this?' he asked, helping me move the massive wine barrel. Fortunately, the table top was separate to the base, otherwise we'd have struggled getting it through the doorway. As it was, it weighed a ton and on clanking it down, I noticed the cleat at my end, protruding ever so slightly beyond the three-board top, had left a temporary indent on the palm of my hand. By mid-morning next day, both it and the food hutch had sold.

Looking through the notes again, I came across a reference regarding an intervention by the law. In his search for the elusive wheel, he'd once been startled by a strange character up on Clee Hill, known for some reason, as Aeroplane Bertie, who had suddenly appeared at a gap in the hedge to blurt, 'Cuckoo!'--- *When the son of this individual appeared in the shop late one Saturday afternoon, to brightly announce he'd chanced on certain things for sale, I had no reason to think anything other than the man had come by them legally. My belief was enforced by the fact, he held tenaciously to his asking price, not budging one penny.*

The deal was done and with all items being currently saleable, John had expected to earn a quick profit when re-opening the shop on Monday morning.--- *Until a constable appeared with the list of recently stolen goods. Reading the descriptions, made me realise I was now the proud owner of every single item on it, stolen from a woman living in a lane, not five minutes' walk away.*

All was gathered up, taken away and the clueless son of the would-be Clee Hill aviator was taken into custody. I was told, once a free man again, part of his weekly dole would be given me, until eventually I had my money back. Needless to say, I never saw a penny.

In the new batch of notes, as mentioned before, I had noticed the name Anne appearing. It seems that just as Mrs. Lockyer had hinted, there seemed to be a problem regarding his mother's appraisal of certain females he met. The greeting given Anne, a local girl of 18, had been icy to say the least and John hadn't dared put her through the ordeal of staying the night in the shop. It had all been rather embarrassing.

He writes:---*On one occasion we'd both made a bit of a night of it, on a wander round the pubs, the Tavern, Keysells, the Bull, the Rose and Crown and with turning up at the shop likely to put a dampener on things, we drove up Whitcliffe, first pull-in on the right. There was a dreadful, 1930's walnut veneered, demi-lune cabinet in the back, that had come in a deal for nothing, but no matter, we hauled it out and spent a pleasant night in the estate car. The following morning, I wondered what Anne had suddenly found so funny. Not only, apparently tickled by my interpretation of showing a girl a good time, she pointed to a sign nailed to a branch above us; 'No camping.'*

There were other mentions of Anne and the exciting atmosphere in the town at the time. A particularly lively and inventive generation was growing up, parties were frequent, often quite impromptu, plus there were trips up to a club near Knowbury, with a name that suited the times, The Exploding Ferret. Touring musicians performed there and one night on offer, was even an hilarious stand-up comic. Life in general, seemed more carefree back then.

Some spells in the shop, however, were not always a fun way to see one's life drift by. Often, days could drag unmercifully and I came across one section where it seems, John Dodds suffered slight discomfiture, thinking he might get his lights punched out.

It was over a matter involving an engagement ring and it must have put the wind up him, for a full account was given in the notes, although I did realise, at time of writing he'd obviously recovered sufficiently, to see the funny side. That written below is in the main, faithful to the original text, with just the odd touch from me.

---*He was a brawny, unforthcoming piece of work, the type you can imagine not needing a jacket in the winter. The £3 I'd offered for his engagement ring brought such a writhed look of hatred, I felt sure he was about to use me as a cathartic instrument of therapy, unleashing all his pent-up anger at being jilted.*

I backed off, fearing the ring, with its cheap diamond chips, brandished between thumb and forefinger, might later need retrieval from a nasal passage.

'I gave 24 pounds for this, now you're offering 3 fucking quid, you robbing bastard!'

I explained it was now only worth scrap value and his silence when I suggested he return to the jeweller he'd bought it from, told me he already had.

With it not being hard to imagine a fresh gaping hole through a shop window in the shape of the jeweller, I should have left it at that, for even preceded by the ameliorating, 'It's nothing personal, you understand,' the divulgence, that most people considered, rings from broken engagements unlucky, couldn't have invited greater wrath, had I referred to him as swamp breath, which in fact would have been the truth.

I was saved by the shop bell ringing and couldn't have been more pleased to see the particularly dreary regular from Leominster, had he been Rod Stewart, spikey haired, bedecked in tartan. Standing aside, in fear of being knocked over by the spurned bruiser making a hasty departure, he asked, 'What was all that about?'

I explained and added, that that would be the last engagement ring I'd ever make an offer on. The slight elation at seeing this new customer, soon evaporated however, for he was the one we referred to as Black Hole, having the ability to suck up every bit of atmosphere in the shop.

There was another called, Creepy John, who gave the feeling he belonged to some strange cult that convened every full moon to dine on babies. There was another regular that hardly ever bought anything and just seemed to stand there, only shifting when you got the hoover out and another called Gus, who was friendly enough, had an eye for quality, but would hang around in the belief his persistence would wear you down to such an extent, you'd let him have your latest prize for virtually nothing.

Another, you wouldn't want to get stuck in the pub with, specialised in pine retaining its original Regency paintwork, a growing trend I'd noted and was happy to have his custom, but the way he'd just stand there grinning, head at a slight tilt, earnt him the nickname, Sweety Pie.

There was one old dear, I'm glad I'd shown patience with, even though she'd regularly call, simply to pither about with things in the window and tell me she had a Ming pot in her place of residence, just below Clee Hill Village. She was as deaf as a post and her defective hearing aid, when it whistled, could make a brass jam pan ring. Then one day I was up Clee Hill way and knowing where she lived, called in. The Ming pot was a misshapen pottery, evening-class ashtray that the maker had scratched ming on the underside, probably as a joke, but in her larder was a stack of old biscuit tins, another thing that had recently become collectable, especially when like a few in the haul, they resembled toy vehicles. I left her holding three, one-pound notes, looking dumbfounded that anyone should pay money for such old junk.

I came across another reference to Fred, the dealer who'd driven him to London all those years before. From the few details, I got the impression Fred was no longer married and that drink might have been the cause.

John Dodds writes:---*He no longer had a shop and in fact gave the impression he'd been resting, as thespians are known to say when not in gainful employment. Although still chipper in his manner, it now had a slightly false ring to it, not helped by the fact he was dealing in things he'd once have derided, the likes of, marble topped washstands, jugs and basins and towel rails, bought for an American shipping firm based in Gloucester. The oversize cheques he signed were in the firm's name and as he was working on commission, the more he paid, the larger his share. Of course, there were limits, but with the notion of pushing those limits to the limit, he suggested we visit a few of my regular haunts, my reward being, a share of his commission.*

We had a few lively outings and I suspect he enjoyed my company, for he said it reminded him of the old days. One of the calls, I wouldn't normally have taken a rival dealer to, was Minsterley, which in actual fact paid off quite handsomely, for from the garage and old chapel they rented, we rooted out a few things I wouldn't have dreamt were saleable; numerous single kitchen chairs, old shovels, garden forks and can you believe it, aluminium watering cans, saleable as long as they retained the sprayer. I found a few items for the shop, with those trips, usually on a Thursday, being quite fun and something to look forward to as we headed through the Autumn. Then a few days before Christmas the firm's cheque came back unpaid. It was a large amount, for I'd chanced on quite a haul of stock they specialised in, plus best of all, the deal had included, something I thought I'd be buried with, the wine barrel. Apparently, there had been no sign of Fred or the goods. When the cheque was returned a second time, stamped refer to drawer, I realised it was just a worthless piece of paper. As you can imagine, it put quite a dampener on Christmas.

Then who should appear one dank, dreary January day? Deerstalker. He was flush with money from his annual shares dividend and looked keen to spend a portion. Of course, I was only too glad to help and managed to get him on a bit of a roll, offering a man most found impossible, a few suggestions as to things likely to enhance his abode, which following a moments' pause he'd say, 'Very well, add that to the list, oh and those others on the shelf there, and these little green medicine bottles.'

Medicine bottles? But who was I to argue? He looked like he hadn't had as much fun in months and with a beaming smile, even bought the mule chest.

'You do realise, this should have drawers?'

'Yes of course, but it's still an extremely useful piece of furniture.'

'Very well, add it to the list. I'll just drape a bit of cloth over those openings.'

I delivered all his purchases the following morning and returned, the car almost drifting along on air, to find a fresh cheque had arrived from Fred's shipping firm. This time it went through.

It all put a bit of a spring in my step, but even so, I wasn't fully prepared for the next piece of good fortune. It wasn't that the factory time piece had cost that much, it was just that I'd eventually become party to the fact, I could have bought five for the price paid and had become heartily sick of the ridicule. The man was over from The States visiting family and asked if I could arrange to have it shipped to Hawaii? 'Carry it there in my bare arms if I have to,' came immediately to mind. The catch was, I'd have to trust him to post the cheque. Thinking about it for fully half a second, I agreed. He seemed a person you could trust and my judgement wasn't wrong, for about two weeks later the cheque arrived. Seems like luck, good or bad, runs in patches. I'd even made £5 profit on the damn thing and no longer had to listen to the ding of its bell, accompanying a question like, '45 quid? How many more of these would you like?'

CHAPTER NINE

The next year John Dodds describes as being the year of the Irish and 'That hot summer.' It also culminated in him moving shop, but we'll come to that later. First in his notes, he dealt with the subject of visitors.

---*You never really knew who might call in the shop; occasional visits from M.P.'s you recognised; then those unassuming types wandering in, giving no hint, they were renowned authorities on certain subjects; also, there were serious collectors, with more expertise in their field, than the majority of those in the trade; the lively, imaginative, cast-members of the Shakespeare play, performed each year in the castle, would sometimes light the place up, but I must admit, I hadn't expected the drayman. Following a screech and crash of glass, I found him sprawled in the shop window. The truck attempting to reverse up the alley had been that far off course, it had rammed the man through the plate glass, which was fortunate, for had he been flattened against the brickwork, it would surely have killed him.*

Helping the stunned man rise from the shards, I suggested he made a more conventional way back out to the street. Onlookers asking after his welfare, picked bits of glass off him and visibly shaken, the truck driver advised me to ring the brewery and put in an insurance claim. I was clearing the window of jagged glass and pottery, when the storeman from Boots chemist turned up. He was the dilatory idiot who never cared about the time the Boots' delivery van spent blocking the lane; a man infuriatingly deaf to any reasonable approach and so, when not having offered one word of consolation regarding the recent disaster, he chirpily asked if he could have the larger pieces of glass for his garden seed trays, he received a two-word response, the second of which was, 'OFF!'

The insurance assessor arrived and was that disparaging about my valuation of the pieces broken in the accident, it made me regret not having included a Locke's Worcester potpourri pomander bowl I'd broken the year before. They did pay up, eventually.

There then follows a section where Anne was the main subject. John was now temporally running the shop single handed, for his mother had at last moved north. She did turn up with the odd deal, but the profits didn't come close to the 50% she still received from all his efforts. Anne often stayed at the shop, especially at weekends. He mentioned:---*One Sunday morning when exiting Keysells wine bar by way of the rear door leading into the alley, nought but a stumble away from the shop's back door, we were both stunned by bright sunlight. We fell against each other laughing, realising, carousing to near breakfast time, we'd almost drunk ourselves sober.*

Anne went with him on various explorations to Shropshire hill forts and also to a landmark that had always been his ambition to visit, Flounder's Folly. Local legend had it, the prominent tower on Wenlock Edge, had been constructed on the whim of a Victorian shipping magnate, to enable him to observe his ships on the distant Mersey. I looked it up on the internet and found the shell John Dodds had visited, put up by the man with the strange surname, Flounder, has now been fully renovated with an apartment at the top.

Now we come to the that uncommonly hot summer, when the Irish travellers had descended. The gathering of the clans was for an important wedding and they camped everywhere; along Darky

Lane; in the abandoned quarry up on Titterstone Clee and in the old railway cutting where a branch line had once gone via Tenbury Wells to the Severn Valley. Many of the families owned huge pantechnicons which, harking back to their caravan roots, always had a bucket swinging at the rear. John Dodds had written:---*Like monsters blocking light to the shop, they'd park outside and if one weakened and stepped within those cavernous interiors, beyond the heaps of feather mattrasses, the piled tangle of metalware and furniture awaited. The one smiling and seeming so genial at the outset, would be joined by at least three others and the haranguing would start. Of course, no dealer could be asked to buy a pig in a poke, but with each item being so difficult to extricate, the pressure to reward time and effort spent dragging items out into the road, intensified alarmingly. The four besuited, as if having slept in the things, standing tall in their platform soled shoes, would almost dance in their insistence at having their ludicrous valuation of an item, countered with an offer, any offer, just as long as you took the bait, allowing them to start reeling you in.*

Even when inured to the smell of unwashed feet, I instinctively knew I shouldn't have succumbed and beginning to feel uncomfortably trapped in the back of their wagon, cursed myself for having foolishly become ensnared. It was a nightmare and I can't remember the exact words, but it went something like the following.

'Have a look at the fine cabinet there, sor.'

'I'm sorry, that's not for me. I don't want it.'

'How can you be knowing that if you've not seen it properly. Danny, help Joe get that cabinet out so the gentleman can have a proper look at it.'

'No please---'

'No trouble sir. Will only take a few seconds.'

119

With it now down on the pavement, I reasoned, 'It's not the sort of thing I buy.'

'But if it was, sor, how much would you be giving for it?'

'I'm sorry, but------'

Then the others would join in, 'Just tell him a price, sor. It can't hurt to be making him an offer.'

'I've already told you I don't want it.'

'What? After the trouble we took, for him to be looking at it!!' Says the previously genial one. 'What sort of fookin', gobshite dealer does the man call hisself?'

Offering a comforting arm, another of the band would say something like, 'Now don't be worrying about him, sor. Just give us your best offer.'

'Look I'm sorry, I wouldn't even want the thing for a tenner.' Which I immediately cursed myself for uttering.

'Now there's no need to be like that, sor. Would you be wanting it for 50 pounds?'

'Don't be mad Danny, leave the man a profit. We can't be letting you have it for a tenner, sor, but would ye be willing to part with 40 pounds?'

Alarmed as to where this was leading, 'No I'm sorry. I really don't want it.'

'Give me your hand, sor. Go on give me your hand. Twenty pounds. We can't be fairer than that.'

At this point the once genial member of the outfit, storms off yelling, 'You're all friggin' mad letting him have it for that price. I'll not be witness to you giving the thing away!'

'Don't be worrying about him, sor. I'll take your twenty pounds. Give me your hand, sor, 20 pounds.'

This is loudly chorused by the others and turning to go I hear, 'Will you give 15?'

A sense of panic wells at hearing, 'Take his tenner Danny. Let the man have it for a tenner.'

Not quick enough back into the shop, I hear a hand slap and, 'You win, sor, it's yours for a tenner. Help me into the shop with it, Joe.'

Shortly afterwards one of my regulars asks, 'What are you doing with that? Doesn't look like your sort of thing.'

In fact, almost immediately, I made £5 on the dreadful piece of machine-made Edwardiana, with its art nouveau tulip in the bottom panel, but the trouble was, once you'd dealt with one of them, they'd brag to their cousins, saying you'd been an easy touch and then there'd be swarms of them, not helped by the fact, their favoured meeting place was the Tavern, not a stone's throw from the shop. They'd pack every nook and cranny and no locals would dare venture within, but it has to be said, when the landlord announced closing time, the head of the clan would stand, tell the rest and they'd all dutifully file out. Although a menacing prospect, for any unwittingly wandering into the scene of revelry, there had been no reports of trouble, no fighting and the landlord later told me, some of their rounds came to over an eye-watering £100.

I heard that Knowbury village hall hadn't fared quite as well. The damage was talked about throughout the area and I don't know if some poor soul actually cleaned out what was found in the piano, or whether they just dumped it. No doubt some of the young buckos had thought it a great gas, to leave the villagers with a few bum notes to sort out

As said before, I found it easier to deal with those traders who'd learnt how to handle them. Two I regularly visited, had extensive country piles and would ask for all truck contents to spread out on the drive. Items of interest would be haggled over and the rest ordered back aboard.

I'd assumed the feather mattresses, they all seemed to have stacked at the rear of their wagons, like huge grubby sacks, were just their way of getting into the houses, but found they were actually able to turn them into cash, selling to a firm that made duvets.

I've included a slight lament from John Dodds.---*It seemed a shame to have all that mass of goods on offer and yet not take advantage. Truth of the matter was, however, I hadn't accumulated the knowledge to enable me to do so. With some of the crazy prices being asked for furniture, they could have you bankrupt in the space of an hour. One new to the business had let it be known, he was prepared to lose £30,000 in order to learn the antique furniture trade. They took him at his word.*

I was quite staggered to read just how much was inveigled out of farmhouses and barns. It seemed amazing they were ever let in, in the first place. I needed to find out how it had happened and made a note to ring Mike. What I did work out was, a hundred-pound round of drinks back in what I assumed to be 1976, would be the equivalent to a mind numbing, one thousand today, so at least 100 of them, ordering something like beer and double whiskey chasers, must have been packed in the bar, lounge and back yard and the £30,000 spent learning the ropes by the novice to the trade, could have bought a Georgian town house in the area.

Before continuing with the tale, I sat and thought for a while, trying to piece together all the facets of John Dodds' character. I had found no image of him on the internet. Would I ever get to meet the man? With his interest in local hill forts, I felt certain we'd have plenty in common. Certain details in the notes had hinted, an embryonic business styled on his personal taste, had started to evolve. I noted his dislike of certain things, bought simply out of profit motive, also, with now having regulars, he must have become a trade call. Someone to keep an eye on and with one of those regulars saying, 'It doesn't look like your sort of thing,' it also hinted at a certain style developing.

I'd picked out a few further clues. Other than the two trading from their country piles, he'd described visits to two other large establishments, where the stock was bought almost exclusively from the Irish travellers. One commanded a wide sweeping corner on the main road through Leominster and the other was a massive building in Hereford that had once been an hotel.

---*The serried ranks of oak, with hardly enough room to squeeze between, lacked any hint of charm and in fact, almost seemed repellent. Pewter platters, in abandoned piles, resembled towers of dull grey poppadoms. Both places gave the feeling, if you weren't prepared to load a van with goods bought by the pound, you weren't worth the bother.*

Here's another example.---*Mother happened to be staying once again and asked, why I'd dragged a salting trough up the street? I'd spotted it outside Don's shop, located half way up the hill and without hesitation, had bought it.*

'*I like the shape and just look at that colour!' I answered. It had relatively low sides, with an inviting spread and standing on turned legs with spoked metal wheels, it was reminiscent of a child's drawing of a powder-blue railway wagon.*

'*But it's got a wrong leg!'*

It wasn't a leg in fact, but a riven piece of planking with an original wheel on the end. 'I don't think it will matter,' I said. 'For some reason it has a lucky feel about it.'

I was right, by end of the week it was gone.

He also had a similar instinct regarding an armchair, bought from the same contact.--- *Don must have recently done a house clearance, for there were electric lamps, rolled-up rugs, a tea trolley, three armchairs and other typical pieces of collateral damage, spread either side of the steps to the shop. I found him inside, arranging the better goods from the call. His prices could be imaginative to say the least and so I limited my enquiries to one of the armchairs outside. It stood proudly, wide-seated on mahogany legs and had a pleasing bulbous roll at the base of its high back. It cost very little and I carried it up the street. My gut instinct, that it was early 19th century was endorsed by the most renowned local dealer of period furniture asking the price. It became my turn to be imaginative and Mr. Paul Smith bought it.*

I also found references to the fact, he had started stripping a few pieces of pine. A note on the front door directed customers to where he worked in the alley. Not only did it help pass the time, but the note deterred constant interruptions from what he referred to, as the three P's and once polished, the pine sold immediately for treble the price he'd paid for it. He writes:---*I did get some strange looks from Trevor Lockyer, mind you, as he sailed towards me on a course of alcoholic headiness, having exiting via the rear entrance of the Tavern.*

A bit bleary eyed, he asked, "Whatever's you messing with that stuff for? I oodna 'av that if it was gid me!"

I sensed John was breaking away from the traditional and had started riding a new wave, dealing in what old school traders found baffling. One had asked, '*How can you make a living out of this rubbish?*'

'*It has to be the right rubbish,*' John had replied.

I also sensed he was becoming more of a dealer's dealer and have included this as an example.---*Apart from polishing the oak and mahogany I chanced upon, I no longer considered having it restored. To do so would have invited a severe bollocking off traders who wanted the stock, just as it had been found. Restoring it, took away that magic, fresh to the market feeling.*

So old Percy round at Dinham had been consigned to history. I did find another reference to him, mind you and even though it goes back years before John Dodds was even in the business, I've decided to include it.

In the days before the shop was even thought of, his mother had chanced on a Georgian straight-legged oak dresser base.---*Well, the legs were straight until she'd negotiated the entryway to the Feather's Hotel. It was strapped, like a dead horse, legs to the sky, atop the roof of the old Bedford van and as she roared through, all four legs snapped off like carrots. Her friend, whose antique shop was immediately below the entry to the hotel carpark, surveyed the damage and being a no-nonsense Lancashire lass, suggested the corpse be taken around for old Percy to resuscitate. This he did, gluing the legs back on and the piece, on the second time of asking, sold, to continue its merry way through the trade.*

At this point, I gave Leon Jones a quick ring, to ask if he knew what had been meant by the three P's, mentioned.

Laughing, he said, 'Browsers. Pick up, put down and piss off.'

'Thank you, Leon.'

'No problem. Best of luck with the book.'

We now enter, what John Dodds describes as, 'That hot summer,' meaning I'd been right, as regards the above date, when estimating the year of the great Irish gathering, for I found on the internet, the record breaking 3 months of hot weather had occurred in 1976. From his description, the town seemed to take on a complete, carefree, Bohemian feel, with the glorious weather putting a smile on everyone's face. He'd written three versions of the following and with two crossed out, I'll give you the one he was finally happy with. I've made a few adjustments, but basically, it's as found.

---*Remembering tales of old, before any had notions of foreign travel, a time when families picnicked on the banks of the river Teme at a place known as Batty's Island, many of the town's youths revived that tradition, going there almost daily.*

Where the river had wound its way for centuries through pastureland, an island had obviously once formed and even though the only trace left is a dry curving indentation where ancient willows still stand, it is still known locally as Batty's Island. The waters, ever eroding, had forced a way through the far banking further upstream, the constriction giving the river enough pace to be ridden on. Some days there would be as many as twenty, sploshing upstream in old shoes, to float back down on the rapids.

One afternoon Anne and myself went there, more for a stroll and the company, rather than a swim. As usual, wine and beer were on offer and later, just for the hell of it, we took a dip. My underpants, other than being decidedly droopy, didn't draw any attention, but when Anne emerged, Pre Raphaelite tresses clinging, bra and knickers transparent, a few of the lads certainly perked up a bit, raising themselves on an elbow, but from the young ladies adorning the green pastures, I noticed looks of opprobrium glinting.

Those acting in the summer play, put on annually in the castle, gladly shared in the lively spirit current at the time, and a few of us, when wangling our way into after show receptions, held in the Blue Boar, got to know some of the minor players quite well. Lesley Ann Down, star of the production, bought a brass-bound camphor trunk from me and another of the cast, one in the infancy of his career, invited Anne and myself to the final, end of festival party, held at a property down in Dinham. We were challenged at the entry of course, but said, an actor called

Tony had invited us. Members of the cast were permitted a few courtesy invites.

'Tony who?' we were asked.

We hadn't a clue in fact and could hardly say the nickname we'd given him. With Tony refusing to tell us his part in Hamlet, we'd joked that really, he was probably just a scene shifter.

'No, a bit more than that,' he'd said, laughing.

We made a few more guesses and he nearly choked on a mouthful of beer when I asked, 'What about a tree then? That's it. That's why you won't tell us, you're all leafed-up, rustling like a tree.'

We'd all had a bit to drink and the new name Anne had dubbed him, 'Tony Tree', he took in good part.

Well, announcing we'd been invited to the Dinham party by Tony Tree wasn't going to gain us entry, but fortunately, just then, I could hear his voice echoing in the lane.

The gateman asked him, 'Have you invited these to the party?'

Tony Head said that he had and we gained admittance, not leaving until dawn's grey light heralded, we were well on our way into new day.

By now, I worked out John Dodds had been in the business three years. It had seemed like an idyllic way to make a living. Admittedly one had to survive on one's wits, but life in the town sounded fun and he'd even found time to play rugby for Ludlow first XV. He had gained in confidence and I found in the notes, a willingness to now back his instinct, when catching first sight of something, for if receiving a feeling, described as, the piece almost calling to him, that innate sense never seemed to prove wrong.

Here's an example.--- *Although having an unconventional configuration of cupboards and drawers, I'd had no qualms of chancing my arm on an oak dresser base, that sat looking quite neglected out in a milk parlour. It was a bit of an oddball lot, but something about it had appealed and even when a few regulars gave it scant regard, I'd not felt the slightest bit daunted. Old Wilf, a smallholder on Clee Hill had taken me on the call. I'd met the man by chance, when searching for old wagon wheels and he'd been a useful contact ever since.*

I couldn't believe it when Wilf told me, how he found most of the things he alerted me to. With his face a picture of sincerity, he divulged, it was whilst on his rounds, delivering Avon cosmetics. Of course, I thought he was joking. In his grubby string-tied mac and wellies, Wilf must have been the strangest Avon lady on the planet. One day when calling, I was taken by the sight of a shaded flock of sheep, peacefully bedecking a small mound, looking like a Sydney Cooper painting come to life.

'That's a fine sight, Wilf,' I said.

To which, with a slightly disconcerting smile, he slowly replied, 'Yes,--- pretty ain't they?'

So how did John then fare with this strange dresser base from off The Bonk? That name, I discovered, Ludlovians often used when referring to Clee Hill. I'll hand you back to the man himself.

He writes:---*I was locking the front door of the shop when a Land Rover pulled up. Luggage was strapped to the roof and there were children crammed in the back. A lady in an all-enveloping frock bustled in, followed by her husband. Although merely divulging, they had been holidaying in North Wales and were now heading south, I could instantly tell they were in the trade.*

After a bit more bustling, I was asked how much was wanted for what was described as, 'That strange thingamy in the back room?'

Her eyes didn't seem to focus as you'd expect, giving the impression she may have been asking someone standing adjacent.

My answer didn't cause much of a stir and the husband, not a big man, helped me heave it into the alley for closer inspection. His wife squinted fussily into its interior, inspected its backboards, looked into the drawers and declared it to be, 'quite an oddity.' Her dark hair stood out frizzed, as if having been dealt a slight shock from the experience. Well anyway, after a good half hour's deliberation and my assurance there was a profit in it, they bought it. Then, following the reloading of luggage, packed in tight around the children, we heaved the quirky item up onto the now vacant roof rack. Luckily the ironmongers was still open and I bought them a hank of washing line to secure it with. The first pint that Saturday evening slipped down particularly well.

So it seems, John Dodds was finding his feet. Another example was a mahogany three-leaf wind-out table, a Victorian turned leg variety that, other than for scrap, were supposedly unsaleable.--- *The thing was a good colour, near perfect condition and with the leaves in, could easily seat twelve. It seemed stupid for it to be deemed unsaleable. Avowing this belief and promising to have it back if my customer became stuck with it, I sold it to one of my favourite regulars for £45.*

There were storm clouds gathering, however.

---*The long glorious Summer was at last coming to an end. We had all enjoyed it, but now looked forward to the promised rain. The land was parched, trees were prematurely autumnal and the river no longer made it over the weir, its only flow being via the sluice gate. So, the front heading our way across the Atlantic brought no concerns, but a visit from our landlord's agent did. I was at pains to show him the leaking valley roof, ancient wiring, holes through the brickwork and primitive sanitary arrangement. He simply stared back and said nothing.*

With the rain imminent, I hauled in the dreadful chaise longue from the alley. There had been no room in the shop and a short spell in the summer sun would hardly have hurt it. Whilst parked on the cobbles far side, it had been a regular spot of sweet repose for one of the Tavern regulars, needing to sleep off the day's intake. The man was from a good Ludlow family, but over the years, booze had reduced him to a dithering wreck and almost tramp-like appearance.

When Anne and I discovered the man's little friends glistening, like segments from a wet blackberry, the couch went straight outside again, for a whole container of flea powder to be shaken over it. The thing had come in a deal for nothing and so I didn't care if it got soaked.

The rains were tumultuous and next day Anne and myself rushed down to the river, overjoyed at seeing its brown tumbling flow in full spate once again.

I looked through my notes to discover the fate of soggy couch, but was left to assume it must have somehow sold, for now the main focus of attention was the letter received from the landlord's agent. Admittedly, the shop had been on a peppercorn rent, but it wasn't so much the huge increase that worried, it was the fact the new contract was a repairing lease. The whole roof needed stripping and renovating and the rotten valley section also involved part of the neighbour's roof, so the whole job, if insisted upon could have bankrupted him for the sole benefit of the owner.

John Dodds took the trouble to visit the lady in question, a sweet little thing, looking like she couldn't harm a fly, living in a cottage over by the racecourse. He asked, instead of renting, would it be possible to buy the building?

---As her words, with its veiled message sank in, I watched her smile freeze into a rictus, as inviting as a strand of sugar-coated barbed wire. Basically, stripped to its true meaning she'd said,

'As never in her life, had she ever knowingly done anything to benefit others, why should she start now?' I was truly worried.

The next phase was to ditch as much stock as possible, find another property to rent--- and quickly. Luckily a small shop in Corve Street had been empty for a while and although John Dodds didn't initially like the feel of the place, had little choice and took on the agreed monthly rent with nothing more than a handshake. The accommodation problem was solved by taking a room in a mate's flat round by the church, a flying rental above Barclay's Bank. When he eventually rang his mother, telling her of the new arrangement, she was aghast, in fact angry, but it wouldn't have been her name on the new repairing rental agreement. She was safely ensconced in the terraced cottage he was still paying the mortgage on, in Lancashire.

Here's another piece of reasoning, directly from John Dodds.

---Often, you don't truly know mates until going on holiday with them, when an emerging side you'd never noticed before, can become that apparent, it makes you want to distance yourself from them, the moment you return home. The same can be said when sharing accommodation. After numerous enquiries, I found an alternative arrangement in Linney, a ground floor flat in a house immediately below the old town wall. Not only could Anne stay, if she had a mind to, there was also room in the garden to strip pine.

It seems, that from once being simply something to pass the time, pine stripping had become a major part of the business and also, the first phase of John Dodds' antique career looked to be complete. For ahead now lay, the new dealing days in the Corve Street property, but before we move on, I'll just detail a few things John, with hindsight, wished he had have bought. They give an insight, for one setting out with such limited resources, of how difficult it was to make the right decision.

First, he describes a huge case of stuffed birds, that with having no love of taxidermy, he'd dismissed without examining properly. If he had have done, he might have seen, amongst the list of contents neatly labelled on the back, the collection included a passenger pigeon, many years extinct in the USA. A dealer near Leominster bought a new Volvo, with proceeds from the deal. Second, was the huge 8-seater oak gateleg table. There had been many warnings regarding made-up items and with the table top being decidedly planky, he'd turned it down, then had to listen to how well the man dealing from nearby Castle Lodge had done with it. The non-deal that hurt the most, however, was a comical looking, 9" dial, brass faced, one handed, oak grandfather clock, so slender, it had slits cut in the side and wooden triangular boxes applied, to allow room for the pendulum to swing. Had he been offered it a mere 18 months later, he'd have snapped it up, being exactly the sort of quirky look he'd become confident with, but when offered the clock, it had been in those days of running shipping goods north and he'd been fearful, the thing had been made up. We finally come to the non-deal that worried the most. It was a mahogany bureau, turned down because the linings of the small interior drawers, looked startlingly fresh and he'd concluded the piece to have been out of period, an Edwardian copy. He heard, an established furniture dealer in Broad Street, had bought it, proving his judgement had almost certainly been wrong and being on friendly terms, John visited, in the hope of learning a lesson for next time.

Stanley Woolston's reply to his enquiry, 'Sometimes things can be a bit misleading,' didn't exactly inspire him with confidence and he wondered whether he'd ever be able to tell, the original, in pristine condition, from a later copy. So, it was not just what you bought that could be a terrible error, it could also be what you didn't buy. A wise old friend's words did bring a little comfort. 'Any dealer who says he's never made a mistake, is a liar.'

Finally, I had heard of the actress, Lesley Ann Down, but wondered who the actor Tony Head was? I looked him up and instantly remembered something from childhood. He'd been the man in the Gold Blend advert.

PART TWO

CHAPTER TEN

It seems from the notes, that John Dodds had great misgivings about the new shop. Even when he'd painted the walls, it still had the feeling of an empty front room, which of course it would have been, before its conversion to a photographic studio, back in the 1950's.

There was still an oval mark on the single, soulless, vertical sheet of glass, where the advertising sign had once been glued to the atrocity that replaced the original Georgian window. The place had also been a fruit and veg shop for a while, then a frozen food outlet, until the profits had been drunk.

Access was via four stone steps, through a Georgian panelled door, to a passageway and then an immediate right turn through a panelled door, which led to the 10'x 12' selling area. There was a back room accessed via an extremely narrow passageway, 30" wide by 5' long, down the left side of a massive Georgian chimney stack, that contained two flues from the ground floor fireplaces, blocked and plastered over, two more from the first floor and a further two venting from the small bedroom fireplaces. It was a monumental brick barrier to any idea of easy connection of front and back rooms.

Anything wider than 30" had to go down the house passageway, where stairs rose to the landlord's living quarters, but anything wider, had to be taken down a neighbour's alley, hoisted over an 8' high brick wall and eased in through a large back window.

The place didn't initially have any feeling of luck whatsoever and the logic of having had no choice as regards taking it on, had to be constantly invoked, otherwise the move felt like a depressing mistake. It wasn't helped by the first shelf John Dodds screwed to the wall, falling, crashing to the ground. Luckily, the broken crockery was more decorative than especially valuable, being Indian tree and Willow pattern.

With the remnants from the old shop in a pile on the bare boarded floor, it felt like nothing could possibly sell, plus annoyingly, the landlord kept popping his head around the door to see how things were going. Beneath a hearty bravado, he was the nervous type who didn't quite know how to make an exit and the man had an unfortunate habit, if helping lift something, of giving an unnecessary commentary, accompanied by strange hoo-hoo sounds. 'That's it hoo-hoo hoo. Have you got it? Up a bit, ho-hoo and so on. One of the first jobs would be, to change the lock.

Knowing the move was imminent, John had knocked out as much stock as possible, and was very careful regarding new items bought. Things that had turned out, rather on the faithful side, had been dumped in the Codsall saleroom, over by Wolverhampton, far enough away not to be recognised.

Dealers bought most of the antique furniture, put up for sale at auction and the local trade would have spurned his castoffs, not wanting the stigma of being landed with another dealer's old stock. He had used Codsall in the past, taking things that were more sought after in the heart of the Midlands, to return with the quirkier type of lot, if available.

They were evening sales and extremely wearing after a day in the shop, but had the advantage of being run by a local dealer, the same Don as previously mentioned, who would transport the items there in his van. When the lots sold, payment was immediate and many's the time John Dodds' car had returned at midnight as if riding on air, with him having that wonderful cathartic feeling of having got out from under, yet another particularly burdensome lot.

The dire feeling regarding the new premises wasn't helped by the fact, another antique dealer, well a complete novice in fact, had taken his old shop. He couldn't believe the man would have been naïve enough to have signed a repairing lease on such a money pit, but there he was, however, looking like he'd won the pools and worse than that, had somehow latched on to Trevor Lockyer, who was taking him round all his mother's old calls.

Mrs. Lockyer was absolutely incensed at her son's treachery and John Dodds wasn't best pleased either, as most of the supply from that quarter dried up. The whole move to the new shop felt ill-fated and depressing.

All the above, I summarised from John Dodds' notes, but now, with just a slight touch added here and there, I hand you over to the man himself. It's virtually as he wrote it, well in fact, typed it and was obviously composed many years after the event.

---*So, sitting there wondering what on earth I'd done, my thoughts were invaded by the ringing of the telephone echoing loud in the empty back room. I'd managed to get our old number transferred and a man with a broad Herefordshire accent, announcing who he was, blurted a strange place name, then cursed as the phone pips cut him off. A few days later it happened again. When mother next rang, I tried to describe what I'd heard, 'Billevans eer, from Errdro. We got some stuff…beep-beep, beep-beep, beeeep.'*

She said, 'That sounds like one of the two old boys I bought those four-poster beds off. You remember, you lent me the money for them. There's a lot of stuff there. You need to follow it up.'

'Fine, but how?'

'They live near some quarries.'

'That's a big help.'

'I'm sorry dear. It was a while back now and I can't remember for the life of me where it was, other than it's sort of in hill country and the old farmhouse is opposite a telephone box. You know the sort of place I mean, where you don't know whether you're in England or Wales.'

'Thanks, that narrows it down a bit.'

'Well don't blame me. It was a place Trevor found. He said he wasn't sure about old beds and took me on the call, but because he couldn't read the road signs, we went all over the place until eventually, out of nowhere, there it was. He told me, the only way he could ever get back to a place was by retracing his steps.'

'Well Trevor won't be much help. He's acting as guide and advisor to that bloke I told you about. The one in our old shop.'

'Told you moving was a crazy thing to do.'

I thought, 'Thank you mother.'

So, I asked around regarding quarries lying to the west of us and of course searched on O.S. maps. Then closing the shop one mellow, early summers' eve, Anne and myself set out in search of Errdro, beep, beep, beeep. The obvious start was over by Presteigne where there are extensive quarries and we drove endlessly, all around the area, asking at various farms, but got nowhere. We explored every road in the region of the quarry, but saw no sign of a stone farmhouse opposite a phone box. The only lane we didn't try was white from limestone dust as it led into the quarry itself. Other workings had been mentioned and we drove for miles exploring those, but in the end, I said, 'It has to be the Presteigne quarry. That's the only one that makes any sense.' By now it was gone 9 and decidedly gloomy.

We drove back to check if I'd somehow missed a lane and was about to give up, when I thought, having come this far, we might as well take the only option left and drive into the quarry itself. To my *amazement, far side of the workings, I saw a wonderfully normal looking strip of tarmacadam leading between hedges, out into the countryside. A little further on was the sign, Yardro and then, just as mother had described, standing there, as if accompanied by a heavenly choir, was the phone box, with the elusive stone farmhouse directly opposite. People were still up; I could see a welcoming slab of light, angled in the hedge, opposite a ground floor window.*

'Where d'you get to?' asked a cheery red face at the door. 'Thought you wanner comin'. Nearly gave up on yer.'

With being two brothers, Bill and Sam Evans, living alone, I could immediately see the effect Anne was having. They stared at her as if I'd brought some exotic, rare feline from the east along with me. We were shown around the downstairs rooms, the small dairy and then up the narrow wooden stairway to a landing where the dumpy bulge of the old feather mattress and covers on the Edwardian oak bed looked in desperate fear of the massive weight, bulging down from the ceiling.

Anyone actually in the bed, if needing to turn over, would have rubbed their nose on the plaster, a constant reminder that tonight could be the night the whole thing crashed. The upstairs was a bit of an obstacle course of steps up and down to the bedrooms and having seen all that was on offer, I started making a list. They were actually moving a couple of weeks hence and so wanted the place emptied fairly quickly.

The ordinary jugs, bowls, washstands, dressing tables, pine chests of drawers, chamber pots, oil lamps and towel rails were easily dealt with. The double ended Victorian black couch was not for sale at any price, as their sister wanted it. I could hardly contain my sorrow, but the two pieces of furniture of real interest to a budding antique dealer were thankfully available; a small panelled oak coffer and a Jacobean oak chest of drawers with moulded drawer fronts.

The latter was not one of those repellent black things that have been got at, the sort I used to sell to the Dutch trade at quarter price, but was dry as a bone, its pallid colour simply itching to glow from the application of clear wax polish. It stood tall and untouched, as if having spent much of its life in a church; had generous mouldings, both beneath the overhang of the slender top board and those skirting above the turned feet. It retained all its original escutcheons and brass axe-head handles and a quick peep within told me, decorative moulding, that had succumbed to gravity over the years, had been safely stowed in one of the top drawers.

There were two snags, first the purchase of the two prize lots had to include a black lump of a coffer made from old floorboards and secondly, at the time in question, I hadn't a clue how much to offer. I needed to tease a notion as to what was wanted from the two old boys, or I could have been in danger of losing the lot. To give time to think, I suggested we return to the dairy, where I was on more familiar ground. From door-knocking days, I'd discovered, the best way to buy an array of items, when dotted here and there, on stone floor, wooden shelves and slate slab, was to gather all together and offer a tidy sum for the lot.

So, piling the sycamore bowls, two butter prints, butter roller, wooden ladles, butter tub, bread board, sycamore chopping board, cider costrel and small glass butter churn together, I offered an overall price and was relieved to see it brought a flicker of appreciation. With that little engagement won, we returned to the main battle awaiting upstairs. The small coffer was first in the reckoning, made tricky by them not being willing to sell it without inclusion of what, judging by the rat holes in the back, had once been a homemade grain bin.

'You do realise that it's been made out of old floorboards,' I said.

'Happen it is. But you'm an antique dealer. You shouldna 'ave any trouble getting rid of it.'

Ignoring what could have been taken as a slight, I decided to give the unlikely beauty and beast pairing a rest for a while and concentrate on the main lot, the Jacobean chest of drawers.

'How much were you hoping for it?'

'It's up to you, you'm the antique dealer.'

'Well I recently saw one sell for 120 pounds.'

'That all?'

'Admittedly it wasn't as nice as this one. How does 150 sound?'

'Two 'undred more like it?'

Relieved at having at last coaxed a price out of them, I said, 'What? With all those mouldings missing?'

'They ain't missing, thaim in the top drawer.'

Opening the drawer fully and rattling them forward, I said, 'Oh, so they are. More here than I thought. So, would 180 buy it?'

'No. Give us the round two hundred and it's yours.'

'What about the coffers? You surely can't still be expecting £200 for them. If I pay the £200 for the chest, put the coffers in the deal at £150. That's £350 the lot.'

Looking one to the other, they agreed.

All the smaller items were packed in the car and I said I'd return for the rest the following evening. They refused payment until the entire deal had been completed, which with the use of my friend Leon's trailer, it was, the following night. They'd even rooted out a few more lots, earthenware bowls, cider jars, circular japanned spice tin, fenders and fire irons.

Everything flew out except, having sold the good coffer for £150, I was left with boarded embarrassment as profit on the two. The deal, however, brightened both myself and the shop, with the latter at last, beginning to feel lucky.

Perusing ahead through John Dodds' notes, I found a few other references to those early days in the new shop. He still made early morning forays, attempting to be first in line, at Mrs. Brown's, the lady near Tenbury who bought her stock entirely from Irish travellers. He had started venturing into new territory, concentrating on the prestigious lots of pine furniture; cupboard dresser bases, Georgian chests of drawers and linen presses. The new craze was becoming that prevalent, a Georgian pine version of a piece was often worth more than its oak equivalent. Many old heads in the trade were sadly shaken at the craziness of it, but John Dodds was happy to ride the new wave, being particularly pleased with things like the Orkney chairs, that sometimes arrived on the Scottish loads.---*Wooden seated, with drawer below; their curved, woven-straw backs gave them a wonderfully ethnic feel.*

There were also the other curiosities that seemed to fit in with the new fun way of dealing. With the change of business location requiring printing of new trade cards, he'd driven to the only printers active at the time, which from the description I read, operated from a precarious looking prefab on the left as you approach Church Stretton from the south. The boss just happened to ask if he might be interested in the trays he'd rooted out, earlier that morning. They were loaded with old printing blocks, copper on mahogany. He said he could do with them out of the way and was happy to accept a tenner the lot. Many dated from before the war, showing old buildings, classic cars, prize bulls and horses. John Dodds, on taking careful note of his progress selling them, found when totting up three months later, the profit from that ten-pound outlay had covered the shop and living expenses for a complete month.

Another deal of similar happenchance, came his way when driving down the steep hill in Ludlow known as New Road Bank. On seeing people loading a trailer with furniture, he'd decided to put his door-knocking experience to good effect and turning the car round, did a loop and pulled in behind the trailer.

John Dodds had been that taken by the illogicality of the episode, he'd written down the details.

---I apologised for intruding and enquired regarding the fate of the items they were removing.

A bitter faced young woman, with a strong Birmingham accent replied, 'It's all going to the tip.'

'Well that seems a shame. If you're agreeable, I could buy some of this stuff off you.'

They looked quite dumb-struck, but then, Mrs. Bitter Face asked, 'Which bits exactly?'

I answered, 'Well take that chest of drawers for example, I could give you ten pounds.' Which at the time, allowed me £5 profit.

'It's worth more than that,' she snapped.

Slightly angered, at things so recently viewed as no more than worthless junk, now being coveted like the crown jewels, I literally begged the rest, giving a pound here, 50 pence there and loaded it all on the car. Rounding the corner, bottom of hill, on impulse, I pulled onto the broad pavement outside Leon's shop. I sold him the lot, asking him to leave it on full display, hoping Mrs. Bitter Face would stop and look at the prices.

Another piece of luck, was a call almost on his doorstep, down the bottom of Corve Street, again not antiques in the classic sense, but something John Dodds was fully in tune with: enamel advertising signs, highly decorative framed prints and a whole cache of pre-war tinware toys in near perfect condition.

He wrote:*---Some calls could take you to places you never knew existed. It was beyond Clee Hill Village out around the back of*

Titterstone Clee. There was an old gate, made from riven timber, a length of terracotta drainage pipe lying horizontal in the hedge for the newspaper delivery and a path beyond, which led across a field to a white cottage standing in its garden. An enclosed piece of habitation in the wilderness. As I approached, I heard the resonance of barking from what sounded like a particularly large chested dog and on nearing the garden gate, could see that the slavering hound commanded the centre of the perfectly round, brown patch, it had described whilst patrolling the full extent of its leash. As I went to lift the latch, a hysterical cacophony accompanied an aerial performance as the huge creature at the end of its chain, sailed past, teeth bared, clearly intent on ripping chunks out of me. At the third pass, I was relieved to see a woman appear in the cottage doorway.

'Dunner open that gate," she warned. "Whatever you does, dunner open it! You'd better 'op over the fence and come this way, through the string beans.'

Trying to make light of it, thinking if I'd have timed it right, I could have dodged the beast mid-flight, before it came in to land, I said, 'Well surely I'd have been safe enough with it being tied up.'

'Oh no,' she said. 'Damn thing bust 'is chain and 'ad the postman a cuppla wiks back. We've 'ad to fetch the mail from out the 'edge-pipe since then. My 'usband can 'andle 'im, but I daresn't go near the brute. Nor 'ull any other bugger for that matter.'

There was, of all things, a chapel organ for sale, which I didn't want at any price, a few minor items of which I've lost all recollection, but as long as I live, I'll never forget that dog.

I'll include one other section from this period, for it gives a glimpse of how John Dodds' taste was diverging from the norm.

---I was returning to the shop and made a slight detour to see what Leon might have bought recently.

'Sorry mate, you've missed it all,' he said.

He'd had a Welsh call and all the usual pine furniture, chest of drawers, boxes, dressing tables, washstands and tables were still arrayed, awaiting collection.

My heart sank, for there amongst it all, in original light greens, greys and muted red paintwork, stood the most charming little cabinet, looking lost and completely out of place amongst the other pine furniture. Its panelled doors concealed, graduated shelves and bold beneath its cornice was painted, 'School Library.' It looked like something William Morris could have designed.

'D'you think they would sell me that?' I asked, completely crestfallen.

'That's the one thing they didn't want,' said Leon with a broad grin.

I couldn't believe my luck. Not only had I chanced on the prize of the load, I'd probably saved it from a dip in caustic soda. Obviously, I was glad of the profit; you could basically name your price, for you'd never see another, but I was actually sorry to see the charming little oddity go.

So, from such an inauspicious start, I could sense John Dodds was turning the new little shop into quite a success. I made a note to give his friend Leon another ring. I sensed he would be a mine of information.

Sifting through the notes further, I began to realise, the shop was not what we normally associate with the word; a commercial building, open to all, nine to five each day, it was more a place to store the latest purchases and do a deal with the trade, before locking up to go in search of goods worthy of filling it again. With John Dodds being way down the pecking order and having limited resources, it was imperative he be first there, grabbing the chance of whatever it happened to be, before it passed too far along the trading chain beyond reach. So, when told of an item available, he had no choice, other than shut shop and follow the lead, before someone else beat him to it.

One such instance, was the tip-off that the landlord of a pub over in Shobdon, wanted rid of a built- in double corner cupboard.

---I grabbed a few tools, locked the shop and arrived at the pub well before opening time. The landlord didn't expect much for the cupboard, it was more a matter of getting it out of there. I was shown into the back snug and espied, in all its glory, a Georgian, floor to ceiling, pine four-door corner cupboard with original simulated oak paintwork. It was that artfully adorned, I had to check, it was in fact pine. It had an attractive interior, with the patinated leading edges of the shaped shelves blending pleasantly with the blue interior. There emanated a reassuring musty smell, probably from the years of booze and smoke and it had obviously been specially made for that particular location, for the bottom section had no floor, other than the boards of the room.

The large screws, holding its back to the wall, fortunately turned easily enough, but I then had to slice down the layers of wallpaper either side of the cupboard's slender returns, before able to prise it from where it had stood for the last 180 years. Tipping it at an angle, with its front uppermost, I dragged it to the door, eased it over the steps and once at the car, tipped it to lean against the roof rack and being careful not to rip the front off, lifted and levered it up to lie along the rack's length. Once it was securely roped, I went back inside to put all the furniture back in place.

Seeking out the landlord in the gloom of the bar, I counted out the four five-pound notes in payment and suggested he follow me. I wanted to ensure he was aware of the fact, the vacant corner now needed some attention.

'You've done it!' he said looking truly amazed. 'I was going to help you with it onto the car.'

I apologised for the mess, but he said not to worry, as the room was soon due to be completely redecorated.

My slight elation at having at last successfully procured a complete Georgian corner cupboard, rather than just the top half of one, was dampened slightly by the fact, with it being all in one piece, there was no chance of it fitting in the shop. I decided to call on a friend, whose shop was just below the Broad Gate and luckily found him in residence.

It was the same dealer who'd acquainted me with the term 'breaker,' when first espying the railway carriage of a coffer from the north. He'd given up oak a while back, to now concentrate on the latest craze, pine.

'You like 'em big,' he said with a smile, as we slid the cupboard to the pavement. 'It IS a big boy.'

I'd imagined, I'd take a quick £100 profit and leave him with the problem of stripping it, installing a floor and selling it. After all, it was a fine Georgian cupboard with a very pretty interior, so why was he standing there scratching his head?

'How do we cut it? That's the problem.'

'Cut it?'

'Well yes. Not many houses can take a thing this size and it would be far more saleable, if cut into two sections. I can adapt its waist moulding, so that's a start.' Peering inside, he said, 'Looks like it was screwed to the wall.'

I said, 'Yes,' and fishing in my pocket handed him one of the screws.

'Marvellous,' he said.

I was a bit nonplussed, as he seemed more taken with the fixings than the item they'd fixed. 'Here, I kept all of them,' I said, not wanting to deny him the set.

Holding one up for my inspection, he said, 'Blacksmith made. They're the original. See how the cut in the screw head is slightly off centre. No machine would have turned out a screw like that.'

Meanwhile, with the corner cupboard standing patiently waiting, I suggested we lower it, before a gust of wind did it for us.

'Yes of course. What did you want for it, by the way?' he asked at last.

On telling him, he said, 'Well I can't really say no, can I' and feeling a wave of relief, I helped him inside with it. He said he'd figure a way of cutting it later and would strip the front by hand, not wanting to lose the wonderful colour of the interior.

What follows is the reason why I've included this account in full.

---A few days later, one of my regulars, a dealer from over Wolverhampton way, called in the shop. He said, a little bird had told him, I'd recently chanced on a Georgian double corner cupboard and had sold it to a local dealer.

When I said, I had, grabbing me half in jest by the scruff he said, 'Well don't do that again! Next time you find anything like that, give me a ring.'

This illustrates just how difficult it was finding the right stock. Dealers were daily combing the whole area and from what I'd gathered from the notes, would then almost dine out on descriptions of what in later years, would not be considered particularly important finds.

Another item chanced upon, proved significant for two reasons, first it shows he was starting to get his eye in, as they used to say and second, it illustrates just how far he still needed to go, if wanting to be judged remotely close to becoming a period furniture dealer.

---*There was something about the wooden chandelier I'd found down at Leon's that seemed to say something to me. It was painted a dull duck-shit grey colour, but something about its faceted detail shone through. I decided to lean it in the window, rather like a lure and see what happened. It worked. Paul Smith, the dealer who'd bought my Regency armchair the previous year, called in and lifting the chandelier for closer inspection, asked how much I wanted for the scruffy looking thing?*

It had cost a fiver and I was in completely unknown territory, so imagining what my average customer would have paid, I trebled it.

'Drop it round to the shop, would you? Betty will have a cheque ready for you.'

I did as asked, taking it to a small store up a side alley and then entered the shop, by way of the door off Church Street. First time I'd ever been in there, in fact. It was one of those slightly forbidding interiors, that makes one aware one's shoes need polishing. The furniture was sparsely arrayed, arranged as if in a home setting, with each piece having a deep glow, sense of rarity and standing there in such a gentlemanly manner, you wouldn't dare ask the price.

As Paul's wife was busy with two customers, I feigned huge interest in a massive oil painting depicting a noble looking couple beneath a tree, with their grand stone pile, peppered with countless windows, some distance behind. I heard Mrs. Smith apologising to the couple, she was sorry, but they only had six of the chairs, not the full set. This jolted me somewhat and taking a squint at the supposed inadequate items referred to, I felt truly humbled. If I'd have driven home with just a pair of them, I'd have been elated, never mind six. With the realisation of what a huge mountain needed climbing, if I was to eventually call myself an antique dealer, the triumph of the chandelier paled somewhat.

I was talking to a couple of dealer friends in the pub later and on relating the tale admitted, that apart from those dreadful Edwardian chairs you could pick up for nothing, I'd never handled a set of six antique chairs in my life, never mind eight or more. Then remembering five oak chairs I'd had the misfortune of once owning, I told them the following.

'Talk about ugly; they were that ugly, I hadn't dared put them on display. They'd come in a deal with other stuff and I'd shoved them up out of the way, in the top room of the old shop. It was only when in the throes of moving, I remembered the damn things and was actually in two minds whether to take them to the tip.

Whilst out on the pavement awaiting my verdict, you'd never guess,--- they caught the attention of a passer-by. When he popped his head in to ask the price, I knew I couldn't make them too cheap, otherwise he might think they were a load of rubbish, which to my mind they were, so I steeled myself and said, "Thirty pounds."

"They look as if they're fresh in," he said.

"I've only just put them there." You know me, I don't actually like telling a porky. Well, the bloke not only bought them, he took them away in his car. No need for delivery.

Well, you can imagine my horror can't you. A few weeks back, in comes the same man,---it was into the new shop this time and he says, "So there you are. Wondered where you'd got to."

He looked around and then after a bit asked, in that tone people tend to employ, prior to divulging something that's been seriously niggling them, "You know those chairs I bought from you?"

"Ye-es," I answered, fearing the worst.

"You wouldn't be able to find me any more like them, would you?"

"Well, they were quite unusual," I told him. "Could be tricky, but I can give it my best shot."

When he left the shop, I looked up and gave a silent, "Thank you Lord."'

This little anecdote helped me build a mental picture of John Dodds. He didn't exactly come across as a bit of a Jack-the-Lad, but there again, there were signs he was learning to think on his feet and was certainly becoming one of the boys, an accepted member of the new band of up-and-coming dealers. And it still sounded like the business was fun.

The likes of himself and his friend Leon, must have made what they were doing look easy, for John Dodds put in his notes that some of the more established members of the trade seemed a little put out by the amount of business they were doing. Some even chanced their arm at buying similar, but like everything, it's not always as simple as it looks.

He was driving past a fellow trader's shop, mid-Old Street and noticing a painted bookcase and a kitchen table for sale on the pavement, stopped to look, but on seeing the bookcase was pitch pine and the turned legs on the table had a deep red finish, to simulate mahogany, turned both down. He hadn't bothered to inform the shopkeeper, the same Don as mentioned previously, caustic soda, used for stripping pine, sent pitch pine an unattractive dark colour and time spent removing the red stain from the table legs, would have made the thing more trouble than it was worth. Only when they'd increased in value and more sophisticated sanders had become readily available, did the stripping of that type of kitchen table become viable. I also saw from John Dodds' notes, that pine wardrobes still didn't sell, but the little episode where that became apparent, didn't happen until early the following year.

Meanwhile, Christmas was approaching. Autumn had been kind and with Anne's help, he'd stripped quite a considerable amount of furniture. None of it had been sanded or polished, he'd just taken it to the shop to give all a rub down with vinegar, to neutralise any remnants of caustic soda and for it to dry out. Business had faltered and the only dealers calling had been at the carrion end, sniffing out carcases to pick at. So the shop had become full, most of his money had become tied up and the usual emergence of Springtime fair-weather traders seemed an awfully long way off. Pre-Christmas was also a time, when the Irish traders returning home, threading their way to the Holyhead boat, were rather keen to cash in any remaining stock.

John Dodds wrote:---*It's amazing how an impending boat trip could bring them to their senses. I was able to buy things they would normally ask crippling prices for.* He named, what sounded like, surprisingly humble pieces; a Georgian oak taper-legged side table, an elm sword chest and an oak wall cabinet and went on to say--- *Trouble was, I was almost out of money. I'd already bought enough food and wine to see us through the festive season, but apart from that, we had just £12 to last until things started selling again.*

I'd had a couple of pints up in the Bull Hotel, well it was Christmas Eve and then returned to the shop to make sure I'd left nothing in the yard and to just sit and think for a while. Outside was now pitch black, the heat from the gas fire was quite soporific and I could feel myself nodding off.

The shop bell gave me a start. It was way past closing time and I hadn't realised I'd left the front door open. I went through the narrow passage to the front room expecting to see the big bear of a landlord, Geoff, in one of his lingering 'Hoo-hoo- hoo' moods. It wasn't; it was a dealer I vaguely knew from Leominster. He explained, he was thinking of getting into pine, almost sounding like some sort of cupboard fetish and asked how much the items in the shop were. I apologised, that none of it had been finished, but he said he preferred it that way. He would do his own finishing.

Nothing was ticketed, but you know how it is in the early days in the trade, I could remember to the penny what everything had cost and also knew to the penny, as regards pine that is, what it was worth. Well, no point in going into detail, the man bought the lot, from both front and back rooms, paid by cheque and said he'd have it collected early in the new year.

As said, Anne and I had only £12 to last us over the festive break, but it turned into one of the best Christmases either of us had ever had.

CHAPTER ELEVEN

---I'd noticed in my short time in business, that the first dismal days of the new year can give one the feeling, enough stock to fill the hungry maw of the antique trade, will never ever be available again. At the first sale I saw advertised, held in Knighton cattle market, I found four lots of moderate interest, but counted a staggering twenty dealers there to buy them. What often happens in such a scenario, with nothing better to compare them with, such items can take on a splendid allure, rather like the village beauty syndrome and thus can end up being considered, worth more there than in any other place in the country. I wondered, 'Would there ever be enough stock available again to provide a living for so many dealers?' The prospect seemed unlikely and most depressing.

Luck was with him again, however, for a few days later, someone called in the shop to say, they'd heard a cottage over Clungunford way needed clearing. He followed the directions and seeing the well-worn track leading out across the field, realised he'd arrived at the right gate. With the field looking decidedly soggy, he opted to walk, for fear of getting the car stuck. Going through the next gate and walking on the grassed ridge between the muddy wheel ruts, he followed the trail down to a cottage in the trees. He was shown the house contents and was about to make a list, when told not to bother, for as long as he cleared the lot, it was all his for £50.

This of course was a Godsend, but did pose the ticklish problem of how to get it all out from there. He had nothing else to do that day and so, packed the small items into drawers and making several journeys, carried all up to the car. They showed him where they'd leave the key and said they needed the furniture out by the weekend.

'Not a problem,' he'd said, but it was only when lugging the final drawer-full of lamps and brassware up the muddy track, that the solution suddenly struck him. He had been thinking of paying a farmer mate to fetch it all on a tractor and trailer, but the answer was simpler than that.

He set off at seven the following morning, steered carefully down the ruts, loaded the car and drove back out, to continue to the shop for off-loading. The following morning, he went back for the few bits remaining, which included a rather pleasant single door, pine wardrobe. The things still didn't sell, but it retained its original paintwork, simulating satinwood, he was later informed and was useful, so he decided to keep it.

The ground was still frozen solid, as he exited the second field to the lane.

This time, he returned to the flat they were renting. Anne helped him in with the wardrobe and they both snuggled back into bed for half an hour to warm up.

Studying the notes, I realised a store now came into the scheme of things. He didn't say how he'd come by it, but just that he was now using it. He described it as being located off a lane in the centre of town.

The lane must have been narrow, for he says:---*As useful as the store is, it can be tricky gaining access, for if a Woolworths delivery van is off-loading all you can do is wait, as with it being a one-way street, other than breaking the law, there's no other way to the store. Also, loading and unloading has to be sharpish, otherwise, those waiting to drive through can become a little irritated.*

So, his store must have been near wherever Woolworths had once been located and here's another reference.---*Bought a van load of wooden children's chairs from Leon. He'd cleared an old school in Wales. We stacked the lot in the store. They were not that old, probably about 1910 or so, but with turned back rails, splayed legs, bentwood top rail and quite thick seats, they had a certain charm and bringing them out in sets of four, I polished and sold them in the shop. Took a while, but when they'd all gone, I realised I'd trebled my money.*

The chapel pews weren't such a wise buy, however. Should have sat in one before I did the deal. Their backs caught you right under the shoulder blade. Probably designed to stop the congregation nodding off. But as the old dealers always said, 'Everything goes in the end.'

I'll include this next bit, for it shows John Dodds was coming to terms with the professional responsibilities of the job.

---*Mr. Berry called and asked me to take a look in the back of his van. He wasn't like the rest of the Rathkeale travellers, being calm, measured and didn't generally ask ludicrous prices. He had an oak double corner cupboard, lying prone and I should have known when he asked a mere £80, there could have been a strong underlying reason for it being so reasonable.*

He knew the store's location and I said, rather than all being crammed in the front of the van, I'd go on foot and meet them there. Walking down the narrow lane, I realised he and his wife must have already withdrawn and erected what I'd committed myself to, for I espied an ominous dark column reaching up to the underside of a protruding first floor bay window. Feeling dwarfed, I realised you'd need climbing equipment simply to access the top shelves. If there had been a national competition for tallest corner cupboard in the land, this would have certainly come away sporting the rosette.

'I'm sorry,' I said. 'I can't possibly buy a corner cupboard that big. I'm really sorry, but with it being half covered up in the van, I just didn't realise the sheer size of the thing.'

Wagging an admonishing finger Mr. Berry said, 'You shouldn't really do that you know.'

'I know. I'm sorry, but it won't even go in the store, let alone in the shop. I'll help you back in with it.'

'We can manage,' his wife replied, almost barging me out of the way.

I had broken one of the unwritten rules, 'You don't renegue on a deal.' I had, by now, also taken another rule on board. If one expected to be considered a respected member of the trade, it wasn't done to fly a kite, price-wise with one of your regulars and then sell the item for 50% less when realising one had been a little over-ambitious regarding its value. Word got around and it was a certain way to lose a good customer.

Another thing that dawned on me about this time, was why all the best china and porcelain in a house clearance, often seemed to be held together by rivets. I used to wonder, 'Didn't they ever break any ordinary stuff?' Well of course they did and flung it onto the ash tip. Quality pieces broken, however, would have been safely kept until the plate rivetter did his rounds.

It seems that with so many dealers chasing so little stock, certain merit was awarded where it was not necessarily deserved. Just to keep the expenses paid and with not having the knowledge or funds to compete for the best lots, John Dodds was often forced to compromise. He didn't like handling satin walnut, but some weeks, with not much else available, he'd little choice. I looked the term up and found, satin walnut was a dense grained import from the south-eastern United States, thus its other name, American Walnut.

A massive quantity of Edwardian bedroom furniture had been constructed from the timber. John Dodds wrote, that he particularly hated the pressed steel, bronzed backplates, that often had the handles missing. They were fixed by what looked like screws, but were in fact small nails, clenched so tight in the grain, they were almost impossible to lever free without scarring the soft timber. Replacement brass handles came from a Birmingham firm. John Dodds writes:---*They were garishly bright and far too thick, needing their backs filing and colour toning down, but in those days I didn't know of an alternative.*

An indication of how little, in reality he'd progressed, came from his description of a foray up Ruthin way, to a farm sale he'd heard about.

---There must have been at least 30 dealers in attendance and I only recognised one of them. He was from Llandovery, but as he only dealt from the back of his van, could turn up virtually anywhere. He was generally known as Luffy, a shortened form of his surname. He told me, there were two groups of traders present, 'The North Wales boys and the Chester mob.' Apparently, they didn't always get on. Having viewed everything in the house, plus the lots laid in rows out in the garden, I felt fairly certain I'd valued everything more or less within the bounds of reason and so felt rather dumb-struck by what ensued. The two rival trade groups certainly didn't get on. The prices bid were staggering. For instance, a round mahogany table, only large enough to seat four, made an extraordinary amount; further along the row, Luffy paid £280 for nothing more than a small rectangular, oak wall cupboard; small central door between two panels and then way down the line, three mahogany table leaves, leaning against the hedge, commanded a colossal sum, with things almost coming to blows. A female member of the Chester mob screeched, 'You're just bidding out of fookin' spiite!'

I came away with a couple of pine chests and an oak settle, with the realisation on collection of the latter, it was completely home-made in the most charmless manner and I felt like as if I was driving home with a roof-top stigma, advertising my ignorance along every mile. I was completely shell-shocked by what had ensued and was in two minds whether to stop and fling the wood-butcher's construction, over the hedge.

It was only when I'd calmed somewhat, that a light of reason came on in my head. Remembering a strange vertical split in the fussy pedestal of the mahogany table, I realised it would have had an opening mechanism and for some reason had been sold separate to its leaves. So, that explained the spite retort. The north Wales boys had run the price of the leaves up, for the table would be vastly overpriced without them. But what about Luffy's expensive cupboard?

Mother had been looking after the shop that day and was chatting with one of our regular callers, Gay Walker, who had stayed on especially, being keen to see what exciting treasures I may have brought back from the North Wales trip. The dark, nailed-up piece of seating furniture was lowered to the pavement and taking a deep draw on her cigarette, she said, 'No. Thank you for showing me, John, but it's not for me.'

Having felt she'd let me off extremely lightly, I explained my astonishment at prices paid at a sale, so far away, up in the hills. On being told about the small wall cupboard, she enquired about the hinges.

'Sort of butterfly,' I said.

'Obviously an early one.'

An early one. I realised if I was to progress, I had to gain a working knowledge of what exactly was meant by the phrase. She was one of the landed dealers mentioned earlier, who was able to handle the more reasonable of the Irish travellers.

I'd wondered why John Dodds' mother was now back helping in the shop? Then found the reason. A cottage had been found and movement to it was imminent, but it was in need a huge amount of work. The grant offered by the council, by John's estimation, would cover the materials, but not the labour. Even though never having done anything like it in his life before, he'd had no choice other than to do the renovation himself and with there being a cut-off point of two years to complete the work, or lose the grant, he needed to be quick about it. His mother managed to negotiate a very reasonable rate, to stay in a guest house belonging to a friend, bottom of Corve Street.

Before moving on to the cottage phase, I must tell you this bit. On one of his favourite calls, to the dealer who did house clearances, Ann Heath, up in Minsterley; amongst other things, he had returned with a sofa. It wasn't a thing he'd normally buy, but felt certain this was a Regency example. On reaching the shop, however, he realised there was a snag. There was insufficient room for it in the main selling area and so it would need to be eased down the side passage that led beyond the house stairway, to the back room. John took one end and Anne the other. Between the stairs and passage wall, the thing became jammed.

"*Careful,*" he warned. "*We don't want to scrape the wall. That's it. It's coming free. Hey, can you imagine if Geoff was lifting this? He'd be going, 'Hoo-hoo-hoo. Up a bit, hoo-hoo. Ooh that's it---hoo-hoo-hoo.'*"

John Dodds continued:---*When the sofa was finally free of the constriction and lowered, standing at the other end, glaring at me, was Geoff, the landlord. Behind him, Anne was sitting on the second step of the stairs, clutching her sides, rocking backwards and forwards, trying her best to suppress the laughter. My sudden fit of coughing, with a few hoo-hoos thrown in, attempting to cover my embarrassment, simply made her worse.*

CHAPTER TWELVE

I worked out, that in the space of four years, John Dodds, although having a very thin knowledge of antiques, had accumulated enough money to put down a deposit on a cottage and had also generated enough financial credibility to obtain a small mortgage. Further forward in the notes, I'd found a reference to the fact his mother's debt was still ongoing and presumably, he was still paying the mortgage on the small terraced house in Lancashire. That wouldn't have amounted to much, however, as the purchase price had only been £2,200.

The cottage basically needed the lot. It was damp, the roof, with slates awry and in many places missing, had that sad abandoned look. There was one cold water tap, one ancient power point, but it did boast a pair of outside lavatories, having once been two cottages. With it being a Herculean undertaking, there was a great deal in John Dodds' writings regarding how this had been achieved, but as this is a tale about his progress as an antique dealer, I decided to include just a few snippets.

Here's a description of his first afternoon there, as it captures just a little of what he was up against.

---*We drove out to the cottage with all our worldly goods on the car and trailer, the latter having been borrowed from friend Leon. The faithful Baby Belling cooker was eased into the alcove, left of fireplace, as that was the location of the only power point in the house. Thankfully there were four working lights. The only tap and sink were on the back wall, directly opposite the main entry to what we called the kitchen. Waste water went straight out through a pipe to soak into the foundations. I wondered how people had managed to cope in such conditions. Apparently, a family of eight had been brought up in what would have once been called, next door. It comprised, one main room, with two bedrooms above, no electric lighting and no running water. Even the mains water for the larger cottage hadn't arrived until the 60's, by which time I presumed the two cottages had been knocked into one.*

Our few bits of furniture, plus clothes and bedding were carried inside and Anne prepared a ham salad. We were both starving, but at the first mouthful, I put down the knife and fork and said, 'I'm sorry, I can't eat this until we've cleaned up a bit.' The kitchen window was enshrouded with yellowing cobwebs and countless dead flies littered the sill. It felt like I was eating them, along with the dust and plaster detritus scattered across the ancient linoleum floor covering. Half an hour later we were able to continue the meal.

John spent the whole summer re-roofing the cottage, while his mother tended the shop, but as his resources gradually drained, hardly any money came back in. Not only was there a mini-slump in the antique trade, but with no fresh stock arriving, sales tailed off to such an extent, one week the total takings amounted to a mere £28. Not even enough to pay the rent.

During the following Autumn, his mother returned north and after each day trying to revive the shop's fortunes, John Dodds would return home to work on the cottage interior. He had run the wiring, which an old friend from school days had connected and he'd made a start on the boarding and plastering. They still had no bathroom, however. I realised this must have been the case, for following an assessment of his plastering efforts, he'd added a little tale regarding sanitary facilities.

---I became quite a dab hand at plastering, specialising in an interesting lunar finish, minor impact craters and the odd Sea of Tranquillity. I was always fooled into thinking I'd mastered the art until the plaster dried, revealing I'd inadvertently created a moonscape once again. I thought emulsion might reduce the effect, but in fact it actually highlighted it, drawing one's eye, as do skin blemishes.

We both had to be careful of liquid intake approaching bedtime, being mindful of the fact we only had what used to be referred to as a 'guzunder,' for light relief. For anything more serious, a trip to the outside facilities was called for. One bitter night, with the north wind rattling the window, Anne, suffering from stomach cramps, held on for a while, but then realising there was no alternative, begged me to give moral support and light the way. Donning coats and boots, we ventured to the rear of the cottage. Taking the torch, she asked me to wait and stand guard. A few seconds later, I heard a tiny shriek. Hunched on the seating board of the first lavatory, were three rabbits sheltering from the cold. Leaving them undisturbed, she used the neighbouring facility.

Going back to the notes, I found, there was still the odd deal with Mrs. Lockyer, but she complained bitterly at how her son had betrayed her, even to the extent of buying a pretty oak bureau she'd always been promised. There were things to be had from those two connections previously mentioned, supplied by the Irish and he constantly checked for news of fresh clearances at Minsterley, dropping everything and driving like mad up the back roads, to be first there. On one visit, an unusual country chair was in the deal. For some reason, its charming simplicity appealed and even though not knowing quite why, he decided to keep it.

An interesting addition to the notes: *Years later I saw something similar in the American Museum in Bath.*

On another deal, gut instincts told him to take a gamble on a yew wood box commode with dinky little barley twist legs, joined by

163

similarly intricate stretchers. It cost £120, way beyond the £40 he'd first reckoned it, but decided, if he was to learn the job it had to be done on items of such rarity. The profit margin was but a secondary consideration. The first dealer to ask its price, went off in a huff, telling him he needed to be more realistic, but the second on the scene declared it to be simply gorgeous and paid the £145 asking price. He wrote,---*Simply gorgeous would not have been a term I'd have used for a box commode, but there again, it was a little gem.*

So, did I find at last, John Dodds had seen a way forward and from now on would only be dealing in the better end of the market? Seems not. He wrote, that he would dearly have loved to have done, but there simply wasn't enough stock of that ilk, made available to the likes of him, to achieve it. His friend, Gay Walker gave him a list of reference books, which he managed to obtain with the help of the Castle Bookshop, but meanwhile he was stuck with things such as pine and satin walnut. He'd had an order for 25 pine chests, stripped and polished, from a Warwick dealer, but to give you an idea of the state of things; when a satin walnut wardrobe had blown off the roof of his car, whilst driving into Ludlow, he wrote:---*I glanced in the rear-view mirror to see it sailing majestically, to implode as a flat-pack in the middle of the A49. I was that skint, I gathered the debris and glued all back together in the shop, where it sold for £15.*

Another reason for him not being too picky about where the profits came from, was the fact in the August of that year, there arrived into the world, another little mouth to feed. As regards the nest the baby boy was to be brought to:---*I had finished the roof, including building a dormer window above where the bathroom was to be, had built a septic tank, underpinned the walls, but the entire ground floor was a muddy pit, awaiting both damp-proof membrane and concrete, plus worryingly, not a single bedroom had been completed. I drove home from the Shrewsbury Hospital, absolutely elated, but mindful of the fact, if a permit had been required to have children, our request would have definitely been denied.*

I picked up a hitch-hiker at the Meole Brace roundabout, but not particularly taking to the chap, didn't share my news with him. I wanted the first person told, to be someone I liked and respected. It was my farmer friend, Richard Griffiths from down the lane. And no, I didn't wet the baby's head. Feeling mentally and physically drained, I went to bed.

I read that, Anne and the baby were given accommodation by friends in Ludlow, allowing John enough time to at least get the kitchen floor in and one bedroom completed.

The following year, I realised, was when the Bunker Hunt brothers had attempted to corner the world market in silver, for he noted that some of the items bought from Mrs. Lockyer, brought more money as scrap than they were worth as objects. His feelings on the matter:---*It seemed criminal, but with such a feeding frenzy, the rewards were immediate.*

He kept back the pretty Swiss fob watches, as once a friend had cleaned the works and got them going again, they sold quite well. He also had the Fusee movement, Hunters and Half Hunters restored, but the ordinary 19th century silver cased pocket watches, if not in working order, went for scrap as did all the gold-strapped ladies' wrist watches.

Joined to the rear of their cottage, back up in the hills, was a handy shed, plus another just down off the road. Along the lane was a deconsecrated Methodist chapel he was able to rent and so the Ludlow store with its awkward access was abandoned. Pine was hand stripped in the garden and left to dry in the small brick shed by the road, whilst that awaiting his attention was stored in the back shed. Meanwhile each night, work on the cottage continued. People commented on how drawn he had become. The mixture of 12-hour days, caustic soda fumes and pine dust was getting to him and yet even with countless hours he'd spent stripping furniture, he found there were still lessons to be learnt.--- *Some of the more fragile pieces, on being swabbed with hot* *caustic, simply fell to bits. Gluing them back together proved a great lesson on 19th century construction methods. Other pieces could turn out to have had an infuriating inclusion of mahogany in their fabrication, not evident until showing as ugly, deep purple when exposed to caustic soda. This necessitated a little carpentry, to replace the offending portions with old pine. Not really an innate skill of mine, but I did eventually manage progress into the area, I'd once judged as being, much needed room for improvement. Another lesson, bitter experience brought home, was, never buy painted oak. The caustic soda turned the light medullary rays, black, so a bookcase I'd stripped sat like a massive malevolent starling in the back room of the shop. Even scraping paint off oak rarely works, for the last 1%, showing as white flecks in the grain take more time to remove with a pin, than the thing is usually worth. Any thought of simply polishing over the blemishes, brings forth an annoying reminder of failure, as if from a myriad of tiny stars.*

When the time came for the council's inspection of the near-renovated cottage, luck shone once again, for the Building Regs. official happened to be an old mate from junior school days. John Dodds had completely run out of time and money and writes:--- *Not only had I not been able to paint two of the bedrooms, the kitchen, apart from an old cupboard and a sink supported by laths, was a bit of an embarrassment. The man might have been a friend from distant school days, but was now operating in a professional capacity and to this day, I can still hear his voice echoing in the unfinished bedrooms, asking, 'What about the painting? You could surely have slapped on a bit of emulsion.'*

He must have seen I was absolutely exhausted and petrified of being denied the £2,000 grant, for he said, 'I take it you prefer the dried plaster look.'

'Yes,' I said. 'For now that is. I don't expect any favours, but trust me, it will be done.'

'Well it's not up to us to determine rules of taste,' he said and ticked the box.

Back in the kitchen he drew aside the curtain hiding the sink's supporting laths. 'Interesting arrangement. I take it, it's only temporary.'

'Everything works and I've a piece of furniture that the sink will fit into perfectly.'

Another tick in the box and the ensuing grant money paid back the loan from the bank. I'd actually acquired what was to become the cupboarded sink unit three years previously, thrown in a deal for nothing as its top boards were missing. It had proved to be a handy work table, when stripping pine round at the Linney flat and was now, perfect for the kitchen.

I was amazed to see, that despite all the cottage renovation and running of the shop, John Dodds still had time and energy to play Rugby for Ludlow and if partaking of a little light refreshment afterwards, as was the norm, he'd return to the cottage along back lanes. To be banned from driving at that stage, would probably have been the end of his antique career. For that same reason, when needing a break from the never-ending grind during summer months, he and Anne had often trundled down the country lanes to Leintwardine, where up by the church was a homely little pub with welcoming locals. Not once the baby had been born of course and here's his description of the Christmas when his son was 16 months old.

---The Baby Belling had done excellent service, but with the turkey, bought from an old school mate, being a whacking 14 pounder, we'd had to jam a chair against the oven door as we'd not been able to force it completely shut. Anne had made a delicious sherry trifle to follow and I'd said, 'Just look at him.' Slightly red of face, paper hat askew, my son waved his spoon in time to the music playing on the radio.

167

'I think the pudding's got him drunk,' Anne said with a tremulous look and a laugh.

Any sense of liberation one would expect, having virtually finished the cottage renovation, leaving him free to concentrate on the business, seems to have been staunched by the ominous cloud of VAT. The amount of business he was now doing had taken him well over the limit. He'd made a number of references in the notes, regarding ringing the accountant and on a few occasions, being that worried and frustrated, he'd walked round to his office in town.

---The man seemed to be suffering from amnesia, for he always asked, 'What's the matter old chum?'

'Same as before, I'm over the VAT limit and worried sick about it.'

'No need to worry about that, old chum. Just leave it with me, I'll get it sorted.'

'You said that last time.'

He'd send me on my way with a reassuring pat on the back and I'd carry on, shutting the out problem until one of the shippers would ask, 'Would you like me to pay the VAT on that?'

'No, I'm not VAT registered.'

There would then follow an astonished, 'What? You want to be careful. They could take the lot off you.' And then on hearing scary details of dealers who'd been raided, I'd be on to the accountant again.

Shuffling back through the notes, I realised I'd missed a significant entry. Again, it was the result of the pages being in the wrong order, probably happening when that gust of wind blew them off the table. Referring back to the recent Christmas, John Dodds had written:---*As regards it being a proper home, the cottage was far from finished, for even the kitchen was still fairly basic, but although having virtually nothing, it was a time of true happiness. It almost felt dangerous to experience such joy, lest some invisible malignant force might be watching and take our lovely son away from us.*

I wandered the house making a mental note of all the work, yet needing completion and the hours required to achieve it and I also added up the value of the stripped pine stored in what was to be the sitting room. The roof of the little shed by the road had decided one night it was tired of clinging on and had collapsed, meaning, the drying pine now invaded our living quarters. The value, when sanded and polished, came to a few hundred pounds, but when I'd worked out the time necessary to achieve that, I realised, such a way of carrying on, meant we wouldn't starve, but the truth suddenly hit me, we'd never get ahead.

The above explained why all his pine was now taken to Gay Walker. Her brother had installed a huge galvanised tank in one of the barns and was doing a regular hot-strip of furniture. No longer having to scrape and wire wool the paint off by hand, freed up countless hours, but a considerable draw-back was, pine furniture left to soak in hot caustic often fell to bits and thus required reassembling. Also, the wood could swell, meaning the drawers no longer fitted. John Dodds wrote---*If I'd not known better, I'd have sworn at times, certain drawers could not possibly have originated in the carcase they came back with. Hours were spent, with the orbital sander sounding like a Wellington bomber reverberating on the drawer sides, before they would slide back and forth freely again. If impatient and forcing them, with the handles having been removed pre-stripping, it meant there was no way of extracting them again, so short of prizing the back off the chest and thumping each drawer from behind, they remained stubbornly jammed.*

Also, when at Gay's, it gave the opportunity to peruse the latest stock and he'd often return with the '*a bit of a gamble,*' as he put it.

---I would cautiously venture into unknown territory and trusting her advice return home with the odd piece of oak or metalware. Also, items she judged to have been in stock for too long, would be knocked out at cost or less and with me having more passing trade, the items usually sold fairly quickly. There again, as regards the better pieces, I was constantly made aware of the gulf between my knowledge and hers. One that comes to mind was a sampler. Even though framed, it must have spent its life in a drawer, because the colours were still amazingly vibrant. Realising I was taken aback at the price, she said, 'But John, look at the condition and it's an early one.' That phrase again. I needed to grasp a full understanding of what exactly, 'an early one' meant, because the term seemed to apply to different dates, all according to the item referred to. From the reference books I'd bought, I'd established that the cupboard Luffy had spent so much money on, was in all likelihood c1680, my yew wood commode you could also class as early, being c1710, but the sampler Gay had referred to, was only c1820. Not far off being Victorian. Once in full command of the term 'early', it seems you could name your price.

My chance of putting it to the test, came when buying two 18th century oak chests of drawers from the Craven Arms Saturday sale; they and all the other purchases, arriving fresh to the market the following Monday morning. If the weather was fair, I'd leave the bulk of the latest haul on the street and what didn't sell, would be heaved in at night. Many's the time I'd spread sheets of newspaper on oak and mahogany following a shower, the paper being ideal for absorbing the droplets without leaving tell-tale speckled marks. Well anyway, an oak dealer asked the price of the two chests and launching into first usage, of what I'd learnt, I asked a third more for one than the other.

'Why the price difference?' he asked.

Showing him the horizontal backboards of the one, compared with those vertical on the other, I said in an assured manner, 'This is an early one.'

He bought them both.

While on the subject of the hottest selling space of my new premises, the pavement outside it, I'd often put a box of junk there, with a ticket, '£5 the lot.' Nobody would ever buy the lot, but during the day I'd have constant enquiries, 'How much d'you want for this piece?'

'Well done. You've selected the best item, two quid.'

By the end of the day, I'd often be a tenner better off and still have a box of junk.

Sometimes, in the notes it was a job to know which year was being referred to. There was mention of Saturday sales where he aimed to come away with the more prestigious lots. It was his best chance of a gamble paying off, for unless receiving a tip-off regarding items of particular rarity, the big hitters in the trade didn't even bother viewing them. The fairly regular examples were, Craven Arms, Bishops Castle and of course the farm sales. The goods bought were fresh to the market and gave an impetus to the following week.

Also, by now, John felt confident enough in his knowledge, to write out cheques amounting to much more than he actually had in the bank, gambling, that by the time they were due for clearance he'd have sold the majority to cover the deficit. It was a constant tightrope, but he reasoned, antique dealing wasn't for ninnies and if he was to break out of being ever reliant on stripped pine, he needed to be bold.

This next little tale, with references to certain restless feelings, *'having been cooped up long enough,'* I assumed it must have occurred in the Spring of the following year, possibly 1981. He wrote:--- *The shop was being given a good sort out and as often happens, when we put old stock out on the pavement, to give us room to rearrange things, it seemed to be looked at, quite literally, in a different light. Initially, I'd diligently tell regulars, 'You've already seen that,' not wanting them to get lumbered, as seemingly*

I had done. But then I realised, if it appealed to them in its new setting, why deny them the chance of buying it? It was in fact, like an act of liberation, letting the thing go to a new home. That's not why the little brass and iron cot sold, by the way. The lady who bought it, a doctor from West Wales, was a completely new customer. When I said to mother, 'We're finally rid of the cot at last. I'm sick of seeing it stacked, gathering dust in the back room,' she said, looking a little alarmed, 'You haven't sold it? What if the original buyer turns up to collect it?'

'I'll just give him his money back. He can't expect us to hang on to it forever.' Its first time of selling had been back in the old shop. I actually got twice the amount second time around, but the trouble was, I'd promised to deliver it to Newcastle Emlyn.

Mother didn't share my cavalier spirit, however, saying I could end up in court. I wasn't aware of the law, stating in such cases, you were duty bound to hold on to goods, for a minimum of 6 years. It also applied to items reserved with payment of a mere 10% deposit, which was handy to know, for from that time on, I never accepted deposits, unless slightly less than 10%.

John Dodds gave details of further purchases from Leon, bottom of town, a few deals with Mrs. Lockyer, glad of the fact, the dealer who had taken over his former shop had now left town, meaning the traitorous Trevor was no longer working against her, but I'll take you fast forward to the West Wales trip.

No sorry, must slip this bit in. Sometimes Mrs. Lockyer would receive letters from old customers she'd accumulated during all those years traveling the lanes. The note would be taken round to a trusted friend, who with being literate, could explain exactly where the letter had originated. With as yet, no rapprochement between her and traitorous Trevor and another son who'd often driven her, doing a custodial term, she called upon her husband Ted to drive her, just like in the old days. Often, when John and his mother were dealing for the silver and jewellery in the back

172

sitting room, they'd hear a dull thud and groan from the room above.

---*'That's the first one gone,' Mrs. Lockyer would say with solemnity, followed by a conspiratorial grin.*

Apparently, after the rigours of the day, once all was unloaded, Ted would take to his bed, armed with quart bottles of cider.

But now the reason for including this. With the Irish having picked much of the area clean and Trevor having gone behind her back, buying off her regulars, she couldn't see the point of carrying on much longer. Sadly, an era was coming to an end.

When I'd read about the offer of the cot delivery, it had seemed quite a magnanimous gesture, but then realised it was actually treated as a buying opportunity, a business trip, plus Jessica's son in law had originated in Pembrokeshire and so it would also be a family reunion, staying with his parents. The things they bought from shops en route didn't amount to much, for just like back up on the Marches, anything decent was immediately snapped up by the trade for shipping to America or to be sent along the chain to end up in places like Cirencester, Burford, Stow-on-the-Wold or Chipping Norton. On reaching Neyland, however, their place of stay, their luck changed. When it was known, two antique dealers from Shropshire were there for the weekend, not only did locals bring things of possible interest to the door, the two intrepid visitors were invited to view items in situ.

---*On the second morning, when hearing a caller being told not to pester, for the guests had travelled far and needed a rest, mother was instantly on her feet, making it perfectly clear, the two visiting dealers didn't mind being pestered one little bit.*

All the items bought were nothing more than what you'd see in an antique hobby shop, where the main income was a fat pension, but the market was hungry and given time you could sell anything

173

of that ilk, even the dark Edwardian mahogany envelope, card table, neither of them would have personally given houseroom to. It soon became obvious, they had far more than a car load and so arranged a further stay for the following weekend, when they'd return with a trailer. The hospitality they'd been given was heart-warming and the general friendliness of all those they'd met, put some of their English compatriots to shame.

It was the return trip that actually brought the biggest financial reward, but far more than that, the experience seemed to have opened John Dodds' eyes.---*It was late Sunday afternoon and we were on the verge of leaving, needing to fill up with fuel before all the garages closed, when a neighbour arriving, said a relative who dabbled in antiques would like us to call. The man had a few bits, which were added to the load, but more importantly, he then told us of another local dealer who operated from a farm building in the next village. We said we'd have a quick look, but time was running short, a garage was essential, for the fuel gauge showed less than a quarter full.*

What they'd chanced on, however, was an untouched cache of purchases hoarded since the previous autumn. By the time they had picked their way through it all, stacked for economy of space rather than goods being shown to advantage, they realised pieces of interest needed extraction for examination by torchlight, before even thinking about opening negotiations. As always, they had to ensure tops and bottoms had started out together, rather than being a marriage. When squeezing between the piles, viewing by dim bulb light, instincts told them they really ought to be moving, doing the sensible thing and returning the following weekend, but the more they explored, the more they didn't dare let go. Who's to say the stuff would still be there next weekend?

'What's that glazed cupboard down there?'

'Oh, top half of a bookcase, the base of it's over here.'

'And what are those drawers. Looks like a desk top?'

'It is. The pedestals are over in that corner, under the table.'

By the time it had all been dealt for and packed on the trailer, it was way past 10 o-clock and their only chance of fuel was an all-night garage in Swansea, over 50 miles away. This was obviously not the most direct route back to Ludlow, but they had no choice, as there was no chance of a garage being open that time of night, in places like Llandeilo, or Llandovery.

John Dodds described doing what most drivers do from time to time, with the needle hovering on empty, he'd started talking to the car. *'Come on, you can do it. Don't let us down now.'*

They were pulled in by the police, who as ever, couldn't imagine what seemed to be nothing but a massive pile of rubbish, being worth the amounts shown on the two receipts they had. Their intervention proved quite handy, in fact, because they explained exactly, how to get to the only garage open.

It was gone 2am by the time they reached the cottage, but even so, John was away early the following morning and by 10, had sold all the pine they'd bought from that final lucky call. He'd not bothered with chests of drawers and blanket boxes, too much haulage for a couple of pounds profit apiece. What he'd concentrated on, was the pick of the cache they'd stumbled upon, selling the two linen presses, bookcase, long kitchen table and partners desk to the man who'd opened a business, operating from a barn, beyond an arched entry virtually opposite. So all they had to do was carry it across the road.

I hadn't realised how rare pine partners desks were, until reading in the notes, *'With it being as rare as rocking-horse poo, I dreamt up a crazy price and he was glad to pay it.'*

Apart from the lucrative nature of the deal, however, I could also sense it was opening John Dodds' eyes. He'd made a massive profit on items of pine furniture, without the slightest whiff of caustic soda having been involved.

Another piece of luck that had come their way that Spring, was purely on account of the sale of a smallholding south of town, not having been properly advertised. John Dodds viewed it and passed on the prices to his mother, before heading north to an evening rugby match, a knockout game in the Shropshire cup. On reaching the shop next day, he was handed the receipt for all goods bought and trying to keep a straight face, his mother said, '*You might be in need of Leon's trailer again.*'

---*I was absolutely staggered. It was one of those sales all dealers dream of, for apart from ourselves, not one single trader had turned up. Mother had bought everything of antique merit for the princely sum of £33.50, having had to shell out £3 each, for the pine chests of drawers, but the washstands, dressing table, towel rails, blanket boxes, side tables and kitchen table, had come in for a pound apiece or less. The set of kitchen chairs had been the most extravagant buy, costing £7. All the pine flew out and again, without any notion of stripping it.*

It was the same Spring, Mrs. Lockyer had taken him on a call. She'd said, '*Ted canner manage it, not with 'is knee and I inner givin' Trappy the benefit.*' *Trappy was her name for Trevor. We drove up the lanes into hill country between Tenbury and Cleobury Mortimer and parked the car in the small farmyard.*

Mrs. Lockyer rapped on the oak boarded door and giving me a wink said, 'Ees in there. Dunner you fret. 'Eel come to the door in a minute.' She knocked again, calling, 'Come on, I knows yume in there. It's no good you 'iding.'

The door slowly creaked open. 'There you am. Brought you a visitor.' Then turning to me, 'Come on in, 'ee ooner mind.'

I followed her bustling figure, through the porch past the boots, wellingtons, walking sticks and old coats into the gloom of the kitchen, where the coals in the iron grate gave a rosy glow to the backboards of a settle and nearby flagstones. The old farmer swung the fire crane forward and with a piece of rag for protection, hefted a massive encrusted, black kettle off its hook and poured surprisingly clear, steaming water into a teapot.

'Ees come to look at that owd box o yorn up on the landing.' She shouted. Either the man was deaf, or this was her normal way of dealing with old bachelor farmers. 'Betcha thought I'd forgotten yer, dincha?' she shouted, flicking me a wink. 'You anner gone and sold it as yer? You knows you olluz said it was mine.'

'No, it's still up there,' he said, pouring the tea.

'There, told you he was a good un.' She said to me. Then shouting again as if owning the place, 'Go on up and 'av a look at it. 'Ee ooner mind. You dunner mind dus yer?' Another mirthful wink, 'Course 'ee dunner.--- Go on up and 'av a look.'

On the landing was a pretty little oak panelled coffer. I let Mrs. Lockyer deal for it and we carried it to the car. The tea by the way was just like tea ought to taste and no, the settle wasn't for sale.

Driving back to Ludlow, when I asked what profit would be required, she said, 'Just give me what you sees fit. I ooner be greedy.' I got the impression, it was the act of pulling the piece of furniture that mattered, rather than financial gain. Sadly, it seems that was her last call, for Gary was never again seen in the shop doorway, proclaiming, 'Our Mum's got some stuff for yer.'

I saw mention in the notes of a few prestigious pieces that had been stripped and polished; a small Georgian pine press cupboard; an impressive kitchen piece with a row of spice drawers running along the base of the glazed top; a fine dresser base with 2" thick sycamore top, which he sold to a friend Gerald, in Broad Street, but the days of endless stripping of chests of drawers and washstands seemed to be over.

One slow Thursday, he'd said to his mother, on impulse, '*Let's just go on a little jaunt and see what's about. Has to be better than just sitting here. I tell you what, if it works out, I shan't strip a piece of pine again.*'

They locked the shop and heading out of town, called first at Leon's. There on the pavement was an oak coffer with a top panel missing. They knew a man who specialised in fettling problem pieces, putting them for sale in his shop in Belbroughton and they bought it, but I was amused to see a little addition to the notes:--- '*I wouldn't have dreamt of buying a coffer with a panel missing in later years. There were too many good ones available, but by then I'd customers, my immediate competitors hadn't and so could pay that bit extra for the best.*'

On first reading the notes, I had underlined that important last sentence, to make sure it was included, for it spoke volumes.

They called on the two traders still operating in Clun and came away with a couple of unusual oddities, but in Bishops Castle, there glinting on black velvet, mid-window of a small shop was their star lot of the day, a silver chatelaine. It had its thimble and needle cases, silver handled scissors and all the rest of the implements, spread in full array.---*It was a struggle to come to a deal, because the man had gambled a fair bit for it, but it was so complete, it seemed a certainty you would never get stuck with it.*

The one-eyed coffer, as John Dodds had called it, was kept under a blanket for when their contact called and once sold, he said, '*That's it. From now on, no more pine stripping.*'

Bottom of page I saw another note.---*Years later, a local dealer, nickname of Dithery Dave, told me he'd had that very coffer dropped on him in the knock-out. He'd been that irked, that on his way home, he'd dumped it at Leons', with the instruction, 'Just get rid of the thing.' As for us, seems it was a case of, 'Where*

178

ignorance is bliss.' Ironic, that a lot I really shouldn't have bought, proved a bit of a life changer.

I paused here and checked back through the notes to see if I'd missed anything. What prompted it was, I'd heard of the Bunker Hunt brothers' attempt to corner the market in silver, for in some quarters their name had become synonymous with folly, but I'd seen no reference to the overnight collapse in John Dodds' writings. I looked up the exact date it had happened, March 27th, Silver Thursday, 1980, roughly about the time work on the cottage would have been completed. I think therefore, it is safe to assume, with John having been intent on finishing the house renovation and with scrap silver not having been a major part of his business, he'd not felt the impact and so of course, hadn't at this point, made a note of it.

I decided to give his old mate, Leon Jones a ring. He was away again on a trip, West Wales this time. We were cut off, as ever in that region, by a poor signal, but a short while later the phone rang.

"Got a bit of a signal now and I've pulled into a gateway. How can I help?"

He told me that, prior to the silver market collapsing, things had gone quite mental. Some dealers had completely abandoned their normal operations to concentrate on the metal. They chased around the shops and attended all the sales, weighing the tea sets, salvers, coffee pots and the like, to work out whether they were worth more for scrap than they were as items; buying in bulk and working on the tightest of margins. He said the collapse hadn't affected him, as he'd never much bothered with silver and jewellery.

What had made a bigger impact, roughly about that time, in fact, had been the police raid on a dealer's ring down in Carmarthen. "Shook the whole trade," he said. "They got hefty fines, tax investigations and a saleroom ban for a year. Never affected me personally, like. But it made a good few of 'em think a bit, I can tell you. Had enough on m'plate dealing with the Irish boys.

179

Didn't have time to sit around in salerooms. Some of them were complete bastards, any road. I'll never forget one of 'em, swapping price tickets on my clocks. Our mum would have been none the wiser and when I got back, I found the cheating swine had robbed me blind."

He was about to end the call, but then said, "Sorry, I was rambling on a bit. But anyway, just remembered, roughly about that time, don't hold me to a date, there was a similar boom and bust on mahogany furniture. Stuff nobody had reckoned much before. Victorian wind-out tables, dressing tables and four-door sideboards, all shipped to Australia. Went that mad, Victorian sideboards ended up fetching more than flamin' Regency ones. What was selling for a thousand, cost twelve hundred to replace---then fourteen---then sixteen in an upward spiral. But what none of 'em reckoned with, even though Australia's a huge place, there inner that many folks what lives there. So of course, it all went tits up and then deadly quiet for a bit until the Italian market kicked in."

I thanked him and he said he'd definitely like us to meet up, but when, he didn't know. He was always on the move.

The call from Leon proved invaluable. It led to me finally pinning down a couple of things that had evaded earlier efforts. There was the purchase of a particularly rare bed, plus the sudden appearance of his old friend, Fred, turning up as if back from the dead. The same Fred who'd taken him to London all those years before.

--- *After his disappearance just prior to Christmas a few years back, I never expected to ever see Fred again. He'd lost a lot of weight and didn't look a well man, but when he smiled, I could see the old Fred was still in there. He examined a straight legged oak lowboy in the window and an oak wall rack nearby. 'You haven't put enough on those, lad. I'll send you a customer, but ask another £200.' With a wink he added, 'You can give me half the extra. I need the odd little earner now and again.'*

180

I was a bit wary, as I didn't want, what I considered an unnecessary extra amount, hampering their departure. The two items had cost me a fair bit and I needed a quick sale. I needn't have worried mind you, for his contact, Peter, didn't flinch at the prices and also left me his telephone number. I hadn't realised it, but the man had taken over a massive building in Leominster and apart from dealing in traditional furniture, was also going into pine in a big way.

A few days later, Fred appeared for his £100 commission and that was the last I ever saw of him.

Going back to the notes, I looked for more references regarding this Peter who had recently come on the scene. I remembered having seen the name a number of times, but couldn't work out exactly where he fitted into the scheme of things. Each time I saw him mentioned, I'd underlined it, for ease of locating the relevant passage again. Here's one reference and you can see why it didn't exactly jump off the page.

John Dodds wrote:---*I was surprised to hear, Peter had been roped in on that Carmarthen incident. I would have thought he'd have had enough on his plate, setting up his new business, without sitting around in the Ivy Bush Royal Hotel.*

This was obviously the auction ring case, Leon had told me about. I rang another contact I'd been given, a certain Charles, who had apparently once strutted his stuff around the salerooms. He was initially wary to say the least, "And may I enquire, who exactly it is, I'm talking to?"

I told him and the reason for making the enquiries.

"So you're nothing to do with the boys in blue then?"

To try and reassure him, I gave names of those I'd already contacted and relaxing a little, he said, "That boys in blue,

181

utterance just now, was just a little jape, dear boy. Anyway, the sale you're referring to, if I remember rightly, was a Peter Francis venue and the negotiations afterwards were convened in the Ivy Bush Royal Hotel. Unbeknown to the protagonists, the local constabulary were filming them by way of a camera hidden in the ceiling lamp fitting. Way before my time, old bean. All way beyond my comprehension. From memory, I think I was going through my cracked jugs and basins phase. Not a thing I'm proud of, but one has to start somewhere."

I liked the sound of this Charles and was glad he agreed to a meeting sometime in the future.

The next reference to Peter from Leominster was regarding a huge pine cupboard, with a clock central to the upper section. It had been offered John, by his farmer mate, Richard Griffiths, who had actually sold him the cottage. Being a monumental 8 foot long and 7 foot tall, there was no way he could entertain the idea of doing the deal himself and so took a commission off Peter for the call. When he'd been asked, was there anything else? He sold him the dresser base from the cottage kitchen and a Scottish pine press cupboard from his back shed.

John Dodds had written:---*I was told that housekeepers' cupboards containing 8-day grandfather clocks, were a Shropshire speciality. The dresser base I sold Peter had been a c1700 oddity of Scots pine and oak construction. I'd always meant to tidy it up, but like the builder who never seems to get around to jobs needed at home, I hadn't found time to do it. Same with the Scottish press. It was the slightly high waisted type, with an attractive drawer arrangement, the two larger, in the upper row, flanking a dinky little candle drawer. I'd always had it earmarked for the house, but with it needing stripping and finishing, never found the time. When Anne saw the bare back wall of the kitchen later, she was devastated.*

On finding another reference to Peter, I realised I was well on my way to pinning those dates down. John Dodds, thanks to a tip-off from a friend Tony Craig had bought a particularly rare four poster bed and not knowing what to ask for it, had decided to put it into McCartneys Antique auction and let the trade fight over it. For that to happen, he needed to ensure competition, otherwise the ring could buy it for next to nothing and knock it out between them.

Here's what John had written:---*I hit on the idea of ringing Peter. Although banned from salerooms for a year, the ban didn't extend to a sneaky preview and after having a word with Mr. Talbot, the auctioneer, we were admitted to the hall. Peter had said, there was nothing against his right-hand man buying the bed and then supposedly selling it to him later. To have actually turned up in person on sale day, however, could have earnt him a custodial sentence.*

Before we go to the actual sale itself, I'll give you John Dodds' description of how he came by the bed. Yet another rare triumph, where incredibly, no other antique dealers had turned up.

---*The sale was held in an abandoned Victorian school building and there was pine furniture, which I could now rate to the nearest shilling, a huge bundle of useful pine mouldings, a stack of Victorian match boarding, twenty-two pine fireplace surrounds dating from c1820 to c1920 and the bed. Carved vines adorned the slender fluted front posts, the frieze retained its original pale green and* gilt *decoration and there was a domed canopy, which other than seen in reference books, I'd never come across the like of before. It was of course disassembled as was my brain, for I had not one clue what to pay for it. When the bidding paused at £45, I expected a voice to say, 'Fooled you,' before it all restarted in earnest. As I watched the auctioneer, gavel poised, my heart was hammering and I hardly dared breathe. It was the same man who had needed persuading to include my 'railway carriage' coffer in that Leominster sale all those years before. He was obviously guesting in this Much Wenlock charity auction for the day. With obvious reluctance, he quietly said, 'Sold.' Tony Craig and I looked at one another, unable to believe what sweet charity had befallen us.*

The bed, worthy of a grand country residence, resided in the old Methodist chapel, near the house while we decided what to do with it. I did approach the Leominster rooms, now relocated at Rylands Road, but a narrowing of eyes warned me to come to my senses and not actually broach the subject of the bed, as it would have been rubbing salt in the wound. It would not have been kind or in the long run advantageous, to have made it obvious, an esteemed Herefordshire auctioneer had let a rare bed go for next to nothing.

One extra bonus of having had Peter take an interest, had been the fact he bought all the pine moulding, the match boarding and the best of the pine fireplace surrounds. Those had also been bought for mere buttons, by the way and like all lucky deals, the luck persisted, with even the flimsiest in the stack selling quite quickly. My partner in the deal, Tony, often watched Ludlow first XV's home games and would grin broadly as approaching the touchline, I'd call, 'Another three gone, mate.' He knew what I meant.

The actual day the bed sold was horrid in the extreme. It was cold, dank and pouring down. Mr. Talbot the auctioneer, noticing my glum look said, 'Don't worry. They'll be here.' The bed cleared £2,200, after commission, bought by the Cambridges of Cheltenham, underbid by Andrew Wakeman from Wolverhampton. A note bottom of page:---*It was one of the things I should have kept, but how was I to know?*

I spent some time at this point, searching Welsh newspaper archives and felt slight elation at finally being successful. With the court case regarding the illegal knock-out of antiques in Ivy Bush Royal Hotel, having taken place in July 1981, it meant the last meeting with Fred was probably in that same year, with the sale of the rare four-poster bed being in the Spring of 1982, sometime before the end of the Rugby season. QED, I said to myself.

CHAPTER THIRTEEN

I had noticed certain sections in the notes had been written as if short stories, with possibly the intention of compiling them later into a book. This particular part was called, 'Travels with Trevor' and that below is more or less how John Dodds had written it, for as with previous extracts containing the Shropshire dialect, with not being qualified to amend it, I'd thought, 'Best leave well alone.'

---*One morning Trevor Lockyer made an unexpected appearance in the shop and asked, 'Ood you be interested in an oak dresser?'*

Of course I was, but there were two drawbacks, first, with never having yet bought a conventional version, I wouldn't have a clue how to rate the thing and second, I didn't have the cash available, but of course didn't admit to it. He said, it was in a house in Malvern and if I drove, he would show me its whereabouts the following morning. 'You needs to bring cash. About £800 should do it.'

He said, 'The moosh inner keen on selling it, but the sight of all that dosh could turn 'im. Canner promise nothing, but at least we can give it a go.'

Obviously Trevor was out of funds. Our previous source of immediate readies had moved back to South Wales, leaving me with the only option of enquiring about the possibility of an

185

overdraft. I'd had a loan when renovating the cottage, backed by the council grant as guarantee, but this would be a request for an unsecured loan, a big step into the unknown.

I was shown up to the bank manager's office and explained why I needed the money. We chatted generally about business, until obviously satisfied, he said, follow me. Down in the engine room of the bank, he had a quiet word with, what I took to be the head cashier and told me, 'I've set you up with an overdraft facility of £1000 pounds. No point messing about with just £800.'

I thanked him, withdrew £800 and walked back to the shop feeling absolutely loaded. At the call over at Malvern the following day, the owner of the dresser, which was a rather spiky, straight legged thing with a skeletal rack, did waver at the sight of the money, but in the end held firm and we drove home empty handed. I wasn't exactly sorry, for in my humble opinion, the word dresser, had stupidly inflated its value. A few days later, I banked the cash, putting myself back in credit in real terms, but just as importantly, in credit with the bank manager.

It was in the Tavern one evening that Trevor suggested we go out door-knocking. He said, to get us started he would take me to a few old calls where there were goods available, but as they'd not been things he understood, he'd left them behind.

I withdrew £500 and mid-morning next day, we set out for Penybont. At one of Trevor's old calls, a grand brick house near the common, we were given tea and made welcome. I was able to buy two 1897, porcelain commemoration mugs and with both being early, that word again, they were instantly saleable. I also bought; blue and white platters; a miniature pewter tea set and from the attic a Victorian cabriole legged armchair, surprisingly, the first I'd ever possessed. At another call, I spotted the ends of four turned oak posts and with them having steel pins protruding, realised, the triangular roof space of the shed, could be harbouring a pair of four poster beds. We dragged them and the plain back posts out, then *using a ladder, I fished inside for the side and end rails. They were only single beds, c 1820, but the farmer virtually gave them us, saying, 'You might as well 'av 'em. Thaim doing no good up there.'*

We came back with quite a car load and Trevor asked mystified, 'Can you sell all this tack?'

Careful not to show any sign of elation, I said I would do my best and asked how much he wanted for the day's efforts?

In fairness he said, 'It's mostly stuff I oodner bother with. Just give me a drink on the cab-leg chair. That'll do me.'

We went out each weekday and touring the lanes, it amused me to see him as alert as a terrier, spotting signs of habitation, that I might have noticed if walking, but not when trundling along at 50mph.

On one occasion, he said, 'Stop a minute. Back up to that gate.' He got out and dragging it open, beckoned me onto the track. It wound in a gentle curve down to a farmstead, half hidden in the trees. The final approach was between two lines of abandoned cars, carts and farming equipment and as we pulled into the yard, cats flitting up into vantage points, eyed us warily. The farmhouse was half timbered, built on a stone foundation of massive boulders, thick mossed where slewed, rusted gutters had allowed water to disgorge.

'Hello!' Trevor called, his voice echoing sharply off surrounding buildings. After a while a man appeared from one of the barns and walking at a measured pace towards us, asked the reason for our visit. Trevor went into his usual patter, 'We've come around buying owd furniture. Oak, mahogany, washstands, dressing tables, owd clocks. We dunner come around beggin',' he said almost shouting. 'We pays good money.'

The man said, he'd love to have a deal, but had nothing to sell.

187

Trevor wasn't to be that easily put off, however. 'No owd jugs and basins. No big meat plates?'

Shake of head.

'Dressing tables. Marble top washstands?'

Anything, just to gain entry, enabling to spot what lay within, before offering the lure of cash.

'I'm sorry. I'd love to 'ave a deal, but all the old stuff's gone.

'What about the dresser?'

'Went years ago, my sister 'ad it and she wouldn't be for lettin' it go.'

There followed a protracted silence while Trevor's brain whirred, trying to figure an approach from a different angle. 'Have you still got the pig bench?'

I could see the question had struck home.

Looking rather reluctant, the farmer led us to a barn and there upended, leaning against a wall, was a pig bench of magnificent girth. Hanging from the far wall-plate beam I spotted a cider costrel, an adjustable fire hook, wool scales and a steelyard.

With now having entered into the spirit of things, the man ferreted in a tack cupboard to produce, as if a magician, a set of wooden butter scales. They needed restringing, had a bit of worm, but neither he, nor Trevor would have realised, how incredibly sought after they were. I asked, if he minded me having a look and spotted, forgotten in a corner, a sycamore butter print with a cow crisply carved on its underside; to him a forgotten relic; to me a gold nugget. There was also a butter scoop, with stylised flower incised into the flat, circular handle.

188

We were shown the kitchen, but the man had been right, for apart from the breadboard with the word, BARA and wheat ears carved, there was nothing of antique value. As we drove back out, I spotted how Trevor had known a dwelling would be at the end of the track. He'd seen the improvised mailbox, a terracotta drainage pipe, horizontal in the hedge.

Like many things in life, luck ran in phases. We had a golden spell, especially when calling at brand-new brick bungalows, standing alone and looking slightly incongruous in such a rural setting. Using government grants, families had been glad to abandon the old traditional homes in the valley and move up out of the mud to live beside the lane, where mains water had recently been made available. The things they left behind tended to be the old bedroom furniture and they were glad of the money and to have us take it away, for if left there for much longer it would surely have rotted. In one abandoned house we first had to drive the cattle out and then wade through the muck carrying chests, washstands and wardrobes, brought down from upstairs.

It wasn't all success mind you. Nothing ever is.

When suffering completely blank days we'd try and remember the houses where we'd been offered monstrous mahogany veneered, Welsh chests of drawers. They often had glass handles and a cushion moulded top drawer. You could almost imagine sitting down and playing the things. As they took up the whole roof rack, we treated them as a last resort, collecting them on the way home to pay for the day's petrol. A friend of mine, Graham Hayes, would give me £25, using them as breakers, to manufacture useful items such as, small chests of drawers and pairs of bedside cupboards.

Entering a bad run it could last for days and I'd begin to think the whole thing futile. I'd learnt about objects never handled before, oak curved back settles, sets of Victorian chairs, burr walnut duchess dressing tables, grandfather clocks and Victorian sideboards, for which I was grateful, as the knowledge gained, *further liberated me from pine stripping, but long days of nothing began to get quite depressing. If things weren't already bad enough, fate then seemed to taunt us. Early one morning we chanced on a cabriole legged, oak lowboy idling away in a barn. Negotiations, however, were halted by the man's wife suddenly intervening, to declare in a broad Welsh accent, 'If that liddle table leaves y'ere. Then you can rest assured, so shall I!'*

I almost felt like saying to the man, 'Now's your chance,' but with her being rather a handsome woman, I knew the deal to be lost. That particular day was made even worse by finding on the final call, what seemed like a life saver, a fine taper-legged, three drawer dresser base, languishing under a Dutch barn. Trouble was, the man wouldn't take a penny less than £1400 for it. At the time we'd have been lucky to have got our money back.

Then came a change of luck. It was down to Trevor's persistence once again. The silence between him and the man leaning on his farm gate, that morning, had yawned into realms of embarrassment and I was about to suggest we leave him in peace, when Trevor asked, 'What happened to the dresser?'

'My brother's got it. Pride of place along his hallway.'

After another long pause, 'What happened to the rack?'

'Oh we've still got the rack. It's in that woodshed over yonder.'

'Can we have a look?'

We were in. The dresser rack was virtually buried beneath logs, with just the lively fretted frieze and cornice visible. The man said he'd clear a way to it and we'd be able to see it properly, if we returned after lunch the following day. Of course, following such a barren spell, I was eager to disinter it right there and then, but Trevor urged patience. Experience and instinct told him, we weren't about to lose this particular deal.

Driving away, he said, 'Dunner fret. 'Ee ooner go back on 'is word. Once these folks says something, they sticks to it. We'll be able to buy it.'

Which we did, the following afternoon and even got sent on to a neighbour's farm where we bought more, to finally drive home with the car absolutely laden.

Trevor said, 'If youda gone rushin' in last night we probably wouldna 'ave got all this other tack.'

I'd noticed that many of the farmers we called on, were actually keen to have a deal. They seemed genuinely frustrated when they couldn't. I suppose, with buying and selling livestock all their lives, it was in their blood.

Often as we drove along, Trevor would point out places of earlier successes. With all of it, now gone from the countryside for ever, it was actually quite depressing. On one dull grey, fruitless day, he said, 'Some mornings over the years, I've been sat there at my kitchen table, racking m'brains wondering where to go next. I think I've been along every lane up in these 'ills. You couldna get me lost. I knows them like the back of me 'and.'

Looking at his proffered hand and with not having a clue at the time, where we'd roamed on such a gloomy day, I asked, 'Where exactly are we, Trevor? Which way is north?'

'If I'da knowed you was gonner ask me that, I'da brung a compass.'

One morning, with the weather set fair, I suggested we pick up one of the monster Welsh mahogany chests of drawers, hoping it would lend us an aura, advertise success and give the appearance of us being winners, rather than just chancers. If we then happened to strike lucky, we'd just have to shove it in a shed somewhere. So, having paid the £15 for the incumbrance, now prone on the roof rack and me passing the drawers up for Trevor slide into place, he said, 'Hope you knows what yume doin. We used to chuck things like this over the 'edge. They wonner worth luggin' 'ome.'

Thankfully the tactic worked. At a smallholding mid-morning, I could see our burden was being eyed and with the farmer hardly likely to know its value, I wondered, would it have the desired impact? It did, for swinging a barn door open he answered Trevor's entreaties with, 'Any of this tack any good?'

By lunch time, having deposited our mahogany edifice in the barn for temporary storage, we left the man's yard, with a pine kitchen piece, comprising 3 cupboards above an all-drawer base; an elm dough bin; oak pig bench; pine kitchen table; curved-back settle; unusual oak food hutch and smaller items such as a wooden bushel measure, swan butter print, butter tub, milking stool, milk tin and cider costrel.

Success breeds success and it was decidedly gloomy as we headed Kingsland way absolutely laden, with the swaying load on the roof rack, being a good 5' high. A Volvo approached, obviously a dealer's car, unmistakable on account of its roof-length furniture rack. A flash of lights, was followed by a hand waving us down and I recognised Gay Walker emerging. For some reason she had one of the Belgian dealers with her, probably taking him to a call, where the asking price of an item had left her stumped. She scanned our load and asked a few prices, but with not being able to see any of it properly, didn't commit herself. Instead, out of Trevor's earshot, she said, 'John, I can understand the reason for you calling round the farms, but why do you take him with you?'

I answered, 'If you went rabbiting, wouldn't you take a ferret?'

'Good point,' she replied.

It sounded derogatory, I know, but the truth was, if it hadn't been for Trevor and his thick-skinned   persistence, I would not have been a quarter as successful. In fact, with the Irish travellers having had all the easy pickings, I would probably have given up after a few days.

Following a particularly lucky run, Trevor would go missing on a long, wet spell, getting himself bleary eyed in places like the Bullring Tavern. It gave me chance to send the residue stock on its way and thus build up a financial reserve. I also had my own calls to do and the books to keep up to date, which I dreaded as it was a frightening reminder, I was still not VAT registered. With the accountant still horribly blasé about the whole issue, I had started to put funds aside in a separate account, a cushion for when the inevitable big hit came. Also, with the shop doing so well I'd been able to reduce my mother's debt. She still received a share from my efforts, but keeping the fact secret, I'd been siphoning some of her tranche, to reduce the overdraft.

Once Trevor had caroused his way through the money, he'd be back, suggesting we hit the road again. With what I'd learnt in such a short space of time, however, it gave me the confidence to entertain the notion of attending the better antique auctions with the view to buying furniture, rather than, what had once been described as, just squitter. Their attraction was growing, for at least an auction provided the certainty of there being goods to buy, while our success relied on not much more than sheer chance. It was near end of day and like many before, one of slim pickings, when Trevor suggested, we return to one of his old calls. We were on our way back from the Welshpool area and would be passing a house where a particularly good clock, quietly ticked away on a cottage wall. He'd been after it for years, but thought it was at least worth giving it yet one more shot.

Being welcomed almost like an old campaigner, he beckoned from the doorway, suggesting I join him. We usually approached the houses alone, not wanting to appear mob-handed. Many's the time I'd watched from the car, amused at Trevor's remonstrations, looking so animated in the downstairs windows, then voice *ringing from up in the bedrooms, while I'd pondered on his chances of success.*

The old lady made us tea and her husband, a bit shaky to say the least, told us the battle for the clock was not to be resolved that day, it was staying put. It was a magnificent triple-weighted Viennese, walnut cased wall clock with the carved horse pediment, splendidly rampant.

Trevor went into his earnest entreaty, that they'd obviously heard before; saying he didn't go around begging goods. He then surprised me somewhat, offering £600 of what was my money for the purchase of it. They thanked him for such a generous proposition, but indicating the female making strange noises by the fire, explained the clock had been left to their granddaughter.

It was a job to put an age to her, for even though she noisily sucked a thumb as she rocked back and forth, she must have been at least 20. I noticed Trevor looking at her, weighing up the situation.

"Look! I inner bein' funny,' he said at last. 'But wouldn't you be better off banking the cash for 'er now? Dunner want to sound insulting, but the pair of you inner gonner last forever. What use is the clock to 'er then? First robbin' doorknocker ull probably 'ave it off 'er for fifty quid. Like I said, I inner bein' funny, but 'ow's she gonner know what it's worth? Look. I'll give you 700 quid right now. In cash.'

All attention was on the girl rocking back and forth and I was beginning to feel particularly uncomfortable.

When he followed it with, 'Just look at 'er. What use is the clock gonner be to a poor wench like that?' I started eying the door, ready to get out of there.

The long silence, broken only by sucking sounds and silky ticking of the clock, seemed endless. Suddenly, the girl's grandmother said, 'You're right. We'd be better off putting the cash in a savings account for her.'

The clock weights and pediment were removed and lifting it down from the wall, we carried it between us, very carefully, to be wrapped in blankets in the car. Going back to thank them, I noticed the wad of notes still on the table, but also a long, very fresh-looking rectangular patch on the cottage wall where the clock had hung all those years. I had very mixed feelings.

In the car I asked, 'Are you sure there's a profit in it? Seems an awful lot to pay for a wall clock.'

'It inner one of them piddly little two weighters---thisun's a three weighter. You probably ooner get the chance of another.'

'What about you? How much do you want out of it?'

'Get it sold first. We can sort that out later.'

As I'd noticed on the call his mother had taken me to, the success of at last hooking something they'd been after for years, seemed to mean more than the actual profit. I sold the clock for £850 to the dealer from across the street, for although he bought pine furniture, clocks were his speciality. Knowing how I'd come by the time-piece, he'd tried his best to chisel me down on the price.

'I paid £700 for it,' I told him. 'It was Trevor that actually did the deal.'

'What him? I thought he always begged the stuff.

'No. If he can see a quick profit, he won't leave a good thing behind.'

'You know it's right on the money?'

'Sorry, can't be helped.' I could see in his eyes, he'd have to buy it, couldn't possibly leave it behind, for the desire of owning such a rare item in pristine condition, outweighed all thoughts of profit. He did persist of course, but I refused to budge, knowing he'd capitulate, which he did. I had obviously read human nature, rather than the article, but as we carefully cradled it across the road, I wondered how Trevor, a man who couldn't read or write and without the aid of a shop to give him continual feed-back, had known how to rate this rarity?

When I told him of the £150 profit made, he said, 'Just gimmee fifty quid. That'll do.'

Another deal, remembered for prickly embarrassment was at a call over by Kington.

The white cottage at the end of a crazy-paving path could have been from a 19th century painting of some lost bucolic idyll. Trevor explained that the man generally didn't like callers such as ourselves knocking on his door; if he had anything for sale, he'd carry it to the gate. Trevor called out in his usual manner and eventually the owner of the cottage appeared.

Trevor greeted and asked if he'd managed to dig anything else out for sale.

The man growled, 'No and I never shall! Not to the likes of you, anyroad!'

'Oh, and why's that?'

'I'll tell you why,' he said, angrily pointing a finger. 'Last time you were here you bought the bureau.'

'That's right.'

'It was you and that other fella and I said I'd always promised it to your mother. To which you said, 'That's no longer possible, she's dead.'

The man looked absolutely enraged and I was all for heading back to the car.

He asked, 'How d'you think I felt when your mother turned up one day? Thought I was seeing a ghost!'

Obviously, there was no way out of this one. Not even for Trevor.

'I never said she was dead.'

'Yes you bloody well did!'

Feigning anger, 'No I never! I'm tellin' you now, I never said she was dead. If you remembers,--- what, I in fact, said was,------not that she was actually dead, but that 'er was the next thing to bein' dead. It just so 'appens, 'er made a miraculous recovery.'

Well the long and the short of it was, the man eventually went back inside to reappear carrying a jug and basin set; on the second trip a hanging oil lamp with shade and on the third, a wind-up gramophone with horn. It was a story you couldn't make up.

The very last deal accomplished when travelling with Trevor was in the village of Worthen, up by Shrewsbury. We were invited into the kitchen where a young girl was breast feeding her baby.

When suggesting, we might have chosen the wrong moment to call, the girl said breezily, it didn't bother her and her mother said, 'Dunner be so daft. It's just natural aint it.'

Dominating the whole of one wall was a Shropshire housekeeper's cupboard, with the circular face of a grandfather clock in the upper middle panel. I had a fair idea of its value, having had a hand in the sale of the one in the farmhouse, close to home. We tried our best, but they wouldn't sell it. We had to satisfy ourselves with a strange piece out in the hallway. It was an oak, five-foot-tall cabinet, on dumpy turned feet, whose double doors concealed *a bank of graduated drawers. It was obviously an early piece, for the doors were geometrically moulded and within, moulding divided each drawer into framed pairs of panels. What made it particularly unusual, was the drawer fronts had original painted swirled-frond decoration and tiny polychrome figures. It wasn't cheap, but up until then we'd had a blank day and so we bought it. Well more accurately, I did.*

The clock cupboard joined the list of a few other notable things we'd been unable to buy, the most frustrating having been in an absolute hovel up in the Mochdre hills above Newtown. The point-blank refusal to sell the small oak coffer, full of morning sticks in the wood shed had been bad enough, but what really irked was being taunted by the sight of the Queen Anne, oak cabinet on stand, top of the stairway, looking as if absolutely begging to be released from its squalid surroundings, remaining like a pedigree dog chained in a pigsty and the owner seeming to wallow in our exasperation. In vain hope, as I'd occasionally done before, I left the man one of my business cards.

CHAPTER FOURTEEN

At this point I decided to ring Mike, to tell him how far I'd progressed with the story and also attempt to pin down a few dates and ensure I'd got things in the right order. On telling him I'd just completed the section entitled, 'Travels with Trevor,' he said, that on his scanning of the notes, he remembered the parts regarding Trevor and his mother, for he'd found them amusing, but all that had occurred long before he'd started working for John Dodds. I told him I'd found a reference to another storeroom, quite a large stone building, a former smithy's workshop in Onibury and asked, did he have any idea when it had been taken on? He said he couldn't really help as all the stores had been given up, about the same time the whole operation became focused on the big shop in Old Street.

"I've found mention of a trip to Ireland," I said.

"Oh, that trip. He told me about it. He said he was heading west towards Sligo and was surprised by his phone ringing."

"What phone?"

"His mobile. He didn't think it would work outside of the UK."

"That can't be the trip I'm talking about. Mobile phones would hardly have been heard of, back in those early days at the cottage. What happened by the way?"

"It was one of his contacts, a chap called Roger. A bit of a rum bugger, but he had an eye for a good lot. I remember the piece, it was a tall, bow-backed settle. You'll probably see it mentioned in the notes. I think it was mainly pine, but the shaped sides and seat were sycamore. What made it a bit special, was its original green paintwork. I remember it well. Took some lifting because, with the weight of that sycamore and the flared skirt around the back, it was a bit of an awkward lump. It was in a load John lent to one of the dealers doing Olympia."

"Olympia?'

"Not the horse show, the antique fair."

"So are you saying, he bought it over the phone when he was in the middle of Ireland?"

"Yes, that's right."

"Sounds like a different person to the one I've just been reading about. Before you go, Mike, can I ask a favour?"

"Yes ask away."

"I'm struggling in places to put the things I've found, into the right order. Would you mind terribly if I put a pencil line through the details I've already covered? It would make the job a lot easier."

"Yes, don't worry about that."

"And make notes in the margins, of supposed dates and reminders to connect certain events? I must admit, I've done a fair bit of that already. Hope you don't mind."

"No, go ahead. The notes are there to be used, so do whatever helps."

"Thanks, Mike. Look forward to meeting up again soon."

I spent the rest of the day, solidly crossing through what I'd already covered and putting approximate dates in the margins, plus numbers to try and put some sort of order on how the various references were to be sequenced.

Then I found this. Something I'd missed.---*It had been a particularly foul day and our efforts had produced nothing. Trevor had rendered my mood all the more sombre, insisting on telling me of past successes. I don't know why it got to me, for I was sure he made half of it up, a suspicion confirmed by him telling me of the fantastic run he'd had door knocking on Anglesey. He said he'd bought that much furniture, they'd charged him freight when bringing it all to the mainland on the ferry. I felt too dispirited to tell him the last ferry probably crossed the Menai Straights over 100 years ago. Don't know why I let him get away with it. I should have really rubbed it in by asking, why hadn't he used the Menai Bridge? I suppose I felt too glum and didn't relish his outburst of anger at having his veracity challenged.*

I arrived back at the cottage and burdened with shopping, looked directly down, being mindful not to slip on the cobbles as rain was running down the path in rivulets. Out of the corner of my eye, I detected a movement. My son, having been got ready for bed, had wandered out through the kitchen door and stood there with arms raised to be picked up. Quickly dumping the shopping, I went back outside and scooping him up, felt all the frustrations and gloom of the day immediately leaving me. As I hugged him tight, pretending to chide him for getting wet, I wondered how I would find enough love in my heart to share it with the other little package soon due. I also wondered how I'd cope, leaving him behind for two weeks.

Looking further through the notes I found the following:---*It was good to see cousin John again and the bars he took us to were vibrant and absolutely glowing with life. The conversation, didn't just flow, it danced back and forth, from one to the other, interspersed with wit that had everyone rocking with laughter. I loved the architecture, for even through the Victorian period they'd continued building in the Georgian style, with the graceful terraces having tall sash windows and intricate fanlights above bold-painted doors.*

Suddenly, I knew where he was. He was describing Dublin. This was the trip to Ireland I'd mentioned to Mike.

He continued:---*But as the days went by, I felt more and more as if I'd had part of my innards cut out. I was missing my son that much, I could hardly bear to look at children his age. Hurting thus, it was hard to imagine how full of internal ache his mother must have felt, but there again, her whole being was slowly changing, taking on that splendid radiance some expectant mothers have.*

So at last, I now had a rough idea of when the old Smithy had been taken on, for he'd mentioned having had a deal with his friend Mark, viewing pine by torchlight in the new store, before departing at dawn, to take a few days off. From what I'd worked out previously, this had to be happening in 1981, meaning that the last deal with Trevor, where they'd missed the chance of the Shropshire housekeeper's cupboard, must have also been in that year. Meanwhile, 80 miles down the road, a group of dealers were featuring in Swansea Crown Court. receiving hefty fines and a year's saleroom ban, for operating an illegal knockout in the Ivy Bush Royal Hotel. At last, the pieces seemed to be fitting together. I assumed, there'd been no immediate reference to this in the notes, on account of John Dodds having been almost in another world, out door-knocking. He also of course, wouldn't have known at this point, about a certain rare four-poster bed that was soon to bring such a massive profit and crank up his credibility in the trade. I apologise for having got things in the wrong order, but at least the timing of events have been nailed down at last. Not easy when your using someone else's compositions, jottings and in certain cases, scribblings.

I'm assuming this next section, that refers to the fakes that seemed to be brought around each Spring, was written in that same year, but with most of it being retrospective, it was a job to know.

He writes:---*I got badly caught out by the oil paintings, so was on my guard when the Staffordshire figures did the rounds, followed by the ruby glass, then the bronzes. It was always the same story, 'My grandmother has left me this. I was wondering if it could be of any interest?'*

My dealer friend, Wes, happened to be in the shop, that's the old shop I'm referring to, when the man had returned, obviously with more fake oils to stitch me with. Wes was the dealer I'd sold the 3-leaf mahogany wind-out table to, for £45. He'd started specialising in paintings and apologising for being the bearer of such bad news, told me, 'It was better you know the truth;' the five paintings I'd bought were all fake. Removing one from its frame, I was shown where the photographic technique hadn't quite covered the original daub on the old canvas.

It was at this point, the shop bell went and there was the crook, the man in question, standing in the doorway.

I said, 'Wes, let me introduce you to the man who sold me these paintings.'

'Bastards like you need locking up---,' Wes boomed, but never got a chance to say more, as the man was off down the road like a rabbit.

Strange thing was, a BADA art specialist bought the paintings off me. On the one hand, I felt incredibly guilty, but on the other, with her being a member of the esteemed British Antique Dealers Association, I felt it was up to her to make her own mind up.

Sometime in the Autumn of what I'm assuming is 1981, John Dodds had had quite a large cheque bounce on him, courtesy of a

Leominster dealer. When seething about it and showing the worthless piece of paper to Leon, his friend had fished in his wallet, to produce its twin. 'Snap,' he said with a broad grin.

With car and trailer, they paid a visit next day and a few dealers manning the Leominster antique centre, watched open mouthed as they exited, bearing away stock equivalent to the amount owed. The cheque bouncer, a very well-spoken young man, was left thoroughly deflated on a near empty stand and from that point on, seemed to drift out of the business, more proof that antique dealing wasn't as easy as some made it look.

The following gives an idea of how the prices of the goods were gradually spiralling.

---*My strategy of using the profits gained from the bread-and-butter goods to invest in articles, I had only the faintest notion of, was certainly paying off, for I could feel my confidence growing. It came at a cost, however, as the pieces where I'd been a touch over ambitious, were beginning to build up in the store. Thank goodness, that on the more sought-after items, each Spring seemed to bring a price hike and by early Summer, if you'd not gone too mad, most of the previous year's flotsam tended to float away on the Spring tide.*

I discovered that his giving out of the odd business card on his Travels with Trevor, did actually pay dividends, for he wrote:---*One morning the phone went and a man with a distinct Welsh accent asked me to call at a house near Llanbister Road railway station. On arrival, I recognised the house and its occupant, remembered from when Trevor and myself had been on a particularly bad run. The house was to be sold and the man needed it clearing. Thankfully, he said he could manage all the household stuff, but wanted a fair price for the antiques. Although all was saleable, it was pretty mundane apart from a rather fine Georgian mahogany bookcase. It was of course, highly desirable, but for someone of my limited experience, it posed a problem. I know my dealer friend, Mike from Hereford had said, 'You'll never get stuck with a good bookcase,' but the truth was, I hadn't a clue what to offer. Too little and I risked the chance of losing the whole houseful and too much would have tied up most of my working capital, putting me out of action for a while. I desperately needed Trevor's guile. To give me time to think and build up a rapport, I began running through all the other goods, but it soon became apparent, the man's patience was beginning to wear thin. We were up in one of the bedrooms when he finally said, 'This all very well, but what about the bookcase?'*

I managed to wrap up a provisional deal on all the lesser furniture and back in the parlour asked, 'What figure did you have in mind?'

Usual reply, 'It's up to you. You're the antique dealer.'

I thought to myself, "Yes, an antique dealer, who other than having an innate alarm system, as regards paying too much, hasn't in fact, got a clue." I wrote two figures on my hand and revealing one, said, 'I suppose you were expecting that much?'

'Well no, I was expecting a little more actually.'

I breathed a sigh of relief, for his answer enabled me to reveal the second figure, indeed somewhat higher, but still well within the margin of safety. 'I'm glad you said that, for this how much I really intended to pay for it.'

I drove home, car stacked high with goods, feeling mighty relieved and rejoicing at now being slightly further along the learning curve.

He continues:---*A similar, if not so lucrative, drop of good fortune, landing out of the blue, thanks again to a business card, came from a farm up in the hills beyond Bishops Castle. The furniture stood jumbled, far wall of a lambing shed and I had to drag the mahogany wind-out table from under a low, corrugated iron lean-to. Nearby, a sheep dog, chained to a rotting trailer, listlessly wagged its tail. The poor thing, with sad eyed plea and fur as soft as thistle down, looked as if asking to be taken home with me and it was heart rending to disappoint him.*

Back at the shop, I did as usual and unloaded everything onto the pavement. It must have been a Thursday, for that's when a certain Worcester dealer always called.

He'd obviously needed a quick scan of the table top and weighing up the deal with it prone again, legs in the air like it had decided to die there, he said, 'Look, I'll buy it John, but while I'm down, calling at Leon's, could you get rid of all that sheep shit?'

It was filled up to the underside of the winding mechanism with a thick mat of dark green droppings.

The most memorable event of that year was of course the birth of my daughter, early September, in Shrewsbury Copthorn Hospital. I'd been up all night trying to help Anne through the excruciating spasms and in the murk of dawn, came one of the most awful sounds I'd ever heard in my life, a meaty snip of scissors. Out shot my daughter, eyes blinking, looking up at me as if asking, 'What happened. Where am I?'

When swaddled and passed to Anne, her tiny face was just visible and staring wide-eyed she gave a little hoot, bringing an exhausted hug of love and relief, as if all recent agonies had momentarily been forgotten.

We were playing Kidderminster that day, a tough fixture at any time, never mind being first of the season. I was of course asked how things had gone and received hearty congratulations, but not surprisingly, felt a little dazed and was slightly concerned I might let the side down. I had a quiet word with a mate of mine, Mike Davies, 'Don't know how I'll get on today, Mike. I've been up all night.'

Typical farmer, 'Dunt be so daft. Get stuck in. You'll be fine.'

We beat Kidderminster by the way.

So, the arrival of that particular little package, trumped beyond all measure, anything regarding antiques, including the amazing success, back in the Spring of that year, when buying the rare four poster bed. This must have been 1982 and as said, the dates at last, seemed to be slotting into place. The bed's sale had been noted by a few in the trade and as a result, John Dodds had the pleasant surprise of seeing its notoriety reflecting directly on him, attracting callers from higher up the antique pecking order. A few left business cards, writing on the back, details of latest things sought. One dealer from Bath, after buying a few items had said, 'I don't mess about with all that haggling nonsense. If I can see a profit, I just buy it. But if someone asks too much, they don't get a second chance. Even if they suddenly decide to fold on the price, I tell them, "Sorry. You obviously think it's worth what you've just asked, so don't let me stand in your way. You go for it, mate."'

He gave John Dodds a comprehensive list of items he was looking for and said, provided he remained loyal he'd keep him updated on latest trends and not divulge details to any others in the area. The man's name was Stuart and John Dodds didn't know it at the time, but it was the start of the designer phase, fuelled mainly by dealers from New York. Being armed with this knowledge, gave him the edge over his immediate rivals, plus the confidence to follow his instincts. At last, I felt I was coming to the point of metamorphosis, where a dealer that had been grubbing around, living hand to mouth, was suddenly transformed into one of substance.

He was still not VAT registered, mind you and the fear of it often kept him awake at night. I noticed a few references of yet more money being put into the kitty to help pay for the eventual day of reckoning. He was also still quietly paying off his mother's debt.

Meanwhile, I saw his transformation was not quite as immediate as I'd imagined, for he still bought a lot of the usual clutter when it came his way, for of course, old habits die hard. Even so, I could sense a confidence growing, for I read, when buying the usual slim-margin pine from a Clun dealer, he often chanced his arm on other items to further his knowledge. The man had expanded his business and was operating out of two massive farm buildings. From the notes, I gathered, he apparently hoovered up much of the pine that came into the area, but also, as if by magic, procured the occasional early lot and the odd interesting piece of an ethnic nature. Looking at the village's location on Google maps, I found it staggering that so much business could have been generated in such an out of the way place. John Dodds had surmised, he must have been getting a tip off from various traders, when loads were imminent, for with him not dealing directly with the Irish, how else could he have maintained such a vast stock level? Plus, where did the odd period piece come from? John, had surmised he must have blundered into the better lots when buying the pianos advertised for. Pianos, it seems, from being virtually unsaleable, were now desirable and descriptions such as straight strung, over-strung and underdamped crept into certain dealers' phraseology.

John had been happy to leave that particular market niche to those with the muscle and space to store the things, but as said, when calling there, he occasionally chanced his arm on other items to help him along the learning curve or sometimes on a piece that appealed, without him really knowing why. An example of the former was a Regency three leaf extending dining table and of the latter, a mahogany hallstand, so outlandish, it had a flared look of shock as if suddenly realising it was facing a firing squad. On receiving that inner jolt when first spotting it, he knew it would sell immediately, but the table didn't exactly fly out, on account of one of its leaves being stained pine, rather than mahogany. It did eventually sell, for not quite the profit he'd hoped on such an outlay, but in actual fact its purchase eventually proved quite fortuitous.

Fortune had often played a significant hand in John Dodds' career it seems, for I'd found quite a few instances in his writings where pure chance had given him the odd little boost. One example was nothing more than a visit up the road to the bakery.---*It was a corridor of a shop, with bread for sale far end. Payment however, was at the only till near the entry, where the baps, buns and cakes were displayed, bringing constant confusion over whose turn it was to pay. One of the old girls in there, used to shake that much trying to twist the ends of the inadequate tissue-paper wrapping, it made you want to snatch the loaf and say, 'Just give it here! Forget the wrapping!' Patience can be a virtue, however, for while the poor old dear with white fluff on pink scalp fiddled with the paper, I noticed the door behind her had been left ajar. Beyond, standing facing me in the corridor, was something of potential interest and after a word with the manageress, I managed to strike a deal and came away that day, owner of a crispy white loaf and of a 2' 3" Georgian oak chest of drawers. I immediately returned with the car to collect the little gem, before she changed her mind.*

I'd seen elsewhere in the notes, that three-foot-wide, was thought to be highly desirable if buying a period chest of drawers, no matter what wood it happened to be and so one in oak of such a diminutive size, I guessed, would not have hung around for long. He wrote:---*The unusual lots were essential to maintain trade interest in the shop.*

Regarding another occasion of smiling good fortune, some lead garden urns had come his way and with one having a handle adrift, he'd decided it best to have it repaired before offering the pair for sale. Obviously, working in lead was a dying art, but he was told of a retired general builder who'd operated from a ramble of sheds and workshops in an area in town known as East Hamlet, who supposedly still retained the art.

He was a lovely old boy, Mr. Wheel, but other than supply the name of the plumber who had worked for him, had said, unfortunately he couldn't help. Not help? His premises was an untouched, absolute cornucopia of ancient artefacts: Georgian lead drainage hoppers with cast floral decoration; intricate cast iron cistern brackets; lead water trough; a magnificent lavatory pan with overall blue and white floral decoration; a massive Georgian weather vane; a huge brass bell; an ancient painted pub sign, sporting a raven; the works of a tiny turret clock; a small sink in its cast iron stand; numerous stacks of decorated tiles and countless other items amassed over the years. It took three journeys to clear it all.

John Dodds writes,---*Gay Walker happened to be in the shop when I returned with the final load. She immediately homed in on the weather vane, old clock works and pub sign. I had originally intended to put the sign, with its slightly naïve painting, aside for my new contact Stuart, but as Gay was first on the scene, it was only fair I should conjure up a price. Looking almost hurt from the impact she said, 'Surely you can do better than that, John,' and after recovering, fair play, she made quite a sporting offer. Noticing my air of stubborn insouciance, often present when a dealer has virtually begged the goods, my mother had a quiet word, 'Let her have them, John. Don't be greedy. It seems like a fair offer and she has been good to you over the years.'*

I of course gave in and then came the worry I might be getting a bit big sorted. I chastised myself, for it hadn't been that long previously, I'd bought a latish oak press off that same Miss Walker and driving home had pulled into a gateway, needing to climb onto the roof rack in a mad panic, to check and reassure myself I hadn't bought a marriage. So, I thought, not such a big shot really and don't be getting too ahead of yourself, for you know what awaits those that do.

There was another lucky deal that must have occurred in this same year, for he'd said, he was mindful to put some of the items aside, out at the cottage, for his new contact from Bath. The widow of a local dealer had asked him to clear two large sheds adjoining her Brimfield property. Her late husband had often been the buyer of what would have been considered years ago, items not wise to bid on, stacks of old frames, wardrobes, Victorian mahogany chests of drawers, top halves of linen presses, plus countless linen press trays and the bottom half of a tallboy, obviously with the aim of creating something desirable in those sheds of his.

It took roughly ten visits, one per week, to clear it all and most sold to his friend Graham, doing with it, exactly what the previous owner had always intended. The mahogany commode armchairs sold to a Warwick trader who bought them for the burgeoning Italian market, but the maple frames, ship wool-works and samplers from amongst the dusty stacks of old frames, were secreted in the shed at the back of the cottage for when Stuart next called.

The better Staffordshire figures, silvered glass candlesticks, large painted tea tins, ship diorama, spongeware, Wedgewood cabbage pattern plates, majolica and early creamware, bought when visiting local shops and salerooms, also joined the little cache. The knowledge he'd gained, gave him a slight edge; for the time being at least.

As proof of the expanding business, I saw mention of yet another store, this one being a long concrete tube of a room in an old industrial complex on the northern outskirts of town. Proof that his status might also be increasing, came when Peter, the esteemed dealer from Leominster had had a quiet word about a Queen Anne walnut chest, on offer at a Saturday house sale in Luston, a village on the back road to Leominster. He was now in the clear as regards attending auctions, having served his year's ban following the Carmarthen incident, but not surprisingly, was still wary of re-joining the cut and thrust of the ring. Being caught a second time would have earnt him a prison sentence.

John Dodds had been quite flattered at being given such a responsibility, but the price he'd been left, made him sick at heart. Four years earlier, thanks to an advert in an obscure local paper, he'd had the luck to chance upon a sale, no other traders had got wind of. Quite incredible really, for this was the third time he'd been thus blessed. Being on a Saturday in the rugby season, he'd had to view it and leave Anne there to do the bidding, before racing back for the 2.30 kick off, of what was fortunately a home fixture.

They'd won, he'd showered and was anticipating just the one pint, the one that hardly touches the sides, before having to rush off to rescue his maiden fair, when all such notions were dashed.

I'll hand you over to the man himself:---*I was called to the phone and heard Anne's quavering voice, 'I've been stuck in a field with all this furniture and I'm scared. There was this man hovering about. He said he'd help me lift it all to the barn, but I'm scared. What did he have to mention the Yorkshire Ripper for?'*

'What? What's the Yorkshire Ripper got to do with it?'

'He says they still haven't caught him.'

'You're in the farmhouse I take it.'

'Yes. I'm using their phone.'

'Stay there, I'm coming to get you.'

It was in the back lanes over Squilver way, west of the Long Mynd and took an hour to reach her. She had bought the lot for virtually nothing, including the William and Mary walnut chest. Although a murky colour, probably thanks to years of quiet calm in smoky surroundings, it was in otherwise original condition, retaining its handles, bun feet and D moulding, plus the patterns of stringing and veneers could just be detected through the grime.

Standing there in Luston with a price from Peter for a far inferior model, quite plain and with feet missing, I realised I'd parted with the one four years earlier, for a quarter of its true value. I actually felt quite sick. I bought the thing, against the usual suspects, but sent a message asking for Peter to collect it. I couldn't bear the thought of even lifting it into the car.

A quick check on the internet, regarding the Yorkshire Ripper still being at large in the Autumn of 1979, helped me establish the date of the Luston sale, as probably being in 1983.

There were quite a few descriptions of loads arriving at Leon's, as his shop had become a Mecca, or should I say Lourdes, for the Irish Travellers. They would arrive with their brand-new Volvos piled high and some even rattled into sight with what looked like, mobile bonfires on tow behind. I'll just give you two instances, written by the man himself.

---I'd heard a fresh load had arrived at Leon's and so walked down the street to see if there was anything of interest. I recognised the big white van pulled up onto the pavement, which confirmed John, the dealer from Clun must have been given a tip off of the imminent arrival. How else could he have beaten me to the load? Leon was across in the pub car park adding the last items to his list. The furniture was strung out in rows and dotted here and there were lamps, Staffordshire figures, platters, Britannia metal tea services, jam pans, warming pans, copper kettles and clocks. I wandered across, not bothering to look at the pine, as I knew I'd missed the chance of it, but thought there might be at least one thing to reward my effort of wandering down the hill.

It lay hidden beneath a rectangular American wall clock, but I could tell from the hewn stumpy legs what it was and I walked back over to the shop and waited. The Irish, having been paid, went on their way and Leon commenced selling the pine furniture, walking along the rows, adding a few pounds here and there to the purchase prices on his list and when all was done, he asked if there might be anything I wanted. I enquired about a couple of flow-blue meat platters, but checking his list, Leon said they'd been sold and then I asked about my only remaining hope, the little bench beneath the prone wall clock.

'No I don't think he wants that,' and seeing him about to shout across and ask whether my opposition, did indeed want the cobbler's bench, I said, 'Leon, he's had his chance and obviously didn't see it. So, how much is it?'

'It's fifteen quid, mate.'

213

'I'll buy it. Help me over to the shed with it.' We popped it into the garage he rented off the pub. It was normally the resting place for the end of day leftovers, for the problem with buying off the Irish, apart from the usual stress, was the fact they expected you to buy it all, bad with the good, whether split top, wrong leg, worm eaten or stained with engine oil. If you didn't, they took their wares elsewhere. The dag-end deals took up a fair deal of storage space and soon a huge barn out near Onibury needed renting to accommodate the burgeoning accumulation. Obviously as time went on, low end dealers, or those seeking out bits for restoration, climbed their way across it, delving deep, but even so, the pile kept growing. Keeping tabs of what it had all cost must have been a nightmare.

The other Leon episode I've included from about this time, was an occasion when John Dodds had actually managed to arrive before any rival dealers. Sometimes as many as five could be waiting and on one memorable morning, a Victorian Canterbury had been virtually pulled apart by two Devon rivals squabbling over who had spotted it first.

---I waited in the shop, watching from the window, as Leon haggled with the three animated Irishmen haranguing him. He nipped back in for something and I said, 'I don't know how you cope with them.'

With a broad grin he replied, 'Three on to one, mate, but I'm still winning.'

It was all the usual fare apart from an oak dairy table with sycamore top. The two main drawers flanked three tiny middle drawers, two above one. Its top had a generous overhang and unlike most, it wasn't too deep from back to front, so it almost had the look of a dresser base. The first one I'd bought had been in a load off Mrs. Lockyer, way back in the time of the old shop and had been of such massive girth, I'd had to cut it from back to front, after which it sold instantly.

I was paying and noticing the Irish lads were leaving, called out, 'See you next week.' As you can imagine, being regulars, I'd vaguely got to know them.

'Oh no,' says the one and on walking closer, confided, 'We're away to Rathkeale. Tis all very sad.'

'Why what happened?'

'He was a cousin of mine and he'd always been a bit prone to the odd mood. Well, he tried to do away with hisself. Cut tru his own wrist. They got him into the car and were rushing him to hospital, but half way there, the thing ran out of petrol and he bled to death. Very sad. We're all away to his funeral.'

A few weeks later, I saw the same trio down at Leon's and asked how all had gone and the one replied, 'Twas all very sad. We were at the wake and another cousin of mine, ---he'd had a terrible amount to drink, far too much for his legs. The tumble down the stairs broke his neck? We were all after staying for another funeral.'

'Sounds like you're lucky to make it back alive.'

'I know. Tis all very sad.'

I watched them leave, all three illiterate, prone to drinking themselves silly and yet, there they were, driving away in two brand-new Volvos, while mine was distinctly second hand. They were as free as birds and yet I had the daily rigours of the shop to cope with.

John Dodds then went into descriptions of frustrations thus experienced in being burdened with a shop, but rather than trouble you with that at this point, with it being of a lighter nature, I'll include just this one little episode.

---She was a lovely old girl; Mrs Campbell-Dixon from over Stretton way. With having the upkeep of two horses draining her

215

resources, she'd often pop in and ask me to call. When first taking on the new shop, I'd bought a pretty chiffonier and glazed top corner cupboard off her. Out of ignorance, I'd paid too much for the Victorian corner cupboard, but it was all part of the learning curve and it went in the end. I had a mental picture of what was in her house and when satin walnut became saleable, I was able to call and do a deal on the bedroom suite she'd begged me to buy on a previous visit.

Trouble was, she always seemed to call near five o-clock, by which time I was usually keen to lock up and go home. The dear lady was running out of things to sell, but had a free spirit about her and an infectious laugh and so I didn't like to be unkind. One time when I'd been there with my son, she'd entertained him while I carried items to the car and I don't know what game she'd invented, but he was in absolute fits of laughter; well in fact the two of them were. It sounded like music.

So, come five thirty and feeling hungry, having listened to all the items that might or might not have been of interest, I just wanted to politely ease her out. With a sigh of relief, I finally succeeded, but then the shop bell went again. Popping her head around the door, she asked brightly, 'Did I ever show you the lamp in my back passage?'

'No, Mrs. Campbell-Dixon, I don't believe you ever did.'

I did call later that week and bought a couple of things of little merit, but then let her talk me into buying a mirrored wardrobe. It was a good example of its type, but not a thing I wanted to burden myself with. From her imploring look, I could tell she'd probably just been hit with a vet's bill, so I gave in, saying those fatal words. 'Oh, go on then.'

It was only when I pulled it from the alcove that I found it had been cut in half. Skilfully done, even to the point of having metal pegs to locate top to bottom, but cut none the less. At least we had no

216

problem getting it into the back of the shop. It became quite a useful storage space, obviously for coats, but also for wrapping paper, bubble wrap and piles of completed invoice books. Yes, wrapping paper. Gone were the days when customers left with purchases wrapped in newspaper, looking like they'd just bought a bag of chips.

I'd wondered why John Dodds had been beavering away and yet splitting all the profits with his mother. Being a dutiful son seemed quite admirable, but only up to a point, for from what I could ascertain, now the cottage had been renovated, his mother was hardly ever in the shop. There had been the occasional visit, but most of her time was spent in the north. Then in the Spring of that next year, I saw mention of two deals that redressed the balance somewhat. First was the clearance of the offices of the old Co-op building in Carnforth.

He wrote:--- *And so one Friday eve, I and the family went north, as I needed to see what mother had become so excited about. At first sight, when wandering the floors of the building, I must admit, I was not exactly overwhelmed. True, there were numerous mahogany counters and a massive dinner service with the company logo on the back, but apart from a couple of smokers bow armchairs, a rather too polite looking oak table, a bent-wood stick stand and six oak art nouveau style dining chairs with drop in seats, all the other furniture was built in, being drawer units and cupboards. I didn't want to seem ungrateful, but it looked like a lot of hard work.*

I noticed his mother's spirit didn't seem to have been dampened, mind you, for where he saw mahogany counters and drawers, she saw pine desks with polished mahogany tops. He tried to explain that the trade didn't really care for a pine and mahogany mix, to which she'd answered, it wouldn't matter, for they would sell privately.

---*Mother asked me, 'Exactly how many pine, knee-hole desks have you found to date?' To which I replied, 'Just that partners desk we bought down in Pembrokeshire.'*

'You see! For some reason, they hardly ever made the things. These will fly out.'

I had to hand it to her, her enthusiasm was contagious, having already a man on hand keen to help, plus she'd cajoled a retired joiner into doing the tricky work. One by one, the desks were delivered south, free of charge, in the back of a massive truck, wrapped to lie on the scrap iron being delivered to the South Wales foundries. The pine was a beautiful pencil grain, the mahogany tops were silky and she was right, they flew out. I sold them all privately.

The second deal from the north, came from a house in a Cumbrian village just south of Kendal. They were asked to clear the whole contents, most of which was mundane pine and shipping furniture of the instantly saleable variety, but of special interest was the long pine farmhouse table and then strangely, two items that had only been given a cursory glance when pricing everything to tender the offer.

---It was only when I pulled the aged cover off the sofa, that I realised I'd bought a buttoned-back Chesterfield for £2. It was a bit sad in the seating area, but I decided to keep it, using it in the front room of the cottage, until I could find someone to reupholster it. When I prised the greasy kitchen unit away from the wall, I got an even bigger surprise, for when I knocked the spurious cupboard doors off, I was amazed to find I'd inadvertently bought a Georgian pine dresser base for a fiver. The shelves above had been included in the deal. They didn't belong, but even so, they were decent pine wall shelves, grooved to retain rows of plates and had an attractive cornice.

Back in the shop, I was pleased that it happened to be Gay Walker first on the scene and I sold her the earlier bits of pine, plus the table, dresser base and wall rack.

Looking ahead in the notes I could see things were heading towards a huge unwanted crescendo and was eager to plough straight ahead and deal with it, but realised before I could, details of a certain meeting had to be given, as chancing upon that person, was the prelude to that potentially life changing event.

First however, I realised, it was this same Spring, John Dodds had had a bit of a lucky run, in of all places, Clun. The first was at a farm on the left, as you approach from the Craven Arms direction. He describes them as being, a marvellous family, Mr. and Mrs. Collins, selling a few items prior to moving to a new location near the castle. John didn't bother asking why they hadn't called in the local dealer who'd been doing so impressively lately.- --*Why muddy the waters when we were getting on like a house on fire? I felt as if I'd known them for years and leaving my son in the care of Mrs. Collins's sister, could hear his laughter clearly ringing out, even when I and the good lady herself, were up in a far room, dealing for earthenware, cream bowls and jugs in a row beneath the oak dresser base.*

He also bought numerous treen items, a pig bench and various pieces of furniture, that came to quite a car load by the end of the morning and as they required cash, he'd walked to the cupboard in the wall, Barclays outlet still operating at the time. Apart from the warmth he felt towards the family, the call was largely memorable for what he couldn't actually buy, the oak dresser base, an oval slipware dish and yet another of those Shropshire housekeepers' cupboards with a grandfather clock in the upper section.

They recommended him to another family needing a house clearing and the luck continued, as these told him of a house, where following a fire, part of the roof had gone and rotted floors had collapsed. The old boy who'd once lived there, a relative of theirs, had passed on peacefully a while back and John Dodds was told to just go help himself to whatever he could find.

They said, the man had lived there with his sister and the place had been like creeping into a sooty cavern. One of the nurses who'd cared for the old girl before she died, said that when the brother had paid a hospital visit, he'd slapped his hat down, end of bed and asked, 'Now what's up uv ya owd girl?' Finally, when leaving, he'd been completely oblivious to the ring of soot, left on the bed cover, where his hat had been.

When entering and climbing over fallen joists and floorboarding, looking for anything worth carrying away, John Dodds had rooted out a detritus covered, pine washstand and wall shelves from the scullery and looking up saw, teetering above the abyss, a perfectly preserved pine chest of drawers with shaped gallery.

---*I carefully ascended the narrow stairway and stared across the void at a potential £35, one hell of a good day's pay, just sitting there waiting to be picked up, but how was I to reach it without falling amongst the wreckage of what had once been the kitchen? Parts of the floor clung on at a precarious angle around the perimeter of what had been a bedroom and very carefully, testing each portion for strength, I waited until loose plaster had finished rattling below, before putting my full weight on it. Having finally made it to the chest on the far wall, I thought, 'Now what?' Tipping the piece onto its side, I edged backwards dragging it after me, one step at a time. I imagined the headlines, 'Local dealer breaks his neck attempting to retrieve painted pine chest.' Such ignominy! Not 18th century oak, mahogany or walnut. I'd be remembered, for snuffing it, while trying to extricate nothing more meritorious than a piece of Victorian pine bedroom furniture. Anyway, I did manage to get it out of there and later, rooting in the shed, found where the two double brass and iron beds had been stowed following the fire and general ruination. One was badly scorched, but not beyond saving. No-one seemed to know how the fire had started.*

Now finally, we come to the fateful meeting. It was at a Saturday sale at Lydham. John Dodds had bought a few of the outside lots, a pig bench, pine settle and the like and was waiting for the better furniture, never sold until all the small items on the front table had been auctioned. Near the food hatch, back of the room, he happened to fall into conversation with a dealer who was also waiting for certain lots. They spoke a little about business and the quirk of fate that had led them into the trade, but it was when making comparisons of early mistakes, that it became clear, this meeting would be remembered as being significant.

---He introduced himself as, Ron Baker and told me he traded from Montgomery, renting what had once been a warder's cottage, remnant of a 19th century prison.

I realised, this referred to the grand, long abandoned, Victorian scheme George had mentioned on the day I'd been regaled with the Ben Evans' stories. Anyway, I digress. Back to John Dodds.

I told Ron about the travails of renovating my own cottage and as it became obvious, we were both being quite candid as regards our antique dealing skills, I divulged my railway carriage oak coffer mistake, my drawer-less mule chest encounter and how I'd been lucky to climb out of a deal where one of the table leaves had been pine, not mahogany.

Ron asked, 'Out of interest, how much did you pay for that table?'

When I told him he muttered, 'The robbing bastard! You didn't happen to buy it off a certain John from Clun, did you?'

I said that I had and he told me how he'd been unmercifully bid in the nuts, on account of the table having had a wrong leaf. Well from that moment on, I seemed to be his new best customer. With him being almost on home territory, I let him bid on what he wanted and when he dropped out on a couple of the better bits, I took over and bought them. He told me, he made his living from house clearances and would give me a ring when he chanced on the next good deal.

It suddenly dawned on me; I'd struck gold. I'd inadvertently discovered where the better pieces from Clun had been coming from. I'd chanced on the source, but just to make sure, I told him of a few other things bought from John of Clun and found, Ron had been the supplier of every single one of them.

Suddenly remembering I said, 'There was even a crazy hallstand.'

'You didn't buy that thing, did you?'

'Yes, I loved it.'

That did it, we were almost best mates.

I had quite a number of deals with Ron from then on, but to ensure being first there, needed to drop everything the minute the phone went. Much of the stuff was shipping furniture and ordinary pine, but there were also some amazing purchases, like the pair of Georgian barrel-backed alcove cupboards; the long set of chemists' drawers, with glass handles and labels intact; large white cream pails; white rectangular butter and margarine slabs; small Georgian mahogany kneehole desk and numerous items of 18th century oak and mahogany. I was not always first there, of course and on one occasion had to listen to chapter and verse of what I'd missed, but on looking at the leftovers, saw a stack of Rogers, Elephant pattern plates, c 1830.

'Oh, he took all the Willow pattern, but didn't want those,' Ron said.

It was one of those ten-pound deals worth a hundred. They were added to the goods, saved for Stuart of Bath.

The only casualty of all this seemed to be my relationship with Anne. She became more and more ratty at my leaving whenever receiving a call from Ron Baker. It was bad enough when it was at seven in the evening, but when I sometimes went missing for half of Sunday, I'd pay the price for the next two days. I of course tried to explain what it meant to us financially, for with not having the money or contacts to deal in the same artefacts once they'd gone higher up the chain, being first there to buy goods fresh on the market was essential, but I began to feel we were drifting apart. The more my knowledge and expertise increased, the more I seemed to be leaving her behind. I suppose, being stuck out at that cottage didn't help. I'd have to buy her a car, but before that I realised, I now desperately needed a van.

At this point I realised from the notes how close I was to the crunch week. If John Dodds could have envisaged what lay ahead, he'd have done just as his friend Leon had wryly suggested, but I'll leave that quote until the relevant point in the story. First comes the fact, a van was indeed bought, the first new vehicle he'd ever owned. I noticed, that apart from it making life easier, he'd carried on dealing in much the same way, but then realised this must have been the year he'd made his first visit to the Isle of Man, not a great distance physically, but a huge one emotionally, as for the first time, he'd be returning to the land of his birth.

It had been at his mother's instigation, reasoning that with his grandfather being in his nineties, he wasn't going to live much longer and deserved the chance to see his grandchildren. Also of course he'd be seeing his father, a man he hardly knew. The family had split when he'd been two and a half and he'd only seen him fleetingly, twice since then.

I'm guessing the month was August, although the notes don't actually say, but as the weather was described as glorious and his daughter had taken her first tentative steps there before her first birthday, it must have been then or perhaps the last week in July. A few pieces of furniture were chanced upon for virtually nothing, plus a deluxe double-decker goffering iron and three majolica platters, bought reasonably from a shop in Ramsay; a bull-headed cheese dish from a place in Peel; two generous high backed Windsor chairs, bought from the Ramsay general auction and best of all, from the same sale, a thick seated primitive armchair that shouldn't really have left the island. Even though worthy of a folk museum, it had failed to sell at the previous Crystals' Friday auction. A porter bought it for him for £40 and apologised for having had to pay £15 apiece for the other two armchairs. Needless to say, Anne had not been best pleased with his endeavours, but he'd tried to reason, the time he'd spent rooting a few things out had been minimal and if people left gold nuggets lying about, he could hardly be blamed for gathering them up. Her mood did soften, mind you, when they used the chairs while enjoying a picnic on the lower slopes of Snaefell.

It might have all seemed like a fun way of making one's way in life, but beneath it all was the lingering dread of the VAT. His accountant had still done nothing about his registration and his turnover had gone so far beyond the limit, he'd felt petrified of notifying the authorities, for fear of them seizing everything he owned. All the tales he'd been told regarding customs officials had been terrifying, as if they'd been more interested in administering penny pinching rules and exacting retribution, rather than simply gathering taxes due.

He wrote down his thoughts at the time.---*Anne and I were up in the hills looking across at Cumbria. It seemed that close in the clear evening light, you could almost imagine people being visible, busying themselves like ants, doing their daily rounds. Here on the island felt like a sanctuary, a safe haven, but I realised I'd soon be back across, joining those ants and my heart was full of dread. There of course had to be a day of reckoning, but I feared for the future of my family. Would everything we'd striven for, be taken from us?*

He actually described feeling physically sick, at the thought of having to return to the churning over of such ordinary goods just to make a living; waiting down at Leon's for the next heap of scruffy pine to arrive and hauling home things of limited merit from Saturday sales. His hope of buying just the better lots, was yet all but a dream, as he still didn't have the capital and sufficient knowledge to compete with the more experienced dealers.

Ron Baker still came up with the odd good piece and on one occasion had shown him photos of a bedroom suite with marquetry inlay, that could definitely be bought, but he'd been cautious, for the clients wanted £1200 for it.

---*I was so sick of the run of the mill, I told him, 'Just buy the thing. It's not really my taste, but if I can't sell something of that quality, I might as well give up.'*

It was duly bought and he sold it from the chapel to one of the Chester dealers.

As time moved on to Christmas and the year beyond, it seems he'd recovered from his sickness at heart and had carried on trading in bulk, while selling the better items that suited the American designer trade, to Stuart and the more interesting pieces of mahogany and oak furniture to another friend, Mark Rowen. The latter bought all the pine that could be given the Georgian touch, plus items such as one-piece top tripod tables; or the occasional version with bird cage mechanism allowing the top's rotation on vase shaped stem; or even more occasionally, a table with knee adornment of acanthas, shell or harebell carving.

The pine went to Mark's American customers, the oak and mahogany to his London trade contacts. He, like Stuart, gave useful feedback as regards what made one item worth significantly more than, what to an untrained eye, looked virtually the same. It was Mark who showed him how to detect whether a wine table had started out as such, or had just been a conventional top, later turned on a lathe. To form the shallow dish necessary, the turning process when faking, often exposed the tiny end marks of the attaching screws of the tilt mechanism beneath. A dead giveaway. Also a true Georgian one-piece-top wine table would show slight shrinkage across the grain, not noticeable to the eye, but a tape measure across the grain and then along it, ought to show up roughly an eighth of an inch difference. All these little tips were arming John Dodds for the future.

He was still stuck with the cut wardrobe, mind you, but had put it to another use, for its copious bottom drawer had provided the perfect resting place for his daughter.---*I did find her a Georgian cradle, but even in those most tender months, she showed signs of knowing her own mind, for the little madam definitely preferred the drawer. A customer bustling about in the shop, had requested to take a look in the back room and walking through, asked, 'So what have we in here?' Her drumming footsteps through the short passage suddenly stopped. 'Oh my goodness, it's a baby!'*

As said, Christmas came and went and late May they revisited the Isle of Man. Again, John had found the trip lucrative and also discovered part of himself, realising that certain ways of doing things, plus much of his sense of humour, he'd inherited from his father. The notion of monthly trips back to the island, was flirted with and seemed idyllic, but with the trade not set up the same as in England, having nowhere near the frequency of stock replenishment, he realised it wouldn't pay.

Again John Dodds felt a mortal dread at the thought of returning to the fray in England. In fact, it could almost be described as a depression, for a huge cloud of worry followed him about and invaded his sleep. He was right to worry, for we finally come to that momentous week.

CHAPTER FIFTEEN

---*It was a Monday morning and I was down at Leon's, watching while he bought the latest load, hauled out from the back of a massive wagon parked across the road in the pub car park. A dealer from East Anglia arrived and alighting from his van said, 'Hey, mate. There are two VAT inspectors up in your shop.'*

My blood ran cold and I said, 'You're joking.'

'Believe me, I wouldn't joke about a thing like that, mate.'

Absolutely trembling and probably ashen in colour, I returned to the shop.

Mother said, 'Ah, here he is.'

The two inspectors were quite young and explained they'd been asked to tour the town, making enquiries in all the shops regarding VAT status and annual turnover. The limit at the time was about £19,000 and I admitted, that not only was I over that figure, but also, was not VAT registered.

Answering their polite enquiry regarding annual turnover, I admitted to the handling of £130,000 worth of goods in the previous financial year. They both looked stunned.

Stifling a laugh, the one said, 'No you must have got it wrong. We need to know your annual turnover, not the turnover since you first set up in business.'

'Honestly, it was £130,000.'

'What from this little place?'

'Well, I also sell things from off the pavement and from a bit of a shed.'

'So why are you not VAT registered?'

'I've asked my accountant countless times to register me, but he doesn't seem to listen. I feel like strangling him sometimes.'

'You don't need an accountant to register for VAT, you can do it yourself.'

'Well I know that now, but by the time I eventually realised, I was in it, way over my head and absolutely terrified.'

'Are you certain you turn over that amount?'

'Yes I've the books to prove it.'

'Can we see them?'

'Bit difficult right now as they're out at the cottage. I was working on them at home over the weekend.'

While the one asked the questions, the other took notes. At that point the shop bell went and giving a quick glance, the one inspector said, 'You'd better go ahead and deal with him, we can wait.'

It was Luffy. 'Luffy,' I muttered. 'I've got two VAT inspectors in the back of the shop,' thinking being forewarned, he'd do a *runner. He didn't, he just shrugged. So even Luffy, ducking and diving with deals out the back of a van, was VAT registered. I felt like a complete chump.*

When he'd gone, I locked the front door and put the closed sign in the window. Still inwardly trembling, I returned to the inquisition and divulged the fact, I'd been that terrified of the possible consequences success had delivered, I'd been putting money aside to pay for the fateful day.

'Sorry, I don't quite understand,' said the main inquisitor.

'Well I've been working out each month, what I'd owe on the antique's special scheme, if actually registered and I've been putting the money aside.'

'Let me see, if I've got this right. Your last year's turnover was £130,000?'

I nodded.

'And even though you're not registered, you've been putting money aside, as if you were registered.'

'That's right.'

'This is bizarre.'

I'd obviously inadvertently pushed my business beyond the bounds of wildest expectation, for they both looked stunned. 'Maybe it is bizarre, but it's the truth.'

They summed up by saying, they would hand all the information to their boss and it would be up to him to decide what happened next.

If the decision was to back date the tax for 6 years, as was their right, I had the money saved. If they slapped a fine on me, then I'd just have to find the money somehow, but if they charged VAT on the whole of my turnover, rather than just on the profit, as allowed under the special scheme for antiques, then I would be instantly bankrupt. I spent the rest of the day, half relieved that I'd been forced to grasp the nettle at last, but the other half of me was petrified.

Then the phone went. It was one of the VAT inspectors again. He said, they had mislaid their notebook in one of the shops, had it been in mine? I had a quick look around and answered truthfully, 'No.'

'In that case, I'm afraid we'll have to question you once again. The appointment details will be sent in the post.'

When I rang my accountant with the dreadful news, he said with unfamiliar urgency, he'd meet me out at the cottage that evening, to advise on how to deal with the coming meeting. He had a grave look as we discussed matters in the kitchen that night and although the place was still a little draughty, the room was fairly cosy, for we'd had a wood burner installed and it was going full blast.

The following morning, I discovered our black cat, its flattened face frozen in a grizzly, last look of agony, dead in the lane. Anne was especially saddened, for as a tiny kitten, on his very first night in the cottage, he'd caught the huge rat that had been plaguing us. We'd repeatedly tried to trap the rodent, but it had found a way of stealing the bait without getting caught and the baited cage, it had ignored completely, preferring to nibble at food stains on baby's bibs and gnawing at the soap in the sink. Some nights it sounded as if it was using the kitchen furniture as an obstacle course, until that very last leap when Clarkie had nailed him. That was the name Anne had dubbed the little ball of fur, for even as a kitten, his insouciant manner had reminded her of Clark Gable, but now sadly, the full-grown cat lay alongside the rat, buried in the garden.

On the Wednesday, things were about to get decidedly worse.

---*Ron Baker had told me about a house sale over by Aberystwyth and suggested we both go in my van. I was aware, that at times, Ron supplemented his living by receiving payments from the knockout, but told him, as for me, it would be out of the question. I was in enough trouble as it was. If I got caught in the KO, as it was known for short, my antique dealing days would surely be over. He told me not to be so fatalistic, but I answered, 'You'd be bloody fatalistic in my situation! If you want to have a deal, end of sale, then go ahead, but I shan't be joining you.'*

The auction was held in the music room of an impressive Georgian house set in its own grounds. The offerings were rather sparse considering the grand feel of the place and there was surprisingly little that interested me. There were a few pieces of period furniture, but as the ring usually dominated their purchase in catalogue auctions over in border country, not wanting to stir things up, I hadn't paid them much attention. There were a few interesting prints, a pair of slightly offbeat Georgian chairs that I thought might slip through the net, a celadon dish, Turkish rugs and a few items of pine furniture, but with there being a Leominster dealer in attendance, who competed for the latter as if being his mission in life, there was little hope of gaining profit from that quarter. All I could do was help boost his feelings of self-worth and sanctimonious sense of grace, by fitting them into him as solidly as they would go.

What saved the day, goods wise, was Luffy. He told me he'd bought a 'whole rake of stuff,' down in west Wales and I ought to take a look.

Sliding the van side door open, he said, 'There you go mate.'

I suggested, to deal thus, could be a little one sided, for he was armed with perfect knowledge of the items, while I was largely in the dark.

'What, you want me to unload the van?'

'Well it would be handy.'

The upshot was, I bought the lot and to be honest, left to my own devices, I'd have given Ron a few prices on some prints, pair of chairs, pine etc and driven home. It was not to be of course, for I'd have left my lucrative contact stranded.

During the sale itself, I heard a fair bit of banter between traders and was mildly surprised, that a group I didn't know, were quite cheerfully familiar with those I did. I bought six measly things, that certainly didn't pay for me having spent four hours there and stowing them in the van, told Ron to gather whatever he'd bought, for I was about to leave.

He looked quite offish and told me not to be so hasty, for there were a few items he was still interested in.

'Well go ahead, I'll wait for you.'

'It's not that easy, you'll need to drive me. We can't knock the stuff out here, they're all going to Clarach Bay.'

'Look, I told you, I can't afford to get involved.'

'But I haven't bought anything,' he wailed.

'That's not my fault.'

'There's the oak bureau, up on the landing. It's come in for £80. Surely you want that.'

'Actually I don't. I'm quite happy with what I've already bought.'

The dealers helped each other loading. Two huge ornamental iron gates went on one van, the grand piano, with legs unscrewed, was *heaved onto the rack of a Volvo and there was much banter and mention of Clarach Bay, as if we were all off for a few beers and a quick dip.*

On the short drive there, I again said I didn't want to get involved, not least because I hadn't the faintest idea what to actually do and of course risked looking a complete idiot, if simply standing there.

'You won't have to do anything, it will be a general.'

I didn't say, 'Who's he?' I wasn't that daft, but did ask, 'What's that? What's a general?'

'Each lot gets put up and if you're interested you bid for it.'

'And if you're not interested?'

'It doesn't matter. All the money bid, goes into a central kitty to be divided equally.'

'So those that don't actually want anything, get the same as those that do?'

'That's right.'

I replied, that it was a strange way to be going about things, when really, I meant gutless.

Anyway, all the heavily laden vehicles were parked above the lonely shore and the gathering was quite jocular, with all but myself, enjoying the thought of not only conducting business as usual, but it being enhanced by such a lovely setting. It was suggested we should all take the short descent to the beach and not wanting to appear a complete wimp in such vaunted company, I reluctantly joined them. The general mood was that jovial, there had been no thought of leaving someone up top as a lookout.

The items were put up for general competition and I noticed catalogues being marked to keep a record of who owed what for each purchase. Still shaken from my VAT ordeal, the whole thing made me feel thoroughly uneasy and I stood as far from the centre of the group as I could.

'Not much bidding coming from over in that direction,' growled one of the Cheshire dealers, looking meaningfully at Ron and myself. To show willing, Ron chipped in a couple of safe bids, but never came close to being the proud owner of anything. I was a bit, miffed, at realising, that simply by being there, I had seemingly lost possession of the pair of chairs I quite liked.

All the bidding had been completed and totals were being totted up, when one of the throng asked, 'Why's that fellow staring at us.'

'Well wouldn't you stare at a bunch of blokes gathered on a beach?' Came the reply.

Another, pointing to a chap exercising a large Alsatian hound, said, 'And he's staring at us. Hasn't taken his eyes off us.'

'Look! There's a bloke taking photos!"

We all looked up and a dealer, name of Jack Callan, said grimly, 'It's the law!'

At the top of the rise, a man called down. 'I am in the belief that an illegal auction ring is in operation. My officers will pass amongst you. Please hand over catalogues or any pieces of paper you have in your possession.'

I felt like the sky had fallen in.

Six descended and were joined by the two we'd seen earlier on the beach. I'd secreted my catalogue in trouser waist band and *covered it with my pullover, but thinking again, realised there was nothing incriminating on it and so handed it over.*

We were told, 'Some of my officers will travel in your cars, the rest can follow to Aberystwyth police station.'

My brain was that scrambled, it hadn't dawned on me, that not having actually been arrested, I was quite within my rights to drive home. Wouldn't have got far, mind you, I was almost out of fuel.

We were ushered into the basement of the police station and with two uniformed officers standing guard, told to wait. Any queries in their direction were met by stony stares. We were allowed a phone call apiece and I rang Anne with the terrifying news. Our incarceration lasted about two hours and then one by one we were asked to enter the interview rooms above. I'd thought I'd be in for a grilling, but it was more like answering a questionnaire. 'Why, with you living to the east of the saleroom, did you journey west to the sea? Why didn't you just drive home, etc?'

I should simply have answered, 'No comment,' to each question, but naively thought it smacked of sounding guilty and so instead, prevaricated. 'I don't often get to see the sea and so being that close, didn't want to pass up the opportunity.'

As to why I didn't drive straight home, I'd answered, 'It's a free country.'

After that little process, with all having been questioned, we were free to drive home and I couldn't believe what Luffy came out as we walked through the foyer. To the Chief Inspector himself, he said, 'Don't know why you're picking on us. The farmers are at it all the time.'

I thought, 'Well that's f------d it and watching Luffy walk off into the night, asked that same officer about the possibility of a garage still being open. He couldn't have been more helpful, giving directions to one, just beyond the bridge to the south, suggesting we needed to hurry, as it closed at ten. He followed it with, 'I don't know if we've enough against you yet, it will be up to the D.P.P. to decide, but take my advice lads, pack this silly game in. You're playing with fire.'

We found the garage still open and I drove home, dropping Ron off on the way.

Well you can imagine the reaction when the news got out around the trade. One dealer who I didn't much care for, who made his living by filling US bound containers with dross, jeered, 'From being a bit of a fringe player, you've become fucking notorious!'

Down at Leon's that Friday, I'd bought a few lots and when roping them onto the roof, inadvertently lassoed a windscreen wiper off a passing car. It screeched to a stop and the burly occupant approached in that slightly crouched stance certain men tend to adopt when winding up the notion to punch one's lights out. Meekly handing over the wiper and apologising profusely, I could see Leon, behind the safety of a wardrobe, doubled up with laughter.

'You should have stayed in bed this week, mate,' he said.

CHAPTER SIXTEEN

I paused for a while, taking in the enormity of what had happened. Although the remaining wad of notes seemed to testify, he must somehow have prevailed, it appeared almost inconceivable that he could have done and was keen to find out how he'd managed it. Even his new friend, Stuart from Bath had said he didn't stand a chance, telling him, if it came to a trial, the prosecuting barrister would rip him to pieces and he'd be better off simply pleading guilty. As yet no charges had been formally made and with no money having actually changed hands down on the beach, there could still be hope of the case being dropped.

A rugby playing friend, who also happened to be a plain clothed member of the local constabulary, didn't cheer him, mind you, for he said it had been a masterful piece of police work. He was full of admiration, for all had been netted without actually having been arrested, so no chance of wrongful arrest complaints. John was asked, had any money changed hands and on replying, that no there hadn't, his friend had said, 'You were bloody lucky.'

Without thinking, John had answered, 'I know,' and then worried for the rest of the day, wondering whether that could be construed, as him having definite knowledge of an illegal ring having been in operation. Damning evidence from his own mouth. He was getting that nervy, he was almost jumping at his own shadow, not helped by his cheery detective chum then saying, as if hardly able to believe it, 'You do realise that fraud is first division stuff.'

The VAT interview didn't lift his spirits much, either. They looked a totally different pair confronting him that Autumn morning, probably chastened by a severe bollocking from their boss, for having mislaid the notebook.

'You are not obliged to say anything, but anything you do say, etc'

---*I answered all their questions once again, but this time they asked to see the books mentioned at the previous meeting. I handed over a wad of papers.*

Looking through them, the one pointedly staring said, 'You told us you had books. I took it to mean a stock book.'

'Those are the overall details of the costs and profits per quarter, going back over the last six years.'

'You call these books?'

'I'm sorry. I'm a bit new to all this. I thought that was all I was required to keep a record of.'

Knowing this to be legally correct, he gave a measured look and asked, 'Would you mind if we take these with us?'

'No, not at all. Anything that will help. I just want to get this business over with.'

'We'll make a copy and post back the originals.'

Before leaving, the one said, 'Look, it's not up to us. I don't know if you'll receive a fine or not, but I shall mention in the report, you've been most cooperative.'

'Thank you,' I said and truly meant it.

Having been caught on my very first encounter with the ring, I received a fair deal of banter from my new acquaintances at the Welsh auctions. I had realised, there was a fair chance, the competition could be less intense than that experienced on home territory and thought it worth the gamble of trying a few of the lesser sales, like the Montgomery evening auctions, or the Welshpool Friday, general sales, to see how I got on. In fact, I found them quite lucrative and after a while, not only did a few traders arrive with pine for me to buy, I had an inkling, they left me alone on the odd lot. I thought, if they wanted to knock things out after the auction, then let them get on with it, for occasionally offering a profit to the holder of a good item, was better than getting involved and was quite legal.

Every sale, seemed to have off-duty police officers watching, which was obviously unnerving. They were always in plain clothes, but heavy black boots, tended to be a bit of a giveaway. It made one quite paranoic and I was careful never to openly produce cash in a saleroom, not even when paying one of the lads for fetching the teas.

There was one sale over at Llanfair Caereinion, where I'd needed a fair deal of resolve, mind you. They were selling up an old wool mill and the pine work tables went for virtually nothing, but I had to stay strong and content myself with a few lots they seemed to have left me alone on, for not only did I have the looming court case to worry about, there was also the VAT.

Two of those involved in the Clarach Bay case had had their whole lives put on hold, by in depth tax investigations, to the point one looked like he'd aged ten years.

They had asked, with his shop selling virtually nothing, how had he managed to survive? He'd said, he and his wife struggled, but they managed on her wages. They'd of course looked into her bank details and found that his good lady had spent nearly every penny earnt, on hairdressers, make-up and clothes. So, he'd found himself in an unenviable trap, of either having to admit he wasn't declaring shop sales, or even worse, the truth, he'd been living

239

entirely off knock money. The investigations finished any ambition that he and the other under scrutiny, a dealer from Shrewsbury, might have had of continuing in the antique trade. In fact they finished off the latter entirely, as the mounting stress brought on the heart attack that killed him.

By the Christmas of that year there had been no news regarding VAT or the pending court case and regarding the latter, no news was taken as good news.

In the following Spring, John received a call from a trader he'd previously had dealings with, Richard Cole from Malvern. He wrote,---*Richard had a no nonsense direct manner and told me in his broad Herefordshire accent, 'Never mind the shop. Get y'self over 'ere. I gotta load for you.'*

I'd picked up the fact, Richard often worked with a dealer, Steve from Hereford, but on this occasion seemed to be operating alone. The meeting had been arranged for 11am, centre of Ledbury where Richard then led to where furniture had been stored, in a mate's barn, over by Eastnor. John bought the lot and with just managing to get it all on the van, had been jokingly advised, not to go under any low bridges. With the deal satisfactorily concluded, they talked about latest happenings in the trade and laughed at how they'd once nearly come to blows. As can happen in the school playground, the confrontation had been the beginning of a burgeoning friendship. Richard told him, how he'd been keeping an eye on his progress and came to the conclusion, the pair of them could do a fair deal of business. As regards the KO problem, Richard shared his concern, but said if he managed to come through it, it could be the making of him. John had heard tales of how Richard had been cast out to become a lone operator, having fallen foul of the ring, but was now keen to hear the details from the man himself.

---*We returned to Ledbury and parking the vehicles down by the cattle market, walked back into the centre for a coffee and chat.*

Richard said, 'I'll be quite honest, I was being an absolute pain in the arse, milkin' the odd fiver on the give and take, knowing they'd rather part with a bitta cash, than let me nick the item off 'em. I was used to the odd barb,--- but this one day, one of 'em kept on all morning and in the end, it just got to me.'

'Was that the Monmouth incident?'

'You've got it. That's the one. Like I said,---' He lowered his voice and leant closer. 'That fuckin' baastard 'ad been on at me all morning and I was beginning to boil. I kept a count of the coffees he'd been drinking and thought, he's bound to need a piss soon. Sure enough, down he goes to that public pisser opposite the saleroom and I slipped from the room, close behind. I bided me time, let him finish and zip up, then said, "If you're aiming to get back to the saleroom, you'll have a job, 'cos you'll need to fight your way past me." He couldn't believe it. Thought I was joking. Not when he ended up with his face in the piss trough mind you. It was our dad, taught me to box. He ran a pub, 'ere in town and used to take the gypsies on, for money on a Saturday. It's a simple trick, but it works. Make as if to swing with the right, but catch 'em under the jaw with your left. I'm not as sharp as I was, but never mind, I still managed two more in quick succession, before ee 'it the deck.'

'But I heard you then had another little set-to.'

'Oh him! The reckless rat from Worcester. It was about a week later. We were knocking out stuff in the back of a van and he kept taking the piss, offering his chin sayin', "Come on then Mr. Tough Guy. Come on. Pud-em up." I just sat there thinking,---"Yes, just keep on. Push a bit further and you're gonner wonder what'sit ya."

Well, we all climbed out of the van, but blocking him with an arm, I told him to steady on, not to be in quite such an 'urry, for we still had a little matter to settle. He had that startled rabbit in the headlights look and then complete shock when I chinned him.

241

"Don't try and get up," I told him, "You do and I'll fuckin'-well kill ya!" Well that was it,--- banned from the knockout. But d'you know what, it's been the making of me. I've had to stand on me own two feet, pit m'wits against 'em and it's made me a far, far better dealer. I know it's 'arrd, there's no denying that, but you'll find exactly the same. Don't get involved with 'em. You're better off without them. Half of 'em are just, wankers, in any case. Paper tigers. They don't actually want to buy anything,--- they just follow those around what do and milk the life out of 'em.

Reading this, I got the picture of a tough little package, you'd not want to get on the wrong side of and could sense John Dodds' character emerging; an independent spirit that other dealers were beginning to respect and had now begun to offer furniture to. I also sensed, he was somehow becoming a magnet for the more unconventional members of the trade. Perhaps it was the ingenuous side to his nature, for when he told Richard he hadn't really been involved in the ring that day, but had just been standing there when the law arrived, his friend had been that convulsed with laughter, he'd nearly choked on his coffee. The more John avowed he was telling the truth, the more, with tears in his eyes, he waved an arm in a plea to stop, so he could swallow and breathe again.

Another thing that was becoming apparent, was the amount of sheer luck he seemed to have. Early in that same year, he'd chanced on an advert for a sale over in Chirk and with it being advertised as goods from an engineering plant, no other dealer had bothered to cover it. A sixth sense, however, had told him it was worth a look and he came away with all 16, pine, 6' x 33", work tables stacked inside one another on the roof rack, plus the back of the van filled with other assorted goods, bought for virtually nothing, £204 the lot. The tables needed a little adaptation, but none were oily and he sold them as seen, to the trade for £120 apiece.

To put the windfall into perspective, the average weekly wage at the time was about £150. Meanwhile Easter was approaching and there had still been no news regarding the possible court case.

Not understanding a term, Richard the pugilist had used, I decided to give Charles another ring. He seemed quite forthcoming on this occasion and asked how the book was progressing? He remembered the Richard incidents. Although, not actually there at the time, he said, the news soon went round the trade.

"He wasn't a big chap, but could certainly handle himself. I heard, he never got any bother after that."

I asked Charles, what was meant by a give and take, in the knock out.

"Oh that. It sometimes happened at the end of the KO and the two still contesting would disappear to sort out the last of the nitty-gritty between them. It wasn't usually done openly as they didn't want to educate the opposition. There again, it often happened end of sale when only two traders were still interested in a lot."

"Yes, but what did it involve?"

"Well, the interested party would approach the buyer with an offer. It had to be at least ten percent, so if the item had cost £100, the claimant would say, 'I'll give you a tenner.' This could be countered with, 'No, I'll give you twelve,' thus the original owner would pay twelve pounds to keep the thing he'd bought in the first place."

"Hardly sounds fair."

"No, and in many cases it wasn't. It was just a way of milking the stronger buyers. That's why Richard had got under their skin. But sometimes, the give and take could go into hundreds, almost like a game of brag."

I thanked him and then said, "Before I go, how well did you know John Dodds in those early days."

"Not so well to start with, but as we both got more adventurous, we'd often view the sales together. By the time he moved to that big shop, I was spending most of my time down in West Wales, returning each weekend to sell him the haul I'd managed to pick up. Most lucrative time of my life."

"So you didn't know him when the VAT first enrolled him?"

"Well I did, but was out of the area when it happened. You wouldn't believe the rumours going about."

"What sort of rumours?"

"Far be it from me to talk about others dear boy. You know how scurrilous some rumours can be."

"So?"

"Some say he burnt his own books, but we don't believe that for a single minute, do we?"

"Thank you, Charles. Hope you didn't mind me ringing."

"Not at all dear boy. Any time."

It was at this point in the notes, I realised a strange thing had happened, Anne's cat, Clark Gable had turned up out of the blue.

---*There was no mistaking it, for Clarkie had the most distinctive yowl and there he was, sat on the path announcing his arrival. He looked thin, but other than that, was very much alive. I assumed he must have climbed unnoticed aboard a dealer's van and having been driven away, had by some miracle, found his way home. I rushed in to tell Anne the news.*

'*Anne, you'll never guess, but Clarkie's back.*'

'*What?*'

'Your cat, Clark Gable's back.'

'He can't be. I saw you bury him.'

'Honestly, come and have a look for yourself. Perhaps it's a sign that everything's going to be alright.'

'So what did you bury then?'

'Must have been his understudy.'

Late Spring of that year, when it was hoped the case against the ring had been dropped, a fat, ominous looking envelope arrived. In it were all the details of the case regarding, Queen Elizabeth versus John Dodds. He had stared at it, horrified, for even the Queen was now against him. He already had a solicitor, a no-nonsense man, Mr. Roy Spanner, who successfully obtained him legal aid, but as the trial was to be held in a Crown Court, he now required a barrister.

What really unsettled him the one day, was the meeting he had with the probation officer, the female who, if the worst happened and he ended up with a conviction, would be handling his path back onto the straight and narrow.

---The meeting was in an office of the Ludlow Magistrates Court. The woman trampled on my protestations of innocence as if they'd been nothing more than a wet cardboard box, saying we would need numerous post-trial meetings and she'd certainly need to inspect my house and assess the quality of living conditions. I didn't want that Rottweiler of a woman anywhere near my children and was that shaken, I went straight across the road to see my solicitor. Mr. Spanner, looking rather puzzled, told me a probation officer wasn't supposed to behave like that. I suggested, perhaps she was working for the prosecution. With such an ingenuous observation instantly lightening his mood, he sent me on my way with a patient smile, a friendly pat on the back and the comforting message, 'Don't worry.'

There were eighteen defendants in all and 12 clubbed together to pay for a top London barrister. All intended to plead not guilty, not because they were innocent, it was more a matter of considering the case against them thin. What added a little spice to the whole pickle they were in, not that it really needed any, was the fact the police had been after one of the accused for a number of years. The man had wriggled out of a handling charge, guilty as hell, but free as a bird and the police were keen to nail him. Even the antique trade gave the man a wide berth, not only because of the bad name he gave them, but also, they knew he was a marked man.

The first hearing was a pre-trial formality where legal representation was not necessary. John Dodds arranged to meet Ron Baker in Knighton and from there they would travel to Swansea in the single vehicle. While waiting for Ron to turn up, John had seen a fine set of 8 Regency faux bamboo chairs in a shop window. Using the phone number shown on the door, he rang from a call box to enquire about condition and price, bought them and said he'd collect them later that day. Down in Swansea, to kill time before the hearing, he'd done a tour of the shops and later that day returned home with a sizeable haul. Not knowing, what financial impositions lay ahead, it did feel like putting money into a pocket with a hole in it, but at least it kept his mind off the constant nagging worry.

Ron Baker, wondering how he could consider buying copper coal scuttles, brass fenders and maple frames at a time like that, thought him crazy and later, back in Knighton, when calling to collect the set of chairs, he'd raised his eyes to heaven. The eight included two open armchairs and the authority with which they stood and the quality of the painted decoration made it likely, they had come from a top-quality workshop. John Dodds wrote:---*I didn't realise at the time, I'd blundered into the best I would find at my very first attempt. They, plus the maple frames, went into the back shed for the next time Stuart called. I went on to handle many simulated bamboo chairs over the years, but never again, a set of that quality.*

The actual court case was not until late Summer and to help take his mind of the non-stop worry, another trip was made to the Isle of Man, last week in June, just prior the start of the TT races. Again, he felt the warming balm of tranquillity, but over on the mainland a huge black cloud awaited.

As the fateful day approached, Ron Baker, dropped the bombshell, he was planning to plead guilty. A Queen's Council who happened to rent a nearby holiday cottage had told him, he didn't stand a prayer. Not a hope! Not only would the case probably take a financially crippling two week chunk out of his life, the penalty would be far stiffer than if simply holding his hands up, plus the whole lot of them, would almost certainly get a saleroom ban.

When this little twist of events became known, every single one of John's trade contacts, told him he ought to do likewise, for the guilty plea now blew the case apart. He reasoned yet again, that he had got caught up in it by mistake and couldn't see why he should now have a criminal record for simply giving someone a lift. He was told, the law wouldn't see it like that, for being largely ignorant of circumstances didn't make him innocent.

The Saturday before the trial, he was chatting to a customer, who happened to be a chemist from South Wales. Noticing some moulding planes and a surgeon's saw for sale in the window, plus other tools, he'd asked whether there might be any interest in a brass and mahogany, pill making machine, he was willing to sell? But then added, 'It's hardly worth you driving all the way to Cwm Bran, just for that though, is it?'

John had replied, 'It just so happens I'll be passing your door on Wednesday. I'll call in and have a look.'

On the big day, with his solicitor in the passenger seat, he drove down to Swansea in the van. They were met in the court foyer by his barrister, all smiles, relishing the fray. The eighteen accused were asked to assemble in a side chamber, where the London barrister explained he'd been putting a deal together and could almost certainly get three of his group off the charge, provided the other nine, those with the most damning evidence against them, pleaded guilty. He stressed, it was essential that the nine should include a certain dealer from Cheshire. Suspicions had been right, the police were keen to add this man's scalp to their trophy cabinet. The carrot they'd dangled, was prior knowledge of the fine, £4,000 and the fact there would be no saleroom ban. The barrister left, for the dealers to go to work, putting pressure on the one the police wanted above all else and when he at last capitulated, agreeing to plead guilty, they all returned to the foyer.

It was here that John Dodds happened to meet the chief arresting officer, the one who'd kindly directed him to the only garage left open in Aberystwyth the day he'd been nabbed and following niceties about the fine weather, the friendly Chief Inspector told him the issue was still in the balance.

'You do know who that was, you were talking to?' said one of the partners in crime, forehead furrowed with concern.

I'll hand you over to the man himself, for not surprisingly, he wrote what happened in detail.---*I replied, that the Chief Inspector had seemed quite pleasant and it had only been harmless chat.*

The buzz of negotiations already in motion, could be heard echoing in the lofty vestibule and my barrister was keen to draw my attention to the likely consequence of the latest machinations. He explained, now the big nine were in the net, all the evidence against them would be removed from the case. He said, 'I know it sounds strange, but that's the way the law works. And with five others also likely to plead guilty, it means there's virtually no evidence against the remaining four.'

My spirits immediately lifted.

'However, I'd noticed your initials and the figure £20 appears next to a pair of chairs you bought. It's in a catalogue of one of the remaining four.'

'And that now makes me Mr. Big?'

He smiled and said, 'I'm afraid so.'

'So what happens now?'

'If they decide to open the case against you, I know it hardly sounds credible, but with that being the only remaining evidence against the remaining four, you'd bear the brunt of the court costs.'

'How long would the trial take?'

'Oh, it could last anything up to two weeks.'

'What happens then?'

'You sell your house,' replied my no-nonsense solicitor.

'Look,' said my barrister, 'I'll see if I can get you included on the list of those likely to have the case against them dropped.'

'You mean, if the fourteen plead guilty and save the cost of a trial, they let the minnows go.'

'Hopefully.'

'Like horse trading.'

'Yes, I suppose it is really.'

He approached the largest group in the hall, waited his chance and then put his proposition to the London barrister, who was *still negotiating with the prosecuting council. I could tell by the look on his face, he'd been unsuccessful.*

'I'm sorry, I did my best, but he said, the police didn't like your comments. I told him, "You can hardly condemn a man for being facetious," but unfortunately it did no good, you weren't allowed on the list.'

As the big clock ticked ever on and the moment of reckoning grew large, the barrister explained another of the law's foibles. Apparently, having been asked to state their plea, all would then be asked to restate it, once proceedings were resumed after the recess. If the trial happened to be opened before the break, the judge would take a very dim view, of any who had pleaded not guilty before lunch, changing it to guilty, once proceedings were reconvened. Showing such lack of respect for the court, would probably invite double the fine imposed on the others. If, however, the case was not opened before lunch, there was nothing to lose by pleading not guilty before the break and changing it to guilty, once aware the law was intent on netting the lot of them.

With a hint of relish, he said, 'Come on. They're all going in. I'll try and find out if they intend to open the case before lunch. If they're not, as I explained, you've nothing to lose by pleading not guilty, then changing it to guilty, post recess, at the actual start of the trial.'

Noticing my expression, he said, 'I know it sounds weird, but it's just one of those wrinkles in the law.'

There were that many facing trial, they didn't quite know what to do with us and we were shuffled about this way and that, like first day at school assembly. Initially I was put in the front row, where I would have been blind to any instructions coming from my barrister. I was perched precariously at the row's end next to the aisle and making my discomfort obvious, was fortunately moved further back in the court, where my barrister, sitting two rows in front, was now clearly visible.

The judge entered and all rose as one. Any air of nonchalance or bravado was instantly sucked from the room and looking to my right, I could see a row of extremely worried faces, drained of all colour.

The case was stated and we were asked how we intended to plead. I heard, 'Guilty, guilty, guilty, approaching and I needed to make my mind up--- quickly. With one further plea before mine, my barrister swung round and silently mouthed, 'They are NOT opening the trial before lunch.'

'NOT GUILTY,' I said, bringing gasps of astonishment from all around. By the end, three others had pleaded the same.

Activities were suspended for the lunch break. My barrister was happy to shoot the breeze with his fellow advocates and my solicitor joined me for a snack in a nearby pub. Just before our return to court, a record rang out loud from the juke box, 'I'm still standing,' by Elton John.

I said to my solicitor, 'I have a strange feeling I'm going to be alright.' It was one of those inner messages again and I truly felt as if a huge weight was starting to evaporate off my shoulders.

Back in the foyer, I excused myself, needing the facilities and who should join me in the urinary, but the Chief Inspector himself. Zipping his flies, viciously enough to self-circumcise, he said angrily, 'You're a lucky bastard!'

'What do you mean?'

'You're a lucky bastard,' he repeated and left.

Back in the courtroom the judge announced, 'In view of the number of the accused pleading guilty, the Crown does not think it beneficial to pursue the case against the remaining four. Their names, however, will be kept on file.'

I then heard, 'Come on.' It was my barrister. 'Come on, you're free to go.'

Walking towards the exit, he suddenly turned and asked, 'In view of Mr. Dodds not being found guilty, could my client apply for exemption from court costs.'

That didn't go down well at all, for I could see the judge was clearly enraged and even when hearing the resonance from the safety of the foyer, 'He most certainly can NOT. And if he ever appears before me again on a similar charge, he can rest assured he'll serve a custodial SENTENCE!'---the sheer impact of his words still hit the mark and feeling suitably shaken, watched bemused as my barrister appeared, not just smiling, but absolutely brimming from the little encounter.

'So there you are,' he said. 'You disappeared quickly. Don't you want to see what the others get?'

'No thanks. I just want to get the hell out of here.' Then I asked, 'Whatever did you do that for? I thought he was going to change his mind.'

'No, he wouldn't do that. Don't worry, it's all part of the game.'

I looked at him truly amazed. Although not having the slight sexual connotation as when uttered by Marie, it was that same phrase again.

My solicitor accompanied me around the shops and looked to be enjoying the few deals I put together, even carrying some of the purchases back to the van. On the way home, I stopped at the Chemist shop in Cwm Bran and bought the brass and mahogany pill maker, but obviously didn't divulge the other business conducted that day.

A few days following the trial, another big brown envelope arrived. It was from the VAT office. The contents detailed how *much was owing, going back six years, which as said, I'd saved the money for, but in view of my cooperation, they had not slapped a fine on me.*

The worry I'd felt over the previous year had been that great, so deeply scarring, it took weeks for me to fully realise, the nightmare was finally over.

It was at this point, I realised, yet again, I'd got one of the events out of place. On an occasion when John Dodds had been driving back from Newtown, he'd seen Ron Baker parked at a T junction and had pulled over to ask if anything was the matter.---*He looked truly perplexed and told me he'd heard of a Shropshire housekeeper's cupboard for sale, up towards Shrewsbury, but his contact for some reason had withheld the address.*

'*It wouldn't be over Worthen way, would it?*'

Ron looked astonished and I told him to follow me. It was the same cupboard Trevor and I had once attempted to buy and so my efforts that day had finally borne fruit. I had done no good at all with the early cabinet bought there, it having been dismissed as probably Dutch or German. The deal was quickly concluded and luckily there were two strong men at hand to help load the massive edifice onto my van. Obviously, there was no chance it would go in the shop, so I drove to Leominster and sold it to Peter, giving Ron half the profit. Well nearly half, for I not only had the tax to consider, but now also the VAT.

I realised this little episode must have happened before the trial, for following its conclusion, Ron had said he wanted nothing more to do with John Dodds, ever again.

John had written---*He looked absolutely twisted with bitterness.* '*How can I be guilty and you innocent, when we both travelled there in the same vehicle? It doesn't make sense!*'

I explained, 'Look, if you remember, Ron, I had no wish to be there and when it came down to it, thanks to a brilliant barrister, it was just the way it was played it on the day that brought the result.' I hadn't added, it's all part of the game, for that would have sounded cocky and I certainly didn't feel the least bit cocky. Completely drained and relieved would be more accurate.

CHAPTER SEVENTEEN

I again paused and going back through the notes, realised with certain sections now having been covered, I could put a pencil line through them. I found a reference to an intense flurry of business happening about this time, as if being freed from recent constraints, had caused a surge of energy to burst forth. No less than three mahogany secretaire bookcases were chanced upon in the space of two weeks and then a circular, six-seater mahogany table, that had such a dense array of runners, to the extending mechanism on its underside, it was almost too much for two men to lift. He didn't own it long enough to unwind and ascertain how many leaves it would have taken, but on reflexion, thought probably four would have been the maximum, making it capable of comfortably seating fourteen and possibly twenty at Christmas.

The first of the bookcases mentioned, seemed rather plain, blousy and on the pricy side, so he'd taken a dealer, Ray from Malvern, on the call. He received a commission and the deal had given him a yardstick for the further two, then chanced upon.

The third had been by far the finest and needing to rush off on another call, he'd put it in the shed behind the house.

---*When Ray next turned up at the shop, I took him out to see my prize, telling him, he would find the intricacy of the glazing bars a joy to behold. In the murk of the back shed, however, I apologised, for it now looked rather dull and told him, 'When we were*

*carrying it round here, we were caught by a bit of a shower and all
these glazing bars absolutely gleamed.'*

Ray laughed and said, 'You should have phoned the missus up.
"Quick, I'm bringing a customer out. Chuck a bucket of water
over it."'

*He didn't quibble over the price and stayed for a coffee. He told
me of how, a few years back, when putting together deals, he'd
often ask to have a small object, such as a silver match case, or
card case, chucked in for luck. He said, 'Well anyway, after a
while, I'd amassed quite a few of these and when a Dutch trader
happened to call, looking for items of bijouterie, I fished the
whole pile out. Of course, they weren't officially in stock and so
I told him I'd have to have cash. He peeled off the readies, left
with his bag of silver and once from sight, I went, 'Yippee,'
chucking all the dosh in the air. He'd only forgotten his hat, hadn't
he and stood in the doorway, staring open mouthed, watching all
the notes dipping and diving around me. 'It's an old English
tradition,' I tried to explain. Tell you what though; embarrassed?
I felt like a complete prat!'*

I noticed, it was at this point that the massive deal involving
Regency furniture, Clive from Tenbury had told me about, had
come into the reckoning. Things were certainly booming and he
made mention of the purchase of his very first Welsh oak dresser
and the fact that, with having passed that particular landmark, he
finally felt like a proper dealer. It was only a late, pine-sided thing,
but stood in pride of place on the back wall of the shop. In this
same flurry of activity, he'd been returning from a Cotswold
delivery and driving through Broadway, noticed a couple adding
an X-frame table to a trailer load of furniture.---*Putting my door-
knocking experience to good effect, I pulled in and asked if there
could be a chance of the table being for sale. Better than that, they
told me it was one of a pair, the other having already been taken
to the house they were moving to, further along the road. I bought
them both and driving away, felt like the church mouse that had*

stolen the altar cloth, for I was right in the heart of where such tables made so much money.

I was quite tickled to see, the huge pitch pine cupboard from the Tenbury solicitor's office, also got a mention at this point. He'd written,--- *Although not wanting the thing at any price, I'd given my word to help remove it.* There followed, a description of how they'd got it out without mishap, but he then wrote, with running late for a Welsh sale, how he was desperate to get the thing off the roof rack.

---I drove to the store, the old Smithy out at Onibury; lowered the monster to where a sturdy table broke its fall and from there, slid it to the ground. With a strength brought on by urgency, even though towering over me, I managed to walk it, a few inches one side, a few the other, but once through the double doors, it stood blocking the entrance. Having tied the doors together, I decided, if it was hauled towards me, there was just sufficient room, between two stacked rows of furniture, to lie it on its side. Growling and getting angry with the brute, I suddenly realised, where gravity had assisted previously, it was now not entirely in my favour, for with the leviathan now heading my way, there was no escape route. It was a four-inch nail protruding from a high cross-beam, that halted its descent and probably saved me from entrapment.

Newspaper headline: 'Missing antique dealer, found dead beneath a massive pine cupboard. Career, well and truly over.'

Skimming ahead through the notes, I could see, the sales were still attended and generally, his decision to stand alone was still respected. All were obviously, still very nervy concerning possible police presence, but some dealers, being ring addicts, continued to hold covert knock-outs in back rooms of pubs or down country lanes.

---The fact a few worked together was stupidly obvious, for the initial flurry of arms would immediately cease, once one of their

number had had a bid taken and then that person would continue until the lot was bought, or if having become faint-hearted, the battle would be taken up by one who considered himself, a better judge of the item.

It was at a sale one day, at Hay on Wye cattle market, that the usual banter, was enhanced by the anecdote of recent happenings at a settlement, conducted over in Hereford. Mid-proceedings, panic had ensued, for all had thought they were about to be raided. One of the participants, a certain Frank who'd pleaded guilty at the Aberystwyth affair, had been that spooked, he'd tried to destroy evidence of knock-out details, by eating the paper they were written on.

John Dodds had made the gathering laugh by saying, '*I always suspected, Frank got his prices from up his arse.*'

I found later, regarding certain members of the trade, this same Frank, along with the dealer who sent containers full of dross across the Atlantic, had earnt himself a special place in John Dodds' feelings of contempt. He described how the man would follow him, to the penny at an auction, but be totally useless if offered an item in cold blood. A typical saleroom buyer and there were plenty of them.

It was at this same sale that he bought yet another dresser, a rather skeletal thing with an open rack.

---Dave Roberts from Leominster, eying it up, said, 'You seem to be getting a few dressers around you Doddsy.' I'd noticed him a few days earlier, just standing in the shop, not wanting to buy anything, more as if just weighing the situation up. He'd smiled and said almost dreamily, 'Thank you,' and departed, leaving the door open.

I'm sure I'd been right, for having a rough idea of what my overdraft facility was likely to be, he'd been adding up all the pricier items to assess how close I was to my limit.

Anyway, having shrugged off his assessment of my stick insect of a dresser, I asked him to help me off with the rack. 'Now stand back,' I said.

'Quite a tidy little dresser base,' he said and I could feel a little involuntary respect growing.

Completely tied up with the flow of business, John Dodds had made the usual mistake of thinking he'd remember all the details for calculating the VAT owed, end of the quarter. The mess he got himself into took two days to sort out and from then on, he diligently did his books first thing every Sunday morning.

There was yet another trip to the Isle of Man, far more enjoyable, now the incredible weight of worry had been lifted from his shoulders. On returning, he'd the pleasant surprise of seeing numerous sales in the stock book on items he didn't recognise.

---Mother said, 'It's the stuff from that Clungunford call, you did before you left. They accepted your offer and I cleared it all.' With that and the sale of the goods brought back from holiday, it made for quite a good June, a month, when dealing from a shop in border country, you're lucky to break even.'

'What, with all those tourists?' I was often asked.

'They look, but they rarely buy anything,' I would try and explain, sometimes adding, 'How likely are you to buy an expensive antique, when you're on holiday?'

Expensive antique? At last, with business vibrant, it sounded like he was heading upmarket and the fact he'd put recent troubles behind him, must have been the catalyst for designing a bay window to replace the awful thing that clashed so badly with the Georgian frontage. He had the plans passed and its installation gave the place a look of a proper antique shop.

At this point, I noticed Trevor had come back into the picture. He'd teamed up with his cousin Alf and one of them would call in the shop if they'd been successful.---*The fare on offer was all the usual stuff, either in Trevor's house, or Alf's garden shed, apart from one particular item that stood out.*

It was a mahogany cabinet on stand and something about it spoke to me. I had that feeling, mentioned earlier, coming from deep within. If I tried to make it happen, it could lead to disaster, but when occurring naturally, I knew I was on to a winner. So, flicking through one of my reference books, I wasn't that amazed to find the cabinet's twin. I gave the chance of it to Stanley, from Broad Street, the dealer who had explained, regarding furniture, some things can be a little misleading. Obviously taken aback by the price quoted, he asked with a stern look magnified by his glasses, 'Now!--- How much do you really want for it?'

I repeated my price.

He said, 'Very well,' turned on his heel and left.

I was still wondering whether I had blown the deal, when about fifteen minutes later, I heard the shop bell go. Holding out a cheque, Stanley said, 'Just give me a lift onto the car with it, would you?'

On a completely different note, I hadn't realised at this point, that Trevor and Alf had been helping themselves to my trade cards. It did come to light eventually, however.

Now I saw first mention of a certain Mr. Braddock. John Dodds had often heard tell of the man, for he'd been given almost legendary status by quite a number of local traders, being famous for his skills at extracting goods whilst door-knocking. He just happened by one day and rapped on the cottage door.

---He was a bit taken aback, seeing a fellow dealer standing there, but soon got into his stride regaling me with various tales of

successes. I'd already heard details of his film set ploy, telling those he called on, he'd been given bags of cash to purchase traditional Welsh antique furniture to add authenticity to the filmset, on a big budget movie soon to be shot nearby. Although knowing the story, I let him carry on. Standing there in his tailored suit, gold fob chain glinting against dark mustard waistcoat, he held forth, telling me of how he'd profess to know nothing whatsoever about the value of all this old Welsh stuff. 'I tell them, I haven't a clue and emptying the bag of readies, urge them, "Go on, help yourselves. I don't know what your dresser's worth, take what you think is a fair price. Next time you see it, it'll be in the movies." They stare at the pile of wrappers, but never ever take any and so I count out a few hundred and tell them, "There, that should do."'

Then out of the blue, he asked if the kitchen table might be for sale. Being a pine top on an oak base, it had provided yet another lesson on my learning curve. Although the top was original and it was a 6' Georgian table with ample leg room, I'd become rather stuck with it. In the end, as can happen with similar mistakes, I'd decided to use it at home. Adding the slimmest of profits, I told him the price.

His offer was, to the penny, what I'd paid for it, but putting it all down to experience, I told him it was a deal. He walked up the path, to root under the front seat of his car and returned holding a blue bag, the sort banks swaddle large amounts of cash in. It was absolutely bulging with notes and theatrically peeling off the required number, he paid me. He had told me, the lure of the cash worked miracles and even I was guilty of falling under its spell, for I sold him the set of kitchen chairs as well. Having helped him load the furniture, I returned to the cottage, which now had an ominous hollow feeling. I'd been mindful to forewarn Anne, when collecting her from town later and had dressed up the deal as being incredibly fortunate, but she stood in the kitchen doorway, as if frozen, looking mortified. I tried to cheer her by saying I'd got useful capital back and would soon buy another table and *chairs, but realised ladies don't tend to like having their kitchens devastated.*

Regarding other matters; as is said, 'Every cloud has a silver lining' and three of the dealers caught in the Clarach Bay knockout had become quite good contacts, giving John Dodds a call whenever having sufficient pine amassed to make it worth his while calling. Two were from the Shropshire-Cheshire border area and the other from near Newtown. None of the pine ever made it to the shop. It was all sold on from the store, to either Mark, if having a Georgian look, or to the numerous callers who specialised in stripping and finishing anything at all, as long as it was pine. The demise of the craze was oft predicted, but he wrote,--- *It just seemed to go from strength to strength.*

I was surprised by how far dealers travelled for such humble stock. He sold to London traders; a regular East Anglian caller; Julian from Hay on Wye had several mentions, as did Sam from Leek in Staffordshire and a couple from Ross on Wye. Interestingly, John had made a side note, saying the Ross business was not in the man's name, in fact he didn't officially exist. He'd been a bass guitarist in a rock band that had filled stadiums in the States, but on returning, found the agent had siphoned off the money, leaving the band members with nothing to pay the tax owed. With the Inland Revenue still on his trail, he spent his time stripping and sanding pine furniture, plus making the odd foray for stock.

It seemed strange that such low-end goods, contained a profit for at least two dealers, before being sold to the eventual retailer, but I then chanced on the reason. With John Dodds having once retailed pine himself, it gave him the edge, for he not only knew the look that sold the best, but also how much it eventually sold for.

Although his business was doing well, it was Leon's shop, constantly topped up by loads brought by the Irish travellers, that was the main magnet and then with the Clun dealer opening an establishment in the town, the whole place seemed to be absolutely buzzing. Success breeds success and all three shops had stock brought to them by dealers trading from the back of vans. One of John's regulars was Richard the pugilist, who as said before, often teamed up with a Hereford dealer called Steve. The latter was one who'd flown too close to the sun in the Victorian mahogany to Australia, shipping craze. He'd become horribly puffed up and insufferable, to the point, he had even one day, jeered to a respected gentleman of the trade, Andrew Wakeman of Wolverhampton, 'You can't afford to buy off me anymore, Andrew.' When the whole thing crashed, he was left with a warehouse full of overpriced furniture, near bankruptcy. The sale of the store was what actually saved him. Richard had said to John Dodds one day, with his partner well within earshot, 'Steve's not a bad lad. He's a far nicer bloke when he's broke, mind you.'

The deal I've picked out from the notes, must have happened not long after the pair had teamed up, for it took place late one night while the Los Angeles Olympics were being shown on T.V. It's useful, for it pins down the date when the Australian mahogany boom suddenly crashed, to being almost certainly early 1984, for I read, teaming up with Richard had been the man's way of pulling himself off the floor, following his demise.

---Each time *we successfully negotiated part of the load, I'd rush in to see how Daley Thompson was doing in the decathlon. It was particularly nerve jangling as he could have lost it all on the pole vault. I left there well after midnight, with the van absolutely laden. There were a few star lots, including a magnificent pair of milk churns, that first needed a blacksmith's attentions and then a good burnishing by the absolute godsend of a man, Mr. Owen Williams. He specialised in brass and copper refurbishment in an industrial unit on the edge of town and over the years, made me, a small fortune. The churns came back with steel shining bright and brass tops and etched medallions gleaming. Even with an imaginative price tag, they didn't last a day in the shop.*

I found another reference to the Wakeman's of Wolverhampton.---
*Andrew had drawn up one day, with amongst other things, a
walnut cabriole legged stool in the back of the car. It was not a
thing I'd normally buy anymore, but as we chatted and he
squeezed in a canterbury I'd sold him, I noticed the finesse of
the stool's needlework cover. I asked the price and on being told,
bought it on sheer impulse, only realising when it was fully
withdrawn, the thing was 5' long. It was absolutely magnificent.
I told him about the time, years before, when full of trepidation,
I'd pulled into his yard, driving a small saloon car, with nothing
more than a skimpy aluminium luggage rack on the roof. I'd braved
it into the portals of the massive warehouse, but then froze, feeling
totally out of my depth. I was turning to make a hasty retreat when
Andrew's mother had asked, if she could be of help. I told her I was
an absolute beginner and would be wasting her time. 'Nonsense,'
she said and invited me to wander the full range of the emporium,
which was on a much vaster scale than I'd ever imagined. Patrolling
the rows of mainly Victoriana, I picked out a set of four mahogany
chairs that had finer timber and crisper carving than normally
found, plus I bought a pair of rather forgotten looking candlesticks,
that turned out to be Georgian. The chairs of course, I later realised
were Regency and I made a small, but quite satisfying profit from
the visit, with the abiding memory of the respect Mrs. Wakeman
had given to a complete beginner.*

John Dodds had been worried the local constabulary might have
taken a dim view of his slipping unscathed from the Clarach Bay
affair, but his fears were unfounded and in fact one day, received a
letter of thanks from the head man in Shrewsbury.

*---One bright morning, a wiry looking character had called in the
shop, asking in a broad South Wales accent, if I'd be interested in
goods he had outside in the car. This often happened, but what struck
me as being strange, was none of the glass or china in the car boot
had been wrapped. The fine pieces of ruby glass looked particularly
vulnerable and a sixth sense told me the goods had been stolen.
Thanking him, I said the stuff was not for me and immediately*

phoned the police. They arrested him whilst trying to sell his swag to another shopkeeper. The law had apparently been after him for months, following his trail of break-ins, all across south Wales.

There were yet two more secretaire bookcases in this period, one from an old school acquaintance who'd inherited it and another, from of all places, the butcher's shop up the street. The man had seen the one for sale in the window and said he'd another, not dissimilar, in the storage rooms above the shop. The little antique shop, that had initially felt unlucky, was doing that well, John Dodds had begun to mull over the notion of moving to larger premises. The logistics of getting things in and out of the present one was a constant frustration, plus he competed with the local buses and post office vans for parking. The main stop for the Shrewsbury bus was ten yards up the street and below the shop, was the post office. Also dealers calling often made it impossible to park and unload.

---One day I'd returned with the van piled high and unable to park directly outside the shop, left it, alongside the three vehicles hugging the curb. Business within was frenetic, the phone kept ringing and suddenly it hit me, I'd left the van parked, not beside the road, but actually in it. I flew to the door to see all three cars had gone and there near mid-road, like a ship in full sail, swaying as a huge grain truck thundered past, was my van. I was on fairly friendly terms with the traffic warden, who often warned when I was pushing my luck, but I don't think she'd have countenanced me leaving my *vehicle parked in the middle of the main road through town.*

With still playing rugby, during the season it posed a problem, regarding Saturday sales. At the most frequently held, the Craven Arms cattle market venue, he was pleasantly surprised to discover, he did better by leaving prices with the porter than if he stood there himself. The man was completely trustworthy and appreciated the odd tip, plus they had something in common; he had once lived in the cottage John Dodds now owned. Not surprisingly, water had been their main problem, the only pump being located 300 yards along the lane. As children, if he and his brother went out walking, they carried a bottle apiece and never dared return home without first filling them.

John Dodds wrote:---*It began to dawn on me, that quite a few in the trade, followed the lead of those considered a success, with the reasoning, if the likes of Mr. Dodds can see a profit in something, then going one bid more couldn't do them any harm. By having a quiet word and leaving my bids with the porter, they didn't know which lots I wanted nor how much I was prepared to pay. The one Sunday, following the Saturday sale in the cattle market, I came away with two Georgian oak tripod tables and two early 18th century oak side tables, for half the money I'd left on them. Just like Richard Cole had said, many dealers whether part of a ring or not, can become a better judge of the person buying, than they are of the goods being bought. With no-one to follow, they were lost.*

Whilst still on the subject of salerooms, I'll pop in this little observation. John had often wondered, why three of the strongest dealers in the area, left their prices with three of the most ineffective men in the trade. It suddenly hit him one day. It was because they were incapable of learning, not so much about the goods themselves, but the ultimate value of them. Their timidity made them invaluable, for they were never likely to flourish and become stiff opposition.

Here's a vignette he wrote about a pair of them.

---*The two most well-known characters, making their living from holding other people's prices were Joe and Peter. Both were well into their sixties, perfect gentlemen and had somehow managed to make a comfortable living out of antiques without actually buying any. They survived almost entirely off dealer's commissions and knock money. The well-known joke in the trade was that one day, the pair had chanced on a farm sale where there was a magnificent dresser, long farmhouse table, set of chairs, grandfather clock, plus all manner of desirable antiques for sale. But when no other dealers turned up, they both went home.*

A third, in this category, was Jack Callan. He did actually buy the odd thing, such as table-top sewing machines for £2 to sell to a shipper in Ruthin for £3, but had never been known to launch into being the actual buyer of anything decent, unless of course, when holding another dealer's price. It wasn't actually a particularly good lot, he bought at Machynlleth auction on the day in question, but even so, it seemed completely out of character.

I said to him, 'That was a courageous price you just paid for that chiffonier, Jack,' to which he muttered, 'Don't let on, but there's a particularly rare book I've hidden inside it.'

He'd obviously filched it from a job lot and secreted it inside the pine piece of furniture, which with him now being keen to offload, asked, did I have any interest in buying it? It was a pretty example, but even so, £140 was a bit strong and so I offered him £130, which would leave £15 profit. He took my offer and said he'd collect the book when the sale was over.

Out on the pavement later, he asked, 'Have you found it?'

I answered, 'I've looked, but it's not in there.'

'You're joking.'

'No I'm not, have a look for yourself.'

With some urgency, he did just that and staring at me aghast, said, 'Some robbing bastard's nicked it!'

Another sale of note happened in what I imagine to have been 1986. To reward Anne for all the crazy hours he'd been keeping, he'd paid for her to accompany his mother on a week's break to Rimini, leaving him with no choice other than taking the children with him when viewing or attending sales.

---*It was a Thursday sale at Llanfair Caereinion, where I usually did quite well. As I was viewing, Hannah, my daughter, tugging at my arm, said, 'All those children outside. They're speaking language.'*

She'd obviously found it hard to join in their games, for they were all chattering away in Welsh.

'I want to speak language,' she complained.

A little later, I noticed one of the locals, in order to proceed further along the row of furniture, push a cupboard door closed. When it slowly yawned open again, he tried once more. At the third attempt, he looked inside, laughed and said, 'Aww, come and 'ave a look at this,' and beckoning others over, added, 'There's lovely, isn't it?' I joined them, to see two worried little faces peering out from the gloom. Hauling my two children from the floorless cupboard, I suggested they play outside, but of course, to stay off the road.

The auctioneer, barking out proceedings from the village hall stage, had a particularly strident voice and when I later, took my son for a wee, in the facility off to the left of where he held forth, his voice could still be heard, clearly ringing through the hall.

From beside me I heard, 'Daaaad?'

'Yes.'

'Why's that man shouting?'

'He's selling things and he's shouting so everyone can hear him.'

He took this on board, but then asked, 'He won't shout at us for weeing on his wall, will he?'

Another sale was mentioned, not so much because of the item bought, but for the person actually buying it.

It was a Leominster catalogue sale. I noticed a woman meaningfully enter the room. She spoke to no-one and stood stock still at the back of the hall, sleeves of her white blouse pushed back for action. The main lot of the day, a splendid Georgian mahogany bookcase was the next item up. She interrupted the auctioneer's usual winding down through the prices, trying to coax the opening bid, with the clear, no nonsense, £500 and having taken on allcomers to become the owner, she turned on her heel and left.

'Who was that,' I asked a fellow dealer.

'Rosie,' he said.

Another who'd similarly impressed John Dodds, was the buyer of a small walnut bachelor's chest on cabriole legs that had turned up at one of the Machynlleth auctions. It was obviously rare, but even so, it seemed to make a ferocious price, so when driving through Welshpool a couple of days later and witnessing Ian Anderson loading it into the back of a dealer's Mercedes, it came as a stark reminder, even though he'd learnt a great deal, there was still a long way to go.

I'll deal with one more sale from this period and even though John Dodds found it hugely lucrative, it was mainly the man he met there that made it significant.

At a sale up in the hills beyond Knighton, everything apart from the four-door housekeeper's cupboard had been removed from the cottage and put out in rows on the lawn and either side of the cobbled path. I'd managed to buy an interesting diorama of a room interior, two naïve water colours and every last scrap of pine. Who should approach me end of sale, none other than the famed door-knocker, Mr. Chris Braddock. He said he was interested in the large kitchen piece. He gave it a fair crack, but I declined his offer as it would have left me struggling to earn a profit on the rest of the pine that had come in the deal.

Wagging a finger, he said, 'I think I've misjudged you, Doddsy.
You could be getting a call off me one of these days. You and
I could do a little bit of business.'

There was something here I didn't quite understand and decided
to give Charles another ring.

"Charles, sorry to bother you, but I've a few more questions."

"Ask away dear boy, ask away."

"How exactly did the knock-out work?"

"Well what a thing to ask! How on earth do you expect me to
know a thing like that?"

"I just thought, with all your years in the trade---"

"Well I've heard on good authority, it went something like the
following. End of sale, the interested parties would congregate and
one member would run through the items bought, asking if there
were any claimants. This was always a bit cat and mouse, with
often the strongest buyers staying silent, hoping to put the rest to
sleep. After all the lesser items had been sorted, one might completely
spoil the day of another by quietly saying, 'Before you slip away,
dear boy------.That bookcase you bought. Can I see you on that?'"

"See you?"

"Yes, it was the term used by a claimant."

"But how did the payments work? Did all the money go into a
central kitty?"

"No, not usually. They normally settled up after each piece."

"Sounds laborious."

"Oh no, it was quite good fun, as long as you kept your wits about you. So I've been led to believe of course."

"What I still can't understand is, if money had to be paid out, how did it benefit the eventual buyer?"

"Have you got a pen handy? This is how it was explained to me. Imagine there are ten claimants. If the first five drop out at £30 on, each of the ten would be entitled to £3 each, but being viewed as five who had a tendency to pleasure themselves, their share would be cut back to £2 apiece. Any moaning and they'd be told to bid on their own next time. If a further two then dropped out at £50 on, the extra amount bid, £20, would be split five ways to give those that had still been bidding, £4 each, but again it would normally be cut back, leaving them £3 apiece. Added to that would be the £2 from when the first lot dropped out, making a total of £5 for each. So how much has been paid out so far?"

"£20?"

"That's right, well done, ten paid to the first five to fold, plus the ten paid to the next two out. If the next claimant got cold feet at £70 pounds on, the £20 extra bid, would be split three ways, but again the shares would be cut, meaning that there would only be a further pay out of a fiver, plus his original £5, making the overall total so far, £30. The final two would probably just have a give and take, with the last of the bunch going at let's say another tenner on top, so his share would be a total of £20, making the entire pay out of £50, even though in fact £80 had been put on the item. So the eventual buyer, would in theory, be £30 better off than if he'd slogged it out in the saleroom."

"It sounds quite complicated."

"That was just a simple example, sometimes it ran into the hundreds and you needed a mind like a bookies' clerk."

After a pause, he said, "So I've been led to believe of course. I was told, that years back, there used to be that many claimants, there'd be a division. The weaker bunch had to bid it out between themselves and send a representative into the room where the big boys held court."

"How do you mean a room? I thought most knockouts were held out in a van or nearby café."

"Sorry, I'm talking about the early days, way before my time. At some of the big house sales back in the sixties, the knockout could go on for a full day. They'd rent a hotel room, have food and drinks sent in. At one session I heard about, a dealer, on realising he'd had a lot dropped on him, became that incensed, he ripped all his payment in half and chucked it in the air. They had to gather it up, match the serial numbers and cello tape the notes back together again."

"So things could get quite heated."

"I should say so. I was told of one knockout over Rugby way, held in the infamous Tubby's Café, where all hell broke loose, with fists flying amid a sheer blizzard of money."

"Good grief. What would have sparked that off?"

"Any number of things. Possibly, a few of them being excluded on a major lot."

"So this ring wasn't the same band, constantly touring the sales, almost like a team."

"Nothing like. On any particular day, one of the more established dealers might announce, 'I'm not settling today.' Or he might say, 'I'll sort it out with you three, but you can tell all those other tossers to bid for themselves!'

"What about the auctioneers? They must have been mighty pissed off, with all this going on."

"Some were, but most realised, without the trade bidding, or without running the prices up themselves, the majority of the stuff would get given away."

"Yes I've noticed that in these notes I have. When John Dodds chanced on a sale, no other dealers knew about, the goods were knocked down for virtually nothing."

"Yes, he was always a lucky devil. Most traders dreamt of chancing upon the sale like that. Sadly, I was never blessed with such good fortune. Oh, I've just remembered, there was one division that took place, when I was still fulltime in the business. There was a fine marquetry bedroom suite, a few London dealers had turned up for. Trade at the time was dire and one of the claimants was a certain Ray, who on top of everything else, had been in a bad car smash. He used to drive like a maniac. It's a wonder he never killed himself."

"Would that be a certain Ray from Malvern?"

"The very same. Fancy you knowing that. Well anyway, the London boys said they weren't putting the thing up for the locals to follow them and leech money. The four would have to sort out a price and send a representative to bid for them. When all was done and dusted, the man returned with the question, 'D'you want the good news or the bad news?'

Ray feeling decidedly the worse for wear, said, 'Well I think we'd better have a bit of good news first.'

'It made £24,000!'

'So what's the bad news?' he asked.

'We've bought it.'

He literally collapsed, flat onto his back."

We both laughed and then I asked, "Charles, the main reason for the call was this. Did John Dodds ever participate in the knockout?"

"Now look dear boy, I don't mind explaining about the courses, but don't expect me to talk about individual horses."

"OK I'm sorry. It's just that at one sale mentioned, it reads in the notes as if all the furniture at a sale up in the hills, was sold as one lot. Was that ever the case?"

"Not that I'm aware of. If there were items exactly the same, the buyer of the first could be asked if he wanted to stand on, same price for all the rest, but I've never heard of total house contents being lumped together and sold as one lot."

"Thank you, Charles."

"No bother, dear chap. Quite enjoyed it actually. Brought back a few old memories."

I laughed, because he paused, then added, "Of things I've been told about, you understand."

"One last thing. The sale I'm talking about was over Knighton way, at a place called---. I've got it here somewhere. Ah, here it is, Knucklas. A certain Mr. Braddock happened to be there. Were you also at that sale?"

"I might have been."

CHAPTER EIGHTEEN

With being so busy, John Dodds had almost forgotten about his meeting with the famed, Mr. Braddock. The next encounter made such an impact, however, the section in his writings dealing with it, he'd headed, '*The Tiger's Tail.*'

---*One morning, there came a call from out of the blue. It was Chris Braddock ringing from a call box near Barmouth. He said he had a car load and as he was pulling gear, his word not mine, from all directions, could I drive over and meet him? I said I'd a few things to attend to, but would be there in two hours or so.*

I found the village easily enough, it was the next one on from where he'd rung me and there ahead, half pulled onto the verge and stacked high with furniture, was Chris's car. I was slightly surprised to see Trevor was working with him and even more surprised at the activity in the small place. People all along the street were emerging with items, calling to him, asking whether, what they held, could be of any interest. There were lamps, jugs and basins, a large pair of pot-dogs, brass and copper, blue and white platters and Chris reigned amongst it all, not looking as if he was actually buying, more like directing, as if the villagers were making charitable contributions to aid refugee families. It seemed absolutely unbelievable and if he'd have described such a scene, I'd have been convinced it was just another of his tales.

I was given a cheery welcome, his blond curls and healthy tan giving him almost a cherubic look, but there the comparison ended, for I'd heard of a few who'd come to grief dealing with him. His art at buying, was equalled by his ability to stitch certain items into people, that hard, they seemed destined to be an accompaniment to their eventual demise.

When the frenetic activity finally abated, he suggested we drive to a nearby hotel, where the goods could be sorted undisturbed. Some of the latest purchases, for ease of transport were put into my van and off we drove, to pull into a rhododendron lined driveway of a rather plush looking stone-built pile.

With a man appearing in the grand entry porch, looking none too pleased at the sight greeting him, I waited in the van, expecting to witness a get-thee-hither gesture, accompanied by the rasping of a soldier's farewell. Not Chris, however, puffing on his cigar and striding forward in his expensive grey, fur collared, Crombie coat, he called out a greeting as if walking straight off a film set. Following a few words, he returned, grandly waving instructions to Trevor, who immediately commenced the un-roping. The Volvo was that laden, it wasn't possible to raise the back door until the roof rack was cleared.

It took roughly an hour to negotiate the deal, after which we entered the hotel for coffee and sandwiches. I was regaled with stories of how certain things in the deal had been bought, the goods he had lined up in the pipeline, plus details of the deal I'd missed.

'We tried calling you. Must have tried at least three times, didn't we Orry?'

Trevor nodded and asked, 'Dunt you ever answer the phone?'

'Car was absolutely packed. We had to sell it all, though. Had no choice. Needed the room for the next load.'

'Aa, what 'ee says is right,' Trevor chipped in. *'Car was that packed you couldna 'ave squeezed another thing in there. Not even a butter print.'*

Such talk of course, got me going, just as it was meant to. It took a fair while of dealing with Chris, to differentiate truth from the blatant wind-up. I was told not to worry about payment, but knew he'd not be long in calling for his cash. I had a thousand on me, but with the load coming to just under four, I needed to be pretty nifty selling if I wanted to keep this particular tap turned on.

When Chris left to settle up, I leant across and asked, 'Trevor, tell me something. The one side panel of the dresser? Why is it broken? It looks fresh.'

'Take too long to explain. Look out, he's coming back!'

I was given a hearty farewell and arriving back late afternoon, got straight on the phone to Mike Taylor, a gentleman farmer, who had sold up to put his resources into antiques, dealing from a large half-timbered property in Broad Street. He had often said to ring if I managed to buy an oak dresser and with it costing £1600, I let it go for £1750. It was too cheap, but I needed a quick sale to get the money in to pay for the rest of the deal. The pine was no problem and gradually, the rest of the stock drifted out, refurbishing the coffers. A pine chest, with its simulated mahogany and cross-banded decoration, plus the pair of naïve water colours, were extracted from the load, to be put in the shed at home, for Stuart.

Later in the week, the cottage window was darkened by something massive drawing up outside. It was another load and yet another dresser. By the time the deal was complete, the kitchen table was covered in Staffordshire figures, meat plates, pair of Royal Doulton urns, Georgian cutlery box, pair of lustres, tea caddies, snuff boxes and even silver and jewellery. I settled up on the previous load, but now owed a further £3000+ for that and all the

277

furniture lined along the lane. When they'd gone, I said to Anne, 'I feel like I've got a tiger by its tale and daren't let go.'

I drove to meet them at various locations; an oak double corner cupboard bought from where he'd parked at a café car park near Church Stretton; loads of, mainly pine furniture, from various places in North Wales and I actually accompanied him on a call in Harlech, being quite flattered when asked to pass judgement. It was a rare occasion when the vendor knew exactly how much he wanted and following a nod from me, Chris closed the deal and on helping carry the piece out, could not have looked more pleased, had he just picked the winner in the Derby. It was an incredibly rare patinated pine, chicken coop dresser, another triumph he could regale his customers with. Feeling I needed to reciprocate for all the information passed on by Stuart, he had the benefit of buying it, when really it should have gone to one of the major antique fairs, or I should have kept it.

Not everything bought was fantastic, mind you. Just as with Leon's dealings with the Irish, there were things included, that if left to your own volition, you wouldn't touch with a bargepole. The worst examples were, Britannia-metal tea services, heavy Victorian double ended couches and shipping furniture, at times, that rough, restoration would have cost more than its value. Regarding all these dag-end deals, it was a matter of damage limitation.

It was vital that I still covered the auctions, for I instinctively knew, this cornucopia of goods wouldn't last forever. I couldn't afford to become reliant on it. Of course, I didn't tell my trade customers, where it was all coming from and Chris never turned up at the shop, always mindful to keep one jump ahead of the tax man. All the actual purchases and sales were recorded to the penny in the stock book, for having had a miracle happen as regards the manner of my VAT enrolment, I would have been thoroughly stupid to have abused the reprieve. It's just that the source of the goods was left rather imaginative.

I took the family to the Isle of Man, late May, as usual. Returned with the van laden, as usual, but we were just looking forward to that longed for cup of tea, when the kitchen went dark. A huge van had pulled up in the lane. A swarthy, long faced youth, the sort you don't normally catch sight of in daylight, said he was helping Chris for the day and added cheerily, 'He's just behind me, with a car and trailer load.'

Needless to say, Anne was not best pleased and it was well after dark by the time all negotiations had been completed.

The deals carried on into the Autumn, more spasmodic thankfully, for I'd never have coped with the initial pace. The business would have choked on the volume. As the nights closed in, I bought goods by torchlight and the following morning, would fearfully inspect for damage, tentatively walking along the row of furniture, often stretching 30 yards down the lane.

The man's breadth of knowledge was amazing, being the judge of Georgian jewellery right through to fine furniture. I tested him once on a small enclosed box I'd found in a Llanidloes sale. It was an appealing muted red colour and had only cost a fiver.

He looked at it and said, 'Don't tell me, Jackie. It'll come to me in a bit. I know what it is.' Racking his brains further, he said, 'It's the stand for a Blackamoor figure.'

Apart from the name he'd dubbed me, I was quite impressed, for I wouldn't have known what it was, had it not been for that old warrior, Ben Evans having made a brief appearance, end of sale. He was there for just a day out really, spending most of it in a favourite hostelry and just happened to inform me, what I'd blundered into.

One evening, I arrived home to find Chris and Trevor waiting for me in the kitchen. Helping unload my van, Chris said, 'I know where you've been, Jackie lad.' Pointing to the unusually huge *gallery on a pine chest of drawers, he said, 'You bought that over Barmouth way.' He was right.*

Sometimes, with the price of things escalating, he could be a little left behind, which didn't affect his ability as regards achieving financial gain, for he knew how to ask, but as with the Harlech dresser, he was occasionally hampered when buying. One further example was a Montgomeryshire oak dresser base, he'd been after for years.

'I've softened the moosh up and if you can meet me there Thursday morning, we'll give it a go together. I'll have another rake of gear for you by then.'

I met him at Tregaron and we drove on to the smallholding where the dresser was located. He'd already been there that morning, to open negotiations and I was invited to take a look.

'Now can you help just a little bit?' Chris asked the man.

'No. It has to be £3000. I won't take a penny less.'

Chris looked at me, I nodded, he clapped his hands and the deal was done.

'How much do you want on it,' I muttered as we carried it out.

'Hundred quid will do.'

Yet again, I'd found an example, where the satisfaction of being able to hook an item, meant more than the profit.

One night we were dealing as the frost descended, with goods bought by torchlight glistening all down the lane and I was told there was a double corner cupboard still to come in the load, but as there hadn't been enough room on the car, he'd have to return for it. I was asked to get some readies together for the present deal and he'd be back the following evening.

Seven thirty next morning, hearing a car pull up, Anne groaned and looking out of the bedroom window, I could see Chris beaming up at me, pointing to his roof rack, where a double corner cupboard was roped along its length.

I went down and let him in. 'Thought you said, you had to collect it.'

'I did. I was there at 5.30 this morning. The bloke got quite shirty in fact, but I told him, "I thought you farmers were early risers." His laughter was infectious.

Whether it was the truth or not, you could never tell with Chris, but the fact the ropes weren't frozen like petrified snakes, meaning he hadn't nipped back for it the previous evening, led me on this occasion, to give him the benefit of the doubt. Sometimes, when he was selling, even though doubting the veracity, it seemed almost rude to interrupt, for he'd hold forth, telling the tale, as if a life-long thespian, basking in the laughter it brought. A little light of reality, however, was shed on a few of the deals when chancing on Trevor in the pub one eve.

'That story he told you about pulling that two-foot-wide oak chest. How he turned the bloke by telling him it would take pride of place in the doorway of the Welsh furniture museum he'd opened. He'd have it standing there, ready to put all the customers' cash in?'

'Yes, I remember the tale.'

'All bullshit. I bought that and all the other stuff you 'ad that night.'

'What about the broken panel on the dresser from Barmouth? How did that happen?'

'Well, what happened there was, an auctioneer 'ad been in and told the 'ooman he could get 'er 1500 quid for it and 'ee put estimates

on all the other furniture you bought. Chris turned her, by saying 'ee'd give her three grand for it. When we'd pulled all the other stuff and went to leave, 'er asked, "What about the dresser?"'

'How did that work? I only paid him £1600.'

'Wait and I'll tell ya. He bounced it, din't he. We was pulling it out from beside the fireplace and Chris tells 'er, it's a bit dusty, could 'er get him a rag to wipe it uv? It was all 'er mum's stuff. 'Er lived a few houses along. So anyway, while 'er was off getting the duster, 'ee kicked the panel in. Dunt know 'ow 'er never 'eard it. 'Ell of a racket.'

'I thought it looked fresh. Surely she wasn't fooled?'

'Ee said, "Oh dear, Mrs. whatever 'er name was. Did you know about this?"'

'When 'ee showed 'er, she was most apologetic and Chris looking mortified, said 'ee regretted the position this now put 'im in, for sadly, circumstances constrained him from offering a single penny more than £1500, same as the auctioneer 'ad valued it at.'

'I can just picture him saying that. So in the end, he only made a hundred on it.'

'Didn't matter did it, 'ee'd already pulled all the other stuff.'

'Why does he call you Orry, by the way.'

'One of 'is strange ways. 'Ee just decided 'ee'd call me Horace, one day. His little Orry. Gets on m'tits, but you ooner change 'im.'

'So that's why he sometimes calls me Jack, or Jackie.'

'That's it. 'Ee 'as to make stories up, names up. 'Ee even lies when there aint no need to. I swear 'ee inner right in the 'ead.'

With then not seeing Chris for a fortnight, I knew that was it, just as I'd predicted, he was off to pastures new, one step ahead of the tax man. I couldn't quite see the point, for he was amassing money he couldn't spend. There was the annual car renewal, that he somehow managed to finagle without it flagging up a tax enquiry, but there are only so many new coats, suits, cigars and dinky boots one can buy. What did he do with the rest of the money? He couldn't invest it in land or property, they'd have been on him like a ton of bricks and Trevor told me, what he had back in his rented cottage was nothing to write home about, so what did he do with all that cash?

Having spent roughly four months trading with him, I weighed up one day, what it had meant for the business. On the plus side, it had temporarily made my shop one of the hottest trade destinations in the area; it had vastly boosted my knowledge, but financially, I had come out of it with £16,000 worth of crap owing me nothing. Selling £5000 worth of that would pay tax and VAT on the profits, another £1000 would be swallowed by business expenses, meaning, if I didn't recoup the money on the rest, I hadn't actually earnt a shilling.

CHAPTER NINETEEN

It was at this point that another piece of pure luck came John Dodds' way. His pal, Leon, who he'd never known to have had a cross word with anyone, fell out with a Welsh couple who'd arguably been his best suppliers. He'd arrived one day to find they'd siphoned off the choicest pieces, promised them to another dealer and had expected him to mop up all the leftovers.

Out of the blue, John received a sweet-voiced invite to drive to Machynlleth, with the possibility of taking over from where Leon had left off.

---*I agreed in theory, but first told Leon of the call I'd had, just in case he had notions of a rapprochement. He told me, he never intended to deal with them ever again and so on a Monday evening I ventured forth to try my luck.*

I could see from his manuscript it became a regular trip and on the way, would often call on a dealer living just east of Newtown and the Vaughan's in Llanidloes, before then taking the road west over high-hill country, to finally wend down to the coast. Much of the furniture was pine, but there was also the occasional oak piece, including dressers and the beauty of it was, he wasn't expected to buy it all. So, although not having the same impact as the Chris Braddock deals, this little avenue of profit didn't come with as much collateral damage.

---On one occasion, having my son with me, I set out earlier than usual, but even so, on the return journey could see the little lad was nodding off. I asked him what he thought might be the most important thing on the van.

'The big table?'

'No.'

'That cupboard thing with the shelves?'

'No.'

'The chairs?'

'No, you are.'

'Really?'

'Yes, you're the most important thing.'

He gave a wide-eyed look of astonishment.

John Dodds, at this point described a piece of bad luck, balanced by two pieces of good, followed by an incident that typified Trevor's audacity.

---Mother was helping in the shop. I imparted the good news, that her debt had at last been paid off, for which I received a severe bollocking. She said, if I'd have left well alone, simple compliance with the overdraft arrangement would have eventually paid the debt off in any case. Meanwhile, she could have done with the cash.

You don't know what to do to be right sometimes. Well anyway, can you believe it? She went on to tell me, while I'd been out, a farmer had called in to say, I was welcome to all the furniture, for he was selling up.

285

'Great. Where does he live?'

'I don't know, I never asked him.'

'What? Why not?'

'Didn't think I needed to. He seemed to know you that well, it just never occurred to me to ask.'

'How am I meant to find him?'

'I'm sorry dear, I don't know. He knew you so well. Even knew your name.'

'That's as maybe, but do you know how many flaming farms I called at with Trevor?'

'Well no need to be like that! Surely you can remember those where there was furniture for sale.'

'It would be like looking for a needle in a haystack.'

Fortunately, this was balanced by a call coming completely out of the blue; the chance of a houseful from a farm over Peaton way. On arrival, I was given a pleasant greeting and then, following a puzzled look, was told, 'You don't look much like the bloke that was here before. He was a squat, jowly looking chap.'

'Don't worry, I've been asked to come in his stead.' I realised what had happened. To give himself an air of authority, Alf had been using my business cards and now I had the benefit. A very profitable benefit in fact.

A further piece of happenchance, regarding my shop being used as a trade reference, came from off Long Mountain, courtesy of Trevor this time and he was also the reason for a certain man arriving at my shop one day. I had just locked up and on turning, saw a chap sporting one of those Navaho silver and turquoise *pendants, about to mount the steps. He asked me, would it be possible to see the tribal section in the back of the shop? I must have looked a bit mystified, for he then explained, he'd sold a few items of furniture to an interesting man who had called one day. With his black, straight hair and swarthy looks, he'd taken him to be a descendant of perhaps the Pawnee or Comanche tribes, endorsed by the* fact *he'd described his extensive collection of tribal artefacts in the back room of his shop in Ludlow; moccasins, tomahawks, beads and feather headdresses.*

He looked truly mortified when I told him Trevor no longer worked with me and that I was sorry, but there was no collection for him to peruse.

When he had gone, I smiled, musing over the fact he had probably got Trevor's Indian descent right, but more likely, Rajasthan, rather than Native American. Then my smile broadened further, at the memory of Trevor vehemently avowing Chris Braddock to be a congenital liar.

I surmised, the adjective was probably not one Trevor would have actually used.

Further in the notes, I noticed John Dodds' mother did make slight amends for the lost deal, by somehow chancing on an opportunity in Carlisle. A dealer there had cleared all the pine dressers from a council estate. They were late, ordinary and some even had plywood backs, but the market was that hungry for pine, the whole hired, seven-ton truck load, sold immediately, removed a van-full at a time by Stuart from Bath, who had pre-sold them to a Brighton dealer.

The German beds didn't go so well, however. His mother was offered the opportunity one day, when meeting a Dutch dealer who operated out of Pilling, the same village where John had bought the huge cuckoo clock and overblown oak armchair, years before. With them, not having exactly set the market on fire, he should have taken that as an omen.

---The pine beds sold instantly, the elm beds all went in the end, but nobody seemed to want the heavy oak versions, even though when slotted together, they resembled capacious carved boats. Most of the profit was tied up in them and they'd become a nuisance, blocking part of the chapel. One Sunday afternoon, I decided to tidy the place, but it took longer than expected and nearing day's end, I was struggling to work in that murky winter half-light. The beds were heavy, obstinate and even the sides were a good inch thick. I'd stacked all the head and foot boards and on giving the last a determined shove, a broad six-foot long oak side rail fled from the dark, smacking me, edge on, straight between the eyes. I don't know how I remained standing. I just stood there, feeling sick and moaning to myself as a goose egg lump rose from my brow. The beds went for scrap.

I could see that things still tended to be frenetic, especially with the stock spread out over four locations. Many times, on returning from the Onibury store, he'd see a flashing of Volvo lights, necessitating a U-turn, to return and open up again. Anne often lost track of his whereabouts and felt helpless when traders called out at the cottage looking for him. There were no mobile phones in those days, of course.

One day, Ray from Malvern had called and when she'd apologised, saying she hadn't a clue where he was, he'd answered, 'Fret not, fair maid. He's on his way, this very moment, pursued by a vast posse of dealers.'

In this section of the notes, was a description of how John had skidded to a halt in the middle of the A49, nearly putting an accompanying trader through the windscreen.

---Business had been that frenetic, I'd forgotten my son. The poor little lad looked lost and abandoned in the Onibury school playground.

I noticed the fact, that with Leon's store being out in that same direction, it added an extra dimension to the logistics. The following must have been way back, from the time before buying the van.

---Leon told me he'd dropped a load out at the store, including two pine cricket tables. I said I'd drive out and look, but was urged to hurry as another load was due in at the shop. There was a Leominster dealer there, the one I'd named, 'Black Hole,' but with him being not the sharpest of movers, I knew I could beat him out to the store. As it happens, it was only the cricket tables I was interested in and with my rival's car approaching, I put them side by side on the roof rack, slung a rope through, tossed the store keys to the dreary dealer and roared away to be first back to Ludlow.

It was at about halfway, the gust of wind caught them and I found myself, driving down the busy A road, with the car wearing two tables, like giant spiky earrings. Luckily there was a layby, but on trying to get out, I was faced by two stubborn round table tops and found neither front door would budge. As ridiculous as it sounds, I was firmly trapped by my own purchases. Managing to pick my way through the items in the back, I escaped through a passenger door, just in time to see my rival cruising past to beat me to the next load in at Leon's.

This must have prompted him to write what follows, for again it had happened while driving the Volvo, the vehicle that had preceded the van. I thought, no wonder I'm confused by the order of things, for even in his own writings, John Dodds had put things in the wrong sequence.

---I had bought a number of staddle stones from Leon and asked for the loan of his trailer. The stalks were that massive, we struggled to heave them aboard, but by using an old table leg as a lever, finally managed to line them up in the back. Going through the first of the bends driving towards Onibury, the trailer started to lazily oscillate, swinging like a pendulum, veering the car onto the wrong side of the road. If a truck had been coming as I rounded the next bend, I'd not be here to write this today.

I thought afterwards, it was hardly surprising this had not been written about until way after the event. With the terror of what might have been, he'd probably pushed it to the back of his mind. I happen to know that series of bends mentioned and wouldn't drive through them on the wrong side of the road, for anything, not even a million pounds.

The regular evening trips to Machynlleth continued, but an eye needed to be kept on the weather as apparently, the van was absolutely useless in the snow. John would sometimes ring home from the call box, top of Kerry hill, to say the way was clear and he'd be back in roughly an hour.

A call from that same red phone box had once earnt him five hundred pounds and below is how it happened.

---*There were certain pieces of furniture owned by established traders that by a mixture of rarity and unattainability, took on a legendary status. I'd heard of a small Denbigh dresser and a particularly rare Shropshire dresser base up in Llangollen and another such piece was a Georgian patinated pine Welsh dresser owned by a retired dealer from Machynlleth. It was back in the early days, when I was still a newcomer to the Welsh sale circuit. I was as usual, in a rush, having been held back by all the annoying little jobs involved in running a shop, but couldn't resist stopping briefly to scan items on the pavement, outside the large emporium at the bottom of Corve Street. It was run by a man I wouldn't trust an inch, but had occasionally been successful there. Nothing on the street was of interest, but inside I came face to face with something that glowed with a noble aura, a beautifully patinated pine dresser. Tony, the proprietor, sidling forward, said, 'You know what you're looking at, don't you?'*

It was the legendary dresser from Machynlleth, worth far more than its equivalent in oak, but the trouble was, Tony wanted four and a half thousand for it. First of all, back in those days, I didn't have that sort of money and secondly, he rated it at 50% more than I thought it was worth. I helped him lift it to the back wall. As we relocated the rack, he told me he would adorn it with blue and white and then take photographs.

I continued on my way to the sale, which coincidently, happened to be in Machynlleth. Although late, the auctioneer gave me permission to view behind the rostrum. Ron Baker greeted me, for it was long before our parting of the ways and I told him about the dresser I'd been offered. Word must have got out, for at the end of the auction, having loaded my goods, I was pulling away, only to be flagged down by a dealer standing, literally, in the middle of the road. It was Dave Roberts from Leominster, who hadn't actually been at the auction, but had stopped out of interest, having seen all the vans being loaded.

'Doddsy,' he said. 'I hear tell you've bought something rather special.'

'Really?'

'Yes I've been told you've bought the Machynlleth dresser. I've been after the thing for years, but old Bob wouldn't sell it me.'

Of course, this left me rather stumped for an answer.

'How much do you want for it?'

'Five thousand,' I said, hardly believing my own audacity.

'Drop it round to the shop in the morning, would you?'

Now of course I was in a panic. What if, in the meantime, the dresser had sold to someone else? That would take some explaining. Feeling the complete blundering novice, I actually was and well on the way to looking an absolute fool, I drove at a scorching pace, wondering how I could get hold of Tony. His shop would be shut by now and I hadn't a clue where he lived. At the top of Kerry Hill,

I pulled in and feeling just a little fraught, decided I had nothing to lose by ringing his shop number. Listening to the ring-tone, I prayed he'd decided to work a little late that evening.

I never dreamt I'd ever feel a wave of relief at hearing that particular man's voice.

Trying to sound calm I said, 'Tony, you're working late.'

'Just a few odds and ends to attend to. You sound a bit out of breath. Have you been running?'

'Do you still happen to have that dresser I saw earlier?'

'Yes, it's been much admired, but it's still here.'

'I'll have it,' I gasped.

The next thing was to make sure Dave Roberts paid me. He wasn't the best at coughing up, but I needn't have worried, for when I delivered the stuff of legends the following morning, there was a cheque waiting for me.

'Doddsy,' he said. 'There was no way you were going to get past me, without selling that dresser. You'd have had to have run me down.' He did have the tendency to be compulsive and it was another example of how handling something, could sometimes be more important than the profit.

This had been years before, but with now being such a regular at the auctions over in West Wales, it was only natural that John should be offered goods by those who made their living there. He was often taken to cottages along the coast, or up in the hills, by dealers who had been offered goods, beyond their knowledge or their means. He'd had an amazing house clearance of Georgian mahogany from a shore-front house in Aberdyfi and instantly formed quite a rapport with the Dolgellau dealer who had sold it him, which he sensed might become a problem. If Roger and Joan, at his regular Monday night call, got to hear about it, they'd be furious, for this man was one of their regular suppliers. To have had this one-off deal was bad enough, but shortly after, when just about to leave on his Monday evening run, the same man had rung to notify of fresh stock in earlier that day. It comprised, two cricket tables, a Windsor arm chair, an oak tripod table, two large sycamore bowls and an oak cutlery box, which were all instantly saleable and well worth making the Dolgellau detour, on the way to Machynlleth, but It posed a burgeoning problem, as John Dodds explains below.

---*I was now running exceedingly late and would have to apologise profusely, for turning up at ten o-clock at night. Not only that, the goods I had on board would take some explaining. If they guessed where I'd bought them, I'd have probably been banished, for it was one of those unwritten rules, buying off your customer's contacts, was simply not allowed. Rather than having to invent some spurious story, which Joan, with her feminine intuition was bound to see straight through, I decided to leave the stuff by the gate, located halfway along the track that wound its way up to their cottage. The hedge there was sparse on account of sheep activity, plus the fact it was Winter, meaning it didn't even begin to cover the little array of country furniture, but I couldn't think of an alternative. It was about this time it started to snow.*

The reception was rather frosty, but they did have some soup and bread ready. Deal done and with the snow now spiralling in, we started to load the furniture. I made sure I did the packing within the van, leaving a gap near the side door for my hedgerow fugitives. The load on the roof needed sheeting over and by the time I'd had a coffee and paid, the canvas glistened white beneath the outside light.

I realised I should have turned the van round before we'd started loading, for when attempting to reverse up the slight rise, where I normally turned, the back wheels skidded through to the mud.

On the next attempt, the two tried to push and the van did slew a bit, but still wouldn't go far enough back to allow me to turn. On trying to gain ground going forward, I felt myself being tipped to an alarming angle and heard Joan shriek, 'Oh my God, it's going over.'

I managed to reverse to something more akin to horizontal and Roger said, 'Trouble is, with this snow coming in you might meet the farmer coming up the track. He'll probably want to check on his sheep.'

It was all getting worse, just like the swirling snow, circumstances were hurtling way beyond my control and I now imagined the man arriving in his Land Rover saying, 'Hey, boys, you'll never guess what I've just found in the hedge down yonder.'

It was suggested I stay the night and clear a way for the van in the morning, but going to-and-fro, easing the van a few inches each time, although once again leaning to a crazy angle, I managed to slew it round. I shouted my thanks and Roger wished me luck, saying he'd watch to ensure I made it up the rise leading to the gate. Gaining as much momentum as possible and with back wheels whirring, I managed to snake the van up onto the level part of the track, to park out of sight beyond the gate. Thankfully, my guilty secret was still there, looking abandoned and most incongruous. I dimmed the lights, for if Roger had thought I'd become stuck, he would have hurried to offer assistance. Imagining the sound of his wellies clumping along the track and trying not to panic, I loaded the furniture in through the side door and onto the passenger seat. The snow was still swirling in as I crossed the Dyfi river, but heading east, realising I was now outrunning it, I allowed myself a moment's celebration, at having extricated myself from a complete mess of my own making.

It was that same Roger, who had been the only other dealer at a Dolgellau auction one day. The regular north Wales and Cheshire dealers had never been known to miss it and when all the early bits and pieces had been sold, the auctioneer announced an unprecedented break in proceedings, hoping they'd all turn up, fall out with one another and push the prices up. Not even Luffy or Jim Ash from Llandeilo were there.

---*The half hour wait seemed interminable and I kept eying the double-door entryway, expecting to see at any moment, a silhouetted mob appear, to commence their frenzied rooting through all the lots in the cattle pens. It didn't happen and Roger bought everything of importance for less than you'd dare offer in a house. I gave him a profit, as stated on the invoice, quite legal and as I'd already bought quite a load from his place earlier, I left him to clear it all, which with the loan of a trailer, took the whole of the following morning. The sheer volume of that bought was made evident by the fact it took two visits, to haul it all back to Ludlow.*

CHAPTER TWENTY

Although John Dodds' business had grown out of all recognition, he was at pains to stress, he was still just a small cog in the machine. He called this period, 'Confusing times,' for things were happening in the trade that he didn't understand. Things didn't seem to add up and yet the pace carried on unabated. I picked up the fact, that one of the main driving forces was an itinerant Irishman by the name of Robbie Gemmill. The first mention of this character, was when running oak furniture to the dealer across the street from John's shop. He had made his money in the early days by door-knocking, but now bought from the trade or took the pick of what his fellow travellers brought in from their calling round the farms. Obviously, with all these goods arriving at least twice a week, John Dodds showed an interest and occasionally bought the odd thing that appealed, but in the main, the goods were either not particularly meritorious, or hugely overpriced. What puzzled him was how it all seemed to sell, melting away as if by magic, even the obviously wrong pieces. One example was another of those Shropshire housekeeper's cupboards, in which someone years ago, had decided to replace the grandfather clock with an incongruous looking American wall clock.

He'd written:---*You know the type; a rectangular mahogany veneered case, a maudlin looking woman painted on the glass panel, below the dial and a big label inside, proclaiming the clock to be, from the Ansonia Clock Company. They'd even hacked the central cupboard to accommodate what, to my mind looked like a red plastic nose on an austere gentleman. I'd first seen it in a Cheshire warehouse at Malpas and had been asked the same money as if the thing had been right. Now here it was at even more money in the shed across the road. By the end of the week, like everything else, it had gone.*

I then read, that this Robbie moved on to supply the large shop in Leominster, run by Dave Roberts. Again, it seems, the goods he supplied, were sold on commission and on passing Waterways Galleries, John often saw a parked pantechnicon and men mounting the ramp, burdened by weighty looking lumps of oak. He'd occasionally call to scan the latest loads, but many pieces had that broken-down look, much of it had no hint of a profit left and quite frankly, he found oak furniture stacked in rows, having the only merit of being aged, quite oppressive. Yet mountains of the stuff seemed to go through there, weekly.

For whatever reason, Robbie then returned to Ludlow, offloading his wares at what had previously been a car showroom, the large shop, run by Tony, at the bottom of Corve Street. By this time John found the itinerant's swagger and smug look of disdain, quite insufferable. Plus, what magic wand did he wave to continually have his stock disappear?

Another thing he found baffling, was how certain things he'd personally get buried with, seemed to sell quite merrily at auction. One dealer, who he knew to be a good judge of furniture, would occasionally buy pieces that had obviously been married together, or huge ugly lumps of mahogany that had no merit, other than the wood in them. Mahogany furniture that years before, had been stripped of all character, sometimes made as much money as a patinated piece. It just didn't make sense. Nor did the way many dealers viewed the sales. A quick glance at a piece seemed to suffice and about ten minutes later, they'd be off out the door. At a Leominster catalogue sale, it could take John Dodds a good hour to view, going round, first one way and then to spot things missed on the first circuit, go back through it all again, viewing from the opposite direction. His friend, Gay Walker, even with her years of experience confessed, viewing one particular sale had taken that long, it had brought on a headache.

Quite a number of dealers would turn up for the sale itself, having spent a good two hours in the pub, pouring into the room as if simply on a fun day out. As John gained experience, he was mystified as to how they could buy things that on close examination, he'd found to be just plain wrong and yet move cheerily on as if completely unburdened by mistakes. One example, was a press cupboard that had had its top cut straight through the middle; another was a bureau with a replaced bottom drawer; a chest on chest with drawer linings in the lower section being of completely different wood to those in the upper. All had sold to the jolly throng and yet they were back next auction, half rat-arsed and keen for more. How were they able to keep going?

There were some traders, when having marked their catalogue regarding items of interest, would carry on bidding, taking on the world, until they'd secured ownership, as if any notion of a going rate didn't mean a thing. He was convinced they embarked on each battle with not one clue of what they were prepared to pay, for whenever he tried to sell these same saleroom types anything, they went all dithery as if being asked to venture into the unknown. Even if offered something for half what they'd bid at auction, the very thought of buying in cold blood, seemed to shatter their confidence to pieces. It was as if they gained their strength from those bidding against them, on the basis, if the opposition want it, then it must be a good lot.

A group that obviously did know what they were doing were a quartet of Worcester dealers, who often travelled together. The lesser traders, who hung around for knock money held them in awe, for can you believe it, they pre-knocked the furniture. This it seems was the ultimate in testing one's knowledge. I made a note here to give Charles another ring. I felt he might be able to throw a little light on this and a few other queries I had. One of the most unfathomable being, stripped pine at auction, making less money than it would, had it been painted. John Dodds mentions, he'd frequently taken advantage of this quirk in the market, but failed to explain how it came about.

Going back to the Irish influence, a calm, genuine couple who roved around Scotland in a massive furniture wagon, would journey south and sell all their bounty, to Leon. John, having had the tip-off, would give his friend a profit on the Scottish dresser bases, those with the row of spice drawers along the back, which he sold to Stuart and with Leon having no interest in jewellery, he was able to buy gold chains, brooches, pendants, bracelets, earrings and watches directly off the man's wife, Bridie. A three-thousand-pound investment, could bring a thousand profit and he noted that, dealing with her was not only a pleasure, it always had a hint of luck about it.

Another instance, where luck played a large part, he found quite unfathomable. For some reason, Mr. Berry's tousle-haired son, Tom, had stopped taking his weekly haul to Leon and instead would hove-to outside John Dodds' shop.

He wrote the following:---*Seeing Tom turn up with Volvo and trailer piled high, my heart would sink. He rarely had anything I'd consider buying if it turned up at auction, but he'd alight with an almost bouncing enthusiasm, entreating me to at least consider the better bits. Fully resolved not to buy the chest with a split top, or the small kitchen table painted vivid pink, nor any other of the more unwholesome looking fare, I would relent. But each time, as he worked his way through the load, reminding me that he was being thoroughly reasonable, I would ultimately find, what had once been on car and trailer was now in a heap outside my shop. Passing girls would be greeted with something like, 'Somebody's looking pretty today,' making me curl up with embarrassment, but corny as it sounded, it usually brought a hint of a smile and I can't explain why, but by the end of day, most of his items would be gone. Some dealers were like that, having a sense of luck about them, but with others, even if seemingly having bought a bargain off them, the item could hang around forever, until you were glad to get your money back.*

In this section, he made note of two brothers from the Erin Isle, who unfortunately had a genetic disorder. Their necks, spanned a broad fleshy triangle, from beneath their ears, to the whole width of shoulders, so obviously they didn't call around the houses buying, but survived by dealing entirely within the trade. They would regularly buy off John Dodds, to the extent he was eventually able to look beyond the deformity, to see the person trapped inside. Obviously, his son could be forgiven for what he'd screeched in terror one day, when they'd called at the cottage, 'Mummy! Mummy! There's monsters at the door!'

---Sadly, they were not expected to live long and I often wondered if something could have been administered at birth to alleviate the grossness of what they were burdened with through life.

Other names now came into the reckoning. A note was made, well a tribute really, to two of the Irish traders that stood out at the time, Big Joe and Jim Gore. John Dodds explained, they didn't receive more of a mention, as both sold their oak to dealers higher up the trade echelon, for more money than he could ever think of paying. Big Joe in fact, would often buy from him, giving each twenty pound note a flick as he counted and Jim Gore, if he had anything decent, wanted the kudos of it going to a dealer who'd pay top dollar and be likely to repeat such largesse, not to one still feeling his way, dealing from a tiny shop in Ludlow.

He writes:---*I was up by Dolgellau and saw a Volvo parked in an entryway, with a dresser tied to the roof rack. On pulling in I recognised Jim Gore, who told me he'd made a bit of a detour to look at the church, that supposedly, the Jehovah's Witnesses had erected in a weekend. He said, the dresser had been promised him years ago and the family, true to their word, had recently messaged him, when a recent death had made it available. I did ask the price, but knew he'd want 50% more than I could get for it. When I explained, his valuation left me defeated, he smiled, gave a sympathetic pat on a shoulder and drove off.*

Two other names that came into the reckoning about this time, were Terry and a man from Hampshire, Tim Glenger. He had heard of Terry, but had been advised by his friend Charles, to give him a wide berth, on account of his skill at fashioning desirable items from humble components. When told of a yew wood bureau, that had come into the man's possession, however, he decided to pluck up courage and give him a call. It was virtually on his way home in any case, as he was returning from a Hay on Wye sale.

---Strangely, it was Terry who seemed the more circumspect when I called at his cottage, asking to see the bureau. He told me, that like most small bureaus, it had an incredibly plain interior, but if I didn't mind that, it could be mine for £2,200. I looked at it, couldn't find a thing wrong with it and so bought it. In fact, I made quite a decent profit, which was basically how our dealing relationship commenced. I had the impression the bureau had been in line for an interior upgrade, but actually preferred buying it the way it was and Terry, possibly judging me to be of future use, useful in being on the green side, but willing to have a go, had obviously judged the sale to have greater long-term benefit, than that to be gained from the bureau's imaginative enhancement.

The other name mentioned, Tim Glenger, came across as being willing to fall over himself to be helpful and with him running some of John's goods to prestigious businesses in the south, he seemed a natural choice for him to throw in his lot with. Anne at first sight of the man, had warned, 'Don't trust him.'

John, however, feeling he could handle the man, continued to benefit from mundane mahogany, being run south for immediate profit and Tim found on his travels, things he'd been asked to look out for, pine with original Georgian adornment; blue, green, satinwood, mahogany, anything other than oak simulation, plus on one occasion, a set of faux bamboo chairs, so what could possibly go wrong?

---*Anne, yet again warned me, saying, 'You're teaching the man.'*

I answered, 'He doesn't know who I'm selling the stuff to.' I also of course, hadn't enlightened him to all the other items high in demand across the pond. Here are just a few examples; sailor's shellwork valentines; ship paintings; ship wool-works; early samplers; daubs of Vesuvius; pot-dogs, especially those with baskets of flowers dangling and strangely, way up there, near top of list; Staffordshire figures titled, Uncle Tom and Eva. Also, I have a confession to make here, there was something about Tim Glenger's energy, I found infectious, plus he didn't seem at all phased, regarding launching his efforts into well defended territory and as far as teaching him was concerned, there was certain knowledge he'd picked up in the south, that he was quite willing to share. We sort of, bounced ideas off one another, making the job like an enjoyable challenge and I had no idea, he might have had a hidden agenda.

However, with that brooding look of hers, she said, 'You're being a damn fool and you'll regret it.'

How was it, without knowing a damn thing about antiques, Anne had such intuition? Even when given an insight into the type of compromise stock Tim peddled round the Thames Valley trade, I can only imagine, the fact I'd been affably treated like a co-conspirator, must have been the reason I'd been blinded to what I really should have seen coming. It was obvious, much of what he specialised in back then, had the semblance of what was in demand, but actually, as regards quality and design, missed the mark and when I asked, how he consistently managed to shift the stuff, he'd answered, there were that many clueless traders down in the south, by the time he'd done the full circuit, those he'd originally talked into buying his 'red-hot winners,' had usually managed to climb out of enough of it, to leave them susceptible to another dose. Obviously, when being sworn to secrecy, regarding this, I hadn't realised others, would equally be taken into his confidence, when it came to my turn. Not so much as a recipient of compromise goods, more a recipient of a cunning parasitical force.

Moving on from Mr. Glenger for a while, there was mention of a massive clearance from a house up near Ellesmere. It was Ann Heath's call and having been left the key, she decided to save double handling and sell it all in situ. Half the contents were completely at odds with what John normally bought, burr walnut duchess dressing table, Victorian four-door mahogany sideboard etc, but he knew roughly the going rate and so bought it all, along with the pine kitchen piece, pine farmhouse table and all the other pine crammed into the place. It was as if the contents of a stone farmhouse and a brick town house had for some reason been stuffed into a rambling, dingy 1950's roadside bungalow.

---I sold the brass and iron bed to a rather voluptuous young lady, living near Ludlow and having erected it for her, including heaving on the mattrass, on witnessing her backward leap, crying out, 'Weeee!' I had to remind myself I was a married man.

He was offered another clearance from a pub in the town, which on reading the details, it of course mortified me. I couldn't understand why there had been such a craze for ripping out original interiors, destroying the very atmosphere people now long for. This time it was just the lounge furniture for sale; an x-frame table with a shove-ha'penny board etched one end, circular mahogany-topped cast-iron tables, smoker's bow armchairs, plus tripod tables, of which one amazingly, was yew wood. He'd commented, it was that deeply patinated, it hadn't been obvious at first what wood it was, but of course on lifting it, the weight made him take a second look to confirm, yes it was yew wood. When he'd first thought, in dealing terms, he'd swum the channel, having at last bought a Georgian yew wood tripod table, the first dealer to lift it for inspection, had plonked it straight back down, saying, 'Cedar.'

303

That in fact had sold to a young lad, looking as if not long out of short trousers. His parents explained, he was that passionate about antiques, they'd become caught up by his enthusiasm and were quite happy to finance his endeavours. They were on their way back to Devon, having holidayed in North Wales.

---*I explained the table was cedar, not yew wood, but he replied assuredly, as if having been in the job longer than I had, 'The colour and originality mean more to me, than whether it is constructed from a certain timber currently in vogue.' That first deal was back in the old shop and they became regular callers in the new. His name? John Tredant, who went on to run a vast emporium near Exeter airport.*

Some of the deals done with Mark, from West Wales, would be conducted well after midnight. The man's stamina was incredible. He'd regularly drive through the night, up to Scotland, deal with the Quiet Man who ran the traveller's camp up there, call at various other locations heading south and then finally arrive at John Dodds' cottage. One deal down at the Smithy took until three in the morning and then Mark, declining the offer of a bed, drove the last leg of the journey home.

---*I was knackered just by being up half of one night, so how he managed continue, having been up for two, Lord only knows? It was incredible.*

One deal with Stuart, down in the Ludlow store, had begun at six in the morning, but John Dodds had never sold anything between the hours of 3 and 6 in the morning. It all sounded as if everything was going along swimmingly, but it was in that same Ludlow store one day, that a stark truth hit him.

---*I'd just managed to squeeze the latest purchases into the only space remaining, when it dawned on me, I was effectively trading from no more than one quarter of the area available. With pen and paper, I made a note of what was blocking the rest of the store. It was bad enough that the cost price of those leftovers, totted up to a staggering £25,000, but what I found even worse was, if someone gifted me £25,000, I would not go out and buy a single item on the list. So how had it happened? I realised, with the space available, I'd let my standards slip, speculating on things I'd never want to be anywhere near, if having had to put them in a shop. It had to stop. I wondered if my dealer friend Charles might lend a hand. Over recent years we'd done a fair bit of travelling together, intent on buying the stuff, perhaps he could help me get rid of the residue.*

Later I walked around the town in search of potential shop premises. If one day I was able to move out of the cramped existing place, I made up my mind there and then, if an item hadn't the potential to grace the new venue, then I wouldn't buy it. It had been too easy to simply close storeroom doors on unwise purchases, out of sight, out of mind and the stores and contents all had to go. At the end of my tour of the town, I'd ruled out anywhere in the centre; Broad Street was beyond my means and anywhere else too difficult to access. It left only, what had once been a bike shop, in Old Street. It was large and on the main road through town, so the trade couldn't miss it. Only trouble was, the place was not currently on the market.

During this time, more and more deals came to him, by way of Terry. In the main, it was good period furniture and it puzzled John, how a man dealing from a cottage and a bit of a shed in a remote location, could come by so much of it. Tim Glenger also came more into the picture, actually buying a small cottage in town, a place tucked away from the main thoroughfare, that you'd never know existed unless someone led you to the door. With no shop to run, he was on the road daily, rooting out possibilities. He told John of an evening sale near Shrewsbury and with hardly any traders having knowledge of it, the pair of them had returned with a van full. Tim also ran things to the shop and even though becoming decidedly useful, Anne had shaken her head in disbelief, that her husband couldn't see what she found so obvious. In the notes, I found a short section where Charles had also advised him to be wary of the man, saying, he had no real substance and was nothing more than what John himself had called him, a chameleon.

When attending a Wellington auction, Tim had alerted him to, he was blithely bidding on a Regency grandfather clock, that had struck him as being rather splendid, when his new contact warned, 'You do know you're taking on the best clock dealer around here.'

How had he found out so much in such a short time? As it happens, his next bid bought the clock which went for a good profit to an American client, who then became a regular customer. Also, from then on, he did consistently well up at Wellington, a saleroom he'd never thought of trying before, but Anne still didn't trust the man.

---*I answered, in business, you can't afford to entirely trust anyone. I wasn't a fool and looking back, thought I was in control of the situation, but I'd forgotten the words spoken in that Morecambe pub years before, 'Believe me lad, I can con anyone. Even you.' Being honest with myself, I was guilty of believing I could easily manage the young newcomer who had brought such recent benefit.*

I came across a small section that had an unusual intro.---*Just in case anyone reading this thinks there were never any bad days, then think again, for there were a number, including the following, where believe me, I wished I'd stayed in bed.*

I was at a house sale up at Clee St. Margarete and had bought a few bits of pine and the pig bench, from out in the garden. The auctioneer was trying to tickle a bid on a plain white kitchen sink, when a lady next to me asked, what had I intended to do with a quaint looking ladder I'd bought?

I answered her and then asked the auctioneer why he'd missed selling the pine press cupboard? I had it marked for £120.

306

'You've just missed it,' a bloke next to me said. 'When no-one wanted the sink, he put it with the next lot.'

'Not the pine press?'

The man nodded. 'Sold it for a fiver.'

A helpful soul nearby said, 'I think that woman over there bought it.'

I offered the lady in question a generous profit, but she wore the stubborn look of someone who'd not let it go, even if I'd have crawled across broken glass to offer a thousand pounds. Anyway, trying to put that and the white sink she'd haughtily proffered, behind me; end of sale, I loaded up and heaved the pig bench onto the roof. I was in a rush as Stuart was due at the shop and driving away, down one of those leafy lanes that look so picturesque when sunlight pierces the tunnelled canopy, I heard two distinct cracks. Immediately stopping and getting out, I looked up to see all four legs had been snapped off the bench. It was at this point I realised, in my rush, I'd forgotten the ladder. On returning, I discovered, someone had made off with it.

Back in Ludlow, I was halfway through unloading, when I saw an Irishman passing and on the back of his pick-up, stood the best spindle plate rack I'd ever seen in my life. Being several tiers high, it must have come from the kitchen of a grand country house. It was just the sort of thing Stuart was after. Locking the shop, I raced off in pursuit and arrived just in time to see Leon helping a Leominster dealer tie the item to her roof rack. Her stubborn look when I asked to buy it, made it obvious, any further notions of venturing across broken glass bearing bundles of cash, would have been utterly pointless. Like I said, I wished I'd stayed in bed that day.

I found a short section titled, 'Odds and ends.' He'd given a description of the difficulty of dealing from the small shop, for anything of rather a grand nature, needing to be displayed for maximum benefit, wouldn't make it round the tight angle into the main shop and so had to go into the back room. As said earlier, furniture too wide to be taken down the side passage that ran beside the stairway, had to be taken through the neighbour's entryway, heaved over a high brick wall and then eased through the picture window in the back wall. He pointed out, the whole performance was arduous enough, without having to repeat the exercise when someone wanting to see a piece in situ, decided it didn't really suit. Then of course, getting the thing back into the shop, not only depended on the patience of the neighbour, but on the fact, they still happened to be home when needing to put the hefty piece back over the obstacle course. He'd made up his mind, he had to find new premises.

Included in this, odds and ends section, were descriptions of maidens in distress. The first had rushed in, saying she was desperate for money. She was on her way to Australia and was a pound short of the bus fare. On giving her the money, he did pass comment on it being a strange mode of transport, to reach the land down-under, but not having time to explain, she thanked him, blew a kiss and dashed back out.

The next was a young girl who needed to be in Craven Arms for a dental appointment and her mother explained they'd just missed the bus. She offered to pay for the petrol, but John Dodds had replied, 'He spent that much of his life working for gain, it was nice, just to do someone a favour for a change. For years after, he received gifts of vegetables from the lady's cottage garden. She even put him on to a call at a cottage near a hamlet with the strange name of Cockshutford.

The final short entry, occurred when he and Anne were just about to leave for the cottage. An elderly lady, peering in through his shop window, missed a step and tumbled onto the pavement. They leapt to her assistance and although obviously shocked, they were relieved to find she was not hurt.

'I've had plenty of reactions to my prices,' said John, 'but nothing quite that dramatic.'

All three burst out laughing, drawing some very strange looks from those waiting for the Shrewsbury bus.

CHAPTER TWENTY-ONE

It was at this point I realised I needed Charles's assistance once more. There were a few things I didn't understand.

"It's not the knockout again, is it?"

"Well partly, Charles, yes it is, but there are other things. They've not really been made clear in the notes."

"Knock or ring, I'm always in," he said with a laugh.

"What?"

"Oh, it was just a joke, a saying from way back in those days of yore. Anyway, how can I help?"

"I've come across the term, pre-knocking. It's of course self-explanatory, but I can't understand why it was talked of in almost reverential terms."

Charles was silent for a while, obviously thinking. "What you have to remember is, many of those touring the sales, apart from the things in their particular niche, didn't really have a clue what they were doing. Quite often, when seeing more established traders wandering off in a huddle, they'd tag along without the faintest idea, which of the items bought, had a little leeway left. At the main catalogue sales, as many as three groups, plus numerous lone operators, could be competing and quite often there'd be only one piece amongst the quarry bagged, that had any mileage left in it. So those drawn by the notion of easy money, would pray one in their little band had an inkling, which lot, from the list of things bought, was worth putting a claim on. With say twelve present, the hangers-on would only have to make a fist of bidding it round twice, to draw a few quid, knowing there was little risk of copping the lot in question."

"So they were leeches, basically."

"We all had to start somewhere, dear boy," Charles said with a laugh.

"So basically, those pre-knocking an item, had to have a pretty good idea of its value."

"Well, it could often be a bit more involved than that. Sometimes, if you desperately wanted to hold something, you had to gamble it past what you intended to pay, for with savings being involved, you could easily sell yourself short. Having held it though, you then just had to hope, at the auction itself, you weren't run up to the very last penny, for then, the esteemed item could well be joining the ranks of the long-term investment category."

"Long term investment? Sounds like a pension plan."

"Well not exactly, but it was generally believed, by the better traders, if you overpaid slightly for star lots, it would not be long before demand made them financially viable."

"Thank you Charles. The next query is about pine."

"Ah, that first broad course of the antiques pyramid."

"John Dodds doesn't explain why stripped pine sold so poorly at auction."

"I think you'll find, that again was down to ignorance. Many of the trade competing at the lower end didn't have shops. They relied on running their goods to those that did. Also, back in those days you could dump things in sales and run them up to the reserve price. If you were a regular buyer and then had need to out something, the auctioneer would often show appreciation of your custom, by only charging 5% commission. So a stripped pine kitchen piece could actually be someone's cast-off, perhaps an item taken in part exchange they wanted rid of and if your contact had full knowledge of where it had come from, not only did you run the risk of being lumbered with the thing, you also stood a chance of looking utterly foolish. The same logic applied to anything really. Lower end traders would avoid like the plague, anything with the suggestion of a trade lot about it. It was actually a good way to put the opposition to sleep."

"How do you mean?"

"A phrase such as, 'I know where that's come from,' would often dampen the ardour of someone geeing themselves up to show a little interest."

"Really?"

"Oh yes. Here's another; 'Is that old thing still doing the rounds? First time I saw that was down in Newbury.' Many of the hangers on, would rarely venture out of the area. Going to Monmouth could bring on a nosebleed, never mind Newbury. There were loads of tricks. It certainly kept you on your toes. Talking of tricks, a favourite, was locking the drawer of the secretaire bookcase and keeping the key. That way, it just looked like a piece with a lumpy drawer, rather than one with a fitted desk inside. I once saw the boards of a pot-board dresser being hidden behind the rack, so it looked like they were missing and of course there was the swapping of lot numbers."

"Yes, I was told about that one."

"At one Welsh sale, where the auctioneer was a bit on the slow side, one bright spark bet him 20 quid, he couldn't sell a hundred and twenty lots an hour. He took up the challenge and the dealer waltzed off with the cab-leg lowboy, the prize of the day, while the rest were still languishing in the nearby hotel bar. A similar trick happened when that Australian bubble was on. The short-lived madness for Vicky mahogany. It was Steve from Hereford who pulled the stunt, just before his business went pop. He asked the auctioneer, with him only wanting three lots, 'would anyone in the room mind if the four-door sideboard etc were brought forward?' No-one did mind and so he bought the stuff for nothing. The lads turning up for the afternoon session were absolutely furious at finding all the lots they'd marked earlier, had been snaffled away, heading for a Hereford warehouse."

"That would be the same Steve who once, teamed up with Richard, I take it."

"My, we have been doing our homework. Many of us in fact, shared transport. It lightened the day and of course saved on fuel costs. Way back, can't remember exactly when, I happened to be with Doddsy viewing a house sale and something about it didn't ring true. It had an odd feel about it. The furniture didn't seem comfortable in the place. Jim Gore was there and John said to him, 'All this stuff has the whiff of the trade about it,'

Jim answered, 'As long as the price is right and the things haven't been got at, what's it matter?' You see, back in those early days, neither of us had the knowledge to distinguish fake from genuine. I'm not sure whether Jim could read or write, but he could certainly read a piece of oak. John and I, back in those formative days, would travel to remote sales, feeling triumphant when carrying home the wormy and broken, for at least in that condition, we knew all was genuine. We hadn't a clue really, now I come to think about it, but boy, we had some great laughs."

"With two separate businesses, how did you sort out, who owned what?"

Charles said with a chuckle, "We managed. Talking of which, a favourite venue, was a sale held every few months at All Stretton Village Hall. It was always on a Thursday, by which time, he and I had usually made the week's money, so it was rather like a fun day out. It was all before the job became so damn serious."

"So were you knocking the stuff out?"

"Dear me, we're back to that again. I'll tell you who actually did and it was blatant, right outside the saleroom door. It was the carpet boys. They'd actually stand round the rug they were knocking out, getting that animated it looked like they were doing some strange ritualised middle-eastern dance. At the Leominster sale, they'd go about it, in full view of the police station."

"What about a chap called Robbie Gemmill?"

"Oh, that grimy little Toby Jug. You didn't need to ask what he'd been eating recently, you just had to look at his shirt front."

"John Dodds couldn't understand how the man seemed to continually, make things disappear; even the wrong and the over-priced."

"Well it didn't really matter what it was, as long as it wasn't being paid for."

"You've lost me."

"It all went to the Cotswolds, feeding the American trade. Of course, a certain amount of money was forthcoming to keep the wheels turning and that second hand car dealer type, always took his cut, but by the time there came a sudden hiatus, Robbie was owed over £100,000. A terrific sum, about half a million in today's money. The threat of a knee-capping sent his debtor into hiding, but I don't think he ever coughed up. John would have eventually known all this. You might find it mentioned further forward in those notes you have."

"Second hand car dealer? Would you be referring to a certain Tony?"

"You've got it. He traded out of what had been a car showroom and had the perfect demeanour to enhance it."

"You and John Dodds seem to share the same opinion, Charles."

Looking down my notes, I searched for the next thing that had baffled. 'Here it is.--- I need to ask you about certain dealers on the sale circuit. They sound almost like a travelling circus, drinking, buying wrong lots and yet coming out of it seemingly unscathed."

"Don't you believe it. It caught up with most of them in the end. I'm surprised John's notes don't mention the fact."

"We're talking about the time back in the Corve Street shop. As you say, I'll probably come across a reference to it in the later jottings."

"Oh, if I remember rightly, at about the time he moved, there was a mini collapse. Up until that point, the crew you mentioned would still have been stitching up clueless American clients. Some were just hobby dealers really, sharing a container to ship the stuff back and having got their fingers burnt, you'd never see them again."

"It sounds like the Wild West."

"Crazy days, but good fun. About the time John moved, I also had copious amounts of clutter I never wished to see again and so between us we dumped the stock all over the place, even down as far as Andover. It all had to go. Sometimes the losses were savage,

315

but amazingly, some loads returned a profit. I think John must have lost a bit of money, but it was better than being clogged up with a store-full of missers."

"What about Tim Glenger?"

"What about him?"

"I found a reference in the notes of you likening him to a chameleon. Could you trust him?"

He chuckled, "Chameleon. I think you'll find that was one of Doddy's appellations."

"Yes, I think you're right. It was. Sometimes, trying to thread the story together, it makes my head spin. But anyway, could he be trusted?"

"Far be from me to talk about others, dear boy---. Well, there was this one instance where I just happened to be on hand. I helped Doddsy extricate himself from a deal he should never have countenanced, one item that glittered, but was certainly not gold, that Glenger had stitched into him. It wasn't a thing he had much experience of handling, giltwood. A rather splendid wall-shelf fabrication, rammed into him, right up to the maker's mark, for a ferocious 600 squids. It was his own fault really, he'd taken the man's word and not examined the thing properly. They looked the part, but were in fact, completely made-up from 18th century gilt frames and what-have-you. Well anyway, he had a chat with a local auctioneer and they were entered into a general sale."

"Not a catalogue sale?"

"No it had to be a general sale, for it was at such, that a certain Frank was known to mooch about, buying shipping crap and taking knock money. For the little ruse to work, the rest of the lads loyal to John, had to be in on it."

"So what happened?"

"I remember it vividly. I happened to be standing on a chair at the time, viewing a painting and on seeing Doddsy walk past, I said, 'Doddsy, old chap,---I hear tell, you intend to fit Frank up with those gilt shelves today. He nodded and I told him, 'I find that utterly despicable!--- Count me in.'

What helped was, one of the Worcester lot, who'd been at the Hungerford sale where the shelves had been dropped on Glenger, couldn't work out why, one week later they'd ended up in a junk sale. When party to the little snare being set, he became that enthralled, he decided to abandon his plans for the day and stay and help. Him being there, one of the big hitters, lent weight to the shelves being the genuine article. A man of his calibre wouldn't hang around at a general sale unless it contained, what we used to call, a bit of a sleeper."

"And did it work?"

"Oh yes, success dear boy. Frank got his comeuppance, Doddsy got his money back and the auctioneer received a decent bottle of plonk."

"So, did Frank find out?"

"What, that he'd been set up? Of course. He'd have known instantly and the girl in the office would have confirmed it. Although Frank was married with children, he couldn't keep his dick in his pocket and smarming the fair maid, he'd been giving her a portion. He'd already caused an upset, getting involved with one of the other girls, which is why the auctioneer was happy to play his part. I know £600, plus £50 pay-out doesn't sound like much of a slap, but it was serious money back then. But worse than that, it was the ignominy. Old Franky was never quite the same after that."

"What were the shelves actually worth?"

"I must admit, they had a good look and so as a furnishing item, you were bound to get a couple of hundred, but nothing more."

"Now I'm not asking you to describe in detail what happened that day, but how in such circumstances, would a knock-out work?"

"Well, if you planned to actually drop something on one of the members, I'm told it was best to ensure they sit immediately to the purchaser's left."

"So you did actually sit in a ring."

"Here! Less of the, you! It wasn't always the case, but generally yes. Well, so I've been led to believe, you understand. Also, I've been told, the purchaser never started the bidding, he wasn't required to, it was always the one immediately to his left. To lure the mark in, the bidding would be brisk and the best location for the strongest member of the gathering, would be on the purchaser's right. He'd probably even up the ante slightly, to make it seem like there was no point pissing about. With the purchaser of the item now bidding for the first time, all depended on the victim giving that one extra fatal bid. You can imagine the intense atmosphere. The man who'd supplemented his living for years by reading the buyer, rather than the item; a professional really, having been in countless similar gambling situations over the years--- would he smell the trap? As soon as he opened his mouth, that would be it; the rest would fold like a pack of cards."

"That's incredible, Charles. Would make a good scene in a movie."

"Now steady on, dear boy."

"No I mean it. Most people wouldn't have a clue what went on, back in those days."

"Yes, I suppose it is worth recording. With most of those old dodge-pots having passed on to auctions in the sky, all this sort of information is in danger of being lost. As regards Doddsy by the way, having climbed out from that near disaster, he didn't gloat. That wasn't his way. It would have appealed to his inner sense of devilment mind you."

"You've been a great help, Charles. Thank you."

"Oh, before I go, it was in that same saleroom that Doddsy overheard Frank talking about a Ludlow shop that had just come on the market. Frank was considering putting in an offer on what had been an old bike shop. John left me his prices and drove straight to the estate agent in Ludlow. Well as you will know from his notes, the rest is history."

PART THREE

CHAPTER TWENTY-TWO

I worked out, that during the 13 years that had transpired, since John Dodds had first ventured out that morning with Pete, up in Morecambe sporting £26 to fund their brief partnership, he'd accumulated enough capital and what we now call credit rating, to be able to buy a large shop in Ludlow. The same premises I'd seen on the internet. I rang Mike for a description of the interior. He asked me not to hold him to it, but thought the main showroom had been about 20 feet deep by 15 wide, plus there was a large window display area, roughly 5 foot deep by 12 feet wide. Up a short flight of steps to the left, was another showroom, half-timbered, 20 feet long by ten wide, and beyond that, going towards the rear of the property, was a high ceilinged room, 15'x15' that ran beneath the kitchen.

I sketched a plan from details given. Steps off to the right of the main showroom led to a small flagstone hallway, where an 18th century oak staircase gave access to the living quarters. Opposite the stairs, was a step down to another showroom, roughly 10'x 10' and running the width of the building was, what once would have been the covered entryway for horse-drawn carriages, from its past life many years before, as an hotel. Out the back was a cobbled courtyard and murky garden, in which was later constructed a long brick fronted work room with garden terrace above. Off to the right of the courtyard was a garage, ideal for storing sold items awaiting collection. The local library held flying freehold over this and the enclosed entryway. It was basically, a massive Georgian, three storey town-house, that had had its ground floor gutted in the 1950's to accommodate a cycle shop.

With not having had a penny spent on it in the intervening years, the property required a frightening amount of work, including complete roof renovation and fortunately, Barclay's Bank had not only provided a £30,000 mortgage, but also a £30,000 loan for all the restoration required.

John had managed to reduce the stock previously contained in the three large storerooms and the shop he'd vacated, down to no more than a couple of van loads. A good deal of the money had gone, buying his mother out of the business, plus she now had full ownership of the cottage in Lancashire, he'd paid for.

As he stared at those remnants of recent dealings, all piled in a heap, just in from the shop doorway, I'll give you his thoughts:---
I wondered, as I'd done in the previous shop, would I ever be able to sell anything again? My friend Mark didn't help on that first morning, for he'd breezed in saying, 'Well John, everyone I know in the trade is pulling their horns in. You seem to be the only one brave enough to be expanding.

'Or foolish enough,' I thought.

However, mid-morning, Richard Cole arrived with a few things for sale. By end of day, I'd sold most of it, plus a couple items of the old stock I'd brought with me. I was on my way.

There was then a section in the notes, of deep reflexion. He knew he was taking on a huge gamble, but instinctively felt it was the right thing to do. He'd had to give up Rugby, partly because of the massive new responsibility, plus of course age; he was pushing forty. His team had won the Shropshire Floodlit Cup three times and he had plenty of cherished memories to look back on, but no longer would he be turning up for matches with a van piled high with furniture.

One time, with it being an important evening cup match at Shrewsbury, it had caused much mirth and comment. He'd arrived with a colossal load, bought from Pete Andrews, who had minutes before, just concluded the deal for its purchase, with John's friend Ann Heath. To have made such a bold move years before, with not being first in on the goods, would have seemed unimaginable, but in the intervening years, his confidence and trade contacts had improved to such an extent, he'd done the deal, outside Ann's Minsterley house in fact, without batting an eyelid. It seems that this Pete had become quite a regular supplier, for I found references to John calling at his home, in the Shrewsbury suburbs.

He describes:--- *Just inside the doorway was an oak court cupboard, Pete had bought for £3000, just prior to the recent mini slump in hefty oak. He'd been quite philosophical, however saying it was 100% right and would one day come into money. It was just that, at that particular time, the sale of large pieces of oak; armoires, kitchen pieces and court cupboards was in the doldrums. He hadn't been caught out by the slump, years before, in silver mind you.*

Pointing down the length of his mahogany dining table, he told me, every square inch had been piled high with silver, worth more as scrap, than as tea sets and salvers. The man arrived close to midnight, bought the lot for cash and the very next day came the crash. Pete had escaped by the skin of his teeth.

So, here was a mention of the Bunker Hunt brother's silver ambitions crashing, that I'd missed on my first examination of the notes. Then, came a rather wistful recollection regarding rugby, for he knew he'd miss his playing days. He'd felt pride at being an equal amongst such an admirable band of brothers, all brimming with health and as fit as butchers' dogs. A committed ensemble that, although from just a small country town, when at their best, had triumphed over decent Birmingham sides, plus Kidderminster, Hereford, Whitchurch, Shrewsbury, Lucton, Bridgenorth and Telford.

The memory must have stirred something, for he belatedly wrote of a time when they'd been driving to one of the easier fixtures, at Llandod, as they called Llandrindod Wells. Being so long after the event, I didn't even try and put a date to it.

---*When passing the shop of a dealer I knew, I realised he must have recently done a house clearance, for there were a number of decent lots out on the pavement, which included an X-frame table and cricket tables. I was of course, keen to stop right there and then, but with not being the driver and kick-off fast approaching, we continued on our way with me, the subject of good-natured badinage.*

With the game out of the way, I asked to be driven back into town. What a relief, it was all still there and as there'd not been the slightest reason to challenge the prices, the deal was rapidly concluded. I returned first thing on the Monday to collect it.

Also at this point, he realised he'd have to abandon deals with the likes of Tom Berry. No more wormy pine, or chests with split tops, the sort of end of deal stuff he'd been taking down to a dealer in Llanbister to turn back into cash. He could no longer afford to take job lots as he was determined, his days of lock-up storerooms were now over. If it wasn't worthy of the shop, then he wasn't buying it.

There are always exceptions though, aren't there? The hefty pine chests, even if an occasional one had a top drawer missing and the pine kitchen tables, bought for buttons on account of leg-ends looking dog-chewed. If chancing upon these, they were kept in the courtyard garage until his contact from Lincolnshire called. The man was happy to shell out decent money for the above, as the more solidly built chests, would have both top drawers discarded anyway, when converted to bureaus and the limpy looking tables were all cut down to a height of 18", to serve as coffee tables.

There was one last old shop recollection in this section. Just prior to moving, he'd dumped a load of stock into McCartneys auction. Considering the circumstances, he was happy to take a bit of a hit, but when one item, a Georgian oak side table, was being sold far too cheaply, he'd bought it back in.

---*Three of the usual suspects approached, end of sale, saying they knew I wasn't settling, but just for once, would I put the oak table up to them. My reply was savage in the extreme, but put politely, my reasoning was, 'Why hadn't they simply bought the thing, when drinking coffee off it, in the back room of my shop a few days earlier?' They actually looked a little chastened, for even they realised, with not having recognised what had been right beneath their noses, it proved those particular organs, although not tuned in to sniffing out profits when entering my shop, became strangely vigilant, come the whiff of knock money.*

Adding to that, end of first day, lucky feeling in the new shop, was a little something in the post the following morning. A cheque from Philips Auctions, London. The bag of golf clubs he'd bought from a Hay on Wye cattle market collective sale, the day his mortgage had been approved, had contained an unusual early rutting iron. It had sold for £1200 and with the £200 he'd got from selling the two snare-headed putters, the total return after saleroom commission, plus cost of photo, came to well over a thousand-pounds, for a £40 outlay.

He explained, *the putters at the time were relatively common and with the saleroom not being interested, they sold from the shop.*

The new shop had a hollow empty echo to it, but it immediately had begun to feel lucky. His children loved it and Anne was glad to be back in town.

The notes referring to the following two years, contained interesting details, but didn't really explain how he'd coped trading valuable antiques from what must, at times, have been a building site. Not surprising really, I suppose. With all that renovation going on and the hours spent travelling trying to find enough decent stock for the cavernous interior, he was probably glad he'd managed, without having to actually write about it.

As regards establishing the new shop, his contacts, Richard and Charles helped. The former turned up with the occasional good lot, but Charles was a Friday regular, with loads from West Wales. Some of it, John had bought blind, trusting descriptions phoned through during the week. It was how he managed to maintain a fairly steady flow of rare pieces such as comb-backed Windsor armchairs, oak cricket tables, the occasional coffer-bach and large sycamore dairy bowls.

The corner dresser, missing its rack had been a little too cavalier, mind you, for although extremely rare, the time had arrived when folks asked, 'What exactly do I do with it?' Or, 'What the hell have you brought that home for?' Not many houses had corners simply waiting for a Welsh corner dresser. Also, anything with a domed top, no matter how much it might have glowed, didn't exactly fly out, on account of not being able to put anything on the top of it. This same logic made work tables hard to sell. Marvellously intact Georgian interiors, became a little pointless if table top adornments needed removing, before being able to display the contents and alternatively, when left open, they became fiddly dust traps.

Another thing that had changed drastically, was the attitude regarding, acceptable condition of items for sale. Remember how he had written, years before, the trade wanted the goods as found? Well, now it seems, they wanted stock ready to display in their shops or at a fair. They didn't mind the odd small defect, but didn't want the hassle of having to lug average 18th century furniture to restorers, wait months and then lug it back again. An exception was of course made on the incredibly rare. Then they just wanted immediate hold of it, for the mark-up would be that great, the waiting time was worth it.

Now he had a decent showroom, there was the chance of selling to the occasional private customer and there was of course, no point in showing them something with a bit of a lurch, or doors hanging off. 'This can easily be put right,' didn't pass muster, it simply lost a potential sale. John had said to himself, '*If it's easily put right, then get it done before displaying it.*' His recent contact, Terry was a genius at cheering things up, but as he pointed out in the notes:--- *It was no use taking him the mundane. An ordinary Georgian chest of drawers, or side table would just sit there in the pile, but a cabriole legged dresser base with a backward inclination, or lambing chair with worn pad feet, would be returned looking perky, within days.*

He continues:---*Every Wednesday, Adam from Macclesfield would call. He specialised in the potential winners, if all had still been present and correct, or things that had been frightfully good before the accident. Occasionally there was the odd lot snared, refreshingly unblemished, whilst toiling to swap out of, that recently swapped for, but in the main it became a question of; was his compromise stock, better than the latest disappointments, I wanted rid of? Profit wasn't really the motive of these protracted Wednesday deals, it was more tantamount to a constant cleansing programme, for with the value of the swapped items tending to be on a slightly inflated estimate, the potential thoroughbred that ill-fortune had reduced to worn out of nag, could then be knocked out for less than the purchase price and yet still return the original cost of the recently flushed items.*

Tim Glenger still rang when buying a decent lot and even suggested John Dodds should remain in the shop, constantly at hand to run the nerve centre, thus allowing Tim to be his main supplier. In reply, he'd said, *'Tim, I've heard, those carried around in sedan chairs, back in Georgian times, became that cosseted they almost lost the ability to walk'.*

A sinister feel was burgeoning, for Tim Glenger now operated from John's old shop. He'd wanted a friend from Wales to have first chance of it, but found out years later, Glenger had slipped the landlord a few quid to swing things in his favour.

A few of the Clarach Bay brethren still rang when having amassed enough decent pine to make it worth John's while, to devote half a day travelling to negotiate a deal. They were easy going affairs as the dealers in question knew he had to make a profit and to keep the business ongoing, did their best to leave him one. Sometimes amongst it, was an item worthy of putting in the showroom, but in the main, it was stacked in the covered entryway through to the back yard, ready to be taken away by the likes of Mark or the couple from Ross on Wye. It all helped pay for the cost of running the shop, but didn't exactly enhance the look of it. There again, at least he wasn't storing missers anymore.

He was surprised how the Clarach Bay 'guilty', hadn't remembered he'd not been convicted that day in Swansea Crown Court, often asking if he'd managed to pay his fine. He didn't bother to disabuse them and with the way his business was burgeoning, almost felt he was being treated like their star pupil.

George, from up by Nantwich, on completion of a deal one morning, suggested they both go to Wilson's catalogue sale that happened to be on that day. They made it just in time to view and then once the sale got underway, John Dodds received what he called, a rude awakening. The Cheshire trade were that desperate for goods, he couldn't get near the prices they were prepared to pay. As the bidding became more frenetic and prices spiralled, the memory of the hollow ring of empty regions in his shop began to haunt, until he felt completely out of his depth.

He did manage to buy a Georgian mahogany mule chest, with its Gothic raised panelling and turned corner columns, almost lending it the majesty of a sideboard, but as his friend Mark pointed out, 'You know those things don't really sell, John.' He did soften the blow slightly by adding, 'But I can see why you bought that one.' John hadn't needed telling. He knew, he'd only been allowed to buy it, on account of it teetering close to the edge of the misser classification.

The other thing bought, was a magnificent Regency cast iron garden bench, that had lurked in the passageway leading to the saleroom. Initially, he'd not been sure, whether it was in the day's sale, or waiting for the next, but his spirits were lifted when it slipped through for £800.

--- When loading, the porter, who kindly gave a hand, told me how fortunate I'd been. He'd been left a commission bid of £1400, but having rushed to the aid of an old lady, who had tripped and stumbled outside the saleroom, he'd missed the sale of it. It was an excellent item for the shop window, but I couldn't really rely on old ladies and pure luck, if I expected to keep the shop stocked.

There was still the Monday evening Welsh run, but he now had much further to travel, as Roger had left his partner Joan to move in with a lady dealing up in Criccieth. It was quite a trek following a day's work and when returning with items of particular merit, he didn't dare leave them on the van overnight. If it was a particularly heavy item, like a dresser base, Anne would be woken to help drag it into the shop, often at well after midnight. Obviously, the drawers would be removed, but they were still a hell of a weight, so at a slant, with Anne grimacing at the lower end, it would be hauled in, to be dumped, just inside the doorway.

One piece of unexpected good fortune was the rapprochement with Ron Baker. He had taken on a shop in Montgomery, the one Mike had pointed out to me, that day I'd been regaled with those Ben Evans' stories. To give the shop a flying start, the Georgian mahogany bookcase he'd bought years before, the tiny yew wood gateleg table and the yew wood child's highchair, John Dodds had always coveted, were put up for sale. He couldn't believe his luck, for at last, he was also able to buy the 26 rushlights Ron had amassed over the years. When it was all collected, John proudly made a window display of yew wood, that included the set of seven 18th century chairs, he and Tim Glenger had bought. A professional photographer produced photos worthy of a magazine and that was John Dodds' first advert to the wider world. Just to add a little colour, he'd included a walking stick, the handle being a carved polychrome piece of folk art, depicting a shepherd with a lamb on his knee. It had come from one of those Wednesday deals with Adam from Macclesfield, two lots of ordinary, swapped for a wild gamble on a £1200 walking stick. Expensive? Well at least, better than the elm dough bin and set of meagre Regency chairs he'd swapped for it.

The only direct result of the advert was Robert Young from Battersea, ringing to buy what had been added to the composition, simply to add a touch of colour; the walking stick for £1450. Strangely, he hadn't even asked the price of the yew wood. Of course, the table and high chair sold almost immediately, but not the dining chairs. What he'd heard Betty Smith say, years before, 'Sorry we don't have the complete set,' was a lesson, that on this particular deal, was rubbed in that deep, it almost left a scar.

---At the sale in question, held at Lampeter Community Centre a few months previously, bidding for six yew wood dining chairs and the carver, Tim had said to me, 'One more should do it.' It certainly did. £12,000 and they became welded to me like an anchor, that didn't exactly snag the seabed as such, more like one that drifts and can never be cut free. Interestingly, the vase shaped panel in the back of the carver had a small coffin shaped patch. Folk-law had it, such a rare feature meant, the original owner had loved the article that much; at his death, the original piece had been slipped into his coffin. I began to feel the patch in the chair was likely to be slipped into mine.

The salerooms were still a vital source of stock and he now even progressed from the Halls of Shrewsbury, low-end general venues, to chance his arm at the catalogue sales, leaving prices on the unusual, rather than run of the mill, that most experienced traders knew the value of. Sometimes, on hauling in the net, he was pleasantly surprised at how reasonably certain items had come in at. It wasn't always the case of course, for at some auctions, the results were that poor, he didn't even relish having to collect the *'flaming things.'* He'd rather he'd have kept a clean sheet, but by diligently persevering, there did come sufficient reward to make the endeavour worthwhile.

When viewing auctions, he'd never note the lot number immediately. Too many watchers. He'd move along the row, to something ridiculously ordinary and only then would he mark his catalogue. Also, to save time, he'd no longer turn mahogany pieces inside out to find out why they appeared wrong. He made himself a rule, if they looked wrong, then they might as well be wrong. Not with oak, however, for there were numerous examples of the quirky, the odd-ball even, being as right as rain. One 1720 side table in a McCartneys auction had the turned portion of one front leg, half as long again as that on the other, exactly as it had been made. Occasionally, the back legs of a table could have mortice holes, where no tenon had ever entered. Either a craftsman's mistake or use of reclaimed timber. As Stanley from Broad Street had said years before, 'Some things can be rather misleading.' John Dodds, however, was starting to get the hang of it. The interior of a carcase looking far too fresh for something 300 years old, he no longer found daunting and occasionally, had even found, on the inner face of 17th century panels, the original bark sitting proud of the chamfering, as if the tree had been felled yesterday.

Other time saving ploys were, ignoring card tables with smiling tops, anything with warped doors, chests and tables with badly split tops and sofa tables where top shrinkage gave the side flaps, the Deputy Dog look.

When buying at the Leominster sales, he'd worked out an understanding with the auctioneer. There were two dealers in particular who used to dog his steps and so, to 'put them to sleep' as the saying went, he'd stop bidding at about two thirds towards his rated value, but the auctioneer, Roger Williams, knew, a biro held to the lips, meant he was still in the hunt.

John Dodds, began to regularly range further south, taking in places like the Carmarthen saleroom and forgetting Luffy had been banned, on suspicion of being part of a dealer's ring, John had asked him one day, if he would be attending?

---He pulled himself to full height, puffed out his chest and proud at thinking he'd mastered a Latin phrase, said very grandly, 'I'm personally not granted there.'

Luffy had rung John one rather hot Saturday afternoon, saying he ought to drive down and view the recent purchases in his new shop in Llandovery. Of course, he was interested, but before travelling all that way, had asked for a run-down of the supposedly tempting acquisitions. They all, in fact, sounded rather mundane apart from mention of a pretty little coffer.

'Luffy? That coffer,---exactly how small is it?'

'Oh, a lovely little thing.'

'Well granted, but you couldn't just run a tape across it could you?'

'What? You mean, you want me to go into the shop and measure it?'

'Well, it's a lot less than you're expecting me to do.'

He gave a 'Humph' of frustration and while waiting, I braced myself expecting to hear 42 inches, rather than the optimum 36.

'Sixty-six inches he said.'

Having avoided another potential wooden railway carriage, I thanked him and said I'd call next time I was passing.

There were still a few deals done with Stuart from Bath, but some of the prices being paid for the items he'd recently been supplying, had become that ridiculous, he couldn't see the point of joining in the madness. A few years previously, he'd raised eyebrows when paying £1100 for a Mintons majolica strawberry server, comprising the main dish, inset with four small bowls and ladle.

It had been in mint condition, but now dealers were gambling up to twice as much on inferior items requiring restoration.

John had enjoyed his couple of years ahead of the pack, thanks to Stuart's information, hot from New York and he certainly didn't want to sully it by joining in a mini, Bunker Hunt type frenzy. He now tended to sell him, brass or leather-bound camphor trunks, Georgian pine with original decoration, pine cricket tables, X-frame tables, small Irish dressers with original paint, recent colourful imports from Austria and Romania and on one occasion, even a pine Shropshire housekeeper's cupboard.

One day, he'd needed a fair deal of mental agility, for amongst the latest goods, bought from Richard, was a Victorian child's toy, a dappled painted pony with pedals and spoked wheels. Mike Taylor, the loyal customer from Broad Street had bought it in a flash and had asked John to drop it round later. No sooner had he gone, than Stuart had unexpectedly pulled up, his van lurching half onto the pavement. First thing he did, was enquire about the toy, for being exactly the type of thing he was looking for, it had pulled him like a magnet.

John wrote:---*My brain was whirring. If I told Stuart the horse was sold, as good as we'd always got on, I'd discovered he could be a funny bugger at times and realised I could well be in danger of him going off in a huff. But, there again, if I sold the thing twice, I'd offend Mike Taylor. A lovely bloke who wouldn't harm a fly.*

Suddenly, the solution came. I added a sizeable margin to the original selling price and Stuart gladly bought it, plus eventually, three thousand pounds worth of other stock. Later that morning, praying Mike would understand, I walked round to his shop and explaining what had happened, handed him his profit in cash, which thankfully, although looking stunned, he accepted.

John Dodds' fears regarding lack of stock began to abate. It seems the more successful he became, the more goods he was offered. He now handled 18th century oak and mahogany, much as he had once done, the masses of pine, moving it on quickly at 10% mark up. All the goods were streaming towards London or the Cotswolds and he looked upon his intervention as being nothing more than a slight diversion, taking a cut, before letting it continue on its way.

It wasn't an obsession as suffered by his Leominster neighbour, Dave Roberts, whose desire to control the dresser market had almost been taken to religious lengths. John had found him one day, head in hands, disconsolate, *'A good dresser got past me today, Doddsy.'*

The man's stock level was huge and his appetite seemed insatiable. At times he would bid in the auctions almost as if the whole messianic experience put him into a trance. John remembered years before at a Nock Deighton sale in Ludlow, the man had stood beneath the rostrum, facing the room with an almost insane grin on his face, bidding with flick of finger over his shoulder until he had bought all the oak in the sale. It was stacked in the saleroom for months as he'd not been able to pay for it. He would dominate the Leominster saleroom for a while and then suddenly disappear from the scene, obviously out of funds, but at about the time John Dodds had taken over the new shop, Mr. David Roberts, enjoying a long golden spell, had taken on a Grade 2 listed building near Talgarth, set in its own grounds. John, on being shown round one day, was definitely awe struck by the panelled rooms, original 17th century moulded ceilings, two fine hunters in the stables, but sensed an eery, unsafe, Great Gatsby atmosphere. *It was almost as if Dave was crying out for help, 'I can't stop now, I'm in too deep.'*

John Dodds had found out where Terry was getting most of his stock from. A man operating from a large Georgian property in Kenchester, a village west of Hereford, advertised for house clearances and antiques in general. Terry was constantly on the phone to him, keeping tabs of fresh stock and with obviously not having the set-up to cope with complete clearances, he'd then be on the phone to John, telling him to drop everything and get round there immediately. On one occasion the van had been that loaded, when carrying on to Terry's cottage to purchase what he'd previously hooked out of the recent haul, he'd needed a ladder to crown the huge pile with Terry's star lots. As he roped it all into place, he'd said, '*This might look like a man making a fortune or it could be one going spectacularly bust.*'

A good loyal contact, Jim Ash from Llandeilo, would ring if chancing upon an interesting lot. He was the perfect man to leave prices with, for between him and his brother Gary, they covered all the sales in the area. It was Jim who had secured for him, the pair of domed, barrel-backed alcove cupboards, from a sale in Brecon. The lofty upper sections were open, with pretty shaped shelves and below generous waist mouldings, each had a pair of panelled doors. John actually attended the sale that day, but had stopped bidding to throw the pack off the scent. Putting in another couple of bids, Jim secured them and then quietly asked the auctioneer to book them down to Mr. Dodds. Tim Glenger had also been present, but at that point, John Dodds was still a couple of jumps ahead. He was watching and learning, however.

It had been whilst driving back from Jim's one clear night in early April, not long after moving to the new shop, that John had thought his end was nigh. He was due to leave two days hence, taking the family on their first foreign holiday. He had never had the money previously and certainly not the time, but having grasped the nettle and booked the Spanish trip, early that year, he'd no choice when the time came, other than go ahead with it. Trouble was, heading home, he felt as if he was about to pass out. Opening the driver's side window wide, strangely made things worse. He started to sweat; his heart felt likely to burst from his chest and he'd had to stop at least three times. On one occasion, looking up at the stars, he'd prayed to be spared, just long enough to at least take the family on the holiday they deserved. Even with the lights of Ludlow beckoning, he had been forced to stop again, pulling into Overton Grange entryway with heart pounding. His desperate stoop to splash his face with water would have sent any onlooker into hysterics, witnessing a full-grown man tumbling to head-butt an inch deep puddle. At the shop he couldn't even summon the effort to find his keys and instead leant on the bell. Anne, seeing his white, haunted look and grazed forehead asked, 'Whatever's the matter?'

'Call a doctor!'

The examination showed, strong heart, no abnormal blood pressure and the doctor, being a little mystified, advised him to just try and relax.

He found the reason for his condition the following morning. The rubber seal on the back door of the van had become completely mangled and when he'd opened the van window, it had sucked air in from the back, meaning the exhaust fumes had been basically gassing him; carbon monoxide poisoning.

The holiday did go ahead and with it being the inaugural flight of Air 2000, I was able to look the date up; April 7th 1987. His son had been so taken with the roar and thrill of the take-off, that was it; hooked for life. He went on to become an airline pilot.

To maintain the stock level, John had secured a hefty overdraft agreement of £50,000, but it was rather more open ended than that and each time it hovered near the £80,000 mark, he would visit the bank manager to explain why.

He remembered a time not so many years previously, when he'd had an urgent call from Dick Gannon who ran a massive shipping business from two properties in Bishops Castle. To keep the bank off his back, he'd needed to sell, with some degree of urgency, all the antique oak he'd furnished his house with, for his overdraft had gone through the £100,000 barrier. The figure had seemed horrific to John and yet there he now was, blithely gambling in that same stratosphere. The shop was still mainly a trade destination and if lucky, a day's takings of £20,000 could immediately right the ship once again, but it still felt like a dangerous balancing act.

One year end, with the property restored and the workshop built, he'd sat down for a few hours with the books. Surprisingly, considering his close call years before with the Customs and Excise, other than the regular checks, he'd been told to expect, he'd not been troubled by VAT inspectors. In fact, the rigour with which the books needed to be kept, actually did the business a favour. John Dodds worked out, that 60% of the previous year's trading had been carried out with the same 12 customers, 20% of the rest with others in the trade, 10% with American clients and 10% privately. If anything drastic happened to those vital 12 main customers, he would be in very serious trouble. Also, at this point, he realised, he was in a tax trap. Each financial year end, his profits were tied up in stock and so to pay the tax bill, it went on the overdraft. Simply earning enough to pay that off, automatically put him into the highest tax bracket, 40%, which with the VAT and National Insurance added, meant he was paying the Government 60% of his earnings. As said, he was in a tax trap and with annual profits never topping 15%, it meant there was very little margin for error. To an outsider, it might have seemed he was earning a fortune, but the truth of the matter was, unless the stock was strictly controlled, he would soon be swamped and insolvent. He gave thanks to heaven, he'd had the sense to get rid of all those storerooms, where lingering mistakes, drag a business down.

I realised at this point, two years must have elapsed since first taking on the new property, for it had been renovated and redecorated throughout, the latter job, having been done by Anne and himself. He'd set himself two years for the job and I was assuming the target had been met. Not only had the stark, minimal 1950's plate glass frontage, been replaced by the Old Curiosity Shop look, I'd seen on the internet, he'd also found the old sign that had originally adorned the front of the building, the one dating back to when it had been a pub. His friend Stanley in Broad Street had bought it, but on closing his shop, suggested John should put it back where it rightfully belonged. When prizing up a floorboard to secure the sign's stud to a floor joist, John was amazed to find the original nut and washer still lying there in the dust. The workshop and terrace, mentioned earlier had also been completed and the antique trade was entering into a new era, as most dealers' cars now had mobile phones fitted.

Tim Glenger had sold his tiny cottage and bought a property down by the river Teme. When he told John Dodds, he and a neighbour had been offered a good price for half their gardens, John suggested they fund and manage the building project themselves. They teamed up with a local builder and plasterer, all went ahead swimmingly and by the autumn of 1989, all but one of the six starter homes had sold. As this story is about John Dodds the antique dealer, I nearly omitted this little enterprise, but then I noticed something.

When the final house did eventually sell, he was the only one of the four to pay the higher 40% tax rate on his £10,000 share, meaning Tim Glenger's business alone, was not generating enough profit to finance the transformation, shortly to follow.

I'd read, that John had had an instinctive feeling regarding this, but what I discovered actually proves it. QED, I said to myself once more.

Regarding the state of the antique trade at the time, John Dodds had written,--- *We had roared out of the slight trough of three years previously and didn't realise it at the time, but all were blithely sailing towards the following year, like the Titanic heading for an iceberg.*

CHAPTER TWENTY-THREE

At this point, I again made one of my pauses. I re-read what had transpired, not quite able to grasp the amazing transformation of the business. I found a note referring to the final year's turnover in the old shop, £350,000, which was quite remarkable for such a small place, but after a simple bit of reckoning, realised, that for John Dodds to have been in the highest tax bracket at the end of his second year in the new premises, with no more than an average profit of 15%, he must have turned over something like £800,000, in what at times must have been a building site.

I tried ringing Mike, hoping to verify this, but couldn't get hold of him. Next best bet, was Charles and as I'd been alerted to a farm sale up in border country, suggested we meet up.

"Wigmore?"

"Yes Charles, I've been told there's a farm sale near there and I've always fancied taking a look at the castle."

"I'm not much of an open-air fiend, but I suppose it will make a change. There's an inn there. We could have a bite to eat."

"Probably best if we meet up in the village carpark, I've looked on the net and there's one below the castle. Would be easier if we go to the sale, in just the one vehicle."

It was early on a Saturday morning and the lone car parked, didn't look like the sort, an ex-antique dealer might be caught driving. I was texting when I heard the scrunch of loose stone and an old estate car with a dealer's full length roof rack pulled up alongside.

I alighted, to be greeted by a cheery, "Good morning, dear boy. Hope I haven't kept you waiting."

Charles was dressed in brown chords, leather-patched tweed jacket and I noticed his brogues must have seen at least half a lifetime's use, for they had been diligently stitched, with pieces let in and had that well lived-in look, as if having bent themselves to become part of the owner's personality. His face obviously bore the marks of time, but when he smiled, a boyish impishness still glinted.

We drove in his car to the sale and I left prices on an attractive wrought iron garden gate and a set of sack scales with original wooden pans and iron weights. Charles knew the auctioneer and assured me he wouldn't run me up, so leaving him commission bids, we now had the rest of the day free. As long as we could get clear of the place. Time and again we had to reverse into gateways to allow Land Rovers and trailers to edge past.

Back in Wigmore, we ordered a snack at the Castle Inn and I began my questioning.

"Bloody Hell! You've got a list."

"Sorry Charles, but I'm bound to forget something if I don't write it down."

I asked him if my estimation of John Dodds' turnover in the late 1980's had been right? Of course, he wouldn't have been party to the actual figures, but his description of the sheer amount of trade being done, confirmed the turnover must have been massive and added, how the business had burgeoned so incredibly in such a short space of time, it actually confounded quite a number in the trade. A few joked, he'd found a little abandoned gold mine in the cellar, but the truth was, the shop itself was the gold mine.

I then asked, "Didn't all the work going on at the time, put a dampener on things?"

"Oh no, dear boy. Those building lads were a cheery lot. All part of the fun."

"I doubt John Dodds saw it like that."

"Well no, don't suppose he did. In fact, he had more the demeanour of a classical conductor, battling to bring a rather avant-garde piece to some sort of order."

It sounded like something I'd have enjoyed being part of, but on the verge of delving deeper, I reminded myself, the book was about antiques not building renovation and feeling boringly diligent, returned to my list.

When we'd last spoken on the phone, there had been a couple of questions I'd meant to ask, concerning baffling things done in auctions and I enquired, why certain dealers, supposedly knowing right from wrong, sometimes bought parts of things, obvious marriages and occasionally, even huge lumps of ugliness. John Dodds had been baffled by this and I'd found no hint that he'd found the answer.

"Oh, Doddsy would have known. He'd have figured it out, but I expect, with everything else going on, just didn't bother to write it down. There was one dealer in particular, from down Reading way, who along with the better stuff, would purposely buy parts and marriages on the cheap, then once a month, there would be a grand marrying up day. If tops and bottoms could be married successfully, a bit of titivation would quadruple their money. Those ugly lumps you mentioned, they were probably just bought for scrap. You could fake the outside of something, but not the backs, drawer linings or frames. I've seen huge, worn-out Regency sofas sold in an absolutely frightful state. It was the rails they were after. You can't fake the way beech and hornbeam looks after 200 years and the rails would have been used to replace those rotted on a valuable sofa or armchair."

"Thank you, Charles. That tidies that bit up. Going down my list;--- in the details of the new shop there are quite a few mentions of a man called Terry."

"Oh, that weasel! There's no doubting, he was a gifted operator, but John used to bemoan his little deceptions. On closer inspection, he'd often find Terry had just given the goods an artful makeover. In fact, he often said, he'd rather have bought them in their original state, as he often had to undo Terry's work, to get to what really needed doing."

"But he could do a good job?"

"Undoubtedly, if he put his mind to it, but he could never completely quell his artful side. He'd always screw you over in the end. In a perfect public schoolboy manner, I hasten to add."

"Why did some stripped mahogany sometimes make as much, as if it had been patinated. John wrote, that he found this baffling?"

"Can't really pin that one down, dear boy. There could be a number of reasons. In the first place, the London trade often finished Georgian mahogany as if it was brand-new. But there again in a saleroom situation, you can never really be sure. Two boneheads, thinking they were the only two to realise an 1880's Georgian revival looking piece was actually the real thing, could fight it out, just to show how clever they'd been. Silver teaspoon in the box of junk scenario. An ordinary hallmarked spoon in one of those tin hut sales, would often make double the amount it would have done, had it been up on display, in a cabinet. Another reason for leeched looking mahogany making silly money, could be, a poor description given to a trader over the phone, or there again, it could be a desperate attempt to fill an order. It was a frequent happening when the Italian boom was on. Some of the Warwick dealers would sell a piece, three times over, gambling they could find a replacement before the shipping date.

There was one, another of those gentlemanly, classically educated types, who was notorious for it. He'd sell a good sideboard, but then put an absolute dog in the load bound for Italy. As long as it had the right shape, he didn't give a toss about the condition, just painted it all over with red stain. Dangerous game mind you, because I expect you can guess what was funding that Italian antique boom. Wouldn't have fancied messing with those boys, I can tell you!"

"I think I know the type of gentlemen you're referring to. I had no idea all this went on. It's only since delving into it, embellished by your tales of ring bust-ups, I've found it wasn't all a sedate world of gentlemanly conduct."

"In some cases, far from it. You had to be a bit nimble to cope. Certainly kept you on your toes. Doddsy wasn't bad at that, mind you. Don't get me wrong, he wasn't into stitching people up, but there again, he was no mug. Far from it."

I waited and a smile slowly widened, before Charles continued. "It happened to involve a certain cove, Jack Callan."

"I've seen his name mentioned."

"The White Rabbit, I always called him. Well Jack often teamed up with Ben Evans for the odd venture."

"Ben the thirsty, the one from the old school."

"You've got it. He's obviously had a mention in dispatches. One of those ghosts looming from the past."

I nodded.

"Well at a sale up in the hills beyond Wistanstow,--- it's a village just beyond Craven Arms, I'd bought two mahogany pedestal desks for John and who should turn up late, but White Rabbit and Ben Evans. Ben could be an awkward customer in drink, which was most of the time and demanded I put the desks up to them."

"You mean to buy them?"

"No, dear boy, to knock them out. They were after a bit of knock money. And being very insistent about it. Well I got hold of Doddsy on the blower and then handed the phone to Callan. Basically, John told him to get stuffed."

The waitress at this point, came to clear away the plates and asked if we wanted coffee. After she'd gone, Charles, leaning forward said, "Well it was the devil's own luck. Shortly after, there happened to be a sale at Penybont Village Hall and on offer was this magnificent oak farmhouse table. Doddsy arrived in a rumble of dust, but was a few lots too late. Well, as you can imagine,--- sweet revenge. It made the White Rabbit's day. He was grinning from ear to ear and gloating in the most sickening manner. I could see Doddsy weighing things up and when Callan was safely back inside the hall, he beckoned me over. 'Charles, what do you rate that table at?'

"I think I said something pathetic like £1800."

"Now Charles," he said, "Don't be silly. I think you're a far better judge than that. What you meant to say was £3200."

"It made me laugh and I remember saying, 'Well if you say so, Doddsy, old chap.' Needless to say, I delivered the table to his shop later that day."

"So let me get this right---"

"It's no good you digging any further, dear fellow. It must be old age creeping up on me. My mind goes a complete blank at times. Apart from the fact he gave me a cheque for £2400, that is."

We settled the bill and walked to the castle. I'd looked up its history and had found, for a very brief period, it had been the family seat of the de-facto ruler of England, Roger Mortimer. He'd teamed up with Edward II's wife, Isabella and after the most horrible murder of the King in Berkeley Castle, 1327, was basically in control of the kingdom. He moved his power base to Ludlow, but it was from Wigmore in 1277, his grandfather had marched west and along with those garrisoning his outpost at Montgomery, had besieged and taken Dolforwyn Castle, perched on the far side of the Severn.

As we followed the path winding its way up towards the remaining gaunt shards of the castle-keep, I asked Charles about the Irish travellers that had once swarmed across the country, stripping out antique furniture. I couldn't understand how they'd ever gained admittance.

"Crafty as a wagon load of monkeys. They'd get into the houses saying they were after feather mattresses or marble washstands. For years, people in Wales thought marble slabs were worth a fortune. What they'd often do, was bid daft money for something virtually worthless, like a washstand or scabby old sofa and with the householders thinking they must be a bit soft in the head, it left the way wide open for negotiations on what the motley crew was really after. If the going became tough, they would start offering crazy prices, just to get the stuff outside. Then having established the goods were indeed for sale, they'd then start the real negotiations, pointing out the furniture was riddled with worm. Of course it wasn't,--- certain sections would have been darted, to make it look like an infestation. Another trick, when no-one was looking, was to jam one of the chairs from a set, down hard on the path, jarring the front leg joints from out of their sockets. Easily put right with a bit of glue, but by making such a song and dance about it, they'd insinuate it was the poor folks who were the crooks, not them. This whole well-worked charade, they referred to, as getting the goods on the bounce."

"Yes, I came across the term in the notes. What about the sofas they'd bid crazy money on?"

"Oh those. The folks would be told to hang on to them, until the special truck came round to collect. They'd be given a few bob, with the promise of payment in full on collection. You can imagine it can't you, the admonishing finger as they left, 'Now don't you be selling our sofa to anyone else.' They of course took the feather mattresses with them, for although they'd been mainly bought just to gain entry, they were actually able to sell them."

The view out across Herefordshire was magnificent and at that point my phone went. It was the auctioneer telling me I had bought both lots and just as Charles had assured, I hadn't been run up on the prices. Back in the carpark, I thanked Charles for his help and could see he truly meant it, when he said, he'd thoroughly enjoyed the little outing. Giving a cheery wave, he drove from sight. He had been good company and I don't know why, but driving back to the farm to collect my purchases, I had the strong impression he'd never been married. The scales I had bought would be an amusing item to hire out as a piece of wedding decor, perhaps, guess the weight of the mother-in-law, but once having smartened the garden gate up, it would go for sale on the internet.

Over the next couple of days, I went back through the notes looking for loose ends. I wanted to complete the picture before going onto the next phase. Cheery details of successful business deals, before what John Dodds described as financially, being almost like war zone.

The two years spent renovating the shop and building the storeroom, he'd likened to an area of swamp that needed crossing in order to reach firm ground. He could either pick his way carefully or take a run at it, hoping sheer momentum would carry him un-mired to the far side. Fortunately, he chose the latter option and somehow still managed to keep trading amid all the building chaos. I had a sneak preview of what lay ahead, regarding the Titanic reference and realised, if all the shop renovation hadn't been completed on time, his business could well have suffered the same fate as that famous ship.

To further his education, he'd paid an annual subscription for London saleroom catalogues and went through them diligently, trying to stay ahead of the game. There were still huge blank spots in his knowledge, knowing little about early ceramics, bronzes, period mirrors and surprisingly, still only had limited experience of handling early oak. I took that to mean, pre-1700.

One clear illustration concerning the ceramic deficiency was detailed in the description of a call on a Chester dealer.

---*It was that maverick cove, Mike Melody and having bought some his oak furniture, also took a punt on a job lot of early Staffordshire for £2400. I'd already made occasional visits to the London rooms when thinking I might have something a bit chancy and so decided I'd try my luck with the Staffordshire haul.*

I unwrapped it all and arrayed it on the Christies' objet de vertu counter. I wasn't expecting to be told I had just hit the jackpot, but there again, didn't expect complete disdain. 'Three to four hundred,' was said in a haughty voice and I was too stunned to tell the young madam, offering so little, whilst on a house call, would probably have me shown the door.

I tried my luck at Sothebys, with much the same result, but at the Phillips' rooms, I was given directions to negotiate the tangle and found my way to a small office on one of the upper floors. I was made cheerily welcome by the two men within, who were busy examining ceramic artefacts.

On having unwrapped my haul yet again, the man examining began moving them like chess pieces, sliding them into two separate groups. The main ensemble had all the larger compositions and I waited expectantly for judgement.

'May I ask how much you paid for all these?'

I told him.

'Oh dear. You see, in this main group, all are either fairly common, or Victorian copies of Georgian originals.'

'I hadn't a clue early Staffordshire was being copied in Victorian times,' I said aghast. I knew copies of early pewter had been churned out at that time, but not Staffordshire.

'Oh indeed, yes. It was quite a thriving industry.'

'I thought all the copies were fairly recent.'

At that point, the man across the far side, swung round and scrutinizing the damage, asked, 'What's that funny little chap there? Is it right?' After a screwing-up of eyes in concentration, he said, 'Yes of course it is. Now that could be a bit of a winner.'

The first man picking it up, said, 'It's a comical little thing. It's meant to be a lion, but whoever made this obviously hadn't a clue what a lion actually looked like.' He handed it to the other expert, who absolutely beamed, 'What a little gem.'

'We would be glad to enter that into our next sale, plus these other five items,' said the first man.

The upshot of it all was, the little lion made £1200, the other pieces made a further £600 and so after having paid commission and photo costs, I was left having to claw back roughly £900 on the rest. The genuine, but ordinary early pieces, such as fat babies with crisp bocage, I sold in the shop and all the large pallid models, of which I'd held in such great store, I put into a

Leominster general sale, where those who were the kings of the tin hut auctions strutted their stuff. If they had been entered into a catalogue sale, they'd have almost certainly not sold, or gone for virtually nothing. Offered in a general sale however, they were perfect bait for the likes of Frank and I'm happy to say, he rose manfully to the task. I hardly made any profit on the deal, but learnt a huge lesson.

Whilst on the subject of reproductions, I found in the notes, how certain items once avidly sought after, were rendered almost unsaleable by the number of fakes flooding the market. Amongst the casualties were ruby glass, Mary Gregory glass, puzzle jugs, frog mugs and pastille burners.

To counter this, there were other items that surged to the fore and if you could get your hands on them, they were instantly saleable. In fact, John Dodds commented, they were in such demand, you had to decide, who should have the benefit of buying them. For a start, anything incorporating the word chemist or spice in their description, flew out. Other items trending, included brass-bound mahogany ship's wheels; model Noah's arks; architectural bird cages; early doll's houses and decent quality doll's house furniture; footbaths; Grand Tour bronzes; phrenology heads; tiny globes in treen cases; cold-painted bronzes and traveller's samples, such as miniature trivets, pots, pans, kettles and fire irons.

John had had to abandon the sale of jewellery and the smaller items mentioned above were kept out of sight until the right trader called. The shop was that large, it would have only been a matter of time before he became a target for thieves. He already removed items of silver from the window at night and in the end had the lower glazing bars discreetly reinforced with metal, for ram-raiding had recently become a fashionable mode of entry.

Not at the Ludlow premises recently taken on by John from Clun, however. It was quite large, having been a garage and the thieves had gained entry via the roof.

John Dodds had obviously not been that impressed with the man's stock, for I found a few lines he'd written.

---*I was down at Leon's and jokingly said, 'They caught those thieves, you know.'*

'Really? I've not heard that.'

'Yes, they caught them trying to get rid of the stuff.'

'Where, at an auction?'

'No, up at the tip.'

Leon laughed, shaking his head as if to say, 'Doddsy, you'll get yourself into serious trouble one of these days.'

Just as John had hoped, the new shop attracted the more esteemed members of the antique trade. Paul Hopwell regularly called for oak furniture, Ivor and Sally Ingle came looking for fair-worthy pieces, Andrew Jenkins for anything that was a few cuts above average, the Phillips's from Harrogate proved they weren't just saleroom buyers and one busy Saturday John had been asked by a rather irate gentleman, 'Is anyone serving here?'

---*The place was packed and I said, 'Yes, make a list, I'll be with you in a minute.'*

The reply was adamant in the extreme, 'I have made a list and would now like some prices.'

The gentleman said he'd buy all six pieces and swept from the shop.

Monday morning, the van arrived and the driver handed me an envelope. Inside was a cheque signed by Richard Chester-Masters.

I looked the name up and found the man in question had been one of the most revered dealers in the west of England, dealing from a shop in Cirencester. From that unlikely start, he became a regular customer.

Here's an excerpt from the notes:---*One deal, involving Ivor and Sally Ingle, that stands out, was on a walnut tallboy I'd just bought. I'd been promised it by the man who, years before, had briefly taken over my first shop, just a few doors up. He now ran goods obtained whilst door knocking and told me his offer on the piece of walnut had been accepted. He would call by with it later that day.*

When Dave Roberts rang later, asking if anything interesting had turned up, I told him about the pending deal.

Well, it didn't materialise and when Dave rang again next morning, enquiring about how I'd fared, I simply said, 'I've been double crossed.'

There was a long silence. Finally, David said, 'Doddsy, you'd better drive to my shop.'

I did and there looking resplendent, was the walnut tallboy. Dave apologising profusely, said, when offered it, he simply couldn't help himself. I later found out, he'd actually stood in the road and waved the door-knocker down.

Well anyway, I bought it and now had the Ingles debating whether to take a punt on it. As you can imagine, being a beautiful colour and entirely original, it wasn't cheap and as they stood there thinking, backs to the window, I was horrified to see their bull terrier was absolutely ripping the shit out of the back seat of their Volvo, triumphantly tossing bits in the air. If they'd have turned, to see why my eyes had suddenly widened, the deal would surely have been lost. They didn't; they bought it and carriers picked it up. That particular dog; a wilful bruiser, possibly irked by the encumbrance of a puppy's name, Bo-Bo, was a serial car wrecker, by the way.

It was Andrew Jenkins who bought the other walnut chest on chest that Spring. My old mate Wes, who many years before had bought the three-leaf wind-out table for £45 and then later, had broken the news regarding the fake paintings I'd bought, told me he had just inherited it. I drove to Presteigne, walked into his morning room, and knowing the provenance of the noble piece, mentally bought it at first sight. With surface rippling like gold and original etched handles blending into the patination, its look of complete, undisturbed composition, was magnificently stunning.

I had literally, just put it in the shop window, when Andrew walked in. Of course, he homed in on it and so I left him to his task. He was very much, his own man and I'd learnt, it was pointless saying anything more than the bare minimum. In fact, on one occasion when I'd tried to make life easier, by telling him a breakfast table was just a made-up furnishing item, he'd still asked if I minded him taking a look at it. Anyway, after ten minutes of diligent inspection, he mounted the steps, to the little space I used as an office and told me he would buy it for the asking price of £14,000.

My first deal with certain renowned dealers from London, was on a 7-foot-long oak farmhouse table. I had only just heaved the thing in and I could tell, the elderly couple were in the trade, but didn't know anything about them. They said they loved the table, but would I mind if their good friend Mr. David Roberts looked at it for them?

It was that honest, you could tell from the doorway, there was nothing wrong with it, but anyway, I agreed to hang on to it for them. There was something about the lady I immediately took to and sensed the feeling was mutual, but I wondered, would their good friend Mr. Roberts put the knife in, as a certain Tony always did in such circumstances. He was the one I'd had the famous Machynlleth dresser from years before. He kept hold of his clients with a Svengali like tenacity and would never recommend they buy so much as a pair of candlesticks from me, let alone a Georgian oak table.

Fair play to Dave Roberts, he said, 'Now I'm going to be kind to you here, Doddsy. You can consider this table sold.'

That was the first of many deals with David and Miya Seligman.

One loyal dealer and buyer of the interesting was Robert Deeley from Stowe. I would often find him parked outside my shop, dozing in his Mercedes at 7.30 in the morning. I always seemed to find him a lucky deal just prior to the Olympia Antiques Fair; oak chair table; oak settle with small drop-down table hinged to the backboards; sumptuous Davenport dinner service; oak lambing chair; five-foot wide, cupboard dresser base and of course various items of yew wood and treen.

Another new customer, jingling through in his sandals, was an oak dealer called Roger Kilby. I think the term, rough diamond must have been coined especially for him. He had a colossus of a frame and you needed two hands to shake just one of his giant paws. He'd never read a book in his life, but rather like my friend Richard Cole, somehow had an instinct regarding early furniture as if directly related to those who had crafted it. He bought a massive oak table from me, the top of which the two of us struggled to lift and on the second visit he just happened to breeze in as I was unloading an early 18th century oak dresser base.

'How much is that, mate?' he asked with a cockney barrow boy chirpiness.

I told him the price and with a gentle stroke beneath the top-moulding and a tap of knuckles on the top, he said, 'I'll have that.'

I had spent a good ten minutes examining the piece, the back, drawer linings, inside the cupboards with a torch, before buying it and yet he seemed able to weigh it up in seconds.

Regarding the Olympia Fair, I had visited it a couple of times and had been simply overawed by the quality of goods and amount of business being done. Each time, I'd come away with my head spinning, for if chancing on a deal, from amongst the sheer magnitude on offer, I had every intention of buying. My reasoning was, I didn't want to appear like the clueless browsers that wandered round my shop on a Saturday. Trouble was, the higher prices asked had such a brain-washing effect, you were almost lulled into buying something that at last seemed reasonable, until realising, it was only by comparison. I would have to stop and ask myself, what could I actually sell that for back in Ludlow? It was usually a good 50% less than the price I'd been quoted. I did make a few minor purchases, but couldn't get remotely near any of the furniture.

As ever, following the frenetic fun of the fair, Ludlow seemed decidedly dull and sleepy, especially with three summer months yet to endure; a time of hardly any trade customers. It made the seeming endless trail of tourists all the more frustrating. With having a much bigger shop, it could become absolutely packed with people who had not the slightest notion of owning anything, even if you'd given it them. In the end, I had no choice other than put a polite notice on the door, 'Serious enquiries, please ring.' Ok, it upset a few, but carrying on welcoming the world into my free museum, would have put me into, what my old mate Trevor would have called, the loony bin. Plus, with the note restricting the numbers, I did actually make a few summer sales, slowly building up a private customer base. And at least it wasn't as abrasive as the sign on a shop door in Liverpool; 'If you're trade, please knock. If you're not, piss off!'

CHAPTER TWENTY-FOUR

It was at the end of that second year in the new shop, the best John Dodds had ever experienced financially, that a strange opportunity was handed him. He describes it as, *insouciantly breezing towards Christmas*, when his friend Jim Ash had rung with a business proposition. The auctioneer in Lampeter had been handed a boxed tape, a cinefilm showing the tour of two cottages, both absolutely stacked with early oak furniture; grand four poster bed, numerous wainscot chairs, joint stools, a dresser, impressive coffers, boxes, side tables along with various paintings, armaments and pewter. Items you might chance upon over the course of five years, but not all together in one setting. The inventory was pages long and the rough estimates a London dealer had given, totalled in the region of £250,000. Jim Ash had felt it was more than he could handle and so got in touch with Ian Anderson and John Dodds.

What follows, is similar to other sections I'd found in the notes, written as if meant to be short story. I made a few alterations, but most of it, is as found. It does wander a bit, in the early stages, but I left it uncut, for it illustrated how John Dodds was burgeoning into a fully-fledged antique dealer. I hope you the reader, find the details regarding what is and what is not acceptable, on a collectable piece of early oak, as interesting as I did.

---*It must have been an extraordinarily upbeat time to be doing business, for the two of us were completely undaunted, even though the two cottages in question happened to be in a small town, perched on the coastal ridge, to the south-east of Perth, Western Australia. Looking back, we must have been completely barking mad. There was no way of telling from the pictures, whether the goods were right, or just completely made up.*

What had happened was, a wealthy Birmingham industrialist had had the crazy notion of recreating Shakespeare's birthplace and Ann Hathaway's cottage in the sprawling settlement of Armadale, fill it with English oak furniture and open it as a museum. Initially, the interest had been that great, the main highway had been blocked by cars queuing to get there. What hadn't been reckoned with, however, was that Western Australia doesn't have a particularly large population and those living on the east coast, if wanting to view this supposed wonderful collection, faced a journey, much further than that from London to Moscow, with not much in between. Business of course, soon tailed off and the inspiration for it, an aging Mr. Fowler, was ailing badly and likely to die from emphysema, if not able to sell up quickly and move from Western Australia's dry climate. Problem was, he needed to get rid of all the furniture, before he could offer the property. Without the money from this, they were broke, as a certain religious sect, whose name I shan't mention, had had all the rest of his millions.

So, this is where Ian and myself came in. We didn't actually know each other that well at the time. I had been climbing my way up the trading ladder, whereas Ian and his father David were very much old school, perched on the very top rung. They had London traders calling that wouldn't even darken the portals of other local shops. I must have made some sort of impression, for Ian and his father, David, known as D.A. in the trade, occasionally entrusted me with covering sales they couldn't attend. They could no longer rely on Jack Callan, for with him having teamed up with Ben Evans, it would have been like asking a goat to look after your cabbage patch.

Ian often made trips to Dublin, returning with things like huge pairs of brass-bound mahogany peat buckets, a pair of ornate bronze hall lanterns, a wake's table and all manner of Irish mahogany furniture, so, unable to be in two places at once, he occasionally needed someone to rely on. On this particular day, however, he did happen to be in residence, but with a number of important customers calling, thought it best to stay put. 'Some days, you can make more money sitting on your backside,' was one of his phrases.

I did warn you; the rendition wanders a bit. Anyway, back to John Dodds.

So out of the blue one day, he rang asking if I could cover a house sale up by Denbigh. I called in the shop, to be left a number of prices including a fairly strong shout on a pair of walnut salon chairs with sea-weed marquetry back panels. With being a last-minute call to duty, I was too late to view properly. The place was packed and an absolute tangle, making it a challenge to squeeze between those bidding and the lots they were bidding for. I managed to locate all the items on the list, plus a few for myself, but realised there were six, not two, walnut side chairs and although having the same lot number, for some reason, the set had been separated. I hadn't a clue how much to bid, I'd never handled the like of these in my life before, but using Ian's price for the pair as a guide, did a bit of reckoning and settled on a figure. There were no mobile phones to resort to, way back then, remember. Anyway, after battling against a particularly obdurate, famed Liverpudlian dealer, they came in at £2,400.

Back in Welshpool, even though it was now pitch black, Ian was still at it, completing a deal with one of his best customers, Harry Mynott. I disinterred the three lesser items from the back of the van, for Ian to carry inside and he asked, 'What are all those?'

'It was all a bit of a muddle Ian, but I actually found there were six of the chairs, dotted round the room.'

'Oh, well done. What did you have to pay for them?'

When I told him, he asked how much I now wanted and seeing as how I'd not even have known about the sale if it hadn't been for him telling me, I added a mere £200 to the cost price.

'Well done Doddsy, I knew you'd use your loaf.' As we carefully extracted the chairs, he asked, 'What's that?'

'It was an A-lot, Ian, probably added after you'd viewed.' It was a bold 1820's mahogany stool with a beautifully embroidered, contemporary seat cover.

Harry had appeared, swaying slightly and Ian, having bought the stool, suggested he should add it to his list, saying, 'You can't miss with this Harry. A bit of a gent.'

It seems it was phrase of the day, for Harry chuckling merrily and obviously having been imbibing, echoed Ian's description, 'A bit of a gent.' Then slurred, 'Shove-id on the list, Ian.'

As we went inside to settle up, Ian muttered, 'It's been one hell of a day. I've taken over 50 grand.'

I was staggered. At that point in time, I'd have been lucky to have taken that in a month. I was comforted, mind you, for contrasting that particular day's work with the one not so very long before, where I'd been totally confused and disconsolate, returning from that same area of Wales with a wood butcher's monstrosity tied to the roof rack, I had in dealing terms, progressed a little.

Thinking about it. It was probably deals such as the one described that persuaded Ian to trust me as a partner on the Australian venture. His reasoning was, with no chance of doing any business between Christmas and early New Year, we might as well give it a go.

So, let's get back to the tale in hand. I had carefully studied the film we'd been sent and had called on a dealer, now retired, who had supplied some of the furniture. Fortunately, he still lived in Ludlow. The Georgian mansion had once held the offices of the Ludlow Town Council, but was now the residence of Mr. Donald Peerce, once the lurking sole trader, within the gloomy interior of Castle Lodge. I knocked on his door and standing on a lower step, explained the intended mission. I said, I was wondering about our chances of success. He prevaricated a little, wearing the sort of smile, one might, if feeling safe from retribution and finally said, 'I'd give it fifty-fifty.' There was a quiet click of the large Georgian panelled door and he was gone.

I had managed to track down the woman who had done the valuation for the Fowlers and she didn't so much talk as if having a plum in her mouth, it was more as if she was struggling to enunciate, in that deep horsey voice of hers, on account of the thing having become lodged in her gullet.

She managed to haughtily force through the impediment, 'It's worth going there,--- simply to view it all.'

'What?' I thought. 'What planet are you on?'

That should have been warning enough and we ought to have abandoned all notion of embarking on the trip, but I suppose the novelty and sense of adventure got the better of us and we ploughed on, regardless.

We arrived in Perth, three sheets to the wind and finished off the courtesy half bottles of wine for good measure, falling into bed gone midnight. Strangely, we both awoke quite fresh, ready for breakfast and the day's action. The lift was one of those glass tubes, where you can see all in the foyer milling about like ants and the breakfast was served in a jungle setting, in which you could have happily spent the whole morning, sampling all on offer, but with neither of us hung-over or jet-lagged, we decided not to linger, but get stuck into the job that had lured us there.

It was the first automatic I'd ever driven and within seconds of having taken the wheel, nearly put a revered British antique dealer through the windscreen. I'd reverted to that learnt over the years, forcing down the brake, thinking it was the clutch. Damn fine breaks, mind you. Car nearly did a nose stand and the squeal resonating in the lofty entryway, drew the attention of a liveried gentleman and the agent we'd hired the car from, approaching as if likely to suggest we hand the keys back.

Without further mishap, however, we made it out to Armadale, to be given a big welcome by Mr. and Mrs. Fowler, who were obviously used to the heat, but with the sun now fully up, we found it absolutely debilitating. If it ever became that hot in England, no sane person would even think about antiques. Nobody ever did a deal in such baking conditions, for even the odd waft of morning breeze felt like a blast from a hair drier and yet there we were, willing to look at a quarter of a million pounds worth of the stuff. We patiently listened to what a fine collection we had the privilege of being allowed to buy and then had to ask, we didn't mean it as an insult, but would we be able to closely examine it all?

With a shrug, as if wondering why this should be necessary, we were granted permission. As we'd suspected, a good deal of it was not so much, completely fake, it was more a matter of being sufficiently wrong to deter serious collectors, or have it chucked off an antique fair by the vetting committee. Members of the general public don't usually realise, a wrong stretcher on a 17th century joint stool can alter its value from a potential £1200, down to the mere furnishing category of £200. A replaced seat on a wainscot chair would do similar. After an armpit dripping two hours, we had made our list of what was worth shipping back to England and it didn't make for extensive reading.

Mr. Fowler, for one who had made a fortune, whilst running an engineering business, in what used to be called, The Workshop of the World, was actually a quiet unassuming gentleman. Dealing with him, however, was like trying to move an insignificant looking fence, not realising it had been anchored deep in concrete.

A smile spread slowly, as he explained, he wasn't prepared to allow cherry picking, he wanted to sell it all. Instincts told us, this was not the time to be telling the man, 80% of what he had was either not up to standard, or in fact, complete fake, especially his much revered four poster bed.

Instead, Ian asked, 'Where's the dresser, the oak dining table and set of chairs, Mr Fowler?'

'Oh those. I let a dealer out east have them on consignment. If you look, they are not on the inventory you were sent.'

It had been my job to study the film and check the inventory.

'Didn't you see they were missing?'

'Sorry Ian, but no I didn't.' It's in fact quite hard to see what isn't on a list of about 350 artifacts, when being there as large as life on the film we'd been sent. It was mind numbing mind you, for thanks to my error, I had possibly led a very important British antique dealer on a wild goose chase.

It was at this point, bad was made worse, by Mr. Fowler telling us, the reason why we hadn't found the incredibly rare stump-work cap, was on account of his advisor, the one I'd named, Mrs Plumstuck, having taken it back to England. She'd run off with the easy prize and we were left trying to negotiate for the heavy luggage.

We went outside into the baking heat to think up a plan B. By the end of the day, having reached plan E and having got, not one iota further forward, we at least now felt the benefit of a cooling breeze from off the ocean.

What hadn't helped, during our fruitless attempts to negotiate, was the occasional visitor stalling proceedings, wanting to view the place. Most were from Britain and Mr. Fowler would go all misty eyed, talking about the old days back home. Meanwhile, thinking of all the money we'd wasted getting there, we were desperate to verbally prod them on their way and haul him back on track.

By the end of the second day, a Tuesday as it happens, we'd reached plan J and had still got nowhere. Ian was brilliant mind you, for he knew all the old dealers, Mr. Fowler had bought his furniture from and as he described their premises and idiosyncrasies, I could see the man going all dreamy eyed. It's what probably saved us from being told to take ourselves hence, for his daughter informed us later, "You've done a lot better than the Christies rep. He was chucked out on his ear after an hour."

"Couldn't you have a word with him for us?" Ian asked.

"I'd be wasting my time. We've all tried to reason with him, but it's got us nowhere."

On the Wednesday morning, things were getting desperate and Mr. Fowler had taken the stance that it was obvious, we simply didn't have the money to buy his valuable collection. With taking all the paintings and armaments out of the equation, the only concession he'd made; on his given estimates, the furniture still came to £150,000.

We of course didn't have that amount between us, but if the goods had been genuine, could have summoned up enough support from those back home, to get the deal over the line.

We were then asked, why we'd shown no interest in the bed?

Ian, looking him directly in in the eye, quietly said, 'Mr. Fowler. You do realise the bed is not genuine.'

During the long ensuing silence, I realised the fate of the mission, hung in the balance.

Mr. Fowler smiled and said almost in a whisper, 'Well you would say that wouldn't you.'

I dared breathe again.

It was during dinner that third evening, a possible way of unblocking the impasse came to me.

We went to the phone booth and I rang Mr. Fowler's number. I apologised for disturbing him, but said we'd be calling early in the morning to say goodbye.

He was obviously taken aback and when asking why we were going so soon, his voice sounded quite tremulous.

I said, 'It's because you've got the better of us Mr. Fowler. I've dealt with some tough customers in my time, but you beat the lot of them. I take my hat off to you. We've both really enjoyed the tussle.'

'Oh, I am sorry to hear you're going.'

'Don't be sorry Mr. Fowler, we've enjoyed every minute. In fact we were hoping we could buy just a few items to take home as a memento of our trip.'

There was a silence, followed by, 'What items did you have in mind?'

'I'll hand you over to Ian, Mr Fowler, he's written a few things down.'

Ian took over and in a very calm manner, read down the list of the only genuine articles of oak in the whole collection, adding as he went, the prices we were prepared to pay. The early stool, c 1580, was put in at the same price as all the other joint stools.

I heard Mr. Fowler's quiet response, 'That should be alright.'

Gin and tonic? I bet we had a bucketful apiece. I also rang home. The whole experience had been that stressful, I hadn't dared share my frustrations and worries with Anne. The only bug-bear in the deal was, we had to include the bed. Ian negotiated the price next morning, from twelve thousand down to four, but left to our own devices, with it being made from odd 17th century parts, we wouldn't even have considered it for two.

We needed to organise payment, insurance and shipping, but once done, we had free time, spending a day at the beach, riding in on the creamy rollers and also drove down to Bunbury where we were entertained by Mr. Fowler's daughter and son in law. We did have an ulterior motive, I must admit, hoping they'd talk the head of the family into being realistic regarding the rest of the load, but all we got was a little sympathy and sheer amazement at the fact, we'd managed to accomplish what we had. I must admit, as we finally boarded the plane at Perth airport, it did feel like we'd pulled off a 'mission impossible.'

We broke the journey home, spending three enjoyable days in Singapore and arrived back in England just in time to witness the recent floods abating. Normal trading continued and we patiently waited for our shipment to arrive.

CHAPTER TWENTY-FIVE

With the next batch of notes looking decidedly patchy, I rang Mike's mobile, hoping he could fill in a few details. He said he was away, out of the country, not divulging where exactly, but on return, would be spending a long weekend, with friends up in Shropshire border country and then with no further commitments for the foreseeable future, suggested we meet up somewhere. I thanked him and was just about to end the call, when he said, "How does Clun sound?"

"Clun? Fine, but when?"

"The friends I'm visiting live up in the wilds near Clun. They're not the type to mind me slipping away for a while. They're fairly easy going and so I could meet you there if you like."

"Sounds great. What day exactly?"

We arranged time and exact location in Clun and I made a note in my diary for two weeks hence. I of course, already knew where the small town was, having looked it up, for the period way back in the story, when John had still been mainly dealing in pine. Meanwhile, I continued with the notes I had.

John had written---*Why is it, that the things you have so long coveted, become available at the very time you shouldn't be buying them?*

He described a huge load of mahogany he'd bought off Terry, that had included a pair of mahogany bookcases, c1820. He admitted, with one being slightly wider than the other, they weren't a true pair, but considering he'd witnessed the trade buying blatantly wrong bookcases, couldn't see it as being a problem. Obviously, the larger of the two would need to be disassembled, before being shut slightly, but even so he expected them to fly out. They didn't, nor much in the rest of the load that had set him back £20,000. Nor, for that matter, much of the other stock he bought from then on. In the space of a few weeks, he'd pile-driven full tilt, straight into the oncoming recession. Not a time to be shipping in £40,000 worth of early oak from Australia. So at last we arrive at the point, he had described as, being like the Titanic sailing towards an iceberg.

Even two coffer bachs, costing £3000, didn't raise any interest. He commented:---*I realised at this point, why things, having become a solid gold certainty, can plummet in value overnight, for once that particular bubble bursts, an item previously worth £2000, doesn't just sink by just a small percentage, it becomes a job to even claw back £400.*

What had suddenly dawned on him, was how a seemingly impregnable market was often held up by only a very limited number of players. Once they pulled out, the price collapsed. In the end, he put the tiny coffers upstairs out of the way. He'd become sick of hearing comments such as, '£2,200 for that titchy thing! Our gran's got one twenty times that size!'

The Australian load arrived and he and Ian, managed to drum up sufficient interest to quickly sell roughly half, but with neither wanting to put their name to the bed, it was run down to Phillips's London rooms along with two of the rarest pieces, the 16th century joint stool and 17th century child's high chair.

As the year wore on, John became more and more worried, for he realised that tumbling prices had left a vast amount of his stock high and dry. He couldn't simply stop buying, however, for the trade was an incestuous beast and news would soon leak out, he was in trouble. Then he'd be finished. His stock would be stigmatised and avoided like the plague, as no-one would want to purchase his bad luck. He simply had to put on a brave face, buy and sell at the new going rate and try his best to find a way of getting rid of the mound of stock bought at the old prices.

He did a great deal of the sale viewing with Tim Glenger, who also had a stock burden, but nothing like John Dodds had. He was mindful, not to share the details as they drove along, for he'd learnt long ago, in business, you can never entirely trust anyone. The one glint of hope was the Dutch trade. They still bought oak with the early look, not minding the unappealing dark stain that had been applied years before to cover up what was wrong with the things. As long as they were less than a quarter price, compared to the real thing, they mopped the stock up. John almost begged a moulded-front chest of drawers, to be sufficiently wrong, so that it would only cost £350 rather than swallowing up another £2000 plus.

He and Glenger used to leave what they called Dutch prices and even though the profits weren't likely to reduce an overdraft, at least it kept business ticking over and made it look as if both were still in the race.

Things became that bad generally, certain items, even though in pristine condition were turned down by the trade, for many had simply run out of money. A number of these spurned items turned up at John Dodds' door and when it came to small coffers, large gateleg tables and clean sets of dining chairs, he didn't have the heart to turn them down. Obviously, he negotiated the prices ferociously, otherwise he'd have quickly gone bust and was mighty relieved the items on offer didn't include dressers. He'd sold 50 of the things the year before, but the sight of yet another, on the present climate, would have probably made him physically sick.

He still went to the Isle of Man, usual time, late May and bought goods, again at reasonable prices. He reasoned, you couldn't just stop buying, for the good times could be just around the corner and then you'd rue the opportunities missed. Calling at a new contact he'd been told of, he found the man's storeroom was stacked chock-a-block with pine scrub-topped tables, mostly on the fairly unsaleable small side. He was waiting for a certain Bart from Warwick to arrive and collect them all. Apparently, he cut them down to 18" coffee-table height before loading, for that way, they took up less room and in their new guise, stripped and polished, they flew out.

Amongst it all was a bold looking six-seater pine X-frame table. This was John's reaction:--- *It was a bit of a sickener, for even in present parlous times, at the right price, about £650 in fact, it was instantly saleable.*

'Surely he's not going to cut that down. I know Bart. Give him a ring for me and ask how much he wants for it?'

The dealer answered brightly, 'That's the one table he didn't want.'

With a wave of sheer relief I asked, 'How much is it?'

'Is it any use to you at forty quid?'

It went straight on the van. Manx trip instantly paid for.

I don't know if the pressure of business had got to John Dodds, but as said, the notes covering those three years became very sketchy. I was hoping Mike might remember what had happened.

I waited for him in the Clun carpark, far side of the pretty packhorse bridge over the stream. As usual, I'd armed myself with a bit of background history.

It was hard to imagine such a tranquil spot, once having been on the front line, but it certainly had been, the castle having seen more

370

action than most. Pre Norman conquest, the area had been controlled by a man with the wonderful name of Eadric the Wild. I bet he'd have had a few stories to tell, or more likely, tales told about him.

After a few power shifts along the border, the mighty Fitzalan family from Oswestry, took control, only for a marauding prince by the name of Rhys, to torch the place on an away fixture from South Wales, in 1196.

The new castle got a battering in 1215, in retaliation for John Fitzalan joining the rebellion against bad King John and in 1233 managed to withstand a siege by Llywllyn the Great, but again the town was incinerated. I discovered, the Llywllyn I'd read about previously, the last native prince of Wales, was the grandson of the one who'd been able to add, 'The Smiter of Clun,' to his credentials, the lad in question, having been about ten years old at the time. Following his grampa's death in 1240, the story of how he eventually clawed his way to power, reads like a warlord's action novel, including the little detail of his dad tumbling to his death whilst trying to make a break for it, by way of an upper window of the Tower of London. Reading such history sends my imagination into overdrive and I imagined him yelling, "Ahhhhhh! The bastards told me I was on the ground floor!"

Anyway by 1350, the fortunes of the Fitzalans had burgeoned to such an extent, they were now Lords of Arundel way down in Sussex. Thinking all the Welsh bother was over at last, they used Clun castle more like a palatial hunting lodge, than a Marches' bastion. Never pays to be complacent, though does it? It never occurred to them, that come the early 1400's, the likes of Owen Glendower would start rampaging up and down the border. I could just imagine Owen thinking, 'Now where shall we go next? I know,--- we haven't done Clun lately.'

That day I'd met George, back in Montgomery, he'd told me Owen Glendower's forces had burnt the town of Clun. I didn't find an actual reference to that, but I can't imagine they'd have done it much good.

"What are you smiling at?" It was Mike. I'd been that immersed in historical imaginings, I hadn't noticed him pull into the car park.

We crossed the stream by the fairly new wooden bridge and began the ascent to the castle bailey, talking about how the book was progressing, his recent journey and things in general. When in the castle keep, I wondered what it must have felt like in the early days, gazing out to the west from an upper room of the defences, knowing that below, as far as the eye could see, lay dangerous territory. Would a princess, wedded to the family, have mused, as she busied herself with her embroidery, 'Of all the places, how did I end up here?'

We exited the castle grounds, up by the bowling green and Mike pointing to a nearby stone house, told me, John Dodds had sent him there to collect things he'd bought from a family he was particularly fond of. The deal had included a rather fine brass and iron bed and a number of bed rails from ancient four-posters. Why they'd kept the sturdy rails, but not the posts, remained a mystery.

"The house wouldn't happen to have a Shropshire housekeeper's cupboard in it?" I asked.

"Yes, how did you know that?" After a pause he said, "Ah yes, you read it in the notes I gave you."

We threaded our way back down to the river and Mike suggested we drive to a hotel, he particularly liked. He rang ahead, to ensure there was a table and asked if there was space available in the car park. Lucky he did, for they held the last remaining slot and having left his car at the bottom of Bishops Castle, I parked mine in the Castle Hotel carpark.

It was here that he told me about the three recessionary years John Dodds had endured. He knew about the period in detail, for with his boss not daring to share his problems with others in the trade and his wife being thoroughly sick of hearing about it, Mike had been his sole confidant.

That written below, with not having taken notes at the time, was all done from memory, but I'm pretty sure I have the main details correct.

"The late 80's was a time of immense confidence. Property prices were rocketing and people felt they were untouchable, borrowing against their rising assets, which in turn powered the economy. Well, inflation began spiralling, interest rates rose and the whole house of cards imploded. There had been no sign, 'Danger ahead,' so when John Dodds realised the whole country was in the mire, he was technically a quarter of a million in debt."

I'd asked, "How do you mean technically?"

After pausing to calculate, Mike continued, "Well, he had £60.000 borrowings on the property and its restoration, he'd financed the half share of the Australian venture, there was an expensive deal involving a pair of bookcases and not realising so many in the trade had run out of funds, the prices he'd left at auction had been spectacularly successful. With all the better furniture locally, flowing in his direction, his overdraft ballooned to £150,000. He was spending on average, £15,000 a week and so it had all seemed to happen in no time at all. If he hadn't rung auctioneers, asking them to hold onto his cheques for a while, his debt would have topped the quarter of a million mark. His overdraft stabilised at £120,000, plus of course there was the 60 grand borrowed on the property and if it hadn't been for an understanding bank manager, he would have been forced to declare himself bankrupt."

"What about the collateral of the shop?"

"A commercial property? He wouldn't have got the £65,000 back, he'd paid for it. It was generally believed that antique

373

dealers didn't go bust. They certainly did. London dealers were dropping like flies and locally, a big name to fall was David Roberts. He like most, had borrowed against the rising value of his property and to be truthful, had vastly overvalued it.

Actually, the bank was as much to blame. They shouldn't have allowed it, but the country had been awash with cash and with the money they were making in interest, they kept doling it out. A bit like what happened in Ireland recently. Realising the trap he was in, he dreamt up a fanciful scheme of technically selling the property to a fellow conspirator, a local dealer with assets in Bristol. I can't remember the details, but as you probably know, when selling a business, you're allowed a certain time to roll the money over, avoiding the tax due on the increased value of the holding. With the inflated value put on the premises, the capital gains tax would have been more than the actual value of the property. He'd created his own trap and the man he'd finagled the escape with, the one with property in Bristol, for whatever reason, didn't close the deal. The rollover time elapsed, Dave Roberts was hit with a massive tax bill and went bust."

"What happened to the shop?"

"The bloke from Bristol bought it. Dave owed money all round the trade, the local auctioneer included. I remember the day he turned up at the shop. He still had a van and hoped to continue at survival level, by running goods around the trade. He apologised to John for the £4,500 he owed and handed over a walking stick. It was a in fact a horse measuring stick, worth about £40. You could tell the two, actually liked one another, for when Dave said, 'Well at least it's a start,' they both burst out laughing.

John asked me to go with him to a sale one day, it was in Bartestree Village Hall, just to the east of Hereford. He needed moral support. I don't think his nerve had gone, but he certainly looked pale and shaky. There was an early dresser base there and apart from having a middle leg missing, was totally original.

John stared at it as if he'd seen a ghost. He told me, with it being a bit on the murky side, it didn't really appeal, but he couldn't afford to appear completely disinterested. He figured out a plan and approaching his main opposition, a dealer from Leominster, said he'd bid it to a certain price and then drop it to put all the also-rans to sleep. It worked. Ted from Leominster bought it for the very next bid and John came away with the turned leg side table and small coffer, the only two pieces of furniture he was really interested in."

"So did this Ted from Leominster give John Dodds a clear run on these."

"There had to be a little bit of understanding. A little bit of give and take. These were hard times. You can tell how jumpy the whole thing had made him. Halfway back, he said, 'Pull in Mike. I just want to check on something.'

A few minutes later, having slid the van door open to inspect the garden troughs and urns he'd bought, he said, 'No, it's alright. Thought I might have just bought a load of moss covered concrete.' Even though times were hard, they flew out by the way, as did the oak table and coffer. Bought and sold at the new prices and you could see he looked physically lifted by not having wrapped another three grand into an oppressive looking piece of early oak. Heartened by the little outing he'd said, 'D'you know what, Mike. I think the best time to buy is when you're skint.'

He still of course, had wages to find. Two lads tidied and polished the furniture in the workshop out the back and his brother-in-law helped run the shop. I wasn't there constantly, just popping in when needed.

Most of his regular trade customers disappeared, or if they did turn up, were only looking for specific things they had definite orders for. One morning, John had just bought an oak 6-seater gateleg table and he couldn't believe his luck, for moments later, Paul Hopwell's van darkened the window.

'As good as sold,' he thought.

Paul of course looked at it and declared it to be the purest and best patinated gateleg he'd seen in many a day, but with it not being on his shopping list, he couldn't afford to buy it. This shook John rigid, for this blatantly honest confession was actually coming from a man who commanded a position in the trade, John had for years been trying to equal. He later asked me, 'How come I couldn't bear to turn it down and yet a man I revere, can?' It was all very scary. Another main customer that disappeared at that time was Robert Deeley, as if vanishing from the face of the earth.

Oh, nearly forgot. It was that same table that did give John chance to have a wry laugh. A lady had been really taken by it, but said, she needed time to think. John told me, she'd returned on the Saturday to buy it, but came up short in the doorway, saying, 'Oh you've moved it.'

'No, I'm sorry,' says John. 'I've sold it.'

He told me, she'd had tears of rage and stamping a foot, had said, 'You can't have done. There's a recession on!'

It was on a splendid, early oak dining table that a similar thing happened. It was a beauty. Say what you like about those times; at least you could buy the stuff. It was getting rid of the old stock that was the problem. Well, anyway, again it was a Saturday and a private customer arrived with his weekend guests. I say a private customer, some called that often, it was a job to say, whether they were actual customers or not. John told me, he began asking these regulars, what had they ever bought from him? Sorry, he was a bit more diplomatic than that. 'Please forgive me, but with all the buying and selling, my mind goes blank sometimes. I can't remember. Do tell me, what was the last thing I sold you?'

'Oh, I've never bought anything, but I always make sure I come and look.'

Some of them were self-appointed tour guides and amateur antique buffs, as was the case this particular Saturday.

The chap had bustled in, relishing showing his guests what he'd been telling them about, but looking mystified said, 'You've moved it.'

John asked him, 'I'm sorry. Moved what?'

'The refectory table I saw in the week.'

'A dealer from London bought it.' He'd actually sold it to Ma Seligman over the phone. Refectory table, was never a term Doddsy ever used by the way, using a Victorian misnomer, didn't exactly burnish your credentials as a budding oak specialist.

The man looked absolutely distraught and said accusingly, 'But I've brought my friends here, specially to see it.'

John had had a basinful of timewasters that particular Saturday and said, 'I'm most terribly sorry. Perhaps I ought to remedy the situation by charging an entrance fee. Then I could leave everything exactly the way you last saw it.'

John told me, a few of the man's guests had looked that ready to burst out laughing, he'd almost been tempted to allow them a squint at it, where it stood awaiting collection from the garage out the back.

He had begun to realise, that as long as he was careful, he was able to bounce along the bottom in self-preservation mode, but somehow had to rid himself of the old stock. The official interest rates at one point went up to a crippling 15% and he was shelling out more like 18%, good money after bad, holding stuff that had cost him too much money. One year he paid £40,000 in interest payments to Barclays Bank. His manager lightened the blow somewhat by telling him, 'At least your tax bill will be less.'

One day he said to me, 'I think I've found the answer.' The plan he devised, was to isolate a certain section of old stock and try and figure out ways to make it saleable. Everything was rendered perfect, each piece was polished until it gleamed and then put in the selling hotspot, straight ahead of you as you come through the door. He'd created a separate account and as each piece sold, to be replaced by the next, the money went into the new account until he'd accumulated £30,000. Having set himself such a manageable target made it like a game and even though he was not making a profit on the sales, he became as enthusiastic moving the old stock as he was the new. The £30,000 was moved to lessen the overdraft and he'd start again. By the Spring of 1992, he was in the black and had even paid off the shop renovation loan. He had realised, that in a recession, try as you might, all one could do, in day to day dealing, was tread water. If you wanted to reduce the debt, it had to be done by hacking out the dead wood."

"So it was almost like tackling a long journey," I said. "If you think about the enormity of driving 850 miles, it seems impossible, but if you do it in 30-mile chunks it can be manageable."

"That's it. Sort of fooling the mind. He was only in the black for two weeks, but told me it felt glorious. The bank manager had said to him, 'I'm not sure how you've managed that.'

He replied, 'Without you I couldn't have done.'

John said, his bank manager, being a dry sort of chap and prone to understatement, had come out with, 'Well I must admit, things did get a bit sticky at times.' Apparently, he would ring John every time he was due off on holiday. His under manager, not having the same leeway, had to play by the book, which left him no choice, other than bouncing John's cheques if straying beyond his limit. It only happened twice, by the way.

Once the crisis was over, John even asked for that limit to be reduced. His bank manager, of course, was completely taken aback. I must admit, I was a little surprised, but he explained, 'Mike, that emergency extension got me through hell. I don't want to ever go back there.'

It was quite a story and lasted through lunch, coffee and beyond. It was a lovely day and so we wandered up the steps into the garden. It was hard to imagine, our location once being the interior of a mediaeval castle. We decided to risk a drop more wine. With all the food we'd had, we were not likely to be over the limit.

I said to him, "When I think about it, it's hardly surprising all the painful details aren't evident in those notes. John Dodds must have wanted to bury the stress and move on."

"Agreed, they were hard times, but there were also brighter moments. Chris Braddock would occasionally turn up with a load and light the shop up with his ebullience."

"From the notes, I got the impression, Chris Braddock avoided Ludlow on account of the tax man."

"Oh no, he'd managed to settle all that. John found out the details, because Chris happened to choose John's accountant, to help him out of the mire. I think his name was Terry Mold. They met up for the ordeal, by the tax office, which was not far from the town centre at the time and Terry, looking aghast at his client's brand-new Volvo, had said, 'That's never your car!' When Chris admitted it was, Terry was absolutely horrified. You can imagine his pained expression and exasperated waft of hand, as he pleaded in disbelief, 'Just get rid of it.'

Apparently, up in the grilling room, the two tax officers had asked for £80,000, but Chris, who had donned for the occasion, a dirty old coat and hadn't shaved for days, declared the figure to be nothing but pure fantasy. He kept this up until one of them asked, 'So tell us Mr. Braddock, how much do you think you actually owe?'

'Well it's bound to come to at least £800,' he'd said.

Terry told John later, he'd never witnessed anything like it in his life. Figures bouncing back and forth like a financial tennis match, until they finally settled on £3000. As he was leaving, Chris asked, 'Any chance of giving me a year to pay?'

'GET OUT!!' the man had yelled.

Turning up the one day, he'd announced in his theatrical way, he'd been particularly fortunate to obtain, what he was especially pleased to offer John Dodds. I remember the deal, because John later showed me what had lifted his mood in such parlous times. He'd chanced on apple tea caddies before, but had never had an apple and a pear tea caddy in the same deal. I happened to be there working late, doing some polishing and Chris regaled the pair of us, saying, he'd just had the good fortune to at last chance on a tasty deal, following a barren run, when he couldn't believe his bad luck. He was just getting down to business, when two Irish lads had turned up. He told them, rather than fall out and lose the deal, he'd buy it all at handy money and they could sort it out later. All he'd be wanting, was a bit of a drink on the stuff.

They were waiting for him up the lane. Blocking it in fact.

He said, 'Angry? They went foot-dancing mad at the prices I asked them.'

Chris loved telling the tale as much as he enjoyed buying the goods and brimming with mirth, he said, 'You know how irate they can get.' He mimicked their response, 'I taught you said you'd only be wantin' a small profit!'

'I told them, "That's right, I am only asking a small profit, a modest mark up on fair prices paid." Well as you can imagine, they were absolutely raving, astounded, that anyone could be so stupid,--- to which I replied, 'I'd felt honour bound to pay fair money.'

He was loving the role now, hardly able to contain his laughter. 'They told me I was a fookin' gobshite! A friggin' eedjut!'

I can see him now, pulling himself fully erect and telling us in all seriousness, 'I told them, "What you have to realise is,--- I've got my good name to think of."'

He laughed that much relating the tale, it set him off coughing, bringing tears to his eyes. Don from the shop down the road, who happened to be passing, was drawn in by the merriment and Chris, calming and giving John a wink says, 'Don. Wonder if you can help me?'

He knew that Don's latest career move, had been to try his hand at fine art. Like everything he'd launched into, apart from the innate gift of somehow making money around the fringes of the trade, he didn't really have the flair for it.

Chris lowered his voice and said, 'Don, I've been offered this painting. I can buy it handy money and it's not a bad smudge, but there doesn't seem to be much going on. A big arched gate, a few Arabs, palm trees and camels, but the rest of it's all sand.'

'Whose it by? Is it signed?'

'Yes I did find a bit of a squiggle. Lumpdough, or something of the sort.'

'Lamplough? It could be Augustus Lamplough. Can you buy it? Offer them £300. No, you might have to pay five.'

Chris wagging a finger, said, 'Donald, if you'd have been a little mousey, you'd have just been caught.'"

I said to Mike, "So, just as John had written in his notes, Chris Braddock did have quite an extensive knowledge."

"Yes there was no doubt about that."

We both sat, thinking for a while and then remembering something, I asked Mike about the Australian deal. I'd found no further mention of how the bed had fared.

"Oh that thing. I collected it and a couple of smaller items from Welshpool and ran them down to London. They reluctantly agreed a £5000 estimate and when, by some miracle, it made the money, can you believe it, the client wouldn't pay up. He did eventually, but they had a nail-biting three month's wait. After expenses, they got their money back, but it was the early stool and child's oak high chair, I'd dropped off, that saved the day. Even in the recession, they brought in £3,500 profit. John said the trip wouldn't be an accountant's notion of value for the time and money spent, but said, he wasn't sorry he'd taken the gamble."

"Any idea of how much they actually made on the whole deal?"

"I vaguely remember, John telling me, it was only about two grand apiece. The plane tickets had set them back a packet, being last minute bookings and they certainly didn't skimp on accommodation. Ian had been adamant. 'We're not going all that way to get ourselves holed up in some flamin' Aussie doss house!'"

I laughed. I liked the sound of this Ian.

Mike continued, "It was all the other stuff that made them the money. It was sent later, on consignment, armaments included. The recession was biting hard and after waiting a few weeks, Ian had told the man---what was his name? Must be old age. I've forgotten it."

"I think it was Mr. Fowler."

"That's it. Well done. He rang Mr. Fowler and said he'd had an offer, his own in fact, but was afraid he'd not be happy with it. The man was obviously curious to know the amount. John Dodds loved this bit. He told me, that Ian had replied, 'I simply dare not tell you, Mr. Fowler.'

He said, 'Well go on, I might as well know.'

'Twenty thousand pounds.'

Apparently there had been a long silence and Mr. Fowler finally said, 'I had better take it.'"

Thinking for a minute, I said, "Mike, if I've got my maths right, this is the bulk of the load that had been valued at over £100,000."

"Yes, something like that and the things from what was called the armoury, valued at £50,000, came in for a mere two."

"Just two thousand?"

"Yes, for apart from a brass-barrelled blunderbuss and a few bayonets, which never used to sell for much, all the rest was fake. The woman who had advised the Fowlers, was supposedly a top London trader, but in reality, she hadn't a clue what she was doing. They bought it all for two and sold it on as a job lot for four thousand.

Strangely, all the cocked-up furniture was perfect for the time. The Dutch trade mopped it up. It actually sold better than the remaining pieces from the original load. They didn't get rich on it, but it at last made sense of going to the other side of the world for what was, to all intents and purposes, a house clearance."

Being a lovely afternoon and feeling a bit mellow, we had another glass of wine apiece and Mike told me of a character he used to collect goods from, living just beyond Lake Bala.

"John gave him the name Mad Tom. In a saleroom, if he fancied something, there was no stopping him, he'd just stand there, bidding until he bought it. Stinking dear at the time, but as prices spiralled upward, it all came into money. Tom Thomas, was his proper name and come the recession, he pulled his horns in and just bought things at sensible money. It was all from fellow sheep farmers and John would have a deal with Tom on his way to viewing the coastal sales.

There's a road beyond Welshpool, where you come up against a steep wall of hills, which John used to describe, as feeling like you were entering a Welsh fastness. I know what he meant, for beyond that upper ridge they don't speak much English. Not unless they have to. I was there the one day and remarked at how quickly Tom's grandson had grown. He was pedalling a little trike and Tom said something to him. Can't remember what exactly, maybe, 'Say hello to the Englishman,' but the lad completely ignored him.

Tom laughed and said, 'I'm a damn fool, isn't it? He doesn't know any English. They don't learn it until they start school.'

John had always warned me, 'Tom's English isn't so good; not until he gets going a bit. Once into his stride, mind you, with the rust oiled, the right words seem to come back.'

If passing through Ludlow, they always called in. John thought the world of them and Mrs. Thomas would usually have a small gift for him, garden produce or some of her delicious, runner bean chutney."

Mike looked quite wistful. I interrupted his reverie with, "What sort of things did you collect from there?"

Oh, nothing that rare, but John never failed to call if Tom rang. He said the deals always had a lucky feel and it was more like a bit of banter with a friend, rather than buying and selling. It all sold quite quickly---dressers, corner cupboards, press cupboards. Like most farmers though, although tough and rangy, he hadn't a clue how to lift anything. Getting an oak press cupboard from out of that shed of his, where he stored the stuff next to the lane, there was severe danger of having your back go or a thumb squashed by a cupboard door swinging open. Lovely family though.

I admitted, I'd had no idea, how tough making a living out of Antiques had been back then. The fairly recent plethora of programmes on the subject had made it seem like nothing but a game.

Oh those things. Never watch them. How can you wander around an antique centre where they're retailing the stuff, then re-enter it, virtually from where they'd bought it from and expect to make a profit? And those supposed experts, advising them; have you noticed? They don't seem to have a clue. I was only a flamin' van driver and yet it makes me cringe with embarrassment, with what they come out with. I heard one idiot, describe a cupboard as Jacobean/ Georgian. Dear God! Like I said, unless forced to out of politeness, on account of being someone's guest, I never watch the stupid things. That's not to say, rarities never turn up in those antique centres. John didn't have time to keep an eye on them, but told me, professionals regularly combed through those and the boot fairs, snapping up anything decent they may have blundered into.

John often told me, the Summers were the worst. As the popularity of Ludlow grew, he found himself inundated. Once he'd reduced the stock sufficiently; it would have been in the early nineties; he put a curtain up, across the entrance leading to the other showroom. It restricted them to milling around in the main shop. He should have put a door there really, for once one crept up those steps to disappear behind the curtain, the rest would follow like sheep and then he'd have a hell of a job, herding them out again. He said, some Saturdays, he'd be worn out, the whole day spent explaining details to people who'd not the slightest intention of buying anything. Can you believe this? He found one lot, hidden from view, picnicking around an expensive mahogany dining table, leaving mayonnaise and greasy finger marks everywhere!

I happened to be there the one day, when a customer had asked about a Lancashire settle. John did tell me, they weren't fast sellers, but hadn't been able to resist that particular one, for the panels glowed with beautiful marquetry.

'Scuse me,' this bloke said in a whiney Brummie accent. 'Forgive me for asking, but whatever sort of person would buy a thing like this?'

I can see John now, as if slowly counting to ten, 'Well, it's hard to say, but even with all the vagaries of life, there is at least one thing, about which we can both be certain.'

'Yes?'

With a broad smile and a tap on the man's shoulder, he said, 'It won't be you.'"

We both laughed, but I didn't pass comment, not wanting to stop the flow.

"One summer was saved by a deal out at Downton. It's a charming backwater in the hills and valleys west of Ludlow. A huge estate had been bought by a French water heiress and the estate manager had been asked to locate furniture, in keeping with the buildings recently restored. It was incredible really; no money spared and with it being tastefully done, it gave a hint of the estate's former glories.

John had met the estate manager and they seemed to hit it off and the upshot was, I took a van load out there. Strangely, it included the finest of the coffers from the Australian deal. The initial customer had come down with a severe bout of financial cramp and so mid-recession, John had bought it back again. Obviously there had been a price adjustment, 6 thousand down to 4, because everyone knew there'd been an implosion in the value of antiques. The goods I left there were in competition with items from two other traders. It was all left for Madame to choose, what she thought suited. John was helped by one of the contenders, having arrived uninvited by helicopter. She'd flown from her massive pile, west of Hereford, thinking it would make a good impression.

Apparently, Madame had said, seeing the thing alighting on her lawn, sending the flower beds ragged, 'I am not paying for zat!' and all the woman's goods were taken out of the equation. My next job was to call and retrieve any rejected items, but in fact I simply collected the cheque. Madame had saved Doddsy's Summer."

I thanked Mike and told him, all this had been invaluable. He took me on a short tour of the upper town. There was a small, fenced off, grassed area with an information board. I looked at the artist's impression of what supposedly, had once been, but it was almost impossible to imagine the castle in the sketch, having stood on the small mound ahead. All that remains in fact, is a section of stone wall. We returned to the Castle Hotel by way of a quaint little passage between houses, that opened up to run beside the bowling green, located on the site of the old castle keep. I drove Mike down to collect his car and told him I'd probably be needing his help again.

"I look forward to it," he said.

CHAPTER TWENTY-SIX

Almost as if compiled out of relief of having escaped from a financial war zone, the notes became noticeably more copious. John Dodds rued the fact, in a desperate attempt to keep his borrowings down, he'd had to sell his two coffer-bachs for a £500 loss. I looked for a description of these and found a coffer bach was a small lidded box, with one, maybe two drawers below, standing on bracket feet. The best had fielded panels in the upper section and of course, were beautifully patinated. At least they had gone to a good home. One of his favourite traders, Mike Corfield from Hampshire had bought them for £2,500. This was more than balanced by money earnt on a book, a facet of the trade he didn't normally deal in. Whilst still in the dark days, he'd called to pick up Tim Glenger at about 7 o-clock one drab morning, to head north, viewing.

---*Tim was in a terrible state, hungover and still half-drunk from the night before. He groaned all the way to Shrewsbury, saying he felt sick at the thought of viewing one sale, never mind the five we had planned. The first was a village hall venue up in the Tarporley direction, that operated for a while, before folding in mysterious circumstances. There wasn't much of interest, but Tim went through the job painfully slowly, saying if he had to bend down one more time to examine a piece of furniture, he'd throw-up. To pass the time while waiting, I took a look at one of the books for sale. It was of atlas proportions, lying on a sideboard, with its dull red cover giving no hint at what lay within. As I carefully turned the pages, I was drawn by the clarity and sheer quality of the photographs.*

'What are you looking at?'

Even still half inebriated, Tim's instincts hadn't failed him. Anne had repeatedly warned me, 'When you're in a saleroom, he never takes his eyes off you. He watches your every move.'

'It's full of amazing photographs, but it could do with a few touches to add a bit more interest. Maybe a few old trucks or cars.'

Tim scanning the publication details said, 'Don't be daft. They weren't invented. The book dates from 1860. Come to think of it, photography wasn't invented much before that.'

I haven't a clue what happened the rest of the day, apart from the fact that a call to a certain lady with the charming name of India, working for Christies' auction house, made us aware we'd stumbled upon a rarity and we bought it over the phone for £1200. It was delivered down to King Street, accepted, ready for cataloguing, but we then had to wait for the auction, not due until the following Spring.

We both went by train, relishing the chance for a bit of a jaunt, the day the book was due to sell. The Chelsea Antiques fair was on and we called in to chat with the dealers, both of us taking note of all the items we'd handled, dotted around the marquee.

A taxi took us to the King Street saleroom and mounting the steps with a feeling of high expectation, we knew a profit was due, but had not the faintest clue how much, for the recession still maintained a gloomy pall over everything. We just hoped that interest from America might spur on the bidding for Mr. Frith's fine albumen photographs. When it made £16,000, even though still early in the day, we felt a gin and tonic might be in order.

389

When we called back briefly, at the Chelsea fair, we must have looked the two happiest antique dealers in the whole of London. It was probably infuriating, for they were still hard at it, trying to grind out a living in such parlous times and we were grinning from ear to ear, having done better by sheer fluke, than they had managed by solid graft.

Back in Ludlow, it took a momentous effort, weaving our way from the station, to surmount the north face of the hill leading up into town and Tim's wife told me later, she'd been in the kitchen ironing and had watched, still holding the iron, as Tim, desperately grasping the board like a drunken surfer, had taken it with him through the French windows, to collapse in a heap on the patio.

For some miraculous reason, I was fairly clear headed the next morning and able to take a phone call. I was told with some urgency, there was a decent sale, way up beyond Porthmadog on the Llyn Peninsular. I was almost there, when my phone rang, late morning.

'Where are you?'

'In the van, Tim.'

'I heard there was a sale on.'

'Good for you. I'm proud of you.'

'Don't piss about. Any idea where it is?'

I made a few attempts at static noises, apologised for the poor signal and switched the phone off. Topping the van load end of day, were two Welsh dressers and with most of the trade still fairly skint, they came in for not much more than half price. Obviously, the dealer who'd given me the tip-off didn't admit to being the reason why I'd turned up out of the blue. He was another of the Clarach Bay brethren, Andy King.

I saw in the notes, that just like John Dodds, quite a few dealers had cashed in good furniture at a loss, just to stay afloat through the worst months of the recession. Paul Hopwell told him, he'd even been forced to sell his treasured rarities, just to keep going.

As with every downturn, however, there are those who specialise in helping the distressed, while in actual fact, milking them. John Dodds didn't name the person who had picked at the decayed and dying with such perfection. The modus operandi, was to relieve them of their choicest items, on the supposition they would be offered to the last copious vein of cash still flowing, far side of the Atlantic. Then the tense waiting game would commence, with the anxious trader being informed, the intended buyer had baulked at the thought of parting with so much money in such parlous times. Could the overall sum be eased a little further, or would they prefer to have their items returned? The stalling would continue, until the dealer became that desperate, they'd be willing to take less than half the stock's worth, just to keep the creditors off their backs. Quite a number of the trade's choicest items, ended up in the States during that nightmare and the person responsible for sending a large portion, having invested no money of his own, earnt an absolute mint.

John Dodds happened to meet the man, at the first Olympia Fair, post-recession. He was asked, '*What do you think?*'

'*It's good to see trade bustling again.*'

'*Huh, most of these dealers, shouldn't even bother to get out of bed in the morning!*'

The man in question, wasn't exactly in the trade, but had more knowledge and dealing nous, than most of those who were. Anne's nickname for him was Brains.

I saw from the notes that the corner dresser had gone at last, as had all the residue of stock bought at so called, Dutch prices.

John had entered the latter into the local auction run by the man he'd bought the Machynlleth dresser off. Tony had given up speculating with his own money and instead, was auctioning goods that others had risked their resources on. Peter from Leominster dismissed him as a bit of a Walter Mitty, whereas John's name for him, was rather more reptilian than that, but there again, he had his uses and all the residue of recessionary compromise stock was flushed away for his money back.

Here's another entry referring to that first year, when those in the trade dared hope again.

---*I suppose, because of the way I'd turned old stock back into money, I was up out of the blocks quicker than most and took up Adam's suggestion of accompanying him on buying trips around Cheshire, Derbyshire, South Lancashire and South Yorkshire.*

I assumed this was Wednesday, swap-day Adam, from Macclesfield.

The trade up in those regions were glad to see someone willing to have a go and I did quite well from the ventures. The loads were fairly eclectic, ranging from a small, 18th century carved figurehead from Sheffield to three pieces of Gillows furniture from Whaley Bridge. There were sets of ladder-back chairs, mahogany press cupboards and all other sorts of middling stock, but it was the Gillows mahogany that happened to stick in the mind.

A London trader by the name of Westenholz appeared one day, had a quick wander round, then vaguely pointing to the three items, one centre room, the other two on the far wall, asked, 'How much are they?'

Telling him, then thinking it best to justify the prices, I enthusiastically added, all three were stamped Gillows. With a look of tried patience, he proffered his card, asked to have the invoice posted and was gone.

His manner was much the same a few years later, when I'd outbid his contact on a job lot of four poster beds heaped in a pile, mid-marquee, at the Clungunford House sale. Later, in the shop, I received a call and was in the middle of justifying the £2,000 profit I'd whacked on, telling him the deal now included other bed parts found in the cellar; only to be cut short by the request, "Just send the invoice, would you?"

I found mention of the fact, John Dodds had the odd deal with Ian Anderson, but he wrote:--- *You had to feel up to it, for with him and his father, DA, being so vociferously enthusiastic, you could come away with your ears ringing, or if having succumbed to the offer of a drop of whiskey, have the feeling you were swimming, rather than driving, down Welshpool High Street. A brim-filled schooner of the stuff soon had your brain in a tangle and colour rising. On one occasion, once clear of town, I needed to stop the van and check what I'd bought.*

John Dodds wrote, that it was in the autumn of that year that a certain American had called. He was over on a business trip and was interested in shipping oak furniture, to sell to his contacts in Virginia. John had been out at the time, but Anne had reserved six pieces for him. The one item was quite a unique oak press cupboard, having below the main drawers, a low arched fretted frieze, flanked by two small drawers. The man returning the following day, seemed to take to John Dodds immediately and buying all the reserved items, asked him to send photographs showing pieces of similar quality.

John wrote: *'This was an unexpected turn-up for the book, for most of the American customers I'd had to date, were as difficult to sell to as the average English trader. It felt like the business had turned a corner.'*

Another milestone in his dealings also came at that time. It was actually in the first days of the following year, those days of limbo where he felt, he'd never be able to buy anything again.

---The phone rang one evening and it was the voice of a rather mellow sounding Roger Kilby on the other end. He told me, he had a piece of oak that would sell better where I was, than down in the south-east. I was of course circumspect, as up until that point, Roger Kilby had always bought from me, spiriting the things away into the upper echelons of the oak trade. It was not helped by the fact, the thing he had for sale was a Welsh Tridarn. I had always found the things, big, hefty and alien to English taste. What we called, Didarns, I liked even less, for their high waisted design didn't fit the accepted notion of being well drawn, but Roger insisted I ought to go and look.

'It's not one of those great fuckin' black brutes, Doddsy. This is about half the normal size and a lovely colour. More walnutty than oak. I wouldn't have you drive down all this way to look at a fuckin' shed, mate. This is a little gem.'

I did wonder at this point, why I was suddenly favoured with this particular little gem. It was generally known, much of Roger's best stock went to Mike Golding from Stow-on-the-Wold. Anyway, with nothing else on at the time, I drove down to Folkstone and being exactly as described, I bought the little rarity and it sold within days.

I looked up at this point, what exactly John Dodds had been describing. I found didarn was an English corruption of the Welsh word, deuddarn, meaning two-part. The full description being, cwpwrdd deuddarn, meaning nothing more than two-part cupboard. I found that tridarn meant three-part. Looking at the photographs on the internet, the cwpwrdd tridarns, with a hooded plate rack above the two lower sections, did indeed look better proportioned than the two-part pieces.

There then came a section dedicated to auctions. Described in quite a matter-of-fact manner, it told of how he and Glenger covered at least twelve major sales a week and on occasions, as many as fifteen. It was only when I put them into two different groups on the map, that I realised they formed roughly, two vertical rectangles covering central England and most of Wales, the first having Anglesey and Chester on the northern side of the box shape with Carmarthen and Cardiff in the south. The second stretched from Beeston to Uttoxeter in the north and from Newbury across to Clevedon in the south. Within these rectangles, there were numerous regular sales. He'd listed; Colwyn Bay, Barmouth, Aberystwyth, Hay on Wye, Brecon, Welshpool, Newtown, Lampeter, Stoke, Nantwich, Stafford, Shrewsbury Wolverhampton, Bridgenorth, Lichfield, Birmingham, Knowle, Leamington Spa, Banbury, Oxford, Bath, Bristol, Cirencester, Cheltenham, Wooten-under-Edge, Tewksbury, Malvern, Ross on Wye, Ledbury, Newent, Hereford and of course Leominster and Ludlow. He described how each week, the Trade Gazette was gone through and the routes planned, with military precision. It took three trips per week, often leaving at six in the morning and not returning until eight at night.

The only thing that made it possible, apart from sheer stamina, was being able to work closely with the auctioneers. If they'd not been allowed admittance, often before the goods were even lotted up and allowed to wander among the on-going work, as early as eight in the morning or way after five, if running late, it would not have been possible. If someone was to be entrusted with their bids, they informed the auctioneer, but if the firm itself could be trusted, they usually left their prices on the book. A large proportion of the goods were bought half share, but John wrote:---*If I realised Tim had missed something, I'd ring the auctioneer later, with a price. After all, we were running separate businesses and it was all part of the game, plus of course, he would do exactly the same to me. Sparring thus, certainly kept us on our toes.*

With spending three days on the road and often Friday evenings covering the sales for the Saturday, they no longer had time to attend the venues in person. When viewing, they'd of course dismiss anything with a major problem; aiming mainly at items, that with a slight tweak and polish, would be ready to go to an antique fair. That's not to say, everything they bought was all up together, for if an item was bursting with potential, it would be bought, for restoring to its former glory.

John Dodds did marvel at the fact:---*It was not unusual, to have goods knocked down to us, in North Wales, South Wales, Birmingham and Newbury, all on the same day.*

The whole thing seemed staggering to me. Even if they covered, the lighter load of twelve sales in a week, it still meant roughly 4,000 lots would need to be considered. I decided to ring Charles.

"Hello dear boy. Are we off on a little jaunt again?"

"Not immediately, Charles. It's just a quick query." I explained what was puzzling me.

"Oh those first Glenger years. That was when I was supplying my Irish customer. I sort of went off Doddsy's radar. But even so, I think I can answer your query. The two of them would have been on the hunt for mainly period oak and mahogany. That put a good many lots completely out of the equation. They wouldn't have even broken their stride to look at Victorian or Edwardian furniture and yes, they might have bought the odd piece of early pot, or large dinner service, but all the rest of the bits and pieces, apart from decent treen, would have been completely ignored."

"So if they viewed, lets say, twelve auctions, how many lots would they be considering?"

"In some of the rooms, maybe nothing, in others, unless a major catalogue auction, a maximum of twelve, I suppose. Twelve sales, you say?"

"Yes, ranging from Anglesey down to Newbury."

"Well, a sale like Anglesey, might have had six lots of certain merit, but Newbury could easily have had twenty, not that they were likely to trouble the scorers much, on that sticky wicket. Not to any great extent, that is. An odd lot would have inevitably slipped through, but generally, the prices at the Donnington Priory sales were that ferocious, they could bring on a nose bleed. Same with auctions in places like Knowle, Bath, Bristol and Cirencester."

"Thank you, Charles. The next question, I think you'll find, is a tricky one. Any hope of hazarding a guess at how many lots they'd have considered in an average week?"

"Let me think for a minute. Now this is purely off the top of my head, but probably no more than a hundred or so."

"And the number of lots bought?"

"There would have been the odd sale where they cleaned up, maybe buying a van full, but generally, probably no more than twenty."

"Twenty? So from viewing sales containing a total of 4,000 lots, they'd only come away with twenty items of furniture per week."

"If that, dear boy. Remember, they were only after specific things and competition was fierce. It was no good going mad for the stuff, for there'd always be more sales the following week.

That reminds me. If you wanted to witness crazy prices, you merely had to attend the Newtown cattle market venues. In the Winter, one of the iciest places in the land, but if it happened to be a bit of a scorcher, you could cook in those tin sheds as the battle raged within. It wasn't always the case, but if the Chester lot clashed with the mighty Jim, you could forget trying to buy mahogany. It was a bloodbath, dear boy. A sheer bloodbath."

"The mighty Jim?"

"Jim Ash. Jim the inscrutable. Lovely chap actually. Regarding oak, if a certain South Wales dealer and a Leominster, Mr. Pompous, happened to lock horns, it could end up being the dearest stock in the whole of our fair country. The former bought Welsh oak with a patriotic fervour and the other goon, not Dave Roberts by the way, would bid without any pre-planned notion of what to pay for a thing. If they'd actually been fighting for the oak, blood and snot would have been flying everywhere and yet at the Welshpool auction two days later, with both back home licking their wounds, serenity. Sheer serenity, dear boy. Sometimes, better goods could be bought for half the price. When those two egos went at it in their stubborn, high-blown fashion, it was best to leave them to it. Keep one's powder dry, as we used to say."

"Thank you, Charles, that's added a bit of colour to things."

"Oh, that's alright,---nice to have the old memories flooding back. Oh, nearly forgot. As regards Newtown, the boss of the firm absolutely detested the trade, well most of them anyway. He thought they were operating some vast ring. The more the goods made, the more profit he thought they were making. Damn fool was often getting better prices for his ragged oak, than was paid in the top London auction houses."

"Do you miss those days?"

"I suppose so, now the scars have had time to heal."

We made a vague arrangement to meet again sometime in the future and I sat and thought for a while, allowing what he'd told me, to sink in.

Going back to the notes, I found a reference to John Dodds, having himself, missed the camaraderie experienced at certain sales, even to the extent of it bringing on a sense of nostalgia. All Stretton, had been written about, with a certain fondness. His version was actually, very similar to how Charles had described it. He'd viewed it as being more of a fun day out, than work. Also, the Wellington sales were referred to in a similar fashion, for he'd often meet up with a Mr. Robin Northcote, son of a Shropshire judge and his eccentric pal, one of the scions of the Pilkington family.

At one auction, the latter had bought a few dusty cases of wine and they'd shared the contents of a bottle poured into plastic cups. He describes the flavour, as being rather belated on the palate, followed by a pleasant warmth to the back of the throat and when later remarking to Robin, how distinct he'd found their little tipple, he'd replied, *'I'm not surprised. It made over £100 a bottle in the London rooms.'*

I realised, he must have been describing a time before he and Tim Glenger had teamed up to cover those vast distances. One day there, with things starting to become a little tedious, waiting for the auctioneer to coax that first silly £10 opening bid, on something worth over a hundred, John had interrupted with a bid of £183 on a brass-bound military chest.

'How much?'

'You heard,' I said, accompanied by a grin. '183 pounds.'

The room went silent, until a tap of the gavel accompanied, 'Sold.'

A few lots later, there was a Penny-farthing bike. 'So what am I bid for this amazing relic from a past age? Do I hear------?'

'Two hundred and thirty-six pounds.'

Again silence; followed by, 'Sold.'

When it came to the elm plank coffer, the auctioneer simply stared down and asked, 'So how much for this then, Mr. Dodds?'

'One hundred and twelve.'

'Now are we quite sure about that?'

'Yes, quite sure.'

'Well if all in the room are in agreement,' he said, looking round, 'Sold.'

'You're putting the flaming kiss of death on this auction, Doddsy.'

I laughed. The auctioneer happened to be an old adversary from my rugby playing days.

There was one sale he did actually attend amongst the frenetic racing around, trying to cover all the main venues. It must have been in about 1994 and was right on his doorstep. He'd clean forgotten it was on. For about three years a local man had run an auction in a large shed of a place, down by the river and when John had eventually wandered through the large portal, the thing was in full swing.

'A bit late on parade, Mr. Dodds,' I heard from the rostrum.

I just grinned, had a quick scan, but realised I hadn't missed anything and there was nothing due for sale, that I wanted. The room was quite packed, for locals tended to turn up for the household goods and latest utterances from the lofty mannered auctioneer. If hearing a child grizzling, he was quite likely to say something like, 'Does that brat need to be taken outside?'

I realised the man was currently selling the monstrous piece of oak, standing just inside the doorway.

I could just see the top of the edifice above the throng. The hammer was just about to fall at £80, when a thought struck me. I needed to wade through the crowd for a closer look and bid £85 to keep the deal alive. Halfway there I bid £95 just to give me chance to reach the monster. At £105, I prayed I wasn't making a fool of myself, then finally, £115 bought me a piece, almost writhing with early carving.

Back at the shop, the lads carefully took it apart. There were four late 17th century caryatids and numerous other early fragments. By the time I'd sold them all, the monster had made me, well over a thousand pounds profit. I even got £30 for the Victorian framework. Like most lucky deals, it stayed lucky right to the end.

A thing John bemoaned losing out on, with no longer attending the auctions, was the occasional feed-back concerning the movement in price on certain items. The instance he detailed was at a Leominster auction.

---There was an oak specialist from the west country, who was that mean a buyer, if ever you managed to sell him a piece of early oak, you knew you'd made a severe blunder. He was as thin as a jockey's whip and had an unpleasant supercilious manner about him. At one auction, where I still kicked with the fray, I watched him buy a 17th century oak armoire for £2,200. If a man, as tight as his clothes, worn as if welded to his frame, could pay such an amount, for what had so recently been yesterday's goods, it meant the things must have started selling again.

Remembering where I'd recently seen three similar languishing, I retraced my steps and bought all at the old money,---less than a thousand pounds each. Certain sales could be like free tutorials, but most had become like purgatory, often surrounded by a number leeches, you had no wish to socialise with.

It became evident to both he and Glenger, that by covering some of the better auctions, Oxford, Cheltenham, Cardiff, Lichfield and Birmingham, they completely outran their local opposition, middling dealers that strutted their stuff in the junkier auctions and village hall sales and goods would regularly come in for less money than if sold in the Leominster or Shrewsbury general sales, where the village beauty syndrome still held sway.

The Phillips' catalogue sale in Cardiff had been the first big name venue, they'd chanced their arm at. Doing a bit of detective work,

I traced it back to the mid 80's, for I'd found in the notes, the shock with which Harry Mynott's demise had been greeted about that time. He had been one of Ian Anderson's main customers, still in full cry, the night John had turned up with that set of six walnut chairs.

He wrote:---*Tim and I were steadily working through the lots in the Cardiff saleroom, when there was clatter, followed by echoing female laughter in the corridor, leading in from the street. Harry Mynott, obviously having partaken of a little something to lift his spirits, almost fell into the room with a lady on each arm. He did a tour, lasting about ten minutes, before sailing back out again, leaving Tim and myself still struggling to ascertain what stock to take a punt on and which to leave alone.*

With Harry's business being wound up, shortly after that, it meant they must have added Cardiff to their viewing list about 1986. So, thinking about it, it was even before the move to the big shop. The description of how they'd struggled to cope with the actual viewing, also ties in with such an early date.

Here's a much later entry and I'm guessing it to be from the early 90's.

Although, sharing the driving obviously made the job easier, it became more and more obvious, I'd have been better off viewing certain auctions alone. Also, regarding our agreement to pass on information of outlying sales, covered when off on other business, I began to wonder if Tim was honouring his side of the bargain. Neither of us were that daft, that we'd say exactly what was in the sale, unless it was such an obvious lone lot, it could be valued to the pound simply on description. What we said was either, 'You'd better take a look,' or, 'Don't waste your time viewing.'

In the early days travelling together, I'd got away with the primitive furniture, which back then, Tim hadn't been able to rate, but now found he was as good a judge of it, as I was. I remember being able to buy a crazy looking mahogany hallstand, from

402

Wolverhampton, he hadn't spotted me noting. Yes, it was outlandish, but it had a look and must have hit the mark, for Andrew Jenkins bought it. So I got away with the odd lot like that, but I knew full well there were quite a few chancy things, he'd have completely missed, if he'd have viewed the sales alone.

For instance, I'm pretty sure he wouldn't have taken an interest in a sumptuous Davenport dinner service, I sold to Robert Deeley, late May one year. At the time, it wasn't the sort of thing he bothered with. I know full well he'd have missed the massive William IV mahogany dining table, in a Saturday house sale. It had been buried by all the crockery and silver plate and you could hardly get to it for the mass of people clustered around it. I waited until Tim had disappeared to look upstairs, and seizing my chance, made enough room to view the undercarriage and find a lot number. Turning, I saw Tim Glenger, like a statue, watching from the doorway. It gave me quite an eerie feeling.

The other thing I knew he'd have missed, was again when viewing a house sale. As we were leaving, I remarked, that considering it was a rather grand Georgian house, you'd have expected the contents to have been better. 'A complete load of junk,' I said. 'Unless------.

Tim following my gaze, finished my sentence. 'Unless those stone columns are in the sale.'

They did have a lot number and the six fluted, 8' tall Ionic columns were bought for next to nothing. The man Anne had christened Brains, bought them, for a considerable amount more than I'd paid.

There again, there was a local half share deal, where I was actually glad of Tim's assistance and of course the lucrative book deal, had been a joint effort. We'd been approached by a man at the Leominster saleroom, his look betraying a sense of urgency, as he told us, recent circumstances were forcing him to sell his furniture.

The house was at the end of a long track in the hills between Tenbury and Cleobury Mortimer. Our overall price was accepted, which from memory was about £3,000, but when we drove to clear the goods, the man begged us to leave the oak cupboard, for a little longer, as it contained all his kitchen stuff. It was one of those early 18th century, two door wardrobes, on an open coffer base, he'd slotted shelves into. Not a thing we'd normally buy, but with it being part of a job lot, were happy to include it.

Christmas was almost upon us and having rung twice regarding collection of the cupboard, only to be fobbed off each time with lame excuses, I said to Tim, 'There's something about the bloke I don't trust.' When, a few days later, I got the same weaselly answer, I phoned Tim and said, 'I know we planned a Christmas drink today, but it will stick in my gullet unless we don't go and collect that cupboard.'

The man was visibly shocked by our arrival and the place had almost been stripped bare apart from a table, a couple of chairs and our cupboard. With a stark-eyed look of one having been caught out, he made a lame attempt at prevarication, accompanied by a weak smile. I felt a little sorry for him, for after all it was nearly Christmas, but it was no use being soft hearted and let him ruin ours. In fact, I was certain, if we'd have let the deal slide into the new year, we'd have never seen him, or the cupboard again. Having put a niggling little problem to rest, we dumped it in my shop and then had a rip-roaring time around the hostelries of Ludlow.

I saw, further on in the notes, the cupboard had been sold for £650, early in the new year, to a Dutch dealer. From my reckoning, it would have been at the start of 1994, with seemingly, everything going swimmingly and yet looking ahead, I saw there was a particularly nasty shock awaiting in the near future.

My mobile rang. I was amazed to see it was Charles's number.

"Good morning, Charles. What a pleasant surprise."

"I have a little tip for the 4.15 at Doncaster," he said.

"What?"

"Just a jape, dear boy. Thought you might like to know, there's a farm sale on this Saturday over by Presteigne. If you like, we could meet up.'

"Yes, I'd love to. I really do need to get out. I've been buried for long enough writing this book."

The sale was near the hamlet of Whitton to the northwest of Presteigne and to my amazement, a certain, (correct spelling this time) Owain Glyndwr, came back into the picture, for about a mile further west, his army estimated at 1500 had triumphed over an English army of 2,000, leaving half the attacking host dead on the battlefield. It is known as the battle of Bryn Glas or alternatively, the battle of Pilleth, 22nd of June, 1402.

Owain had triumphed against the odds, positioning his longbowmen on a hill and hiding the rest of his troops amongst the trees on lower ground. His archers, taking advantage of their lofty position, had showered the advancing English before they could bring their longbows to bear. As they reached the critical point, where the Welsh were at last within range, the rest of Owain's troops attacked from the right flank and rear, to go about their deadly work. Three English nobles were amongst the fallen and Sir Edmund Mortimer, who had led the disaster was taken prisoner.

He was of course put up for ransom, but Bolingbroke, who now called himself Henry IV, was strapped for cash and wouldn't cough up, at which point Mortimer must have thought, 'Thanks a bunch, but while I'm here, best make the most of it.'

Which he did, marrying Owain Glyndwr's daughter, Catrin.

The farm sale didn't have much I wanted, some earthenware jugs, two small spoked cart wheels, an ancient kitchen range, clothes airer, that would make an interesting hanging if those hiring, bedecked it with flowers, plus there was a butter churn.

"Whatever d'you want a thing like that thing for? In my day, we could hardly give those things away."

He meant the butter churn, which if I managed to buy, I could easily sell on the internet. As before, we left prices with the auctioneer and then drove to Presteigne. At the centre of town was the splendid half-timbered 16th century, Radnorshire Arms, but with only wanting a snack, we opted for the Farmer's Inn.

After general chat, I asked about his venture, selling to the Irish customer and then, whether he'd done much further business with John Dodds?

"To be honest, after the late 80's, other than meeting up for the odd chat, no. Our paths rarely crossed. It was obvious he was covering the sales, for it was common knowledge, Richard Cole and Jim Ash were holding his prices. Doddsy kept his cards pretty close to his chest, in fact. The business had become far more serious and a lot of the fun had gone out of it."

"That must have been about the time David Roberts went bankrupt. It must have been a shock to you all. From what I've read, he seems to have been the main buyer of oak in the area."

"A shock? Well, yes and no. I had actually seen the writing on the wall, some time before. Damn shame, mind you. I liked old Dave;--- he was a one off. When he was skint, you'd not see him for weeks and then having wangled more money from somewhere, he'd suddenly appear like a man possessed. At one sale, Llanwrtyd Wells I think it was, he got stuck in, with the fervour of a kid with his first beach spade. Doddsy also attended, so we must be going back some time. He said to me, 'I think Dave's lost it. Look at him bidding on that poxy little X-frame.' I remember the item, because his description had made me laugh, 'legs like hedge sticks.' He and a local dealer were going at it hammer and tongs, until David bought it for £750. Quite honestly, he would have been lucky to have got 80 quid for it."

"Really?"

"Yes. Admittedly it had the right shape, but if two people had tried to use it, they'd have been rubbing noses. A complete and utter misser. Now as it happens, Doddsy had done a call the night before. A dealer in a tiny shop in Bishop's Castle had rung to say he'd stumbled on something special and with it happening to be still on board, John showed me. We untied and hauled it from the van, stood it upright and I thought, 'What an absolute belter!' It was a sycamore topped cider table. The one-piece top was three foot wide and the belly must have been a good fifteen inches thick. Lovely colour, with a pair of lines scribed around the outer edge of the top. Just for devilment, he offered it to the Welsh trader who'd underbid the wobbly hedge-stick thing. He flattered him saying, being an admirer of his good judgement, he felt his courageous effort at underbidding the X-frame table deserved rewarding and suggested he cast his expert eye over yet another piece of Welsh furniture. John asked him £1200. After squirming for a bit, the man declined."

"When I went over to hear the outcome, Doddsy had made me laugh, uttering an expletive of the 'eff gerund variety, that preceded, 'saleroom buyer!'"

"Anyway, the man had done him a favour, for the more he thought about it, he realised he'd have been underselling the splendid thing and later divulged, he'd got £1650 for it. Hate to think what it would be worth now. Ordinary dressers and mahogany are still in the dreary department, but I heard recently, ethnic pieces, such as that table, love spoons and primitive chairs, have gone quite simply, barmy-bonkers.”

We both laughed at his choice of words and then Charles continued, “I’ve just remembered another sale, one where Mr. Roberts launched himself in a similarly spectacular fashion. This little fixture was an enjoyable gathering at Penybont. Of all things apart from the oak he bought, can you believe it, he took on a private customer and became the proud owner of a skinny little 4’ 6” brass and iron bed for one hundred and something quid. It was nothing more than a sheep blocker, worth £30, if that. But Dave had had the money tap turned back on and there was no stopping him. Like I said, the writing was on the wall.”

After a pause, I suspect, whilst considering whether to continue, he said, “Later that day, it absolutely bucketed down and in the car park, between one van packed with shippers and the other full of buyers of the more polite furniture, Dave stood there passing bids back and forth through the side doors. Soaked as a proverbial drowned rat, but with him winding-up one side, then the other, you could see it was probably one of the happiest days of his life.”

“So, they were knocking the stuff out.”

“Did I actually say that? No, now you’re being wicked, putting words in my mouth.”

“Was John Dodds there?”

“Now really! How do you expect me to remember a thing like that?”

As before, my bids at the sale had been successful and thanking Charles for all his help, we went our separate ways.

CHAPTER TWENTY-SEVEN

I found a short section detailing the movement of certain antique dealers during the early 90's. His friend Roger and his new lady had moved to a shop in the Cotswolds, meaning those regular North Wales runs had now ended. Ron Baker had moved to a Ludlow shop, bottom of Corve Street, meaning that that particular mid-Wales supply now came to an end. As mentioned earlier, John from Clun, had also moved to Ludlow, but then transferred the operation to a large building on the southern extremity of Craven Arms. Luffy took on a shop in Ludlow, at the bottom of Old Street and way down in Bath, Stuart was forced to retrench, having severely upset his New York customer. So no more inside information from across the pond.

With all this happening, supply lines cut and loss of the Bath connection, it helped explain why the salerooms were now being combed so diligently. Ludlow was handily situated in the middle of the vast pool of resources, which the trade was desperate for, when stocking up to sell at the prestigious antique fairs. John Dodds and Tim Glenger, were basically hunting for goods, worthy of gracing the stands at the N.E.C, Olympia, Chelsea and Grosvenor House.

This posed a question. Rather than trouble Charles again, I rang Mike.

"Mike," I said, "there's something I don't understand. If John Dodds was supplying so many of the traders doing the fair circuit, why didn't he just do the fairs himself?"

"He often asked himself that very same question, but it wasn't as easy as it sounds. The thing is, you couldn't just book up and arrive; there was a rigorous selection process and a long waiting list, plus he never had the better stock for long enough. It would have meant storing it, which would have starved his business of cash flow. Then once word got about, he was fair-bound, he'd have lost his main customer base."

"So my next question is, why did he actually need a shop?"

Mike started to laugh.

"What's so funny?"

"Oh, it's just a line John sometimes used, borrowed from his mate, Ian Anderson. Ian had said in all seriousness one day, 'Some deals can turn out a bit disappointing.' The shop was there to basically get rid of the middling stock and those deals that happened to have turned out a bit disappointing."

"I thought he'd stopped buying the ordinary."

"Well it wasn't that ordinary. It was all period furniture and basically original, it was just that it didn't exactly lift the spirits. That's another line he'd borrowed; something another friend had come out with. I think he said it was an expression used by Mike Corfield from Hampshire."

"So what you're describing as ordinary, John in his early days, could well have considered good."

"Well now I think about it, I suppose you're right. In fact you are. You've just reminded me of something Doddsy told me about. It was a Queen Anne oak cabinet on stand. The sort with a drop-down front, all the doings inside and a cushion moulded drawer below the cornice. It was from up in the hills, somewhere over Newtown way. Years before he'd tried to buy it, when out door-knocking with a local character called Trevor Lockyer. In his mind, he remembered it as being a tremendous prize he'd missed out on, one that had got away.

Well one day, from out of the blue, the man had rung to say, he was now willing to sell it. John must have left him one of his business cards. Anyway, as you can imagine, he set out on the call with a fair degree of anticipation, but when he got there, Doddsy couldn't believe it;--- he was not looking at the image he'd built in his mind, but an absolute dog of a thing. He did buy it, but said it was scruffy, down at heel and nothing like the quality he'd been regularly buying off the one and only, Roger Kilby. Standards had tightened up and the top end dealers had become far more discerning."

"I remember reading about how dispirited he'd been, when unable to buy it that day. I think, he and Trevor had been on a bad run and that had compounded it."

We were both silent for a while and then he asked, "Early on in those notes I gave you, did you come across the mention of an oak armchair he and his mother bought? It was 17th century, but the seat was missing."

"Yes. Bought up in Lancashire, if I remember correctly."

"That's the one. Well in these latter days we're talking about, it probably wouldn't have been half as saleable. Whoever bought it would have struggled to get it passed by the vetting committee. Chucked off for having a wrong seat."

"Surely it can't be that hard to replace a seat."

"Well basically, no. But John told me, if you wanted it to look like it had grown old with the piece, then it was notoriously difficult. Seats, stretchers, cresting rails, were all the first things the vetters homed in on. Well they used to. Probably all retired or dead by now.

We were both silent once again and then another question occurred to me. "Mike, with now dealing in the better things, why did he bother with what was now considered ordinary?"

"Oh, that's easy to explain. What they were after, needed that first day, sale at Olympia look and competition was fierce. He simply couldn't find enough of it to survive on. He needed the bread-and-butter stuff as well. 'Buying it by leaving catching prices,' was how he described it."

"It sounds like a delicate balancing act."

"It was, especially when they never paid him."

"What?"

"Obviously, you've not come across that yet. He's bound to have mentioned it in those notes I gave you."

"Do you really mean, some never paid."

"Well they did in the end, it's just they knew they had the whip hand. They were top of the pyramid and knew there was nowhere else a provincial dealer could go with the goods and so some used the leverage it gave them, unmercifully."

"Sounds like a dangerous game."

"Believe me, it was. At times it used to worry John, sick."

"One last question, Mike. In the mid 90's, can you remember how many antique shops there were in Ludlow."

I heard him mumbling, "There was Luffy, Stan Woolston had gone by then---." Then clearly, "Sorry, had to go round the town twice in my head. Apart from the tat shops, about ten or twelve I think."

"That many."

"Yes, Ludlow was in the ascendancy about that time. Over the years, Ludlow and Leominster seemed to take it in turns."

"Thank you Mike, you've been a great help."

"Any time, just give me a call."

Returning to the notes, I read they went to the Isle of Man as usual, late May that year, paid for by an amazing coffer he'd spotted in a Shrewsbury shop window. The following sections, had again been written as if intended to be collated into a short story and I've left them virtually as found.

---*The coffer had the most amazing carving, I don't mean smothered in the stuff, it was quite sparingly done, but full of life. I asked the price and the assistant said, 'It's four hundred and fifty.'*

I was staggered and blurted, 'How much?'

'I'll just go and check.'

She was gone before I could stop her, to say I'd buy it.

I knew the shop owner well and expected him to tell me there'd been a huge mistake, but smiling he said, 'As it's you Doddsy, 375.'

I sold it next morning to Paul Hopwell, for £1800. 'I really rate this Doddsy,' he said, making me think that I also, had underrated it. I never minded that too much, however, needing the likes of him to survive.

I realised they must have still been using the van at that point, because amongst other things on the Manx trip, John had bought and returned home, with a Georgian sideboard, constructed entirely from camphorwood. That particular wood happened to be all the rage at the time and yet apparently, the piece had been sitting unsold in one of the Jurby outlets for months.

---*One of the dealers, renting a pitch there, said he'd ring the owner of the sideboard for the best price, but warned me against buying it, as the man had been asking silly money, £1400, far too much.*

I gladly bought it for £1200 and back in the shop, sold it almost immediately for £3,500. It was a piece Stuart would once have bought, but like the fate of many over time, hubris had brought him low.

It was a few weeks later, I received a call from the gentleman from Virginia. He asked, as he was due over on a business trip, could I drive him to a few trade outlets he'd like to look at? Also, could I bring photographs of the latest stock?

I had misheard where I was meant to collect him from, but managing to correct the blunder, picked Byron up from a Droitwich hotel and we continued on to London.

I suddenly realised, John Dodds must have bought himself a car, for he'd hardly be ferrying a wealthy client around in an old van.

Byron had booked a room at the Dorchester, where he was welcomed in the lobby, like a long-lost friend. We were shown up to the lavish suite and I froze in the doorway, for just as in a disturbing premonition I'd had the night before, the room was dominated by a bed, a double king-size. I said, 'Byron, they must have made a mistake. Or perhaps these are twin beds that can be pushed apart.'

Now, I can't be certain whether this was an actual bridal suite, but the simple fact was, the bed was that much of a statement, it was clearly a double and would remain that way. At my obvious unwillingness to clamber up and spend the night beneath the same covers as the man I was escorting, huffing and puffing apologies over the mix-up, he returned to the foyer. Thankfully, we were shown to a room with a pair of single beds and while he was in the bathroom, I pushed them as far apart as the room and furniture would allow.

Whilst we'd been breezing on our way to the Dorchester, on the first occasion he'd given my knee a squeeze, whilst coming out with a friendly rough and roistering, 'Good to see you again, Johnny,' I'd simply put it down to perhaps being an American idiosyncrasy. I reasoned, 'Don't make a big thing of it. Us Brits are a bit reserved and everyone knows Americans are far more tactile.' The second time it happened, however, I began to have my doubts. It didn't help when he insisted on telling me, how much he did for his local church, not once, but three times and then, what a fine upstanding family man he was.

The meal that evening was slightly on the minimal side, but absolutely delicious and he'd asked me to select the wine. I'd gone for a lightish red for about £40, one of the most reasonable, as stinging him for £250 or more, would have been rather rash under the circumstances. During the meal, after perusal of the photographs I'd brought, he selected and bought about 15 thousand pounds worth. They were all my better purchases, post Olympia, which I'd expected to have languishing until trade picked up again, mid- August and what's more they were all mine. The reason for which I'll explain by the by.

Up in the bathroom later, looking at my full-length reflection, droopy underpants and doleful expression, I wondered, 'Why me?' I know Marie had said years before, 'It's all part of the game, but this was going it a bit strong.'

Slipping into bed, I managed to feign immediate sleep and was first up to wander around the lobby at about six in the morning. Byron was up and dressed by the time I returned to the room.

I took him round a few trade calls and we ended up in Brighton, drawn by an antique fair, he'd read about. It was not what you'd call, in full swing, having more of a hollow, more traders than customers feel about it. Phillip Morrison, from the Isle of Man perked up on catching sight of me and tried his best to offload a bureau, a handsome beast, with a stepped and welled interior, but with fifteen grand back in my pocket, I was now loathe to shell out three, for the privilege of holding such a hefty piece until the Autumn.

On Lenny Cato's stand, gliding up as smooth as you like, he guided my client with an enfolding arm, to a set of Georgian chairs, the very, very best, he'd just happened to chance upon the day before. I was quite full of admiration at the way he finessed, probably his only sale of the day, on what looked like a particularly desperate, scorcher of a Saturday, at the Brighton Antiques Fair.

On the Sunday, I dropped Byron off at Heathrow and drove back to Ludlow, underpants intact, fifteen grand to the good and the wheels of my car hardly touching the road.

So now I suppose you're wondering, how it transpired, that my best stock was no longer half share with Tim Glenger. Well, it all started when he'd told me not to bother viewing a Bridgnorth evening sale, as it was all, using his words, 'Nothing but a load of crap.'

A few days later, I spotted a pair of fantastic garden ornaments, surmounting a pair of generous lead balls, resplendent in his window and couldn't understand why Tim had gone all evasive, when I'd tried to coax a price from him. Later that day, a friend of mine, Chris Harvey, who sold jewellery and porcelain, stopped me in the street and said, 'Have you heard about Tim Glenger? The police have been round there. Those garden ornaments in his window, were nicked.'

'Never!'

'Not by Glenger, by someone who'd put them into the Bridgnorth auction. You'll never guess where they were stolen from------ Michael Heseltine's garden wall.'

Armed with this I went straight round and asked Tim, 'Was there anything else apart from Tarzan's Balls in the Bridgnorth auction?' He looked truly mortified and even worse when I told him, our little arrangement was over. If he couldn't be trusted, then that was that.

Next morning, white faced at my shop door, he said he'd not been able to sleep and asked, would I reconsider. I simply patted his shoulder and said, 'No. Thanks, mate. You've actually done me a favour.'

John Dodds then quoted something his mother often said, 'As one door shuts, another door opens.'

I read that Terry had rung and wondered, 'Which Terry?' It soon became obvious it wasn't the accountant, for John picked this particular Terry, up from his cottage south of Hereford.

---I was amazed at Terry's contacts. With all my extensive travelling, I'd never before stumbled across a dealer in Leamington Spa, presiding over a vast emporium like it was his fortress. Terry warned me to tread carefully as he was an unpredictable package and mid-deal, had often been known to suddenly turn nasty, telling those perusing the place to, 'Just get the f--- out of here!'. The stock was stacked haphazardly, on all three floors of the house, plus out in the sheds, rammed into vacant spaces, with no thought of display. His existence amongst it could only be described as Dickensian. We made a mental note of what we'd spotted and returned to his lair to enquire about prices. Some of the things he could remember, others we had to show him.

'You don't want that, it's made from part of a clock case,' he rasped at Terry.

'Could I possibly see it?'

He nodded ascent and being the tallest, I clambered over the clutter and hooked it down from the wall.

When I asked about a pine bureau I'd seen under an awning, he snapped, 'So, you've been out the back!'

Terry said, 'Well the back door happened to be open and so we assumed that all those acquisitions, arrayed in the sheds, were also for sale.'

He calmed down and not daring to haggle over the prices, we were allowed to buy six items between us. Georgian, patinated pine bureaus were exceedingly rare and with Terry's application of genius, it alone returned enough profit, to pay for the day. His supposed portion of a grandfather clock trunk, was in fact a tiny oak wall cupboard, missing its bottom moulding and fair play to Terry, he'd somehow sensed it was right, even though initially not able to examine it.

Once restored, I gave him a profit and it didn't last a day in the shop. The sumptuous piece of late 17th century marquetry he'd also bought, I was certain I'd see at a later date, with portions incorporated into various pieces of otherwise dreary oak, for he would have considered it negligent, not to have given such poor things a lift.

Now I was in no doubt, which Terry he'd picked up that morning.

Another of Terry's contacts, patrolled the sales down in the west country and we met up in the London Road, Bath. Stuart's shop was still there, but he wasn't. There was another name over the door. I still had the van, which was fortunate, for the main lot was a set of twelve Swedish, white and giltwood chairs. I made a display of them in the main shop window and the sheer impact sold them.

We made that trip quite a number times and occasionally chanced on profitable lots in the Bath antique shops.

The best deal of all came from a smallholding, buried deep in the Quantock Hills. I thought Terry was partaking in one of his wind-ups when he told me the man we were calling on, was one of the country's top authorities on early clocks and that his wife had once been a stripper. Every word of it true, mind you and I came away with one of the best oak farmhouse tables I'd ever owned. It was that long, we had to heave it up onto the roof rack.

I of course, still viewed the sales, all the harder now I had no-one to share the driving with, but didn't regret my decision.

Apart from Terry suddenly coming to prominence, I discovered another little surprise from about that time. Out of the blue, David Roberts had rung to tell him of a call he'd chanced upon over by Bartestree. An old trade contact of his had died and his daughter wanted rid of a few pieces of oak.

---He warned, I'd not find the goods cheap, but there ought to be a profit, especially as the Montgomeryshire dresser base had been rated at the old money, before their value had started to rocket. What he hoped was, there'd be enough in the deal, costing roughly, £20,000, to pay back the £4,500 still owed.

The dresser base was a bit of a dark, high-waisted, unappealing version, but when things come into fashion, judgement can go out the window and when the whole load had sold, I'd got my money on the debt back, almost to the penny. Bless the man, for as far as I know, I was the only person who was thus favoured.

I came across a section concerning deliveries. I'm assuming they were an eclectic mix from over the years. He'd had no problem delivering the wardrobe that had once cradled his daughter, for the fact it had been cut in half, was the entire reason why the couple had bought it. It needed to go up a difficult stairway, impossible, had it still been all in one. As the old dealers always avowed, 'Everything goes in the end.'

Another wardrobe, Georgian this time, he and the lad helping, had got it stuck, halfway up a Ludlow staircase. They'd had to take the doors off, then the back-panelling and it had been that complicated, twisting and turning the thing, John pinned a note inside, explaining how it had been done, just in case the customers, one day needed to extricate it.

Regarding the Jersey press cupboard, delivered to a house up the Corvedale; he'd been asked to leave it in pieces downstairs, as the bedroom it was destined for, was still being decorated. A few days later, he received a cry of help from the lady. Her son had been unable to get the back panel up the narrow stairway.

---*I had reassembled the thing, by the time the son arrived to give me a hand.*

He asked, 'How the hell did you manage that?'

'All depends if you're the buyer or seller,' I replied, at which he laughed.

Probably, one of the most difficult deliveries I had, was concerning a hefty piece, full of drawers and pigeon holes, I'd bought from Ian Anderson. It was delivered to me in a cattle truck and even though the driver was obviously being paid, it became immediately obvious, he no longer thought the amount sufficient. He crashed the truck's ramp down into the road and four of us, using webbing as slings, somehow managed to lift it far enough from the truck floor, to advance it out onto the street. After taking a breather, we tackled stage two, just managing to get it into the portion of the shop, leading straight out to the back yard.

'Don't know what the fuck you're going to do with that!' the deliveryman tossed over his shoulder, as he stomped back to his truck.

I must admit, a similar question had also crossed my mind.

It was a good-looking thing and useful, but the weight could bring on a hernia. I sold it one Saturday, to a pleasant couple of regulars who lived in rolling hill country, over towards Tenbury Wells. They were Birmingham solicitors and it was perfect for documents they needed to store. Trouble was, it was destined for a top floor room of their house.

There was no point messing about; I rang a carrier I frequently used, Pete from Hereford. He arrived with two strong lads to help and with lifting heavy items being integral to their job, we got it onto the truck's tail-lift, fairly easily. It was at the house, that Pete said, 'Up There? You gotta be joking!'

The first stairway wasn't so bad, struggling a step at a time, as long as we didn't let it slip. Rumbling on its way, escaping to the garden, it would have crushed the two heaving from below. Pausing to mop brows on the welcome respite of a small landing, we eyed the next flight. It was much narrower, as were the gasped expletives from those wedged against stair rail and wall as we inched upwards. On the even smaller top landing, we took a well-earned breather and surveyed the remaining task ahead. It was not helped by a triangle of plastered ceiling below a roof valley, limiting headroom, but by swivelling the brute, there was just room to tip it on its side, before offering it to the door leading to the attic bedroom. With one ahead, guiding and three pushing, we progressed half into the room where it became perfectly jammed.

'What are we going to do now?' asked Pete.

Remembering a line from way back in the Lancashire door-knocking days, I said, 'Oh, just paint it white and leave it there.'

'What about me,' came a plaintive cry from inside the room.

'Don't worry, said Pete, 'We'll fetch some sandwiches.'

'They'll have to be thin buggers, mind,' muttered the other lad helping.

I don't know how we did it, but somehow easing it a quarter inch one way, a quarter the other, we managed to edge it on its blanket, into the room. When at last, standing upright against the wall, Pete said, 'John, if ever they want that fucking thing moving from here, don't go ringing my number!'

I left them to tidy up a bit and feeling light as a feather, descended to the kitchen to collect the cheque and drop off the receipt. Writing the details, I heard further banter coming from Pete and the lads and said, 'Oh, they got down here quickly.'

'No, they're still up there.'

'Well it sounds as if they're down here in the hallway.'

'We must have forgotten to turn the baby monitor off,' said the man's wife, hardly able to keep a straight face.

The final delivery in this section, was to return three oak drawers that had needed a little fettling. John Dodds had sold the lady six items and a few drawer mouldings of a dresser base had come adrift. Every time he'd tried to return them, the lady had been away on business and on the day she did happen to be there, for some reason she'd failed to mention a six-foot-high snow drift blocking the drive. The van was hopeless in just a sprinkling of snow, never mind all the slush lying about, but he did manage to turn it, and the crease put in the bodywork as the vehicle slewed against a stone column, was not massive, but still annoying. Back at the shop, he tried to ring and explain why he'd failed to make a delivery, but all he got was the answer phone.

Eventually, with snow melted and weather set fair for a delivery the following day, he knew he shouldn't have, but as Charles had mentioned, always being prone to a touch of devilment, he'd left the following on her answerphone, *'I'll drop your drawers around, about eleven in the morning.'*

422

CHAPTER TWENTY-EIGHT

I realized time must have moved on, for Tim Glenger seemed to have wormed his way back in, not to the same extent as before, but there was obvious collaboration on certain deals. It was hardly surprising I suppose, for their paths were bound to cross, so a pair of bookcases from Wolverhampton and a pair of chancy looking cabinets from Monmouth were bought half shares and sold to David Bedale who would probably have sold both, opening day at Olympia. It was the £12,000 desk from Abergavenny, however, that John said, brought the greatest satisfaction, for with the auctioneers help, he'd traced it back to Sir Benjamin Hall, Big Ben as he was called; him being the reason why the famous clock was thus named.

---*The desk had burr oak panels and would have graced the more Welsh than Welsh house Sir Ben had had commissioned. Trouble was, even though only Victorian, it must have had a distressing existence once its glory days were over, for its colour was faded and it had that absolutely fed-up look. It cost £2,000 to cheer it up and when lent to my good friend, Ruth Macklin-Smith it sold in the opening hour at Olympia for £24,000.*

Initially it had looked as if they had done exceptionally well financially, but using detail from further ahead in the notes, I was able to work out how relatively little, they actually earnt from the deal. Let's assume, the lady who had fronted the item, would have received a minimum of £2,000 for selling it, meaning, end of fair, she would have parted with a cheque for £22,000. To anyone not party to the details, it would have looked like they'd made £10,000 between them. However, I'd found out, by that time, buyer's premium at the main auctions had become established, meaning their £12,000 bid would have actually have meant paying more like, £14,000. Then came the restoration mentioned, making the total cost £16,000, but on top of that came the VAT, charged on the difference between the initial purchase price, £12,000 and the final selling price, £22,000, roughly £1500 between them. There would have been carriage charges, to and from the restorers and down to London, so they would have each profited by not much more than £2,000, but what a satisfying deal it must have been.

As regards money, John Dodds wrote,--- *You couldn't fault Glenger, for he sometimes sold the items we'd bought, for far more than I'd expected,--- it was trickery regarding his version of the truth, that made listening to him a liability.*

He continues---*I had purchased quite a van load off Richard Cole; he had bought a smallholding at Little Malvern, a lovely location to do a deal and have a chat.*

I wondered if I'd got the date of the story right, for I'd assumed that, roughly about this time, the van had been sold. With further mentions of it, however, I realised it must have been retained for occasional use. Anyway, back to the man himself.

---*Richard was explaining the renovation done on what had been a ramshackle shed, when my phone went. It was Tim Glenger, telling me not to bother with the sale that night at Knockin, for the spice cupboard he'd been told about, he described as being a terrible looking thing.*

I told Richard, I'd have to cut short our conversation, needing to leave immediately for a sale in north Shropshire, a good two hours away. I'd been that busy recently, I'd forgotten the sale was on.

Of course, it was well underway by the time I arrived, but easing through the throng, heard that I hadn't missed it. The traders there, knew what I'd come for and one pointed it out, up on the stage.

Catching sight of me, the auctioneer smiled and with flick of head, mouthed, 'Go on then,' and I climbed up to examine the cabinet and a few other items of interest. The piece itself, had been constructed almost like a tiny building and was the best spice cabinet I'd ever seen in my life. I'm not exaggerating, it was worthy of inclusion in a reference book.

Without going into detail, I bought it and a few other items and had it in the shop next day, not on full display, but on an oak lowboy, up the steps behind the curtain.

First customers of the day were the Bookends, thus named, for their tendency, to always travel together. Each had a shop in the Cotswolds. Their car was facing downhill, so I knew they'd already called on Tim Glenger.

'Anything about, boy?' asked the grubby-bearded one, who had a shop in the square, Stow-on-the-Wold.

I was relieved the cabinet was not on view, for if this particular oak specialist was unable to get to the price of something, he'd bad mouth it all around the trade. He had a depth of knowledge, but no flair whatsoever. My heart sank, for he told me, he'd heard I might have recently bought a spice cabinet and realising where this information had come from, knew it wouldn't have been given a glowing report.

When they both left the shop, with the bearded bookend having completely derided my valuation, it felt that merely allowing the oaf anywhere near the little gem now under my protection, had been tantamount to an act of betrayal. Carefully carrying it upstairs, I placed it on a coffer on the landing, safe from further harm.

Later that day I had a phone call from Robert Deeley. He said, one of the Bookends had been running down an item I'd bought, could I describe it to him and tell him the price?

'If it's exactly as you've just described,' he said, 'I'll buy it.

Robert had made a miraculous come-back since the recession and I'd sold him quite a few items, one of the latest being, a tiny early 18th century oak dresser base, that must have been made for a child's room. Anyway, a few days later, I found him, 7 in the morning, dozing in his Mercedes, outside my shop. He bought the spice cabinet without hesitation and a few other items of oak.

Whilst having breakfast in the kitchen, for some reason we got onto the subject of Roger Kilby and it was only at this point, that a certain puzzle was resolved, for he told me why Roger no longer sold top quality oak to Mike Golding of Stow.

Rob and Mike Golding had gone half shares on a ruined chateau, situated in the hills, south of Toulouse and as Roger Kilby's gifts ranged from purchasing early oak, to renovating old properties, he and two of his sons had been given the job of completely renovating the roof of a major section of the ancient bastion. To see to their needs, they had taken a fair maid of Kent along with them.

Late in that particular Summer, Rob flew down to inspect the work and meet the building inspector, due the afternoon of his arrival. He walked in to find three sheep hanging on meat hooks ready for butchering. He'd already had desperate calls from locals, alarmed at the impact Roger and his boys had made, drinking, fighting and rampaging around nearby villages, but he hadn't expected sheep rustling.

Fearing incarceration if the building inspector caught sight of the carcases, he demanded Roger get rid of them. He'd been that petrified, he'd taken the next flight home and once Mike, his partner, was party to the details, he ordered Roger back *immediately, telling him in no uncertain terms, that was the end of their trading agreement.*

John writes:--- *I knew full well, Roger Kilby was a bit of a rough diamond, having already heard details of how he'd hurled a rival down a flight of stairs in the Haunch of Venison saleroom in London and had left another wearing a large Edwardian china cabinet, but just like my friend Robert, I hadn't realised he had sheep rustling on his C.V.*

I sat there, staring at the straightforward, unadorned account and the thought struck me; if such details happened to be included in a TV series about the antique trade, would the audience believe them?

Then came the particulars of how Tim Glenger, apparently true to form, had informed John, not to bother to view the sale in Harlech, for there wasn't a single thing there worth buying. John Dodds attended the sale, bought the two dressers and the other items of merit and realised at that juncture, there was no point in even listening to what his erstwhile partner had to say.

His friend, Richard Cole had commented, 'Trust him? The man couldn't even lie straight in bed.'

Added to that, Jim Ash had told him, 'It's your own fault! He's your monster, Doddsy. You created him.'

At about this time, a contact in Cheshire came very much to the fore. The name Sandy appears frequently in the notes. Delving a little, I found that Sandy Adams and her husband, having moved their business from Market Drayton to Nantwich, had started on the fair circuit and were flourishing better than most in the trade. John mentions two occasions, at about this time, probably 1994, where he'd had urgent requests for top-up stock at the NEC and Kensington antique fairs. Her stand seemed to have become a red-hot selling area.

Sandy had also chanced on a lucrative deal, requiring goods of top quality, to furnish the house of a wealthy client living to the west of her, not far from the Welsh border. A number of items were taken for approval, including, he could hardly believe it, the yew wood chairs he'd been holding for years. She said, if he could arrange to have a carver made to complete the set of eight, the man would have them. The deal was concluded two days before Christmas 1995, by which time John Dodds knew his marriage was over.

That year, being obviously devastated, he decided not to celebrate Christmas at home, for with it holding too many festive memories, he felt it best to escape.

CHAPTER TWENTY-NINE

I wasn't surprised to find a lacuna at this point. Well, there were a few details, but it was pretty scanty stuff considering we're talking about a span of three years.

He did give brief particulars, of a few days being spent with his sister and brother-in-law in Kent and how he'd journeyed on to Folkstone, for a pre-Christmas deal with Roger Kilby. He'd found him pouring cheap white wine into a pint glass.

---*It was eleven in the morning and he asked if I'd care to join him on such a festive occasion. I declined, bought what he had for sale and was told it would all be delivered in the new year. Can't remember a single thing of what I bought; it's the vision of that wine that sticks in the memory.*

With his two loyal children, daughter 13 and son 17, they then flew to Tenerife, where a closer bond than ever formed in the curing warmth of the Canaries.

There was mention of his bank account having been frozen, for Anne had been a partner in the business, mainly a sleeping partner, but a partner legally, no less. The bank manager had set up an emergency account, but until the partnership was dissolved, he'd walked a financial tightrope.

Another mention of circumstances in the early months of that bleak time, was regarding Tim Glenger.

I was across the street from him and he hadn't noticed me. Having a small paper bag in his left hand, at every couple of swaggering strides, the accompanying swinging right, would dip into the bag to break off a piece of confectionary, which was relished like a cat that had got the cream. I received a jolt within, that innate warning system, alerting me to the fact something must have happened. I hadn't a long wait to find out, for it was about then, he started hoovering up all the Welsh dressers on the market, plus most other hefty oak furniture of note. From some unknown source, unlimited funds had become available.

Apart from one further observation and the details of advice, Bob, a friend in the police force had given, that was it; a three-year gap in what had happened in his life.

---*Bob had been through a similar trying time and he'd said, 'Eventually, instincts will compel you to look for someone else. My advice is don't, meeting the right person will happen when you're not even thinking about it.'*

This was John's observation:--- *In the bleak early days, with my two having left for school and household tasks completed, I would then concentrate on the shop. What never failed to amaze, was, when I finally returned to the kitchen, all would be untouched, exactly as I'd left it. That's when the enormity of what had happened, hit home.*

I worked out the gap had been roughly three years, for in early 1999, he and the children returned by boat from Ireland, following another Christmas escape and he refers to the luck of them having missed the great Boxing Day storm. I looked it up and it had swept across the north of England and Scotland, the day after Christmas 1998.

I rang Mike to see if he could fill in any details, but he just said, John Dodds, with two teenage children to look after, had carried on trading and in fact, one year, if he remembered correctly, had punched dramatically through the million-pound ceiling. He did add, John's daughter, still in her early teens, had taken on the role of being a little mum to them both, doing most of the cooking. He remembered John remarking, how mature she was for her age. One evening, when he and his son had been debating whether the family would ever be reunited, she'd apparently looked up from her sewing to say, 'Mummy, will never be coming home.'

I did find some scraps of doggerel verse, written in the Shropshire dialect, obviously in an attempt to make light of the matter. I've included a little of it.

The following is the first verse of the one poem.

> My missus upped and left me,
> Which I find a mite surprisin';
> Ran off with a bloke from the running club,
> Two dots on the far horizon.

Here are three verses from the second little piece and you can almost imagine Benny Hill reciting them.

> The thought of 'er with another moosh
> Rips me innards now and then,
> But I canner look at another wench
> 'Cos it's 'er I'd choose again.

> To rub in salt, this letter came,
> Now 'es got 'er in 'is bed,
> Askin' for twenty thousand quid;
> That did make me see red!

> I thought, 'I'd 'av 'er back for ten.'
> What injustice cheek and gall;
> Or I'll send 'im fully twenty-five;
> 'Ee can 'av 'er mum n'all!

Then, suddenly, as if a weight had been lifted, John Dodds set to the task of writing again.

---*With relief, I realised, I no longer worried whether I bought dressers or not. Tim Glenger was welcome to them. When all is said and done, they are only pieces of kitchen furniture and the thousands some people are now spending having kitchens re-vamped, doesn't include such antiquated leviathans. He was particularly welcome to the hefty Denbigh dressers, with what are horribly described in the trade, as having belly-racks. Equally nauseating, is a term referring to those with applied panels, which even wannabe antique dealers tend to use when trying to sound part of the business; 'slap on panels.' I never minded the dead-straight pot board dressers being referred to as 'coffin pot boards,' for they were such slow sellers, the term seemed quite apt.*

Anyway, regarding dresser bases of various types, ideal for gracing living room or hallway, I always seemed to have half a dozen in stock without even trying and so anyone putting their mind to the task of netting more of their ilk, plus full dressers, would soon become overwhelmed by the things.

In fact, I gained great satisfaction of hooking out from under his nose, various items of far greater interest. The charming little oddity of a 17th century oak food hutch, from the Wolverhampton saleroom comes to mind; a graceful spread of an 8-seater gateleg table from Stourport and from West Wales, the best coffer-bach I've ever owned. It was slightly larger than normal, looking ready for the off, on cabriole legs and although all the best are constructed, as if in two separate parts, this one actually was, the gothic panelled box-section being removable from its base.

It came in for £800 including the slap, as we traders are wont to call the buyer's premium and Paul Hopwell didn't hesitate in buying it for £3,500.

Jim, bless him, with his gruff manner, actually has a heart of gold.
(I assumed this to be Jim Ash, for the item had been bought in
Carmarthen) *When I asked him if he wanted anything for its
purchase, he'd said, 'No, Johnny. With all you've been through,
you deserve that.'*

Something I'd assumed had been from about this time, I realised
must have been written retrospectively, for it concerns his short
spell, when driving the American client around.

*---With the worst of the trauma over, I can now dare to think of
the last few years, which I must admit, had become a blur. I can
even laugh about memories of those escort days, for with the first
of them coming so close upon what then befell me, I realised, like
many others, I'd pushed them to the back of my mind.*

*On the second occasion, ferrying my wealthy client about,
I actually picked him up from Heathrow. He was keen to explore
the antique shops of Newbury and Hungerford, before moving on
into the Cotswolds, where he'd booked a suite in the Lygon Arms,
Broadway. It was early in the year, cold and draughty and when
the wind whipped under his neat mat, he wasn't quite quick
enough to slap it back down, before the bald truth was revealed,
Byron was a Brynner in disguise. A bit of a shock for any willing
to partake in his night-time manoeuvres.*

*He managed to buy a few items, which as usual, were all ticketed
ready for export, with notes made regarding full descriptions and
prices paid. For my part, I could see there'd be absolutely no point
in trying to buy from such antique outlets.*

*At the Lygon Arms, Broadway, we were greeted like royalty, a far cry
from when I'd done an antique fair in the village years before. It was
one that Don from Old Street, Ludlow had organised in the early
days and he'd enrolled the help of that renowned South Shropshire*

character previously mentioned, Tater Davies, to walk around with an advertising sandwich board. Somehow, Tater had persuaded tourists to ply him with drink and he'd ended up like a circus act, dancing about, surrounded by a huge ring of delighted onlookers, taking photographs. When one shouted, 'You've got odd shoes on,' he'd replied, 'I know. I got another pair just like 'em, back wum.'(home)

I managed to sell Byron a few thousand pounds worth, from my photos, the night passed without any worries, as did the following two and I dropped him off for his business meeting at the chateau Impney Hotel, in Droitwich.

There were a couple more trips, including one to Harrogate, but it was the stay at the Connaught in London, that made my mind up for me. We'd done a few trade calls and he'd bought most of what I'd offered from the photographs, there were single beds again, but before he got into his, he bent down to where I lay and holding my shoulders said, 'I love you, Johnny.'

Grabbing his head, to prevent notions of physical endorsement, I said, 'Think the world of you too, Bryon. Goodnight!' I pulled the covers tight around me, thinking, 'Don't blow the deal, but get the hell out of here as soon as you can!'

Not wanting that accidental on purpose touch, accompanying an exaggerated yawn the following morning, I was up and out of there at six o-clock. It's amazing how much distance you can cover in no time, when trying to kill time. With the Connaught coming back into view and only a further half hour on my watch, I went on a chilly circuit in the opposite direction. When eventually back in the room, I made up a story of having heard a car alarm and had been worried it had been mine.

When dropping him off at Heathrow, he as usual, asked, how much in cash was owed for my time and fuel? As he counted out *the £300 or so, I thought, 'I've had enough of this! I could earn more than that on a pissing pot cupboard!'*

I thanked him graciously, but said, I didn't think I was cut out for escorting duties. I got a bit teeth-gritting here, adding, I was a trader and the demands of the job made it too difficult to take time out driving clients around the country. He looked truly shocked, but I drove from Heathrow with the most incredible feeling of liberation, as if I had wings. Then sadly, I wondered if my dear Anne had felt the same when she fled the home?

It seemed, from what I now read in the notes, John Dodds bought more from the Midlands than he did from Wales. There were frequent mentions of Malvern, Stratford, Warwick, Worcester and Oxford, plus he now even ranged down into the West Country, having a number of successes at the three Exeter salerooms.

I read that, Julian Mynott, now often carried his prices and he did quite well on the items bought from their premises.

---The majority of what they handled was in a price bracket beyond mine, but with persistence, I could hook out the odd thing, such as tall Georgian, four-fold, painted leather screen, being that sumptuous with its foliage, flowers and birds, you couldn't really put a definite price on it.

In another Warwick shop, belonging to Patrick Morley, I'd visited often enough to recognise the new from that having taken root and if sufficient space was cleared, allowing me to stand back, I occasionally found the odd piece, that if given a polish and a bit of carpet to stand on, stood a chance of showing a decent return.

It seemed, his business had changed, going more for mahogany, decorative items and oak with character rather than a plethora of oak for oak's sake. The next little section, must have also been written reflectively, for he mentions two of the secretaries in the

Chester Oak sale having found it hilarious, that a porter, an old boy of over sixty, should be singing the odd snatch of 'Wannabe,' a record just out by the Spice Girls. With the description given below, of how Tim Glenger had arrived with a mate he'd lately teamed up with, Don Knuckles, made it likely we are talking about, early 1997.

---*They were both tanned, having holidayed with their families in the Canaries and arrived wearing matching black leather jackets, like two excited schoolboys talking about Christmas hols. Most of the oak on display, was either sprawling with fatigue, wrong or simply dreary and they were welcome to it. Andy King, collared three decent lots I was pleased with, but I did feel a bit of a dull lump in comparison to Glenger's persona, like a someone really going places.*

I looked further through the notes and found that John Dodds was quite happy to concede that Tim Glenger's new buddy and supplier, was one of the most respected oak traders in the country, which meant, almost unbelievably, with Roger Kilby supplying his own shop, some of the best oak available nationally was being traded through the small town of Ludlow, on the Welsh border. Roger Kilby patrolled the south, including the London rooms, plus East Anglia, while Don Knuckles covered the Midlands and the north. They obviously clashed at certain venues, but most regularly in the south west.

Here's another little snippet, which must have been from those three blank years.

---*I was finding it hard to concentrate on antiques, for it all now felt fairly meaningless and so when Roger arrived one day with a load of oak, I sat on a joint stool staring across at a 17th century dresser base in the back of his van, thinking, 'Why the hell am I bothering?'.*

Roger, watching, said in his broad cockney, 'Eer, you don't 'alf look the part, mate.'

The comment brought me rudely to order. 'What do you mean?'

'Well, if there was ever a bloke, what looked like 'is missus 'as just run out on 'im, then I'm sorry mate, but it's you sat there on that stool. Like I said, you really look the part.'

'Oh, I suppose I'd better try and concentrate.'

'Concentrate? You're not a bad lookin' bloke. Put the word out and you'll 'av 'em queuing at the door. A mate of mine---'ee 'ad what you're going through. I went to see 'im two weeks after 'is missus 'ad run off and was met at the door by this big busty blonde he'd got 'isself.'

There were descriptions of meeting Roger at various locations on the outskirts of London, laybys near Bath, Stratford, Oxford etc; service stations on the M4; M25 and also when viewing sales, such as Clevedon, Newbury and Cheltenham, where it would obviously save the time of travelling on to Ludlow, but it was a rendezvous in the hotel grounds outside Warwick, that a fuller description was given.

---It was early on a chilly, dank morning. We'd co-ordinated arrival perfectly, but as Roger and his son Mark got out and noisily stretched, I did wonder if the hotel authorities would take exception to us using their driveway to conduct business. It took me back to a certain deal with Chris Braddock, up in North Wales. Mark disappeared to relieve himself beyond the leafless trails of a weeping willow, while I helped Roger haul the furniture out.

The deal was a fairly straightforward affair until we came to negotiating the price of a small, rare 17th century oak mural livery cupboard. I told Roger, £3,600 seemed an awful lot for a few turned spindles, a spindle door and a couple of small boards for top and floor. We seemed to have reached an impasse until he said, 'Look, Doddsy, this is really fuckin' early, I've even got to pay out that Knuckles, two hundred quid on it!'

The term early, that I'd once found so enigmatic, Roger had extended, from the unadorned version, meaning c 1720, through to fuckin' early, meaning 1680, reserving really fuckin' early, for oak dating back to 1620 or even earlier. The fact that Don Knuckles would be benefitting from its sale, gave me an idea.

I said, 'Roger, Don Knuckles has owed me £200 for at least three months now. Just knock his £200 off the £3600 and I'll buy it. Even if I just sell it at your asking price, it's tantamount to getting my money off him.'

His eyes lit up. 'I love it,' he said. 'Can't wait to tell 'im. "Sorry Knuckles, but Doddsy's 'ad yer dosh!" Hang on a minute. Just gotta take a leak.'

Rather than go discretely beyond the trees, he headed for the black oil tank, directly below a hotel window.

With steam rising, he yelled over his shoulder, 'I love it!'

I cringed, expecting hotel staff to come pouring forth at any second, gesticulating and telling us to clear off. Mark gave a look of despair and when his father repeated at the top of his voice, 'I love it,' he winced and muttered, 'It sounds like he's having a J. Arthur.'

Absolutely brimming at having got one over his rival, he took some calming and coaxing, before finally willing to reboard the waiting van, Mark had turned in the drive. I was that relieved to drive from there unchallenged, my look around the Warwick trade, was perfunctory at best and by 11am, I was back in the shop.

That evening, came an irate phone call. You can guess from whom. 'Look! you can't just take it upon yourself to help yourself to my £200.'

'Sorry Don, but it's only the same as you paying me what you owe.'

'I'm not having it. You've got no right!'

'Too late, it's done.'

'Who the hell do you think you are, dictating terms?'

I put the phone down and before the week was out, sold it to Paul Hopwell for £3,750. I'd retrieved my £200, made a £150 profit and had put Knuckles's nose out of joint.

Quite often, I'd call down at Roger's house, saving him the slog of travelling and occasionally we'd go round the Kent and Sussex trade, plus view sales if any happened to be on locally. I was able to buy Welsh dressers and press cupboards in places like Deal and Maidstone, for much less money than they'd have fetched in Newtown or Dolgellau. Countless thousands of pounds worth of Welsh oak had been shipped to the south of England in the late 60's, early 70's and was coming back on the market.

Roger's wife Margaret always made me welcome, but I never once stayed the night there. One reason, was Roger's penchant for drink and second was what the drink could do to him.

At my shop one day, he'd told me a little story. It concerned an erstwhile best mate. I already knew some of the details, for on one of my visits, with Roger out of earshot, Margaret had whispered her tale of horror. On the night in question, the happy couple and the man in question had gone to a party where Roger had drunk himself into such a comatose state, Margaret had been beside herself with disgust and embarrassment. The best mate had kindly driven her home, but having somehow hauled himself out of his stupor, Roger set off in pursuit. Once he'd smashed his best mate's car, to the point it was a undriveable, he then set about its owner, putting him in hospital.

'I 'aint got that best mate no more Doddsy,' he said almost plaintively.

I noticed Mark looking down at his boots, thoroughly embarrassed and with Roger staring straight at me, I got the message, 'You so much as look at my wife------'

He was a fine judge of oak, mind you. There again, with no dealer always getting it right, there was bound to be the odd occasion when I found a deal, was in fact a little disappointing, such as the 17th century joined folding table with the wrong top. He'd always swap it back for something else, however, provided I didn't do it too often, or divulge the real reason for wanting out of it.

I was staggered to read how much some of these deals came to. It wasn't unusual for John Dodds to write out cheques for over £40,000, but there again, with some of the items costing nearly £20,000, I suppose it wasn't really that surprising. He gave a brief description of two four poster beds he'd bought, one with a tiny cupboard concealed in the back panelling and another with white painted unicorns adorning the frieze. Both sold on to the trade for over £20,000. Two diminutive dressers, a late 16th century buffet and *'an absolute gem, of a 17th century dining table'* all cost close to the twenty-thousand-pound mark. Then I chanced on something and realised it was another shred of what had happened in those missing three years.

---I hadn't heard from Roger for a while and got no answer on his house phone. I wondered if he might be journeying the dark labyrinth of a whiskey phase, but then eventually received a call.

'Hello Doddsy. If you've been trying to ring me, then you'd 'ave failed. I shot the phones.'

'What?'

'I took them out in the garden and shot 'em. Gave 'em the gun, mate.'

'You're joking.'

'I'm fuckin' not, mate. Shot 'em all in the flower bed. I warned the kids about runnin' up the phone bill. Well anyway, I've put a stop to that. Shot the fuckers!'

I realised it must have been only been a temporary shock tactic, for he was ringing me on his landline. I was told about an incredible, monumental gateleg table he'd bought. It had a solid oak underframe, but the top was most unusual, having patterned oak veneers. I left early the following morning and was outside his house, down on the south coast, before 8am, where he appeared at a bedroom window as if wearing the place. The table was as he'd described and lying on its side, filled the whole back of my people carrier. Driving home, with the roads so eerily empty, it felt almost sacrilegious, having done a deal on such a day, for most of the country was silently watching the course of Princess Diana's funeral on the television. It did actually seem to blight the table, for although entirely original and magnificent, it took a while before I could even get my money back.

So, looking it up on the internet, I found the table must have been bought on September 6th, 1997, just beyond the halfway point of those missing three years.

I found two snippets, referring to John's rough diamond friend whilst staying overnight in Ludlow. On one occasion, John walked down to where Roger had rented a room at the Wheatsheaf public house. Out of interest, I looked it up and found its location to be nestled against the town wall, just beyond the only remaining mediaeval gate.

---Roger's massive frame dominated a bar stool and even though only about 6pm, a few of the tables were occupied by early diners. It was one of those pubs that had broken with tradition, concentrating on culinary delights rather than beer and had gained quite a favourable reputation.

Roger bought me a drink and then interrupted our idle chat with, 'Hey Doddsy! How's that fuckin' Glenger getting' on?'

Seeing everyone had suddenly stopped chewing, I hissed, 'Roger, calm it down a bit. This is a restaurant.'

With a hand clamped to mouth, there came a muffled, 'Sorry, mate.' Then in a whisper that would have been audible even in the furthest corner, he asked, 'Anyway. How's the fucker doin'?'

I suggested we finish our drinks and walk uptown to the Bullring Tavern bar. Not that you would hear much swearing in there, but at least his expletives would have less impact.

On another occasion, we had just heaved an early, not effin early, dresser base up the steps to the showroom behind the curtain, when a female trader asked snootily, 'Mr. Kilby, don't you ever like small pretty things.'

'Yeh,' he said. 'As long as they got big tits.'

I gave a weak smile and helpless shrug to my lady customer, who on that occasion, departed rather quickly, without purchasing anything.

I had heard the tale, regarding half of his house being torched by a lowlife working for a client in charge of nefarious activities along the south coast, a man who Roger had obviously vexed whilst voyaging through a wet phase, but I never thought to bring the matter up. Then out of the blue one day, he told me the details, the extent of the damage and how he'd traced the culprit.

'So what did you do?'

'Thought he might appreciate a little fishing trip,' he said in a chilling faraway voice.

442

I of course, didn't ask for more details, but had no doubt it had happened, for my friend Robert Deeley had told me of Roger's modus operandi, when needing to extract unpaid rent on properties he owned in Dover. He had been in the middle of a deal with him, when Roger's phone had gone.

He overheard, 'We've got 'im dad. What d'you want us to do with him?'

'Take the bastard up and dangle 'im over the cliff.'

Rob Deeley told me, he'd been horrified, especially when the phone had gone again and he heard Roger ask, 'Have you chucked 'im off yet?'

'No dad, he stinks a bit, but he's going to cough up.'

'Well make sure he does.'

John Dodds couldn't understand how villain and genius could reside within the same frame. Taken to extremes, you could almost liken him to, warlord come cathedral builder. He'd pondered:--- *was this larger-than-life character a throwback to the Vikings? Rampaging and slaughtering, before their descendants, the Normans, eventually became the driving force behind this country's magnificent Gothic architecture. Or a latter-day version of Eadric the Wild, from Clun?*

I found his reference to a tiny watery-eyed waif, Roger and his wife had rescued from drug addict parents.

---In the end, they adopted little Clowy and on many occasions, I witnessed the delight on her face as skipping into the room, she'd launch herself, light as a feather to land mid-lap of her hero, as large as any silverback. Eying me with a hint of triumph, it was quite clear, she loved the man.

CHAPTER THIRTY

I now came across a section, once again written as if a short story and John Dodds had given it the title, 'Travels with Harry.'

The Harry referred to, was Harry Mynott, no relation whatsoever to the antique dealer Julian Mynott from Warwick, although he had confessed to John, he'd once spent an amorous night with Julian's mother. The main reason why Harry now came into the picture, was that he had moved in with a lady who traded small antique artefacts from a property in Welshpool High Street.

---*Harry would frequently call, looking for mahogany items he could run down to a customer who operated a vast antique business in Kent. The man had realised years before, one of the foibles of the American antique trade. Unlike in England, where private buyers of antique furniture, expect to at least get their money back, in The States, if tiring of their purchases, they tend to simply dump them into a saleroom, not caring what they fetch. So on average, six containers a year, full of English antiques were shipped back to home shores, where no doubt, American clients bought some of it to send west again. Stuff must have suffered from travel sickness and I know it sounds almost unbelievable, but I can also cite a similarly bizarre example of how an item of furniture can end up almost back where it started from.*

One of the Bookends, the dour one from Stow, had become rather stuck with a Welsh pot-board dresser and asked if I could sell it for him. I did with ease, selling it to his next-door neighbour, the very next day. It was the same dealer who had announced years before, he was willing to lose thirty grand to learn the job. He had since moved from Leominster to Stow-on-the-Wold, directly next door to the bearded Bookend and obviously still had a bit to learn.

Harry would often accompany me when on a circuit, out viewing the auctions. He not only imparted his vast knowledge, but also lightened the journeys with his tales. I learnt, how he'd chanced on the notion of trading in antiques for a living and he also imparted some interesting details of what had happened at the legendary Green Dragon hotel, in the early days, before I also, had blundered into the business.

He told me, he'd started literally, at the very bottom, buying what no-one at the time wanted, chamber pots, washstands, jugs and bowls to sell to a client, shipping goods to America. It had been more like a hobby really, but he quickly realised, it was possible to make more money doing that, than he earnt slaving forty hours a week in a proper job. He occasionally teamed up with a seasoned dealer from Stroud, Jack Smith, who happy to impart his knowledge, gave an insight into the better goods. He told me, that one occasion where he'd had his eyes opened, was when a jug and basin, he'd rated at the maximum of £3, went on to make over £100, which considering the average wage at the time was £12, was an incredible price. Jack, with a wink of one of those in the know, had confided, the reason he'd launched so much money into the purchase, was on account of this being no ordinary jug and basin, but a rather special specimen, from the Mintons factory. It was Harry's job to carefully cradle it on the journey back to Stroud. He had carried the bowl to the shop, as gingerly as if an unexploded bomb, placing it carefully on a table, just inside doorway. Not Jack, however. He'd walked, triumphantly swinging the jug and Harry had watched transfixed, as parting from its handle, it described a graceful parabolic curve, to land with perfection inside the awaiting basin, smashing all to fragments.

Harry told me, he'd been rendered, that helpless with laughter, he'd been in absolute, side-aching agony.

As he learnt more about the job, he'd felt able to rise to the challenge of journeying up to Hereford, where the Irish travellers queued to cash in their hauls at the Green Dragon hotel. It had been taken over as an antique emporium and as the Irish lined up to sell, the English trade waited to buy. Harry would attempt to be one of the first there, buying the choicest pieces straight off the list and selling on to other dealers waiting. On a good day, he'd drive home with a pocket bulging with cash and his van completely empty.

Over the years, as he learnt more, his business went from strength to strength, until in the end he had been turning over 3 million. I was staggered and dared ask, considering that vast turnover, how had it been possible to go bust?

He said, the first time he realised it had all gone wrong, was when his cheque to the milkman bounced. After that, things started to quickly implode and what he divulged helped explain a conundrum that had puzzled for years; how had certain members of the trade managed to buy such vast amounts, with never seeming to run out of cash? Harry supplied part of the answer, which I should have guessed really; some of the major rooms had been giving him and certain others, credit. When he realised the game was up, he'd taken van loads of leftover stock to those same auction houses, hoping its sale would at least pay off some of the debt. He wanted to be able to hold his head up.

A quick calculation told me how the seeming impossible had happened. Harry had been mainly selling to the man in Kent, mentioned earlier, handing over the purchase invoice with just a 3% mark-up. This would have given him a mere £90,000 gross. The VAT on that would have been £14,000, the business expenses, at least £25,000, the tax, at least £15,000, leaving him just £36,000 net on all that turnover. There's not an antique dealer

446

*alive, who doesn't make the odd mistake and so even if only 1%
of that 3 million, went into the rejects corner, a stock build-up of
£30,000 per annum, would have left him with just £6,000 to live
off. He must have had other deals, apart from selling to his main
customer, but even so, why hadn't his accountant warned him?*

*It was thanks to Harry, that I met his brother and the late Jack
Smith's son, both brilliant restorers, working in an old wartime
Nissen hut on a trading estate near Birdlip, Gloucestershire.
Having carefully picked a path through work pending, pushing
open the flimsy screen, led to dim, dusty den where the two
practised their art. Smiling faces would greet, followed by friendly
insults such as, 'So, what piece of old rubbish have you brought
us today?'*

*They had a vast knowledge and it never failed to amaze me, how a
restored mahogany, rosewood or walnut, thoroughbred gem,
could possibly be drawn out into the light, from such a dust-laden
scene of seeming chaos. Like all first-class restorers, there was no
point taking them anything ordinary, or thoroughly distressed as
it would have been left to languish until they suggested, it be
disinterred and taken elsewhere. Present them with something of
quality, however and they'd have it done in a matter of days.*

*They told me tales of the old days, when what they called the
'party gang,' would descend having viewed Leominster, Malvern
and Cheltenham sales, partaking of liquid refreshment at every
stop.*

*I realised they were referring to the ones who'd baffled me years
before, revelling in a day of swanning round the salerooms, hardly
bothering to view properly and often buying wrong lots.*

*Harry's brother, Graham said, 'One day, I hadn't realised they'd
honoured, our little patch, with a visit. It was a lovely afternoon
and so I thought I'd have my cup of tea outside. I was puzzled by
the sound of snoring. Not just one going full throttle, but a*

competing chorus, like a throbbing hive. I found the culprits, all sprawled out on the grass, sleeping off the day's booze.'

'Another time, they announced they'd brought a present and told me to look in the back of the van. There curled up, asleep on the blankets, was some bar fly, they'd picked up.

'And did you?' I asked.

'You gotta be joking.'

Out of interest, on one day when I'd called, I saw they were working on an Edwardian marquetry cabinet of the same quality as that sold way back in my early days for £32. I was surprised, at such a late thing being worthy of their efforts. I was even more surprised when they divulged, their client could get over £20,000, selling it and anything similar, to a Malaysian millionaire.

Harry earnt me quite a steady addition to my income, running Georgian mahogany down to his customer in Kent. I was told, he was not a particularly pleasant fellow, but that didn't trouble me, for I didn't need to deal with him personally. Our prices rarely clashed in salerooms, which was fortunate, for if they had have done, I'm sure an abrupt halt would have been put to that little avenue of financial gain. The one time it definitely did happen, was on a pair of Regency work tables, stamped Gillows. How he'd got wind of them, way up in Colwyn Bay, I don't know, but anyway, I bought them for £14,000, all in. Harry was bidden to fetch them down for the great man to see in the flesh and all I'd put on them was £2,000 profit. I should have known it was just an exercise in putting me in my place, for they came back unsold. It worried me not, for I lent them to my friend Rosie, who sold them, first day at Olympia, for £22,000 and we split the profit.

Harry would regularly run my goods to the Olympia Fair; cricket tables, dresser bases, country furniture with original painted decoration, such as a rather splendid pine and sycamore bow-back settle and some years, I think I did better than many of the stallholders, for the cost of a stand, no bigger than the average front room was enough to put down as a sizeable deposit on a house. I've known some, endure the whole twelve days of the fair and not sell a thing. Always praying the miracle would somehow happen, until those final words of doom, 'The Olympia Fair is now closed.'

One morning, I was up with Harry viewing the Anglesey sale, held in the sheds of Gaerwen cattle market. He'd said, we'd better shut the gates and sit and wait, for the men he pointed to, wouldn't be standing there for no reason. Five, armed with sticks, were in a line across the width of ground that led from the back of the market.

'That's the reason,' he said pointing.

From behind the buildings, a huge Charolaise bull appeared, followed by a cow. The men shouted, waved their sticks, then ran. The colossal bovine escapees disappeared from sight, for the view of that part of the parking area was obscured by a tall garden hedge.

I visibly jumped when a massive horned head appeared about thirty yards ahead.

'That's just the cow,' said Harry.

The mighty frame of the bull appeared, loping towards us as if hardly touching the ground. The car shuddered as it brushed past and turning, I saw it baulk at the gates we'd closed, to instead take the garden route, along with the fence, which it trailed across the lawn.

We drove the short distance to the saleroom door, completed the viewing and on driving back, to the now open gates, Harry laughed, pointing to the trail of destruction, wire fence, children's toys and washing strewn across the garden. Peering, he said, 'There he is and they've put some cows in there to calm him down. He'll be as good as gold now.'

Beyond a 15' foot high hedge, I could see the massive creature, peacefully grazing in the field beyond. It must have gone through the hedge as if simply not there.

Can't remember a thing of what I saw in the saleroom that day, but I'll never forget that massive white bull.

Harry regaled me with stories of his romantic escapades over the years and how D.A. had given him a bollocking, for entertaining the wife of a commissioned officer, while the man was off on military duties.

'Harry, you ought to be ashamed of yourself! The man has taken the Queen's colours and you're seeing to his wife!'

He told me of the time he'd been invited out for supper, by a client, keen to hear first-hand, details of the shotgun pellets in his backside episode, that had made the national press. Also present that evening were the man's wife and a female friend. The host, having got himself thoroughly drunk, went to bed, leaving Harry to entertain the ladies. He told me with a merry chuckle, 'It was two on to one, but I didn't let the side down.'

Some of the ladies he told me about, fine 'gels', graduates from top schools, seemed to take on a different persona in his company, lusting after pleasures of the flesh and it left me puzzling, where did he find such sporting types? Wherever he went, he seemed to generate an end of the races, party atmosphere.

One little tale he related, gave a bit more background detail to a certain Mr. Kilby. Harry had bought a fine set of late 17th century, oak high-backed chairs, but once realising he'd been a bit cavalier with his purchase price, lent them to Roger Kilby, who told him, he'd have no trouble shifting them.

True to his word, they went, for the next time Harry saw them was in a Cirencester shop window, but on sale for less money than he'd paid for them. When ringing Roger, he'd got a rambling reply and then his calls were ignored. He contacted a firm of debt collectors, who assured him they couldn't see a problem, being just a straightforward matter of getting him his money back. Two weeks later, Harry had rung to enquire of progress, but the boss, having delved into background details, told him, 'I'm sorry, but I'm not prepared to send my operatives anywhere near the man.'

The little saga was quite chilling.

Harry and I were viewing Phillips of Oxford one day, when the game changer happened. Initially, all seemed as normal in the saleroom, with the ladies who kept an eye on things, dotted about, or handing small treasures from the cabinets, but it's hard to explain, I could just sense something momentous must have suddenly occurred. The atmosphere in the room changed completely. One by one, people were drawn towards a radio beneath the rostrum. The date was 9/11/2001. From that point on, I knew I had to find a way out of the antique business.

I kept my resolve, letting my prices remain on all the goods I'd viewed that week and with many others having become a little faint hearted, I bought more than I normally would have, the total coming to £105,000. Keeping track of the goods going through the system, I found that when the final item from that particular week had sold, almost a year to the day later, I had earnt £18,000, a slightly higher return than my 14.5% average.

CHAPTER THIRTY-ONE

It still seemed amazing, but at last I had a vague picture of how a man who had once heaved a £1 chaise longue through the town, to earn £2, was now turning over £1,000,000 a year. To anyone looking on, it must have seemed like he had made it, as they say, but in the notes I found a different story.

---I was now alongside, or in some cases had even surpassed many of the people I'd admired when trying to clamber my way up the trade ladder. I was amazed to find, some of those I'd imagined to know their stuff, to be nothing more than blowhards with an extremely thin knowledge, whereas those humble enough to admit, they didn't fully understand certain aspects of the trade, often had an amazing knowledge of their particular niche in the job. If it's the same scenario for all professions, then it's a scary prospect, for who would you trust financially or medically?

I had the same feeling of rude awakening; no, more than that; a shock really, as regards the activities of a number of those in the esteemed trade associations. I don't mean those who genuinely believed their association gave private customers a shield of protection, or even the old rogues who slipped the odd dubious lot through, I mean the real dodge-pots. It was almost as if their rush to join, was to hide what they were really up to. On quite a few occasions, private customers had asked me to take lots in part exchange and with their goods having been bought from respected members of a certain trade association, I thought I had to be on safe ground.

Here are just three examples that happened to stun me; a Georgian oak dresser base, fabricated from a mule chest and other spurious bits; a massive Georgian mahogany break-front bookcase, constructed from three completely unrelated bookcases; a seemingly majestic mahogany chest of drawers, adorned at the corners with three-quarter columns, constructed from the top half of a chest on chest.

There were many holier than thou, plus others in the trade that would pull every stroke possible to denigrate one's business, that at times, made being part of the same structure, quite sickening and disenchanting. Once out of it, I never wanted to see the like of them again. I had often mused over the puzzle, how could such wonderful, ancient artifacts, attract such awful people? I felt disillusioned with the job and now being trapped in a large shop in a town heaving with tourists, couldn't wait to get out.

Some days, I'd have a list of jobs that needed attending to and by the end of day, having sold nothing, found I'd not even been able to complete a mere ten-minute task, the whole day having been spent answering questions from people who had not the slightest intention of buying anything. I'd be thanked profusely and told, 'We must make a point of calling, next time we're in Ludlow,' leaving me thinking, 'Meanwhile, I'll try and hang on.'

Written below, is where I'd obtained the tax trap detail, slotted in at the conclusion of the first two years in the new shop. I don't think it will hurt to now give the full version of what John Dodds had written, for it drives home, how a constant eye needed to be kept on the fine-tuning of the business and how little, in fact, ended up as liquid assets.

---What had started out as a fun way to make a living had become an onerous treadmill. For instance, by the time enough money had been earnt to pay the previous year's tax, I was automatically in the 40% tax bracket and when adding the National Insurance on the first wedge of tax and the VAT due on all the profits, I was paying the Government 60% of all earnings. Out of the remaining 40%, came business expenses and it didn't take a genius to work out, that there was only a 3% margin for error, regarding stock build-up. It didn't mean the stock was wrong, just that for some reason, it hadn't appealed to the regulars, for it was still the regulars, whether trade or private, who kept me going.

The swap deals with Adam on a Wednesday, helped freshen things up a little, but it became scaringly obvious, if I had a build-up of more than £30,000 unsold stock per annum, then I was slowly going down the plughole.

It wasn't possible to just stop for a breather, the regulars wanted a fresh choice of goods every time they called and if you stopped buying, word would soon get out, you were in trouble and then being stigmatised, plus having nothing new to offer, the trade would soon stop calling.

The business needed a weekly minimum of £2,500 profit, just to stand still and to generate that, purchases had to average £17,000 per week, so if for some reason, the trade suddenly stopped, I'd not be long in going broke. Obviously, there were the fabulous deals, with huge profits, but an awful lot of stock, once it had had its time, needed ousting in a damage limitation exercise. Like I said it was a treadmill and 9/11 was a wake-up call. As soon as I could manage, I was getting out of the business.

'Will your children eventually take over the shop?' I was often asked.

I'd explain, they were following other career paths, while deep inside I was thinking, 'Not if I can help it.'

To add to that feeling of impending doom, I'd keep a tally of trade sales compared to goods sold privately and the balance had started to swing towards the latter and so whereas Ludlow had once been perfectly positioned to supply the English trade with goods from Wales and Welsh Marches, it was fast becoming a beleaguered outpost. Would anyone in their right mind, now set up a specialist business in the town, selling rare bronzes or expensive oriental carpets? Of course not and so why should a business specialising in top of the range oak and mahogany survive? Some weeks were saved by a miracle customer appearing just before closing time on a Saturday, but I could no longer survive on miracles, I had to get out.

I suppose, from an onlooker's point of view, with the shop bulging with stock ranging from a few hundred up to the many thousands of pounds, they probably thought I was made of money and didn't need to sell anything.

'Who do you sell all this stuff to? All the big country houses in these parts?'

Or, 'Where do you buy all this from? All those mansions we've seen?'

'Yes they grow it for me and when they've a fresh lot ready, I'm straight round there.'

I only said that once and immediately regretted it, but some days it felt like all the browsers had come on a coach tour, specifically to wind me up. To rub salt in, after a trying day of selling nothing, you could find a couple of valuable artefacts had been stolen. In the very early days in the new shop, I'd had to abandon any notion of selling jewellery and as the years progressed, had to stop buying anything that could be slipped into a pocket. Thank goodness for certain regulars, who kept me sane.

I must admit, I hadn't expected to read this. It seemed, that having striven for so long to reach such an elusive goal, John Dodds was thoroughly disillusioned with what he found there. I decided it was time to give Mike another ring and gain his experienced view of things.

I didn't explain exactly, what I wanted to talk about, but hadn't really needed to, for he seemed glad to help and suggested we meet up. The venue this time was a boot fair at the small market town of Leominster on the Welsh Marches and he advised me to arrive early, first on the scene as the stalls were being set up.

I did as suggested, but then wondered about gaining entry, as there was a definite opening time and I was an hour too early. The answer came when I spotted Mike, waving me over to join the queue at the gate. Clambering into the van, he gave me a cheery smile and paid as we entered, as if being exhibitors. Pointing to the far side of the auction yard, he said to drive and park on the end of the line of vehicles. When a white coated steward tried to wave us into a vacant gap, Mike simply waved back and muttered, "Keep driving." He had parked his car on the edge of town, about ten minutes-walk away.

We were now free to wander amongst all those busily piling things onto trestles and setting up small open-air shops. I bought a few woven baskets, some garden ornaments, only cast concrete, but a layer of moss gave them a certain appeal and Mike suggested I just note my purchases, for collection later, once we'd completed the circuit. There were plenty of stalls, selling tools, toys and clothes that we didn't need to break our stride to look at, but I found a couple more pieces of interest and thoroughly enjoyed the experience.

It was at the back of a van selling what looked like a bit of a clear out, that Mike, pulling my arm, said, "Not so fast, I know this isn't your sort of stuff, but just out of interest, if given the choice; what from amongst this man's fine array would you choose?" He smiled at the person in question and received a tolerant look in exchange.

There were two well-worn armchairs, a standard lamp, metal framed kitchen chairs, small oilcloth covered kitchen table, a spiky magazine rack, a stack of faded looking LP's and various other remnants from what I suspect had been cleared from an old folks' bungalow. I was just about to say, I wouldn't want any of it if given me, when I noticed the vendor pulling out candlesticks from a cheap looking brass coal scuttle. There were two pairs, one fairly stubby, but the other pair was completely different, quite tall and elegant in fact. I muttered to Mike, "That pair of candlesticks."

He picked one up and looking at the underside, enquired, "How much are you asking for these?"

"Twenty-four quid."

As Mike gave a throaty puff of breath, clouding its stem, the man added, "But I could do them for twenty."

Mike paid, popped them in his bag and we continued on our way.

"How did I do?" I asked at last.

"Not bad," he said with a grin.

We collected all my purchases and drove into town against the flow of vehicles queuing at the entrance. Mike suggested we park the van and have a quick stroll through the centre of town. As usual, I had read up on the place and had found yet again, over the centuries, the Welsh had left their mark. In 1052, Gruffud ap Llywelyn had raided and I was surprised to see, Norman warriors had helped the Saxon townspeople repulse the raid. So, just as some of the earliest Saxon settlers had been hired mercenaries, some Normans soldiers must have plied their trade, pre-conquest in a like manner. When you think of how difficult travel was back then, it's staggering, that an overseas party of trained fighting men could have scouted out a lucrative opening, up on the Welsh Marches. I presume it was made possible by traders returning with the latest news, 'Hey lads, instead of kicking your heals round in these parts, get yourselves over the channel.

They're paying top shilling, crying out for the likes of you up in Leominster.'

'Where?'

I wasn't surprised to read, that following Owain Glendwr's victory at Pilleth, his men had maintained their momentum eastward to ransack Leominster, burn the priory and make themselves thoroughly disagreeable in the whole surrounding area. What is now, all but a footnote to history, must have been absolute hell to have actually lived through in this border country. Lives and any attempt to make a living, must have been blighted for decades, with the constant worry, 'What if they come rampaging back again?'

Mike and I wandered down the Georgian street leading to the priory, strangely quiet considering how close it is to the bustle of the commercial centre. After half an hour exploring the church, we headed for the hotel Mike had recommended, The Talbot.

As we waited for the coffee and pastries, he asked, "What made you choose the candlesticks?"

"I don't know. I just liked the design. That one you picked up,--- why did you breathe on it?"

Pulling one from the old cloth bag he carried, he repeated the process and showed me the line of the seam, now clearly visible. Turning it over and pointing to the smooth bronzed patination, he said, "That's incredibly hard to fake and the fact these are seamed, proves beyond doubt they are genuine."

"Mike, I don't understand. How did you know they were in that coal scuttle?"

"I could see the petal base of the one, protruding. Any idea what they are?" Quickly adding, "Apart from candlesticks of course."

"No, not really, but it's obvious they weren't made yesterday."

"They are a pair of Queen Anne petal-based candlesticks, taller than most and in original condition."

I was stunned. "So what are they worth?"

"It's a job to say these days. Everything's different. The value of ordinary brown furniture, including dressers, has collapsed, while small country rarities and things like walnut lowboys, are now fetching crazy money. Twenty years ago, you'd have had no trouble getting £750 for them, but now, with the value of metalware also plummeting, probably £350, tops. You may see similar advertised for more on the net, but if you want to sell them immediately, you'd be hard pushed to get over £300. Would you like to keep them?"

"Well no, that wouldn't be fair, I'd have walked straight passed if you hadn't pulled me back."

He looked at me for a while, obviously thinking. "Then what I suggest is, I sell them and we go half shares on the profit."

"That seems incredibly generous. Shall I give you a tenner for half the cost?"

He gave a withering look and then we both had to make room on the small table, for the snacks had arrived. As I watched him joking with the girl, I wondered if I had judged the man correctly at our first meeting. It's hard to explain, but the way he had handled that Queen Anne candlestick hinted at years of experience, showing the confidence of a vet holding a puppy. Maybe I was making too much of it, but that was certainly the feeling I got.

After we had eaten, I asked about the years in the shop following the world-shaking 9/11 cataclysm.

"I did a fair bit for John in those last few years. I was sworn to secrecy regarding his intentions. Apart from all the van stuff, I helped in the shop when it needed a turnaround and spent odd days polishing the furniture and the metalware."

"Is that how you learnt so much about early candlesticks?"

"I don't know that much. John only tended to buy the small items to set off the furniture. He used to say, 'Mike, this place is looking far too woody. He'd even get wing chairs and sofas upholstered to brighten the place up a bit. There were a number of Turkish rugs, scattered about, for the same purpose. He told me the one day, he'd no intention of being one of those pewter or early metalware anoraks. He showed me an article in the Trade Gazette. A metallurgy analysis had proved a pair of bell-shaped candlesticks to be English rather than Dutch, making them worth £12,000 rather than £2,000. He told me, if the two pairs look identical, what the hell's the point? He had started to become disillusioned about many things. One day, he was writing out a £1,400 ticket for a better than average, oak cricket table and said, 'Mike, you do realise if this was French, it would only be worth £200?"

"At the time you're talking about, did he still have those lads restoring for him?"

"What those in the workshop? No, for various reasons they'd gone. In the latter days, he tended to farm the work out. I remember taking a Regency library chair down to Birdlip to have the frame tightened and castors reinstated. I then collected the thing and took it to Weobley to have the caning restored and finally to Montgomery to have the squab cushion, foot and armrests upholstered. After all that travelling, it sold first day back in the shop for a thousand profit. But many of the things, he'd bought plenty of in the past, like chests of drawers and sets of chairs, he told me, weren't worth the bother. He used to call it, having to make them housewife-proof. It was no use trying to sell chairs with a bit of a creak, or chests, with gappy sides and drawer fronts not sitting straight in the frame. To an outsider, it would have seemed no more than minor detail, but by the time it was all put right, there was hardly any profit left. He used to say, it was more of a customer service."

A thought suddenly struck me. "If John Dodds was out on the road for half the week, who was looking after the shop?"

"He had a lad working for him, but he never sold much. He'd just take down details and John would follow up the leads when time allowed. In the end, knowing he was packing the job in, he let him go. Nice lad, but I have to admit, couldn't have sold less, if paid a commission to fail."

"I noticed from the notes, he was selling more privately."

"Well, what the general public didn't realise in those early years, the reason why they never got a chance of the best stock, when strolling around the shops on a Saturday, was because Doddsy had sold most of it to the trade during the week. But as that trade slowed, following 9/11, a lot of it was still there for them to think about. They of course thought his standards had improved, but what they were actually seeing, were goods that would have normally been long gone."

"Think about? You just said, goods for them to think about."

"Definitely. He did sell things, like the snap of the fingers, privately, but not usually. Even if they'd been looking for years, for that particular sideboard or table, they would always tend to think about it."

"Weren't they worried, they might miss it?"

"More often than not, they wouldn't make their minds up until the Monday. He used to tell me, 'You need four measurers to make one sale.' He wasn't a pushy salesman, but I've seen him produce a sold ticket and say, 'Imagine, while you're having your coffee and thinking about it,' he'd slap on the sold ticket, 'that happens! You're going to beg me to find another just like it, aren't you? And yet, right here, is the very thing you told me you've been looking for.'"

"Did it work?"

"Yes and often, on the next visit, they'd thank him for giving them a bit of a prod. But some of the people could be impossible. I remember one day, a lady coming in because John had done her a favour. He'd found what he could have sold in a blizzard on Christmas day, a tiny Georgian oak corner cupboard and with it being exactly what she was looking for, he'd rung to give her first chance. I don't much like the word cute when describing furniture, but it was. A slightly bow-fronted, cute little thing. She looked delighted at first, but then stunned him by saying, 'There doesn't seem to be much room inside.' He did bite his tongue on that occasion, but late on a fruitless Saturday, when a lady, who had started rocking the top a Georgian tripod table, had asked, 'How do you stop it doing that?' He said, in that dry tone of his, 'Take your hand off it.' Oh, nearly forgot. That tiny corner cupboard. When the woman left to think about it, he got straight on the phone to his mate, Rob Deeley. Bought it without even seeing it. Not surprising really,--- you'd be hard pushed to find another, that small and full of character."

"Did the woman come back?"

"I should say she did, asking, now what's your very, very best price?"

I laughed and said, "I don't think I'd have had the patience."

"You needed the patience of a saint some days and then have to put up with them ringing for a bit of antique-speak on a Sunday night. John told me, that in the end, he used to unplug his phone. Anyway, here I am prattling on. What was it you wanted to know, exactly?"

"Exactly this, Mike. Can I just jot down a couple of notes?" He sipped his coffee as I quickly scribbled down a few memory joggers. When finished, I said, "At one point, I noticed, he wrote about the shop as if it was almost part of the tourist itinerary."

"Oh, he must have meant the coach loads of Americans and those antique buffs living locally, showing their weekenders about. There were the American minibus tours, driven around, especially to hunt out antiques to ship back home, but 99% of the hordes would be hard pushed to take a pair of brass candlesticks back and so used to pour through, using the shop as a free museum. Some of them, babbling away, wouldn't even stop to appreciate anything, as if the shop was just a short-cut to somewhere else. Some days you couldn't get a thing done for them and if it happened to rain, they'd quite blatantly shelter until it stopped. Then on a Saturday would come those self-proclaimed antique buffs I mentioned, showing their weekenders about and imparting what little knowledge they had."

"What are you laughing at?" I asked.

"Just remembered. There was one particularly pompous regular and John overheard him say the word, marriage. You can imagine John can't you, '**Marriage**?' The bloke was referring to a North Wales corner cupboard. Well John had had enough of the bloke over the years and sails into action telling him, it was obvious, he had a fair knowledge; must know a thing or two. He had a bit of a wicked mood on and said to the man, 'I bet you can tell me which part of Wales this dresser hails from. No? Well what about this one then?' Returning to the corner cupboard, he said, 'I heard you use the word marriage just now. Admittedly the panels on the bottom doors are flush, while those above are flat-inset, a peculiarity of the Dolgellau area, but can you explain to me how it can be a marriage, when the carcase is all in one piece?' The cupboard was not particularly tall and so he spun it sufficiently for them to see.

I had to laugh to myself, because with the bloke's colour on the rise I could see his weekend guests giving each other the nudge as if to say, 'That's punctured the windbag.'"

I partook of my coffee and waited, as I could see Mike was deep in thought.

"Nearly forgot. There were the Saturday gloaters. Amateur enthusiasts, coming in specially to tell him, he'd missed buying a lot they'd tickled out from one of the previous Leominster or Ludlow sales. He'd say to me once they'd gone, 'Have they no idea how many lots I view in a week? How do they expect me to remember the reason why I didn't buy their scabby joint stool? If I remembered every reason why I didn't leave a bid on something I'd go more bloody insane than I'm going at the moment.'

I used to feel for him, for there were other regulars, only visiting to price up stock, arming themselves with how much to bid at local auctions. A few came from as far away as Newtown, always appearing the Saturday before the Newtown cattle market venue. There were also those taking sneaky photos, trying to sell his stock without gambling any of their own money. He didn't mind if they admitted they had a client for a particular piece and asked, would it be alright to photograph and take the details? He'd say, 'Yes of course, if it helps sell it,' but it was the sneaky ones that riled him, putting his stock on the internet, under their own name. Selling on the net was just getting started about that time."

"There were a number of occasions, I wasn't always there of course, but being keen to offload his frustrations, he'd tell me the latest thing to beset him. Finding John, head in hands I'd ask, 'What's the matter?' This one time, out of the blue, a major American client had shown up and immediately, it seemed the Gods had conspired against him, for in the middle of guiding the man around the stock, building up a rapport, the place had started to fill up with browsers, with one acting as self-appointed doorman, until you could hardly move. His prized customer, thinking he could be in the way, apologised profusely and out of respect, said, 'Gee, you're terribly busy, I'd better let you deal with all these customers,' and off he went. It could often happen,--- rubber-necks, drawn like moths to a candle, when seeing action within. What made matters worse,--- John had to then listen to excited exchanges of how much money the customer had spent around the town, his purchase tickets bedecking everything. They were usually on a tight schedule, rarely retracing their steps and the browsers, having ruined the deal, all then melted away, having bought nothing.

There was another time. I happened to be there that day. He was under a lot of financial pressure and really needed to pull off the deal with a pair of his best American clients. I could see he was about to lose out, for his punters who'd half a dozen lots in mind, simply couldn't concentrate. It was as if someone had planned it. They stood there fascinated, drawn towards this bloke, who oblivious to all, went from chair to chair to sit eyes closed, until an expression of sheer ecstasy radiated. John, broke off briefly, to politely ask the man, if he could be of assistance, asking which type of chair, did he wish to buy?

'Oh, I don't want to buy any of them,' he replied. 'I just love soaking up the amazing atmosphere in them.'

Well Doddsy flicked me a look and gently leading the chair-freak to the door, I said, 'See that shop down the street?' Giving a little shove, I added, 'he specialises in chairs. Stacked full of the things.' He stood there, mouth opening in silent protest, as I locked the door and turned the sign round, to 'closed.'

Afterwards, Doddsy with a look of sheer relief, said, 'Thanks Mike. I've sold bugger all, the whole week and they've just spent 30 thousand quid. That idiot would have blown the deal.'

Some used to get shirty if he politely asked, if their children could finish their ice-creams before entering. Or if he begged a customer, to please pull out the lopers of a bureau before opening the fall, they could go off in a huff, not even interested in hearing of the horrific damage it could have done. On a number of occasions, he'd ask me with a shake of head, 'How come all the box and caddy openers, don't know how to shut the lids again?'

On the one Saturday, he was dealing with quite a pleasant family and the husband asked, could he find them a three-foot wide, Georgian oak Welsh dresser. He told them he doubted such a thing existed, unless made for a child. Even if one actually did, he couldn't imagine what one that rare would cost. He then asked, 'As a matter of interest, how much were you hoping to pay for this 3-foot dresser?'

'Oh, I'd be prepared to go to £800,' the head of the family declared.

'I'm sorry,' says Doddsy, 'but the only way I could get one at that price, would be to rob an old lady.'

'OK, can I leave you my phone number?'

Honestly you couldn't make it up.

Oh, listen to this one. It was another Saturday where the invoice book hadn't been disturbed and late on, having had enough, John was keen to lock up.

'Excuse me?' the man said. 'I've got this mahogany table. I wonder if you could tell me what it's worth.'

'I'd really need to know a little more about it,' says Doddsy.

'Well, it's got a mahogany top and a leg on each corner.'

John eyed him for a second, then said, 'I own a small cottage in Wales. It's got four walls and a roof on top. I wonder if you could tell me what that's worth?'

'Well! I'd have to look at it first,' says the bloke, getting quite stroppy.

'Darling,' said his wife. 'I think he's trying to tell you something.'

Before Doddsy managed to get out of the business, some of the customers had taken quite a militant turn. Gone were the days when they'd appreciate his advice and respect his years' of experience. I blame the internet. Even in its infancy it had started to delude, giving the impression, everything, even the thing of their wildest dreams, could be available for next to nothing. Also, he was starting to get the stompy ones, becoming quite angry, when asked to please not go upstairs. It of course led to his private living quarters, but they took the attitude, now they were in the building, they had the right to explore every nook and cranny. He even found one up in his living room and on another occasion, two sitting at the kitchen table. It was literally, quite nightmarish. He told me, they'd started to invade his dreams at night, telling him with a look of fury, 'We haven't looked up there yet!'

Once, long after he'd locked up, he'd been on the point of going upstairs, but stopped on hearing voices. Up the steps, behind the curtain, he found a horde of them lounging about, chatting as if in their own living room. They looked quite put out when he explained he needed to close the shop.

He used to tell me, 'If the punters love everything in the place, then you've no chance. But if one's a bit diffident and critical about a piece, home in on them, Mike, for there's a good chance they'll buy it. I did manage to sell the odd piece for him. Here's another tip he gave me, 'If they're dressed up to the nines, don't build your hopes up, but if they're a bit scruffy and truly interested in antiques, they might not buy today, but chances are they will in the end.'

I think what kept him sane, was the marvellous loyal core of customers he had; the knowledge he'd soon be getting out, plus of course, his sense of humour. But like I said, some of the folks were getting quite militant, saying things like, 'How do you KNOW it's Georgian?'

He'd quietly answer, 'After thirty years, you sort of get the hang of it.'

Didn't help with the nutter, mind you. The bloke was absolutely raving, flicking one ticket after another, saying it was disgraceful! A person had no right to charge such prices. Once he started slamming his fist down and looking likely to get violent, he had to go. He was frog marched to the door and with a suitable accompanying phrase, was pushed beyond the portal.

I remember, the Bookends were messing him about one day. He particularly reviled the one with the scruffy beard. Have you come across them in the notes?"

I nodded.

"I think it was a better than normal, turned leg side table, the bloke was pithering about on and Doddsy, almost giving up, said in exasperation, 'Look. if you don't know how to rate it, leave it where it is!'

That did it! He'd got the bloke's dander up that much, he said, 'You cheeky bugger. I'll show you,' and bought it."

"Yes I did get the impression, some of the trade could be infuriating."

"I should say so. Doddsy banned two of the buggers."

Suddenly, glancing at his watch, Mike said, "Gosh, look at the time. I'll have to go."

Then thinking for a while, he said, "I realise, I've just painted a nightmarish picture, but it wasn't all bad. I'm sure you'll find in those notes, plenty of references to decent customers. Some of them could be a real hoot. When certain groups descended, John didn't much care whether they bought anything or not, he just soaked up the atmosphere like a curing balm. Some I remember, were late afternoon returnees from local shoots. Probably, each could have bought and sold him and everything in the place, five times over, but would ask, 'Mr. Dodds, is it alright if we leave our muddy boots out here in the porch? What a contrast to the ice-cream lickers."

As we paid, Mike apologised, for having commandeered a table for so long, while spending so little. The man just laughed and said, he hoped we'd enjoyed our visit.

CHAPTER THIRTY-TWO

It took two days to write all the latest up and another day for the first attempt at correction. That word, correction, it reminded me of the ducking stool we had seen in Leominster Priory Church. The ignominy of being ducked for constant tirades and scolding, would have been as devastating as the quenching cold water the poor dears were plunged into.

I carried on through the last of the notes, underlining here and there and putting a line through what Mike had already told me. John Dodds in fact, hadn't dwelt too much on the problem of the browser plague, probably attempting to block it from his mind.

He did mention, how much he despised a teacher from a local Sixth Form College, who'd regularly lead starry-eyed girls through his stock and explain in hushed tones the ins and outs of what he was showing them. They were always pretty, blonde and obviously extremely impressionable.

---*'Does your wife know you've taken up this antique missionary work?' I asked him, which finally put a stop to it.*

He realised, the way he'd snapped at times when pushed to the limit, had become a bit of a talking point amongst a few other traders in town.

---*'I was beginning to feel like Basil Fawlty, but there again, who cares, for soon I'd be free of the place.'*

The way he'd described encountering a kindred spirit, in the Leominster saleroom one day, I could sense his sheer relief.

---It was well before the sale date and everything was still in irregular rows and heaps, but Roger, the auctioneer on duty that day, said, as long as I didn't mind the clutter and the fact nothing was lotted up, I was free to view. Once having finished, I went over to thank him, but waited, as a local was showing him a photograph of a piece of furniture he wanted valuing.

Squinting at it, he told him, he reckoned it would fetch roughly 8 to 9 hundred.

'Huh!' said the man in disgust. 'I've already turned down three thousand for it!'

'You were a bloody fool then!'

John Dodds wrote,--- *I couldn't believe it. Such abrupt honesty; not suffering fools gladly, but if I dared say similar, it would be round the trade like wildfire. It did hearten me mind you, for I realised I wasn't the only one.*

He then went on to describe some of the customers that he claimed, saved his life. Even though trade deals were diminishing, he still had his 15 or so, regulars. His reason for not listing them, he said, was the fear he might accidently leave one out and thus offend a person who had been part of his lifeline. A large proportion of stock was now being supplied to the prestigious antique fairs rather than to customers' shops and it was regarding this, that he described how he'd strayed into dangerous territory.

---More and more of my most valued customers were asking if I minded waiting for payment. With up to £30,000 going out on a stand at Olympia, plus all the money they'd spent readying stock, they were drained of cash. I was always paid by both them and those I'd lent stock to, end of fair, but meanwhile I was acting as a

free bank, at times giving over £100,000 in credit, with the rump of the debt never seeming to go below £40,000.

The other worry was, to obtain the quality of stock they required, often meant paying more than I could actually sell the item for in the shop. So, if it failed to appeal, I was lumbered. Luckily, as I often told private customers,--- after 30 years, I'd sort have got the hang of it and so rarely got it wrong. If ever fashions changed, however and the fairs became an anachronism, then I was doomed.

My son was now flying for Ryanair and my daughter had left for university and so I no longer felt duty bound to keep the home going. I began to plan my escape.

I found a section where he describes what sheer fun the business could still be. Sometimes a lady he called Mrs. Oakstar would descend with all her weekend guests, reminding him of the Bohemian crowd that used to descend on the home each Saturday, back in the days of Marie and stalls in the Ludlow market hall.

---They all had nicknames for one another, like something out of Jeeves and Wooster and amongst it all Mrs. Oakstar would severely admonish me for the condition of the item she was looking at, 'It needs a terrific amount spending on it, John!' I would just patiently smile, for invariably her husband, a revered Diplomat, fluent in Arabic, would admonish in return, 'Just buy the ruddy thing, woman!'

Meanwhile from around the shop I'd hear hoots of joy and perhaps something like, 'Dear old Tubby would like this. Go on buy it for him. I'm sure Mr. Dodds would quote a favourable price.'

Then another might ask, 'Where's Binky got to?'

'Where do you think? She's out on the tree seat having a fag.'

Another who would light the place up, was a financier called John. He'd bought a cottage up on the Brown Clee and stepping inside beyond the traditional stone front, the place seemed to open up like another world, as if you'd entered a magician's cavern. He seemed to know all the well-connected folk that called in the shop, almost as if he belonged to some sort of South Shropshire Club in the City.

The actor, John Chalice and his wife were always good fun and I enjoyed the bit of banter that inevitably accompanied a deal. They lived in what had been Wigmore Abbey and told me, they were custodians of the remains of Roger Mortimer, the first Baron of Wigmore, interred there in 1282.

I found this detail incredible and went straight onto Google and found that, yes, the very same Roger Mortimer, the right-hand man of Edward 1st, veteran of the battles of Lewes and Evesham, smiter of the Welsh at Dolforwyn Castle, had indeed been laid to rest, with honours, at Wigmore Abbey. After the massacre at Evesham, he'd been awarded Simon de Montford's head and other severed parts, which he sent home as a present to his wife, back in Wigmore. Nice touch. These days, some men do it with chocolates, others with flowers, but reading between the lines, Lady Mortimer, received Simon de Montford's courting tackle as a romantic token, with the head tossed in, to leave her in no doubt as to who had once sported such appendages.

I'll hand you back to John Dodds.

---There were a couple of no-nonsense Tory MP's who regularly called with a view to buying. Like many of my life savers, they would apologise if not finding anything they needed, but I would explain, it didn't matter. If every person who came into the shop, showed as much intent as they did, I'd have been the happiest antique dealer in the country and would probably have stayed in the job.

Two of my favourite customers lived in nearby Orleton. David had been a top advisor, regarding tin, on the London Metal Exchange and he and his partner Susan, thought it hilarious that I'd picked up a reputation for occasionally being abrupt. At times, my serious attempts at vindication, explaining mitigating circumstances, rendered them helpless, almost doubled up.

There was an up-and-coming surgeon and his wife who were that regular, they became more like friends than customers. Mark developed an eye for the job and would occasionally buy interesting oak pieces, to sell on to a dealer in Cirencester. He did better than I did in fact, for when that particular customer called, I could never sell him a thing.

A regular who lived in a large pile tucked in the hills west of Church Stretton, had the most charming way of delivering disparagement. Each time he did, however, I knew there was a fair danger he would buy the piece. He actually had more innate ability than many in the trade.

Another with that skill, was a Yorkshire barrister. His mother ran an antique shop in Gargrave and Paul Smith, one of the original Ludlow dealers, I'd always respected, was his uncle. Simon would often buy a piece of Georgian mahogany, with the same confidence as any life-long professional dealer.

One London trader, specialising in ethnic artefacts and top quality treen, had a strange habit of letting thoughts escape verbally, almost like a mild form of Tourette's Syndrome and so of course, I took to him instantly. I promised, before finally vacating the shop, I'd offer him the items, kept simply for decorative purposes: carved oak face, complete with ladies' head drapery; carved pine Corinthian capitals; a large carved, polychrome, tearoom sign, of a lady in traditional Welsh costume; the small ship's figurehead bought in Sheffield. It was characters like him, expert, but self-deprecating that almost revived my love for the job. I say, almost.

On many a Saturday, I'd be visited by a young chap who lived in a lock-keepers cottage on the upper stretch of the Montgomery canal. We'd exchange anecdotes of my browsers and his boaties, as he called them. I'd say, 'Colin, if you want to have a chat, come away from the shop door. If they see you, they'll be rattling to get in. Honestly, you'll be like a browser magnet. Knowing there's already a customer in the shop, they'll feel safe to come in and mooch about to their heart's content.'

'How will they know I'm a customer and not the proprietor?'

'I don't know, but believe me, they will. Born different I suppose.'

'There's one trying the door. Shall I let him in?'

'No! Get yourself up here! If you let him in, soon, we won't be able to move for them. They seem to send out some sort of pheromone, a bit like bees. Next thing you know, we'll be inundated.'

Tentatively, he sat down opposite, then daring to take a peep, 'He's got his hands cupped to the glass now. He's trying to look in.'

'It's you he's looking for. Now you've given him the slip, should be fairly safe now. It's not like you can even have a joke with them. One came in the other day and told me, he just wanted a little nose.

When I said, "Sorry, the plastic surgeon's not in today," he went straight round to Mike Taylor's, saying what a sarcastic bastard I was. He wouldn't have got much sympathy, across the road, at Ray Cave's, mind you. I know for a fact, he's upset a few. We were comparing business frustrations one day and he said, "When they tell me they're only browsing, I'm afraid I'm quite straight with them--- I tell 'em, 'You'll find no grass in here!' "

Where Colin Canal, a self-effacing lock-keeper, got the money from, to buy the oak I sold him, I never asked, but always enjoyed *our chats and the delivery to his canal-side cottage, usually on a Sunday morning.*

A regular customer, was a blacksmith from the home counties. He'd arrive, by appointment, on a Sunday and always paid cash. Trouble was, he theoretically bought more than he could possibly bang in nails fast enough to pay for. When the pile I was storing for him reached £40,000, I had to put a stop to it. Like many, he thought cash was somehow a magic ingredient. It wasn't, for it all had to go through the system. What had once been mainly a cash business, was now 99% cheques.

When some private customers became insistent, begging me to sell an item, at their offered price; finally, out of exasperation I would show them the purchase invoice or entry in my stock book and explain for the umpteenth time, 'Sorry, I'm not willing to take far less than I've paid for the thing.'

'What if I paid cash?' They'd often ask.

An esteemed architect who had artistically enhanced a farmhouse and outbuildings over in mid-Wales, was another regular as was a lady from over in the Bridgnorth direction who would often pull up in her Ferrari. If she liked a thing, she'd buy it. No messing.

The regular customers who had made their fortunes in the industrial heartland of the West Midlands, all seemed to have one thing in common; not one of them was big sorted. All were millionaires, but you'd hardly guess it, speaking to them.

Some private customers who bought from me, I have to admit, I couldn't see why they'd done it, for the piece they'd chosen just didn't suit their house and I'd feel a bit embarrassed leaving it there, expecting a phone call at any moment, to come and fetch it back again. A Welsh dresser in an ultra-modern sitting room, a bureau with one side jammed tight against a wall and no room to sit at it.

As my trade contacts struggled, meaning more was there for private customers to have a go at, I learnt to say what needed to be said and then leave them to think about it. I'd pretend to read the newspaper, but actually had an ear cocked, waiting for the, 'Well what do you think?'

'Would you like me to slip that onto an invoice for you?' I'd ask cheerily.

One Saturday, I thought I'd saved the day, for a couple were really taken with a Regency, solid coromandel wood, dining table. At the very point they were just about to say, 'We'll have it,' my aged tabby cat, launching itself from off a sideboard, skidded along its entire length, to disappear down into the main shop, like a Davy Crockett hat on a piece of string.

The woman gasped, 'What ever made it do that? Oh, we can't buy it now!'

'But it hasn't scratched it. They're just smudge marks.'

Words wasted. Deal lost. It sold in the end to an English dealer trading in Vancouver, son of the man who had appeared in his underpants, in the Bull Hotel all those years before, 'Asking if he'd been staying in a clip joint?'

Most of the customers, heartbroken at having missed something and begging I give them a ring when next having similar in stock, would turn up weeks after the call, expecting the item to be still there waiting for them.

Not the schoolteacher, living up by Knowbury. I sold him one of the best and purest 17th century oak dining tables, I'd ever owned, bought from Roger Kilby. I also found him a set of 12 dining chairs of a similar period. I'd first managed to buy six in a Hall's catalogue sale and then at the following sale, couldn't believe my luck, for the other six turned up. Quite incredible really.

To cope with the inundation days, I had learnt the art of enquiring what the customers might be looking for, giving them the relevant information and then shutting up. If you bounced with enthusiasm at every enquiry, you'd be a burnt-out case within a month. Only when obvious, they might be seriously interested, did I break from the professional persona and reward their endeavour, by opening up a bit. To give your whole self to all and sundry, would not only have been a complete waste of time and energy, it would have actually prolonged the stay of life-long browsers.

Also, there was no point stocking a bric-a-brac section for moochers to sift through, for with me selling better pieces for thousands, they would reason, my £2 genuine horse brass could obviously be bought for 50p in a junk shop. Wrong. More likely, cost them a fiver and for some reason, they'd be happy to pay it.

The summer months were always more a matter of survival than gain and as business to the trade contracted, you could go through to Friday night, without making single a mark on the invoice book. Something seemed to be looking after me, however, as I always seemed to pull off a miracle at the eleventh hour. Such brinkmanship endorsed the fact, I had to get out. A shop can't survive on miracles.

Also, what the change in circumstances brought about, was to leave one wide-open to the dyed in the wool, life-long fusspots. In former times, when returning for another anguished examination, of the item in question, it would normally have gone on its way, sold to the trade. But not following 9/11. By about the seventh visit, I'd say, 'I'm sorry, there's nothing more I can really tell you. I'm prepared to write a full description on the invoice, I've pointed out the small amount of restoration, I'll deliver it for nothing, what more can I say?'

When first finding, the only genuine antique they owned, was the piece I had just sold them, I was truly puzzled. How, with such caution, could these people walk into such horrors? Get so *horribly stitched up? Then, it suddenly dawned on me; the reason why. Most of the best traders over the years, would have kept their stock moving, too busy to talk endlessly about something that didn't need much talk to sell it. Those selling fakes, however, had all the time in the world and preyed on these timorous folk who trod so warily, probably kidding them they were best friends. Perhaps even suggesting they take a little wander, to compare their bargain prices, with what those other rogues were charging. Those too busy, to answer endless questions. It would have been all smiles and simply nothing being too much trouble: 'Come into my lair, tea out on the patio and let me show you round the garden.' Of course, I couldn't tell them they'd been literally, led up the garden path and each fake they'd bought had probably furnished the vendor with a week's wages.*

For a similar reason, if ever I was taken along by a friend to a supper party and the hosts weren't aware I was in the antique trade, I'd never tell them, for after a few glasses of wine, you'd inevitably be led around the house, to be asked, 'What do you think we paid for that?' Also, you could then rest assured, the conversation around the table would focus entirely on antiques and I was just glad to get away from the subject.

Hardly ever watched the Antiques Road Show either. I'd think, 'Give me a break!'

CHAPTER THIRTY-THREE

The notes I had left were a very slim bundle and skimming through, I began to put items into categories. John Dodds had made it easier, for he'd already portioned certain recollections, off into four separate sections.

It seemed odd, that although there were now quite a few mentions of Ray Cave, a dealer from Broad Street, Ludlow, as far as I could see, there was nothing further as regards Tim Glenger. I wondered if perhaps, he'd moved. I decided to ring Charles.

I found him as jovially avuncular as ever. "Surprised you didn't look it up on t'internet, dear boy."

"I did, Charles, but it's not always helpful, as information tends to stay on there until someone takes the trouble to delete it. It still has a reference to John Dodds, for instance and his shop's been closed for years."

"So what's troubling you?"

"It's not troubling me, as such, it's just that there seems to be no further mention of Mr. Glenger."

"Well it's hardly surprising, I suppose he's simply been deleted, as if no longer a thing of relevance. John told me years ago, the first double-cross was Glenger's fault, but the second was entirely his own. He said, "I should have known the man could never change."

"You mean it was congenital?"

"Something like that. There's no doubt their paths would have crossed. It's bound to have happened; small town; local sales viewed; it's just that when Glenger had risked a blatant deception the second time, he'd not realised, from then on, it would mean him losing track of what Doddsy was doing. He was left behind, mired in his world of heavy oak. By trying to control the dresser market, the stupid blighter had done a classic Bunker Hunt and fenced himself in."

I laughed at the way he'd put it.

"Well it's right. John told me he could still be annoying, but obviously, from what you say about his scribblings, he must have simply risen above it. Not worth giving the chap a mention."

With it having sounded like a deliberate understatement, I asked, "Annoying?"

"Well yes, the way he felt compelled to control; gain advantage by cunning deception. John told me, you couldn't combat it. You wouldn't stand a chance, for he lived and breathed it. Just like you said, it was congenital, almost second nature.

There was one impressionable lad from the Cotswolds, John had taken under his wing. Nurtured him. Put decent goods his way, to build up his confidence. Then there was a dealer from Holland, he was English actually and John had looked after him, after he'd been knocked down by some lunatic woman in Old Street. Broke the man's leg in fact and John took him to Shrewsbury Hospital, returning with him at some ungodly hour. The chap was given free bed and board for two weeks and then driven back in his truck, to catch the Hull-Rotterdam ferry. His parents still lived in Coventry and both came over specially to thank John for what he'd done.

But you know that wry old saying, 'A good deed never goes unpunished?' Well it didn't. John lost both customers to Glenger."

"How could he have managed that?"

"It's hard to say for definite, but he probably used the age-old trick. It starts with, 'Don't let on I've told you this------'

The interested party then asks, 'Let on about what?'

'No, it's wrong of me, I shouldn't really tell you.'

'Well go on. You might as well, now you've started.'

'Promise you won't say anything? Well, I thought you might have already realised, I supply all of John Dodds's oak.'

'Never!'

'Yes, he's constantly on the phone. Gets every stick of it from me.'

'Really. Well, I might as well come straight to you then.'

Simple as that, 'Gotcha.' It takes a while, they think they've got away with it, but it usually catches up with them in the end. They get caught up in a web of their own making and the trade can be an unforgiving lot. A good many of Doddsy's customers made a point of not dealing with Glenger. Considering how independent traders tend to be, each with their own story of how they started in antiques, it's amazing how much they often helped one another. When something tasty turned up in an out of the way sale, the dealer who'd played straight with them, would get the tip-off, but pull a few too many strokes and that's it, radio silence. I know for a fact Jim Ash and Andy King gave John a call when they chanced on a decent Welsh sale, poorly advertised."

"I read that Jim Ash used to rib John. Told him, Tim Glenger was his monster. He'd created him."

"You're right, he did. I'd forgotten that. Must be old age creeping up."

"Charles, I remember in one of our earlier conversations, you referred to Tim Glenger as a chameleon."

"It was Doddsy's description, really. We used to meet up for the odd chat and he'd joke, that if two characters with entirely different traits, invited Glenger out for a trip, viewing, he'd have to refuse. He couldn't be two different people in the same car. Another thing Doddsy mentioned--- a realisation that had suddenly hit him one day,---Glenger couldn't do anything without making it an opportunity for self-aggrandizement. He told me, when dear old Mrs. Evans in Ian Anderson's shop, had broken her leg, Glenger made a point of saying he'd called there specially to give her a little monetary gift. Something to cheer her up.

'Money? Never even clapped eyes on the man!' she'd said, when John asked.

He told me, if ever Glenger drove down south, back to his roots, he'd always claim, it was because his mother wasn't well. Playing the dutiful son.

But like I said, it always catches them out. By pure chance, Doddsy happened to meet Glenger's mother in Ludlow and of course said, 'I hope you're feeling better, Mrs. Glenger.'

'What do you mean?' she said. He told me she was a 'no nonsense woman' and had looked quite put out. Explaining, that Tim had informed him, she'd not been well, she'd snapped, 'Nonsense!' Like I said, it can take a while, but truth will out in the end."

"But from what I've read, he was a good dealer. No need for any of that."

"I know, all sounds a bit sad, doesn't it, dear chap."

"I doubt John Dodds felt much sympathy."

"Well it's strange really. He obviously kept his distance, but divulged one day,--- there was something about Glenger, he couldn't help but like."

"Thank you, Charles, you've been a great help once again."

"Anytime, dear boy."

As I said, I found quite a few references to Ray Cave. John found him almost impossible to sell to, wanting the best things at the price of the ordinary, but the man was a character, slightly eccentric and although John Dodds found him frustrating, when endlessly trying to beat him down in price, he actually thought the world of the man.

Another regular, he had plenty of time for, was a dealer with a terrible stammer, who specialised in oak.

---*Rob, was rangy, super fit, trained every day, was a one-time boxer and now a keen cyclist, but because of the speech impediment, there were certain words he had to avoid. For instance, he always referred to payment as handing out, for any attempt to say pay, would have fired more pees than a pea shooter. One evening, when on his travels, he'd stopped for a bite to eat and the three youths lounging at the bar, thinking his problem hilarious, had unwisely decided to mimic him.*

'So, you th-think it's fu-fu-fu-fuck the lot of you!' He decked the three of them, in rapid succession, no pause for breath, never mind a stammer.

I never made the common mistake, of inadvertently belittling, ending his sentences for him. I'd wait for him to finish. For a man to carry that impediment through life, dealing with the cut and thrust banter of the antique business and thrive better than most,

484

I had nothing but admiration for, plus I'm sure he'll forgive my tendency to see the funny side.

Trudi Weaver and her son Bernard, dealing from a large pitch in Portobello, used to light his days up, as did Ben and Judi Watson on their regular trips over from North Carolina.

John Biggs from north Devon is described as, a hard-working and incredibly thorough dealer, who explained the lengths he went to, to ensure nothing hampered the sale of an item; drawers running smoothly, every lock working and castors re-bushed.

---As he was leaving one day, he said, "I'm surprised you haven't sold this."

It was a settle with cupboard in the back, known as a bacon settle, that none of my regulars had shown any interest in.

Looking at the ticket, he said, 'It's too cheap, John. People will think there's something wrong with it. Put another thousand on it. That'll do the trick.'

It did. Sold within days and I rang and thanked him.

Another who lifted his spirits, more than many in fact, was a young man called Danny, who would arrive like a breath of fresh air on a Saturday. He was a nephew of the famous Robbie Gemmill, one of the original Irish travellers, that had made such an impact on the antique trade. He had a caravan, parked in the camp on the outskirts of Exeter and mopped up all the best, his fellow travellers turned up with. John Dodds, impressed upon him, he would deal with him, but only on the understanding he never divulged who he was selling to. He didn't want a swarm of them descending, as had happened in the old days.

Danny brought him some amazing things from the west country, often first day sellers at Olympia, like the diminutive mahogany estate cupboard with its sliding doors, nooks and cubby holes, that Ruth Macklin Smith had sold for him; the amazing set of Georgian mahogany chairs, the lady in the Ferrari had bought without a moment's hesitation; brass bound wine cooler on original stand and many other pieces of Georgian mahogany.

He didn't always get the oak right mind you, but had a good client for the slightly iffy, in Leamington Spa and never seemed to get stuck with anything. What consistently puzzled John Dodds, was how an illiterate man, barely in his thirties, had managed to gain such knowledge? He likened him to a bright-eyed Cocker Spaniel, having an innate instinct to root things out and once the man had gone on his way, there came that sinking feeling, knowing that on reopening the shop, he'd literally have to force himself to return to the late Saturday afternoon, old Labrador and Bloodhound plodders.

---*One day, Mark, my budding surgeon friend and his wife were there, fresh back from a six-month training stint in Dublin.*

'Did you enjoy it?' I asked.

'Bloody chaos,' said Mark.

'We couldn't wait to get back,' said his wife, in her County Antrim accent.

'Careful,' I said. 'Danny, here, is from Ireland.'

'Oh, don't be worrying about a ting like that,' said Danny. 'Whenever we drive off the Holyhead ferry, my wife says, "Tank the good Lord, we'll soon be home."'

Looking further through the notes, I decided to insert this little excerpt, titled, 'More Kilby.'

---*At the regular Newbury sale, I met Roger, bought most of what he had on the van and continued west, for further viewing. I'd left* *him a price on a 17th century child's high chair in entirely original condition, but with so much interest from the London trade, I knew my chances of buying it were slim. Still, a sporting punt of £9,000, wasn't bad from one dealing way up on the Welsh Marches. Should have kept the one from the Australian deal, but need for cash had been uppermost at the time.*

I heard later, when counting the phones, set up for those aiming to bid against him, Roger had said, 'Eight on to one! That 'aint fair. I reckon, the bloke taking the trouble to turn up and bid, should be given priority.'

At about the £4,000 mark, all in the room, but Roger, had given up and the place went deadly quiet as the bidding crept past £10,000. When he'd bought it for £14,000, he muttered to himself, in that voice, probably even heard in the foyer, 'There! They didn't need those fuckin' phones after all!'

Even well-heeled ladies were seen to splutter a laugh. He sold the chair to a London dealer, over the phone, as he was driving home.

Yet another place, Roger and I met, was at a petrol station on the southern edge of Stow-on-the-Wold. What he had, I just managed to fit into the car. Can't remember it all, but I know there was a tall joint stool, that would have looked imperious amongst the honest, but dreary ones, a Georgian wine table and a tiny 1720's gateleg table in mint condition. We drove to the east side of town, where a swap-shop was underway. I'd often been invited to these affairs, where dealers, all of them well established, took their disappointments in the hope of swapping for something more uplifting. It only worked, because some traders were that desperate to get rid of old friends, it bestowed rose-coloured spectacles for the day, seeing merit where little existed. It was the first one I'd ever attended and of course, all were clamouring for what I had in the car, but none of it was going anywhere, unless paid for with hard cash. Wandering from one vehicle to the next, I quite honestly, could not see one lot I'd have left a price on, had it been in a saleroom. I was glad to drive away and leave them sifting through the mire. No need to give you Roger's verdict.

At a supposed, prestigious house sale down in Wiltshire, most of the furniture had been taken out for display in a marquee. Like many such sales, the grand pile was far more impressive than its contents and I left my few prices with Jim Ash.

I heard that Roger had turned up later, tumbling from the van to lie prone on the grass, before his son Mark, appearing from the driver's side, had hauled him upright. I knew full-well it would have just been an act, for although I've known times when it seemed he'd been drinking to die, I'd never known Roger touch alcohol when out viewing.

It was the sale where I'd left a price on a French armoire, I'd found in a top floor bedroom. I received a worried call from Jim Ash.

'I've bought it for you, Johnny, but I can't get the thing out of there. It won't go round the corner onto the landing.'

'I assumed it came apart.'

'So did I. I've lifted the door and cornice off, but the rest is solid.'

'Will it go through the window?'

'Maybe, but I haven't a rope long enough.'

'Is there a ladder?'

'I'll get back to you.'

I drove on further, cursing the fact, I had £800 stuck in an attic. The phone went. It was Jim.

'I've found a ladder, but it will barely reach the top of my van, let alone two floors up. I'm not sure there's much I can do. I need to

get away Johnny, there's stuff I have to get on with back in the warehouse.'

'Give me a few minutes, Jim. There has to be an answer.'

I realised, going all the way back there with a long rope and someone to help, would cost more than I'd get out of the thing. Then an idea sprang to mind.

'Jim. Does the gravel drive go right round the house?'

'Yes.'

'Is there room to park the van against the house?'

I waited and to my relief, he said there was. 'Why not lower the cupboard onto the roof of the van and then slide it down the ladder to the floor?'

So, that's how he got it out of there and I collected the pesky thing when next in Llandeilo.

Another section in the notes was titled, 'Deals from out of nowhere.'

---Over the years, I'd come to realise, when feeling thoroughly skint and in no mood for going out buying, some of the best deals could drop in your lap. It was a hot sultry day and the last thing I needed was more stock, but giving myself a good talking to, I set out for the Tewkesbury sale. I couldn't believe what I found; a Regency rent table and a massive mahogany circular table, large enough to seat eight. Hidden in the frieze, each with carved foliage adornment, were lopers, which would have once supported four arced leaves, converting the table into something King Arthur would have been proud of. Driving further on to Oxford, amongst other things in the near deserted Mallams saleroom, I found a high-stretchered Regency sofa table in original condition.

Richard Cole bought and delivered the two Tewkesbury tables and the auctioneer procured the few items at the Oxford sale, including the sofa table. I couldn't believe it. The rare dining table had only cost £3,000 and I sold it to Richard Naden from Bath for £8,000 and the sofa table had come in for the then, unheard of price, of £700. On collection, Ben, the auctioneer, giving a wink, had said, 'Well done,'

Incidentally, a few years later, I asked Richard Naden how he'd got on with the table. He'd eventually found mahogany with sufficient width to cut the leaves and after greasing a few palms, it had ended up with an American client, for £160,000. He told me the first attempt at cutting a suitable leaf had ended up like an aeroplane propeller and the whole deal had taken over a year to pull off. 'Well done,' I told him.

Another deal from nowhere, came from Stanley Woolston, who years before, had had the shop in Broad Street. The same dealer that had told me, some things can be a little misleading. He and his wife had become custodians of a massive country house just outside Chipping Sodbury. What I found amazing was, him admitting he was now out of touch with prices and asking, could I make him an offer on the mahogany he had for sale? Can't remember a thing about the goods bought, it was the fact I was now being treated as an established member of the trade, I have as an abiding memory. I drove away from there, smiling at the reminiscences of my bungling along in the early days.

Talking of which. Do you recall that deal years ago, with those travellers camped up at Bitterley station? If you remember, I was then taken up to Bedlam, for a deal on some old metal in an outside toilet, but was unable to buy the oak dresser base in the house. Well, from out of the blue, a man I vaguely recognised, appeared in my shop one day, saying it was at last available. He was now the age his father had been on my first visit and said, 'Dad had always promised the dresser to you and now he's gone, you're welcome to buy it. I was truly touched and felt almost *guilty for taking it from where it had probably stood for half its life.*

In a similar vein, I had a call from someone I hadn't seen in years,--- Gus, the thick-skinned smallholder, who'd been so infuriating in that first little shop, nearly thirty years before. His modus operandi of hanging around until he got what he wanted for next to nothing, must have worked to some extent, for I bought an amazing eclectic mix from his house and barns. He was certainly, an easier man to buy off, than he had been to sell to.

Another deal from a contact almost lost in the mists of time, was the clearance of the little pub Anne and I used to frequent in Leintwardine. The landlady and her daughter were giving up the business and with great sadness, I removed all the antique artefacts and decorative objects that had been displayed to give the small cottage pub, a bit of character.

I must admit, I shared his feeling of sadness. Another fragment of rural heritage, gone forever. The next little section cheered me, mind you, as had his way of writing the above. He'd obviously once had every intention of writing a book and his style almost captures the joy of knowing he would soon be free of the shop. I'll hand you back to him.

---Long gone, were the days when I bought huge loads of pine furniture, but in Rhayader one evening, feeling nostalgic, just couldn't help myself and bought every stick, selling it on to Mark Rowen. However, the deal that gave the real glow that evening, was the purchase of some unique oddities. It looked as if, a hundred years before, someone had constructed cupboards, a bookcase and a dresser base out of all the scraps of timber they could find, in a 'house that Jack built', fashion. They had the innocent charm of a child's drawing, like pieces of folk art. It was certainly not what I normally dealt in, but felt I couldn't miss with them, especially as I bought the lot for something like £120. The usual gang of lads, there that evening, thought I'd taken leave of

my senses, which of course I played along with. If they were in the dark, it was best they stayed there. I'd initially intended to lend it all to Rosie to take to the next Battersea Decorative Fair, but putting on a massive profit, let it all go the following day.

Talking of Rosie, she rang one day and said, 'When you were last here, a customer asked, "Was that John Dodds I just saw driving off?" The woman then told me, "That man was responsible for changing my whole life. If he hadn't have helped with the bus fare years ago, I'd have missed my flight to Australia and everything that's happened since."'

I occasionally bought clocks, but they certainly weren't a speciality of mine. I tended to buy those I blundered into, coming in for lucky money. That certainly was the case in a Cheshire saleroom one day. In the upper room, I'd spotted the works of an ancient automaton clock and just for fun, left a catching price. I think I was heading into Chester when my phone went. The auctioneer's voice came over the speaker, telling me I'd bought the clock works for £280, but there had been a terrible blunder,---they'd missed an important commission bid and would I consider taking £1.000 profit. Needless to say, the man was a recipient of a decent bottle of red, when I next called.

The next little deal of good fortune, came my way when delivering an oak side table to the Leominster dealer, who proudly battled for his oak in places like Newtown cattle market.

He said, 'I don't know why you don't ever call on your way through.'

I thought, 'I do.'

Well anyway, he persisted and tried to justify the notion, by saying, 'I do get the odd private call you know.' Pointing to a particularly small court cupboard, he said, 'Take that for example. I bought it yesterday, out of a house not far from here. I don't put

492

a huge mark-up on things. I suppose that will go out to one of my regulars for £3,000.'

My eyes widened and gulping, I said, 'I'll buy it.'

His jaw, literally dropped, but he couldn't go back on it now. He'd virtually given the thing away. It had unadorned, simple lines, was a lovely deep honey colour, and looked that ingenuously honest, any restoration would have shown up like a black tooth in a smile. I usually avoided court cupboards unless the life within, seemed to call to me and this diminutive little beauty had almost been pleading to be taken from there. I obliged and sold it for £5,500.

One of the strangest deals to come out of the blue, was when I was heading down to collect some bronzes, I'd had mounted on marble, at a workshop just south of the M4. The car phone went and it was Terry.

'Did you just ring me?'

'No.'

'Well that's strange, your number's just come up. Well anyway, now I've got hold of you, yesterday something rather weird happened. Bob Slinger was storming about here in a fit of rage. He was absolutely livid. Robin from Ross had rung him, asking if he'd be interested in two dressers, a dealer from up Llangollen way, had kept for years. Apparently, countless people have tried to buy them, but he'd always refused, saying, they were part of his pension plan. A divorce, looming, changed all that and he'd rung Robin, of all people, to see if he was interested. Robin was a little short of the £25,000 required and on account of his recent impact on the oak market, Bob Slinger had been roped in on the deal.'

'I know the dressers, Terry. One's a small Denbigh cupboard base with a canopy rack and the other's a Shropshire cab-leg dresser-base on stand.'

'You've got it. Well you know how fashions change and apparently by today's standards, the Denbigh jobby was a bit scruffy and Bob wasn't interested, but when it came to the long Shropshire base at £9,000, he couldn't believe it. Honestly, he was absolutely raving, for Robin had piped up, saying he'd have it.'

As they were carrying it out, Bob asked, 'What the hell's going on? I thought you'd dragged me all the way up here, in the back of beyond, to buy the thing.'

'Let's not discuss it here. I'll meet you down the road.'

'What's more, I haven't even seen you pay anything for it yet,' says Bob.

They met in a layby and Bob asks, 'OK, so how much is it?'

'I don't know,' says Robin. 'I'll have to ring my partner.'

'You what?'

'I can't let it go without consulting him.'

Well you know what Bob's like. He raged, 'What the fuck's HE got to do with it? As far as I can see, you've not even paid for it and now you're asking your partner, whose not even seen the bastard thing, how much you can sell it for?'

So anyway, Robin rang his partner and told Bob Slinger, the base would cost him £14,000.

'You're having a fucking laugh! You get me up on a fool's errand and your partner, who's not even clapped eyes on it, now wants five grand profit! What fuckin' planet are you on?'

'I tell you what,' said Terry. 'It's a good job Bob's lady friend was there to calm him. He was that mad he'd have probably throttled him.'

'So this was yesterday?'

'Yes.'

'Do you have Robin's number?'

He gave it me and luckily Robin was still in the shop. He was loading all the parts of a massive oak wall-filler, he needed to deliver and would be there some time.

I arrived at his shop in Ross about seven and was taken through to the back room, where the noble pedigree creature stood against the wall. It was a beautiful mellow colour, long, graceful, a secret drawer up inside the carcase, entirely original and mentally, I'd bought it, the moment I clapped eyes on it. Apart from in reference books, I'd only ever seen one other before and that hadn't been for sale.

I couldn't look too keen and so asked if £14,000 was his best price?

'Well it's a bit political. I'll just nip and ring my partner.'

'No Robin,' I said, realising I could be on the verge of losing it. 'No, let's not trouble your partner. I'll have it.'

It was slightly too long for the back of my car, but I wanted it from there. Immediately.

Sandy, from Nantwich was down early next morning and bought it for £18,000.

When an irate Bob rang later, trying to track it down, I with full honesty replied, there was nothing of that rarity on my property. I had to be careful. I recalled a story he'd told me. He'd been in desperate need of a certain type of early Yorkshire chair to make up a matched set and had bought one blind off the Bookend from

Stow. When having time to examine it, he'd found it had a replaced stretcher and wrong seat. He told me, the Bookend had been engrossed in a deal with an American client when he'd taken the chair back and then, on being given a dismissive wave of the hand and blithe instruction to get himself hence, he'd asked, 'Tell me. Is that your Volvo out there?'

'Yes. Why?'

Raising the 17th century backstool as if a weapon, he'd growled, 'Cough up the money, or you'll be retrieving this chair from the front seats.'

He laughed when he told me, 'The cheque was a bit shaky, but it went through OK.'

The next short section, John Dodds had titled, 'Smarty pants.'

---When recounting memories, one is obviously aware, the reader doesn't wish to plough through details of a litany of ordinary deals that make up 80% of what goes on in a provincial antique shop, yet there again, just describing the better items chanced upon, one is in danger of sounding like, a bit of a smarty pants.

To give a more realistic view, briefly of course; in the latter years, at the end of each financial year I was left with over 100,000 pounds worth of stock, remainder of that bought over the previous twelve months and once most of that had sold, was being taxed on the 30% rump, that I wished I'd never clapped eyes on. Stock increase, was viewed by HMG as an asset, not something you had a job to get your money back on. Considering the amount of trading, most major dealers did back then, it was inevitable the odd mistake would creep in. An 18th century side table, gone over very carefully in a crowded saleroom, could appear perfect, until standing there alone on collection day, with a wrong leg easily spotted from 10 yard's distance, laughing at you. Then there were things you would not normally have considered, but being a forlorn remnant, of the van full just bought, you'd say those fatal words, 'Oh go on then.' Perhaps costing, only £300, but too many, 'Oh, go on thens,' can sink a business. Obviously, it would all gradually sell in the end, or get swapped out of, but it was generally not stock to be proud of.

Also, there have been items, I hate admitting it, but I gave them away.

One busy Wednesday, dealing with two van loads arriving and beset by customers asking prices, I just didn't stop to think and sold a large pair of carved stone urns for the same price, as if they'd been late Victorian cast iron. Mike Taylor from Broad Street bought them. Having instantly realised my mistake, I tried to dissuade him, 'They're a terrific weight, Mike'.

He just smiled and said, 'I think I'll manage.'

Next time I saw them, they were outside Dave Roberts's shop in Leominster and I'd so underrated them, I could have bought them back and still got a profit. Needless to say, I didn't.

An even worse howler, back in those early days in the new shop, was a mahogany partners desk. I sold it on a day when swirling wind and snow made you wonder why you'd bothered to put 'open' on the door. When a mate of mine rang later, complaining of the conditions, asked how I'd been coping, I told him about my little success story.

'You were lucky,' he said. 'You'd be hard pushed to even sell a sledge on a day like today. You said the desk had a carved frieze. Sounds a bit different. What sort of carving?'

'Sort of Chinese Chippendale.------ Oh my good God! What have I done?'

It gets worse. When viewing Olympia on trade day, I'd often hear, 'There goes that John Dodds. Sells unsuspecting London dealers, weird dresser bases.'

497

I'd sold Alistair Sampson one of those quaint oak pieces that sometimes turn up from the Gower Peninsula. We'd have a bit of banter, then go on our separate ways. Thank goodness he had enough compassion, never to mention another item of mine that came his way. He didn't buy it directly, one of his partners did, on a hot Summer's, Saturday afternoon, following a bleak week of sales.

I'd bought it from the doorknocker, Chris Braddock, who said he'd been after it for years. I paid £1,200 and wagging a finger, he said, 'Don't give this away, Jackie.'

It had a hairline crack, but even so, I still got £3,200 for it. These were the days before the internet was so readily available, remember, but even so, as soon as I'd sold it, I had that panicky, white noise feeling between the ears. I'd just sold a late 17th century, slipware dish, depicting King Billy, sword in hand on a rampant horse! No, not sold; gave it away. It was worthy of the V and A. I cringe at the thought even now.

At this point I paused and re-read, with some pleasure, I have to add, the reference to those strange lots, John Dodds had bought from that evening sale at Rhayader. It took me back to the first day I'd met Mike, not knowing at the time, the little cupboard I'd bought, would lead me through the labyrinth I've been so busy writing about.

Sitting there reminiscing, it suddenly struck me, although I had a fair idea of the character of John Dodds, apart from the input his assistant, Mike, had furnished, I'd only had background details from those who had muddled through the early days with him. I was hoping to talk to one of the established trade members, about the latter, more professional days and hear their opinion. I soon realised it was a tall order, for most had passed away, then on the internet I found Ian Anderson's contact details. He still ran a shop in Welshpool.

As always, I looked up interesting snippets, regarding the history of the place and was surprised to find, the original Welshpool castle, now so famous for its magnificent interior and gardens, had originally been a Welsh bastion. It had been put up by Gruffydd ap Gwenwynwyn, Lord of the ancient kingdom of Powys, who actually sided with the English. His son Owain was made first Lord of Powys and probably didn't think too much of Llywelyn ap Gruffydd, claiming to be the true Prince of Wales, whether endorsed by the crown or not.

Musing to myself, I realised Owain was probably on very good terms with Roger Mortimer, who must have paid the odd visit to Montgomery, when patrolling his estates from the family seat at Wigmore and with it enhancing his position, quite possibly passed on the odd bit of inside information. So in 1277, with Prince Llywelyn on the verge of completing Dolforwyn Castle, just across the Severn, did he canter down to Montgomery one day and say, 'Hey Rog, a little bird tells me, those wild mountain cousins who've flung up that bit of a redoubt over yonder, have done so without the consideration of digging a well. Don't let on I told you, but chances are, if you nip across there a bit sharpish, it'll be yours inside two weeks.'

I gave Ian Anderson a ring and as soon as he realised why, couldn't have been more helpful.

"Doddsy? How is he?"

"I haven't actually met the man."

"Well I'm not surprised. Once he packed the shop up, he seemed to disappear without trace. Tell you what though, he couldn't have timed it better. We used to joke; as soon as he shut that shop door, the trade collapsed."

"I don't want to pry, Ian, but I was hoping you could give a bit of simple background information. As a dealer, what was he like?"

"Well, it's hard to sum up in just a few words, but I suppose you could say, he was hard working,--- he'd have a bit of a go.---Yes, thinking about it, he wasn't frightened to get stuck in. And he paid."

"Didn't everybody?"

He mumbled something I didn't catch, then said, "Some of the clients,---well, it was a hell of a job to get money out of them, but Doddsy always paid, right there, on the dot."

I went on to explain, the notes given me and told him briefly, some of the details, Charles had supplied. He asked after Charles in a most affable manner, as if enquiring after an old pal, but I got the impression their paths wouldn't have crossed that often.

When I mentioned the set of marquetry chairs, John Dodds had bought, on the occasion Ian had thought there'd only been the pair, he said, 'D'you know what, I'd clean forgotten about those, but now you come to mention it, that's right, he did use his loaf that day. Well in fact, you could say that was another thing in his favour. I remember dad had called him up one day. He'd got wind of a walnut chest of drawers, in a house sale over at Bala. I was in Ireland at the time, so couldn't cover it. Well, when dad rang him, Doddsy dropped everything, drove over, found the sale right enough, but got there just as it finished. He told dad, the lads had found it hilarious. So having thought the deal lost, you can imagine his surprise, when Doddsy asked him, to please give a hand and help lift the chest from the car. But what tickled dad most, was, he'd somehow managed to pull it, for half the money he rated it at."

"How did he manage that?"

"Used his loaf. What's more, as he wouldn't even have known about the thing if dad hadn't have rung him, he just took a working profit. There's a few, who I won't mention, who'd have gone straight home with it, saying they'd got to the sale too late."

"In the notes, he describes that Australian trip you both went on."

"That! I tell you what, we must have been mad. I wouldn't risk it now. Bloody crackers! What a nightmare. We were on the verge of a hiding to nothing. Dad wouldn't have put up with it. Most of the stuff was wrong. He'd have said, 'The bloke's clearly off his rocker,' and caught the next plane home. Somehow, we managed to squeak a profit, but only by the skin of our teeth."

Ian was quiet for a while and then asked, "Did he mention the lift?"

"No. What lift?"

"He **didn't**? Oh dear, it was funny. That's the thing about Doddsy, he had a wicked wit, but was often funniest when he didn't mean to be. What happened was, we were returning from breakfast and stepping out of the lift, realised we were on the wrong floor. John had pressed the wrong button.

Later that day, after supper, we decided to take a stroll into Bunbury. It was after we'd managed to pull the deal. Well, we'd only gone about half a mile and Doddsy says, 'Ian, I'm going to have to go back.'

He was pouring with sweat and wincing with pain. Obviously, something he'd eaten hadn't agreed with him. Every fifty yards or so, he'd have to stop and I can see him now, face screwed with pain, 'Feels like I'm having a baby.'

Well of course I laughed and he said, 'Don't make me laugh, it hurts. Ahhh! Don't, I'll need a pair of bicycle clips.'

I don't know how he managed it, but walking like his laces were tied together, he somehow clung on. Luckily there was a lift waiting. Once Inside, I said, 'Now make sure you press the right button.'

Explaining in all seriousness, he gasped, 'I have! There's not that much margin for error.'

I think it was that earnest look that set me off. Dear me. I was still laughing when he appeared from the bathroom, beaming with relief and like I said, I don't think he realised how funny he could be.

We talked a little more, with me giving details of what I did and him telling me, I had to make a point of calling there one day.

'I'll bring you a copy of the book, Ian.'

'Wonderful. I'd love that.'

CHAPTER THIRTY-FOUR

The final titled section in the notes was, 'Last Deals.'

---*Things can turn up in the oddest places. Years before, I'd bought a rare dugout chair from Ross on Wye cattle market auction and now found a solid sycamore, Welsh dairy table there. It had the two deep drawers flanking the nest of smaller drawers as usual, but the generous overhang of the top, gave it a joined-hutch appearance, like something from an earlier age. Richard Cole had dropped it off for me and it was still on the pavement, when the husband-and-wife dealers of spongeware and primitive furniture fame, turned up. They had bought the strange thingamy, as it was referred to, years before from my very first shop and as they had almost invented the fashion for what I'd just that minute had delivered, I considered it, as good as sold.*

Well, they huffed and puffed; had me help lift the top off and turn the thing over. Considering it was sycamore, it was quite worm-free and I couldn't quite see why they seemed in such a quandary. I even said, if they failed to sell it, I'd buy it back off them.

In the end, with it being way past closing time, I left them to it and started locking up out the back and making sure the cat wasn't stuck inside. Then I waited. In the end, they plodded back in, still looking befuddled and said they needed to think about it. It was the best example, I'd ever owned and these legends in the trade, were only going to think about it.

When they returned the next morning to hear I'd sold it, they looked truly mortified and asked, would the person I'd sold it to, take a profit? They had obviously presold it.

When I told Rob Deeley, who had bought it on my description, he'd laughed and said, 'That's rich. They couldn't pay your asking price, but now want to offer me a profit? If it's as good as you say, the next time they see it, it will be on the front of my stand at Olympia.'

One day, out of the blue, Byron appeared with his dewy-eyed driver, plus he had his wife and daughter in tow. If you remember, this was the 'I love you, Johnny, Byron.' I could see his wife, tight-lipped, weighing me up and thought, 'Yes, you know his little secret alright, but there's no need to look at me 'in that tone of voice,' he's all yours missus.'

He bought a few things plus a large pair of cast iron urns on swan pediments and that was the last I saw of him.

In that final year, when I'd at last, figured an escape plan from the shop, who should ring, but dear old, Gay Walker. She said, she'd had a call for an incredibly long dresser base over Worcester way and would I pick her up?

Before I continue, I've just thought of something. I bet some of you are wondering why I didn't sell the shop as a going concern? Well the answer to that is, it wasn't really possible. Most in the trade knew, that an antique shop was only what the owner made it and as soon as that person left, any magic they'd built up, went with them. The only exception to this was a good friend, Mike Corfield of Lymington, who was paid handsomely for what he'd built up, but then was actually saddened to witness what his business then became.

Anyway, back to Gay. She stood small in the doorway of her great Hall, looking like a girl waiting to be taken on a school outing. She'd been retired a few years and I could just tell she was loving every minute. The dresser base was a bit on the long side, 9 foot six and a half inches and I had to ease the car through dips in the road, lest the protruding end got caught on the tarmac. On the way back, we called at Ray's shop in Malvern and he'd just bought a small oak, brass-faced grandfather clock. You'll have already read about me and clocks, but Gay quietly entreated, 'You really ought to buy that, John.'

I did and we fed it in, to lie beside the dresser and I could see Gay was absolutely glowing. When I dropped her off, I gave her a share of the expected profit on the two items and almost with tears in her eyes, she said, 'It seems an awful lot, John. Are you sure?'

That would have been Gay Walker's last deal and I'm proud to say, I was part of it.

On my last deal with Roger Kilby, I took my son with me. I bought an early cupboard dresser base and a pert little coffer. Profit on the latter paid for our enjoyable stay at the Bell at Sandwich and the dresser base returned a thousand pounds bonus. Those were the days! My son will remember it well, for with the only room for the coffer, being a very firm fit on the front seat, he'd spent the whole return journey lying in the back with the dresser base for company.

I know Roger had built up a fearsome reputation, but in all my dealings with him, we'd never had a cross word.

In the final year in the shop, I attempted to keep the guns firing, but only on dead certs. I needed to keep what I was doing secret, while attempting to run the stock down. Even with a lower amount traded in that final year, the shop still turned over, £11,000,000 in those last ten years.

Terry knew I was making a break for it and I swapped my vast accumulation of restoration timber, locks, escutcheons and handles for an early moulded-front dresser base he'd found. Made a good profit on it, in fact. Wherever possible I swapped car loads for small rare artefacts, such as early joint stools, !6ᵗʰ century polychrome carvings, pair of inlaid cutlery boxes, with all the innards, plus I burnt my boats, putting all my reference books into the Leominster sale. Following my entreaty, Roger Williams instructed the staff there, not to divulge the source. Then one day, with all the residue removed, relishing the hollow sound of the door closing for the very last time, I was gone.

I must admit, with the notes spread before me, I had an empty, deflated feeling. He'd slipped away and I was left with the endless burden of editing my manuscript, re-reading, looking for clumsy phrases, repetition, missed words and bad grammar. I wished there had been a bit more, like what had happened next. Where did he go, after he left the business? I was told, it was a trade truism, 'old dealers never really retire' and yet it seems he did. You can almost sense the joy with which he wrote about it. A sort of chatty style, in complete contrast to the more formal descriptions of his early days, plus I realised, the scar of the marriage break-up must have healed for I found the following, obviously dating back to when he and Anne had walked up to that tower with the strange name, Flounder's Folly.

> It was one of those places I'd always wanted to climb to,
> The tower, where legend had it, you could see the sea;
> In theory anyway, it was in the wrong spot,
> Yet distant, small-perched, it had called to me.
>
> You had no interest; fences, vistas, hills;
> Other than what I saw in you and you saw in me;
> Not dressed for it either, more dressed for town,
> Pretty blouse, tight jeans, sewn on, seemed to be.
>
> Ruin? No more than what it was built for,
> A Victorian folly, now crumbling, no stairs;
> So, 'That's it I thought, apart from the view,'
> Not my abiding memory after all these years.

Face hot, you followed through waist high bracken,
Wheeling a frond ripped out in a fly-swiping swirl,
Hips swaying, you were topless, dark eyes smouldered
And looking back I remember, 'What a beautiful girl.'

It was a couple of weeks later that Mike rang. He wondered if we could meet up in Ludlow. Of course, I said, yes and just on the off chance, gave Leon Jones a ring. As luck would have it, he told me he was doing a fair that day in Ludlow town square.

As usual, I'd looked up the history of the place, which I found fascinating, but also complicated enough the make the head spin. When the first stone defences had been completed in 1115, apart from much earlier Roman bastions, it made the castle one of the first to be masonry built in the whole country. The de Lacy family, who made such an impact in Ireland, had once held it. It had been used a number of times, as a pawn, to exact loyalty. In 1265, Prince Edward, future Edward 1st, had met up with his supporters there, before setting out to thrash Simon de Montford's forces at Evesham.

For two years, its owner Roger Mortimer, was de facto ruler of the country, until young Edward 111rd, flexing his muscles and deeming him to have overdone it rather, gave orders for his head removed in 1330. Talk about gratitude;--- it had only been the year before, Roger had organised a huge bash, inviting the young king as guest of honour.

Must admit, I did get a bit confused. Too many Rogers. This was a different Roger to the 1st Baron of Wigmore who'd set out from Montgomery to capture Dolforwyn castle. This Roger, who had lost his head, was his grandson.

If you remember, another Mortimer, Edmund had sallied forth from here for an ill-fated meeting with Owain Glyndwr's army, just outside Presteigne in 1402.

What struck me as amazing was, the small market town of Ludlow, had once been the most important urban centre on the whole of the Welsh Marches, putting the likes of Hereford, Shrewsbury and Chester in the shade.

I arrived early and found where John Dodds had traded from in those final years. It truly was a vast property. I walked over the hill and saw that Tim Glenger still had a bit of an outlet. Up in the square I espied a man with a cheerful countenance selling, brass, copper, small items of furniture and knew it had to be Leon Jones. I introduced myself and asking a nearby stallholder to watch over things, he suggested we go to the breakfast van for a filled roll and mug of tea. There were even seats provided.

Leon was slightly reticent at first, but then opening up a bit, said it was at this very spot, he'd last seen John Dodds.

"It was long after the shop had gone and the day sticks in my mind because John, true to form, had made me laugh. Tony's widow happened to be there."

"Tony the antique dealer?"

Leon's eyes widened. "You've got it. You've been doing your homework. He had the big place, bottom of Corve Street. So you've heard about the famous Tony?"

"Enough to know that John Dodds didn't trust him."

"He wasn't alone there. Well anyway, his widow told John, Tony had passed away. Died of a heart attack. As she was leaving, John muttered, 'I'm surprised they found one.' Like I said, it made me laugh."

I could see Leon was deep in thought and so relishing the crispy bacon roll with brown sauce, I waited.

"I've just remembered something else. When Tony and his wife had split up, not what you'd call a clean break in fact, it was a good while before John had packed the job up and she'd told him, she couldn't understand why so many people thought he was so bloody marvellous, when really, he was a complete shit. Well anyway, Tony had come into John's shop not long after, bleating about, after all he'd done for the woman, she now intended to sell his prized dresser base. The one he'd been keeping, special like. He'd been busy, going round the trade, warning them all off it. D'you know what Doddsy did?"

"I think I can guess."

"It was one of those Montgomeryshire pot-board bases, licence to print money at the time and he was straight round there,--- no messing. Tony had stirred things over the years and pulled a few strokes and so John felt he owed him nothing. In fact, he viewed it as just desserts."

Sipping our tea, we watched people browsing amongst the stalls.

"I sold Doddsy one of those bases," Leon suddenly announced, cheerily. "What he used to do was,--- if he chanced on a decent house clearance, he'd buy what he wanted and pass the rest on to me. So when I got something a bit tasty, I'd give him a ring. Worked quite well. In fact, I think sometimes, I did better on the junk than he did on the better bits. But he didn't care. His business wasn't set up for handling all that sort of stuff. On the one call he put me on to, both folks had died and I found three thousand quid rammed inside a bedside cupboard. Wouldn't have been right to keep it, mind. Let their daughter have it. Should have seen her face. Lit up like a torch when I gave it her."

"Oh, just remembered something else. John met Tony up town one day, long after dresser base incident. Tony and a new partner had been living down in Spain. John had said, 'Surprised to see you, Tony.'

'We had to come back,' he told him. 'In the summer, it gets so flaming hot.'

'Heard things got a bit warm down there,' John told him."

Leon's ruddy complexion absolutely glowed as he laughed. "John had heard the Spanish police had been after him. He'd sold an incredibly rare piece of metalware, to a top museum. An aqua something or other, I think it was and it turns out it was a fake. There was a brilliant forger, operating not far from here as it happens and John had seen some of his work.

He told me, Tony had delivered a little package one day, something an American dealer had bought. The same client had bought a load of oak off Doddsy and it would have been daft, expecting a huge truck to stop off in Corve Street, just for one packet. With it only being in loose bubble-wrap, John had taken a look. He told me, it was pair of Queen Anne candlesticks. The sort with the petal bases, he'd stitched into the bloke for £800. John could see, when he turned them up, they were fake. Must have been a rushed job. No attempt to finish them properly. He was certainly a rum-un, that Tony. I still meet folks that say they've been had by him."

Talk of the candlesticks reminded me, Mike had said he'd ring or text, regarding his whereabouts. I checked my phone, but hadn't missed a call.

As Leon was leaving, he said, "That time, when we last met, I said to Doddsy, 'D'you know what, mate? When we were clearing all those cottages, we left the best behind. Those places were going for nothing. If we'd have bought them, we'd both be millionaires now." His laughter was infectious.

Returning to my car, my phone went. It was Mike and he gave me directions to a place known as Whitcliffe. I drove down, over the river and turning immediately right, went slowly up the steep ascent, looking for him. When clear of the trees, I spotted Mike, standing alone, looking down into the town. His tan contrasted with the white he wore. The trousers, slightly baggy, looked like thoroughly comfortable old friends and his shirt, open at the neck, had the sleeves rolled up, obviously with no regard to precision.

"You look like you've just strolled from a beach bar on the Algarve," I said.

"I love it up here. When I think of all the tensions and worries down there over the years. It all seems so calm and peaceful now."

Standing beside him looking down at the ancient castle and houses beyond, packed that tightly, it was hard to make out the street plan, I let my gaze take in the scenery beyond and as happens to many, fell under the spell of the beautiful vista.

Pointing, he said, "Look at Titterstone Clee. When I see that noble, leonine shape, it brings back so many memories and over there, that's Brown Clee. Travelling the countryside over that way, can be like entering a time warp."

"Mike?"

Slowly turning, he raised an eyebrow.

"Mike, there's a thing in those notes you gave me, I find puzzling."

A hint of a smile flickered. "What, just the one thing?"

"It seems strange that John Dodds never mentions you."

"Really?"

"He doesn't. I've checked and there's no mention, not even one. There are plenty of references to a bright and resourceful van driver called Steve Reece, but not you."

"What a rotten swizz," he said with a laugh. "Have you finished the book by the way?"

"All but the endless reading through, looking for mistakes. I had hoped the story, with all its trails and anecdotes, would weave together, rather like a tapestry, but now, when I re-read it,--- "

"What? It's more like a patchwork quilt?"

His words jolted me somewhat, but softened by his glint of eye, I couldn't help but laugh.

"I'd like a copy when it's published. Anyway, come with me. I have a small gift."

He eased into his car and reaching into the glove box, produced an envelope. It was handed to me. Neatly written was, 'Money for candlesticks. Half share, after initial cost deducted, £340.'

"Count it. Check that it's right."

I did and then said, "You told me they were worth £300, at the very most. What about your share?"

"Don't worry, I've got my share."

"I don't understand."

"Well, a few years back, I sold a lady customer of mine, a rather fine walnut cabriole-legged lowboy for a considerable sum of money. Worth every penny, mind you. Prices on small, perfect items like that, have gone through the roof and like I said before, so have those on certain country pieces. Things like cider tables, coffer bachs, comb-back windsors; all fetching silly money these days. Anyway, those candlesticks looked made for the job. Elegant and being of the Queen Anne period, as is the lowboy, they set it off a treat. She was absolutely thrilled."

"Did I hear right? A lowboy, that YOU sold her?" I felt completely baffled.

The door of his car was now closed, but through the open window, eyes filled with mirth, he nodded affirmation.

"I don't understand. You're saying you sold this lady a rare piece of furniture and if my reckoning is right, you also sold her the candlesticks for £700. Well Mike, according to what you originally told me, that's more than double their current value."

Flashing a wicked grin, he said as he pulled away, "It's all part of the game."

Lightning Source UK Ltd.
Milton Keynes UK
UKHW011910301122
413150UK00001B/1